Amsterdam

timeout.com/amsterdam

Time Out Guides Ltd
Universal House
251 Tottenham Court Road
London W1T 7AB
United Kingdom
Tel: +44 (0)20 7813 3000
Fax: +44 (0)20 7813 6001
Email: guides@timeout.com
www.timeout.com

Published by Time Out Guides Ltd, a wholly owned subsidiary of Time Out Group Ltd.
Time Out and the Time Out logo are trademarks of Time Out Group Ltd.

© **Time Out Group Ltd 2011**
Previous editions 1991, 1993, 1995, 1996, 1998, 2000, 2002, 2004, 2005, 2007

10 9 8 7 6 5 4 3 2 1

This edition first published in Great Britain in 2011 by Ebury Publishing.
A Random House Group Company
20 Vauxhall Bridge Road, London SW1V 2SA

Random House Australia Pty Ltd 20 Alfred Street, Milsons Point, Sydney, New South Wales 2061, Australia

Random House New Zealand Ltd 18 Poland Road, Glenfield, Auckland 10, New Zealand

Random House South Africa (Pty) Ltd Isle of Houghton, Corner Boundary Road & Carse O'Gowrie, Houghton 2198, South Africa

Random House UK Limited Reg. No. 954009

Distributed in the US and Latin America by Publishers Group West (1-510-809-3700)
Distributed in Canada by Publishers Group Canada (1-800-747-8147)

For further distribution details, see www.timeout.com.

ISBN 978-1-84670-198-6

A CIP catalogue record for this book is available from the British Library.

Printed and bound by Firmengruppe APPL, aprinta druck, Wemding, Germany.

The Random House Group Limited supports The Forest Stewardship Council (FSC), the leading international forest certification organisation. All our titles that are printed on Greenpeace approved FSC certified paper carry the FSC logo. Our paper procurement policy can be found at www.randomhouse.co.uk/environment.

Time Out carbon-offsets its flights with Trees for Cities (www.treesforcities.org).

Contents

Artis Royal Zoo

home of biodiversity
come and stroll in nature's oasis right in the heart of Amsterdam

natura
ARTIS
magistra

Introduction

'My experience of Amsterdam,' the writer Terry Pratchett once said, 'is that cyclists ride where the hell they like and aim in a state of rage at all pedestrians while ringing their bells loudly, the concept of avoiding people being foreign to them.'

Like those cyclists, Amsterdam assails from all angles, managing to be all things to all people, depending on where you go. It's a druggie paradise for stoner backpackers; it's a bottomless well of live (and interactive) sex and no-holds barred pornography for others; and it's a living, breathing museum (as of 2010 the city's canals were granted UNESCO World Heritage status) for international art and architecture connoisseurs.

Essentially, Amsterdam is a chameleon: while the infamous Red Light District attracts stoners and stag-dos like moths to a flame, more and more coffeeshops are being shut down by the Dutch government in a bid to clean up the area. Meanwhile, many of the city's brothels have been closed to make way for fashion wares from the city's up-and-coming designers. While some feel the government is pulling the rug from underneath the Red Light District's feet, there's still enough razzamatazz going on 24/7 to keep punters happy.

Instead of drugs and sex, the city is busy marketing itself as a capital of culture and arts – not difficult considering there are more museums per square metre than in any other city in the world. Along with the Anne Frank House and the Van Goghs, Amsterdam is teeming with artists, designers, architects, ad world creatives and other culturally minded folks who not only keep the galleries and project spaces buzzing, but add a jolt of art to most of the city's clubs and bars.

These days, the city is very much in continual transition: the industrial Noord, on the far bank of the IJ, is facing a future as a cultural hub with the NDSM-werf creative ateliers and the imminent arrival of a brand new film museum, the EYE Film Instituut. Equally, the Museumplein is getting a makeover with renovations on the city's two largest art institutions, the Stedelijk Museum and the Rijksmuseum.

One thing's for certain: whatever happens in the future, Amsterdam will continue to grow, as it has done since 1200, both literally and metaphorically. Like those pesky cyclists, this city will fling off in every which way – and no one will ever put the brakes on… *Nina Siegal, Editor*

LoS PILoNES

Hot Crowd   Hot Food

Kerkstraat 63
1017 GC Amsterdam
(Leidsestraat)
Tel. 020 320 4651
info@LosPilones.com

1e Anjeliersdwarsstraat 6
1015 NR Amsterdam
(Jordaan)
Tel. 020 620 0323
www.LosPilones.com

Amsterdam in Brief

IN CONTEXT

To open the book, this series of essays explores the city's fascinating history and conveys a sense of the current political and social climate. We look at the paradoxical mixture of forces that shape the contemporary culture of a 400-year-old metropolis, with its reputation as a sex-and-drugs tourist haven, an art and design hub, and its constantly evolving creative culture.

▶ *For more, see pp17-71.*

SIGHTS

As well as in-depth insights into the city's best-known attractions – the Van Gogh Museum and the Anne Frank House, to name just two – the Sights section looks at the shifting character of local neighbourhoods. We guide you through the special areas within various districts, with a waterfront walk, for example, a whistlestop tour of the Jordaan's contemporary art scene and a stroll around the city's hidden gardens.

▶ *For more, see pp73-127.*

CONSUME

This hedonists' haven offers every conceivable type of cuisine. The former brewing centre of Europe is sudsy too, with plenty of speciality bars to suit the connoisseur. Shopping districts with design-minded and haute boutiques are ready to reel you in. Amsterdam also has one thing you won't find elsewhere: coffeeshops, where it's legal to smoke marijuana and hash.

▶ *For more, see pp129-206.*

ARTS & ENTERTAINMENT

Amsterdam could never be accused of being boring. From mainstream theatrical productions or blockbuster concerts to underground film screenings at alternative venues such as De Nieuwe Anita and edgy vinyl-only clubbing nights at Trouw, your daily planner will always be full. Find out too about attractions that are fun for the whole family, as well as queer-friendly destinations in the gay capital of Europe.

▶ *For more, see pp207-279.*

ESCAPES & EXCURSIONS

Although there's plenty to keep you occupied during your stay in Amsterdam, you'd be forgiven for wanting to stretch your legs and head out to find all those Dutch clichés: clogs, cows and cheese. And if expansive fields of tulips make you happy, you can feast your eyes in spring. There are lots of other excuses for day trips, from fine art excursions to beach runs and even a day at a castle.

▶ *For more, see pp281-302.*

Amsterdam in 48hrs

Day 1 Canals, Culture and Clubbing

9AM Avoid queues by arriving early to the **Anne Frank Huis** (*see p96*); the museum offers insight into a profound personal and national history.

11AM Window-shop in the **Nine Streets** (*see p99*), a quaint cluster of local boutiques and speciality shops.

12.30PM Grab lunch at a terraced restaurant on the Canal ring. A waterside table will offer a view: the canals were awarded UNESCO World Heritage status in 2010.

2PM Head south-east to the **Rijksmuseum** (*see p108*), home to Rembrandt's iconic *The Night Watch* as well as masterpieces by Frans Hals, Jan Steen and Johannes Vermeer. For more modern and contemporary art, the **Van Gogh Museum** holds Manet, Monet and, of course, Van Gogh (*see p109*).

4PM Take a breather by ambling through the **Vondelpark** (*see p112*), the city's largest green open space, with wonderful paths, trails and lawns where you can relax and catch some sun.

5PM Grab a late-afternoon *biertje* (beer) at **'t Blauwe Theehuis**, a 1930s café with a sprawling terrace in the centre of the park. Relax and enjoy the people-watching.

7PM Just outside the north entrance of the park, hop on a tourist cruise boat and enjoy the sunset from the water with a guided tour, or hire a cycle boat and guide yourself (*see p78*).

9PM Head east to cultural complex **Trouw** (*see p265*) for a late dinner and clubbing as internationally renowned DJs hit the decks. On the way home, grab a Dutch croquette from **FEBO** (*see p161* **A Bite on the Side**).

NAVIGATING THE CITY
Amsterdam's tangle of cobbled streets and canals can seem labyrinthine. Don't worry: with a little geographical know-how and the right maps (*pp322-332*), it becomes much easier to navigate. Hiring a bike (or *fiets*) is a great way to get around (*see p306*). Mix your biking with tram and Metro rides to get a handle on Amsterdam's topography; free transport maps are available at the Amsterdam Tourist Board locations (*see p208*). And don't forget the canals: although mainly the preserve of tourist boats and local boat owners, it is possible to navigate the waterways on your own or with a smaller tour. For more on travel, *see pp304-306*; for our selection of guided tours, *see p75*.

SEEING THE SIGHTS
To escape the heaving crowds, try to avoid the main tourist attractions at weekends. It is also useful to steer clear of public transport during the rush hour (8-9.30am

Day 2 Sex, Drugs and Shopping for Tat

10AM Kickstart the day at **Dam Square** (*see p80*) and take a tour of the Royal Palace (*see p81*), the occasional residence of Queen Beatrix.

11AM Take a shopping tour of the bustling **Kalverstraat** before popping into department store **De Bijenkorf** (*see p181*) for a coffee and retail therapy.

NOON Head west towards the infamous **Red Light District** (*see p83*), which isn't quite so intensely stagdo filled at this time of day. Try the enlightening **Hash, Marihuana & Hemp Museum** (*see p88*) where visitors can try out the drug in safe confines.

1PM Got the munchies? You're just next to Chinatown, where you can chow down on famous black-bean oysters (a novel was named after them!) at **Nam Kee** (*see p151*).

2PM Escape sin central and head east to the fecund greenery at the **Hortus Botanicus** (*see p118*). Or continue on to the **Artis Zoo** (*see p117*) where you can commune with the animals.

4PM Hop on your bike (or catch a tram) south to hip **De Pijp** (*see p125*), then catch the end-of-the-day sales on popular **Albert Cuypmarkt** (*see p181*) and grab some tourist tat.

5PM In the mood for a brew? Stop off at the **Heineken Experience** (*see p126*) for a tour of the former factory with a free tasting at the end.

7PM For a cheap dinner, head to the ornately decorated former church **Bazar** (*see p162*) for Turkish cuisine, or splurge on dinner at **Ciel Bleu**, the city's Michelin-starred French restaurant on the 23rd floor of the **Hotel Okura** (*see p145*), with a panoramic view of the surroundings.

9PM Cap the night off by settling into a comfy seat at the arthouse **Rialto cinema** (*see p227*).

and 5-7pm), although the humble bike can usually navigate through many a traffic jam, as most of the city has dedicated cycle paths. While the majority of the city's museums and historical buildings charge an admission fee, there are options for those on a budget, including **Amsterdams Historisch Museum**'s Civic Guards gallery (*see p92*) and the **Binnenhof** (*see p294*) if you are in that neck of the woods. Some of the smaller attractions may close early when it is quiet, and many places close all day on certain public holidays (notably Queen's Day), so call ahead to check before making a trip.

PACKAGE DEALS

The **I Amsterdam** pass (www.iamsterdam. nl) provides more than 40 free and 50 discounted offers on major tourist attractions and restaurants across the city. Buy the card online and collect it from the I Amsterdam tourist office at Centraal Station.

WHENEVER, WHEREVER YOU NEED MONEY...

WE GET IT THERE IN 10 MINUTES*

CHOICE IS IN YOUR HANDS

1. Arrange for the person sending the money to visit a MoneyGram agent near them. After sending the money, you will receive a reference number.

2. Find your nearest MoneyGram agent at **www.moneygram.com** or anywhere you see the MoneyGram sign.

3. Give the reference number and your ID** to the MoneyGram agent.

4. Sign the form to receive your money.

MoneyGram. *Money Transfer*

0800 0233880   www.moneygram.com

Amsterdam in Profile

THE OLD CENTRE

Amsterdam's centre is so rich in culture and entertainment, you'd be forgiven for thinking the whole city is right here: **Dam Square**, the **Royal Palace**, and the **Amsterdams Historisch Museum** are great starting points. To the east, the **Red Light District** awaits with its narrow byways and historic buildings, coffeeshops and window prostitutes. The **Nieuwmarkt** area is chock-full of cafés and restaurants, leading to Amsterdam's mini **Chinatown** and gay **Zeedijk**. To the West, on the new side, **Nieuwendijk** and her younger sister **Kalverstraat** are heaven for shoppers, crossing trendy **Spui**, all the way to **Muntplein** and the flower market.
▶ For more, see pp80-92.

THE CANALS

Amsterdam isn't dubbed the Venice of the North for no reason; with 75 kilometres (47 miles) of canals bordered by charming, crooked old buildings, it's also a quiet and romantic place to amble the day away. Recently named a UNESCO World Heritage Site, the **Grachtengordel** is also a vibrant and lively cultural hub, with museums, designer shopping along the **Nine Streets**, a multitude of entertainment options around **Leidseplein**, and a slew of restaurants, many smaller and more authentic than in the Centre – all the way to bar-and-clubbing central, **Rembrandtplein**.
▶ For more, see pp92-101.

THE JORDAAN & WEST

Art galleries, European delicatessens and trendy shops housed in a neighbourhood of cramped doll's houses make the Jordaan a favourite of Amsterdam locals. **Haarlemmerstraat** still offers a vast array of vintage shops and new boutiques, all the way to the lovely **Westerpark** and the **Westergasfabriek**, its beacon of multidisciplinary culture. The Jordaan has a plethora of street markets, from **Looier**'s antiques to **Noordermarkt**'s organic veggies and meats. South of Rozengracht lies the residential **Oud West**, with key commercial streets – **Overtoom**, **Kinkerstraat** and **Jan Pieter Heijestraat** – lined with design-minded furniture and shops.
▶ For more, see pp102-105.

THE MUSEUM QUARTER, VONDELPARK & ZUID

While it may seem unfair to Amsterdam's 50-plus other museums, the **Museum Quarter** is the central nervous system of the city's classical art scene, home to the world-class **Rijksmuseum**, **Van Gogh Museum** and **Stedelijk Museum of Modern Art**. It is nestled at the entrance of **Oud Zuid**, the posh, tree-lined residential neighbourhood where art deco mansions meet haute couture and people-watching restaurants. On its western edge, **Vondelpark** is a 47-hectare (116-acre) breath of fresh air with the perfect ratio of wild to landscaped greenery, bike paths, sport activities and cultural events.
▶ For more, see pp107-113.

Get the most out of your city break and save money and time with Holland Pass!

Holland Pass

- FREE entrance to museums
- FREE entrance to attractions
- FREE 280+ page guide book
- Fast track entry
- Public transport
- Great savings up to 50% discount
- Special offers at restaurants and shops
- Valid until 15 March 2012!

2 tickets:	**€ 24,50**
5 tickets:	**€ 39,50**
7 tickets:	**€ 49,50**
5 tickets KIDS:	**€ 29,50**

Save time and enjoy fast track entry!
Van Gogh Museum, Rijksmuseum, Madame Tussauds, Keukenhof Gardens and many more!

www.hollandpass.com

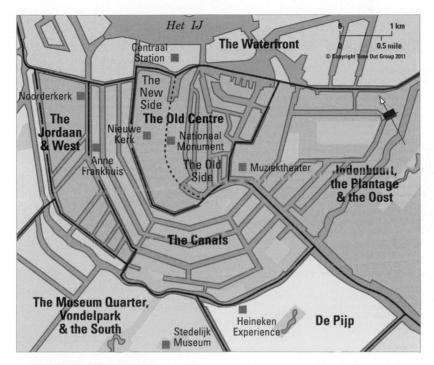

Map labels:
- Het IJ
- The Waterfront
- Centraal Station
- 0 / 1 km / 0.5 mile / © Copyright Time Out Group 2011
- Noorderkerk
- The New Side
- The Old Centre
- The Jordaan & West
- Nieuwe Kerk
- Nationaal Monument
- Anne Frankhuis
- The Old Side
- Muziektheater
- Jodenbuurt, the Plantage & the Oost
- The Canals
- The Museum Quarter, Vondelpark & the South
- Stedelijk Museum
- Heineken Experience
- De Pijp

JODENBUURT, THE PLANTAGE & THE OOST

Former hub of Jewish Amsterdam, **Jodenbuurt** is home to the **Jewish Museum, Rembrandthuis** and the **Portuguese Synagogue**. East of trendy market **Waterlooplein** is **Oost**, a fun mix of cultures and histories. Residential **Plantage** has the **Artis Zoo** and **Hortus Botanicus** garden. From **Oosterpark** to **Flevopark**, through **Dapperbuurt** and its colourful market, the vibe becomes livelier and more ethnic.
▶ *For more, see pp114-119.*

THE WATERFRONT & NOORD

Facing the **Western Islands**, the IJ development combines culture and modern architecture (**Muziekgebouw** and the **Science Center NEMO**). The Eastern Docklands' **Java-eiland** and **KNSM-eiland**, a modern residential area, offer shopping arcades, galleries and yuppy eateries. The area's arty squatters have moved on to **Noord** and creative hotspot **NDSM-werf**.
▶ *For more, see pp120-124.*

DE PIJP

Amsterdam's 'East Village' is centred around the **Albert Cuypmarkt**, selling everything from fresh fish to fashion. Bustling **De Pijp** is teeming with art galleries and creative collectives. A plethora of exotic cafés and late-night eateries reflect its international population, appealing to hip young Amsterdammers. **Sarphatipark** offers a breathing space.
▶ *For more, see pp125-127.*

Time Out Amsterdam

Editorial
Editor Nina Siegal
Deputy Editor Julia Gorodecky
Copy Editors Ismay Atkins, Simon Coppock, Sally Davies, Jan Fuscoe, Megan Roberts
Listings Editors Lake Montgomery, Tim Peterson, Benjamin Roberts, Malcolm Rock, Mark Smith, Arun Sood, Anna Whitehouse
Listings Checkers Catalina Iorga, Alexander Leeuw, Marie-Charlotte Pezé, Ilse Roos
Proofreader Tamsin Shelton
Indexer Jess Fleming

Managing Director Peter Fiennes
Editorial Director Ruth Jarvis
Business Manager Dan Allen
Editorial Manager Holly Pick
Assistant Management Accountant Ija Krasnikova

Design
Art Director Scott Moore
Art Editor Pinelope Kourmouzoglou
Senior Designer Kei Ishimaru
Group Commercial Designer Jodi Sher

Picture Desk
Picture Editor Jael Marschner
Acting Deputy Picture Editor Liz Leahy
Picture Desk Assistant/Researcher Ben Rowe
Picture Editor (Amsterdam) Johanna Nock

Advertising
New Business & Commercial Director Mark Phillips
International Advertising Manager Kasimir Berger
International Sales Executive Charlie Sokol
Advertising Sales (Amsterdam) Katie Burns McAslan, Sabine de Groot, Keeley Warren-Langford

Marketing
Sales & Marketing Director, North America & Latin America Lisa Levinson
Senior Publishing Brand Manager Luthfa Begum
Group Commercial Art Director Anthony Huggins
Marketing Co-ordinator Alana Benton

Production
Group Production Manager Brendan McKeown
Production Controller Katie Mulhern

Time Out Group
Chairman & Founder Tony Elliott
Chief Executive Officer David King
Group Financial Director Paul Rakkar
Group General Manager/Director Nichola Coulthard
Time Out Communications Ltd MD David Pepper
Time Out International Ltd MD Cathy Runciman
Time Out Magazine Ltd Publisher/MD Mark Elliott
Group Commercial Director Graeme Tottle
Group IT Director Simon Chappell

Contributors
Introduction Marie-Charlotte Pezé, Kim Renfrew, Nina Siegal, Anna Whitehouse. **History** Steve Korver, Kim Renfrew, Nina Siegal. **Amsterdam Today** Nina Siegal. **Architecture** Steve Korver. **Art** Nina Siegal. **Sex and Drugs** Nina Siegal, Matt Farquharson, Anna Whitehouse. **Tour Amsterdam** Nina Siegal. **Sightseeing** Charley Harrison, Steve Korver, Christine O'Hara, Nina Siegal, Catherine Somzé, Lena Vazifdar, Anna Whitehouse. **Hotels** Kim Renfrew, Nina Siegal. **Restaurants** Leisha Jones, Steve Korver. **Bars** Erin Farber, Leisha Jones, Kim Renfrew, Tim Skelton. **Coffeeshops** Lake Montgomery, Mark Wedin. **Shops** Karina Hof, Tim Peterson, Nina Siegal, Anna Whitehouse. **Calendar** Willem de Blauw, Sarah Gehrke, Anna Whitehouse. **Children** Georgina Bean, Julia Gorodecky, Jane Hannon. **Dance** Malcolm Rock. **Film** Luuk Van Huët, Marjanne de Haan, Mark Smith. **Galleries** Nina Siegal, Anneloes van Gaalen. **Gay & Lesbian** Willem de Blaauw, Dara Colwell, Mark Smith. Music Steve McCarron, Lake Montgomery, Steve Korver, Mark Wedin, Arun Sood. **Nightclubs** Niels Carels, Joost Baaij, Nina Siegal, Mark Wedin, Christiaan de Wit. **Sport & Fitness** Steve McCarron, Benjamin Roberts. **Theatre & Comedy** Shyama Daryanani, Monique Gruter, Malcolm Rock. **Escapes** Steve Korver, Marinus De Ruiter, Steve McCarron, Kim Renfrew, Tim Peterson Megan Roberts, Nina Siegal. **Directory** Julia Gorodecky.

Maps john@jsgraphics.co.uk except page 336, John Oakey.

Cover photography Alamy
Back cover photography Michelle Grant, Olivia Rutherford.

Photography Michelle Grant; except pages 5, 11 (bottom), 13, 36, 44, 45, 54, 71, 81, 87, 95, 96, 99, 110, 115, 121, 127, 167, 232, 261, 262, 268, 276, 287 (bottom) Olivia Rutherford; pages 7 (bottom left), 144, 207, 236, 251 Wilmar Dik; pages 7 (bottom right), 259 (top), 263, 265, 281, 282, 291, 292, 293, 295, 297, 298 Shutterstock; page 8 Arie de Leeuw; pages 11 (top left), 17, 100, 101 (left), 124, 242, 243 Gemma Day; pages 18, 33 ©Ullsteinbild/TopFoto; page 23 © Sotheby's/Akg-images; page 30 Akg-images; page 31 Rembrandt van Rijn, Self-portrait, 1669, Royal Picture Gallery Mauritshuis, The Hague; page 34 Getty Images; pages 65, 90, 92, 303 Anne Binckebank; pages 77, 79 Photolibrary.com; pages 103, 185, 193, 233, 244 Christina Theisen; page 111 Rijksmuseum; page 113 Henni van Beck; page 116 Roos Aldershoff; pages 117, 172, 180, 199, 200, 202 (top), 224, 235 Karl O'Brian; page 130 The Dylan; page 137 Roel Ruijs; page 170 Heineken International; page 178 Tim Peterson; pages 181, 215, 225, 237, 238, 239 Carolina Georgatou; page 212 SCS/Soenar Chamid; page 213 Roy Laros and Guido van de Zenden; page 221 Stadsschouwburg, Laurent Ziegler; page 222 Stadsschouwburg, Digi Daan; page 226 Cinekid; pages 250, 252, 253, 255, 271 Trey Guinn; page 261 Jos Klijn; page 267 Ajax; page 269 Ajax/Louis van de Vuurst; page 275 Jan Versweyveld.

The following images were provided by the featured establishments/artists: pages 42, 131, 135, 137 (bottom), 143, 146, 205, 274, 277, 279.

The editor would like to thank all contributors to previous editions of *Time Out Amsterdam*, whose work forms the basis for parts of this book.

About the Guide

GETTING AROUND

The back of the book contains street maps of Amsterdam, as well as overview maps of the city and its surroundings. The maps start on page 322; on them are marked the locations of hotels (❶), restaurants and cafés (❶), pubs and bars (❶) and coffeeshops (❶). The majority of businesses listed in this guide are located in the areas we've mapped; the grid-square references in the listings refer to these maps.

THE ESSENTIALS

For practical information, including visas, disabled access, emergency numbers, lost property, useful websites and local transport, please see the Directory. It begins on page 304.

THE LISTINGS

Addresses, phone numbers, websites, transport information, hours and prices are all included in our listings, as are selected other facilities. All were checked and correct at press time. However, business owners can alter their arrangements at any time, and fluctuating economic conditions can cause prices to change rapidly.

The very best venues in Amsterdam, the must-sees and must-dos in each category of this book, have been indicated with a red star (★). In the Sightseeing chapters, we've also marked those venues with free admission with a **FREE** symbol.

PHONE NUMBERS

The area code for Amsterdam is 020. All of the phone numbers given in this guide, when dialled from outside the city, take this code unless otherwise stated. Dialling from abroad you'll need to preface them with the country code for the Netherlands, 31, and then the 020 city code (but first dropping the initial zero). We have stipulated where phone numbers are charged at non-standard rates – such as 0800 numbers (free) and 0900 (premium rate). For more information on telephone codes and charges, *see p312*.

FEEDBACK

We welcome feedback on this guide, both on the venues we've included and on any other locations that you'd like to see featured in future editions. Please email us at guides@timeout.com.

Time Out Guides

Founded in 1968, Time Out has grown from humble beginnings into the leading resource for anyone wanting to know what's happening in the world's greatest cities. Alongside our influential weeklies in London, New York and Chicago, we publish more than 20 magazines in cities as varied as Beijing and Beirut; a range of travel books, with the City Guides now joined by the newer Shortlist series; and an information-packed website. The company remains proudly independent, still owned by Tony Elliott four decades after he launched *Time Out London*.

Written by local experts and illustrated with original photography, our books also retain their independence. No business has been featured because it advertised, and all restaurants and bars are visited and reviewed anonymously.

ABOUT THE EDITOR

Nina Siegal, native New Yorker and former contributor to *The New York Times*, *Wall Street Journal*, *Bloomberg News* and other newspapers and magazines, moved here in 2006 to research her second novel, and ended up becoming founding editor of *Time Out Amsterdam* magazine in 2008. She's still working on that novel.

A full list of the other contributors to this guidebook can be found opposite.

TASSEN MUSEUM
HENDRIKJE
MUSEUM OF BAGS AND PURSES

Enough of Rembrandt and Van Gogh?

Come and admire the biggest collection of bags and purses in the world.

- 500 years of bag and purse history.
- Situated in a beautiful characteristic canal house.
- Museumshop offers contemporary design bags.
- Stylish museum café for lunch or high tea.

HERENGRACHT 573 AMSTERDAM • OPEN EVERY DAY 10-17
www.museumofbagsandpurses.com

In Context

History

From Aemstelledamme, a star city is born.

Technically speaking, Amsterdam is a city that shouldn't really have been a city. The boggy marshland surrounding a rising river wasn't ever a natural support for urban structures, so the locals built a dam and grouped their houses along the River Amstel. What sprang up as a result over the next 700 years is nothing short of a triumph of human engineering: a series of picturesque canal rings holding back the rising waters, and hundreds of thousands of buildings standing on pilings driven 16 to 30 metres (52 to 98 feet) into sand. Pluck a cobblestone out of the streets today and you'll still find seashells right there.

Amsterdammers are proud that theirs is a city built on the sheer drive and ingenuity of its early inhabitants. And its history is something to consider. In its Golden Age in the 17th century, Amsterdam was the centre of the western world. It was the birthplace of the first multinational corporation – the Dutch East India Company – and thereby the hub of all international trade. Not just a business capital, Amsterdam quickly became recognised as the cultural capital of northern Europe: the Old Masters Rembrandt, Frans Hals and Jan Steen gave way to Vincent van Gogh, Kees van Dongen, and later Karel Appel and Piet Mondrian.

Since the Golden Age, the city has gone through many cycles of bust and boom, but it still carries on the tradition of inventiveness, international-mindedness, and a willingness to take risks where risks might seem reckless. The pride in the city's legacy carries over into the vitality and ethos of its current residents. To create, to design, to craft public policy, to imagine a different kind of future – even if there may not be a particularly firm foundation to start with, all of these things are possible.

'After the Amstel was dammed in 1270, a village grew up on the site of what is now Dam Square – Aemstelledamme.'

BOGGY BEGINNINGS

According to legend, Amsterdam was founded by two lost fishermen who vowed to build a town wherever their boat came ashore. They reached terra firma, and their seasick dog promptly anointed the chosen patch with his vomit.

The reality is much more mundane. Although the Romans occupied the southern parts of Holland, they didn't reach the north. Soggy bog was not the stuff on which empires were built, so the legions moved on. Archaeologists have found no evidence of settlement before AD 1000, though there are prehistoric remains further east in Drenthe. Amsterdam's site, in fact, was partially underwater for years, and the River Amstel had no fixed course until enterprising farmers from around Utrecht built dykes during the 11th century. Once the peasants had done the work, the nobility took over.

During the 13th century, the most important place in the newly reclaimed area was the tiny hamlet of Oudekerk aan de Amstel. In 1204, the Lord of Amstel built a castle nearby on what is now the outskirts of Amsterdam. After the Amstel was dammed in about 1270, a village grew up on the site of what is now Dam Square, acquiring the name Aemstelledamme.

BUILT ON BEER

In 1323, the Count of Holland, Floris VI, made Amsterdam one of only two toll points in the province for the import of brews. This was no trivial matter at a time when most people drank beer; drinking the local water, in fact, was practically suicidal. Hamburg had the largest brewing capacity in northern Europe, and within 50 years a third of that city's production was flowing through Amsterdam. By virtue of its position between the Atlantic and Hanseatic ports, and by pouring its beer profits into other ventures, the city broadened its trading remit to take in various essentials.

Yet Amsterdam still remained small. As late as 1425, the 'city' consisted of a few blocks of houses with kitchen gardens and two churches, arranged along the final 1,000-metre stretch of the River Amstel and enclosed by the canals now known as Geldersekade, Singel and Kloveniersburgwal. Virtually all of the buildings were wooden (such as the Houtenhuis, still standing in the Begijnhof), and so fire was a perpetual threat; in the great fire of May 1452, three-quarters of the town was destroyed. One of the few examples of medieval architecture still standing is the Munttoren (Mint Tower) at Muntplein. The structures built after the fire were instead faced with stone and roofed with tile or slate. These new developments coincided with a rush of urban expansion, as – most notably – new foreign commerce led to improvements in shipbuilding.

RADICALISM AND REACTION

During the 16th century, Amsterdam's population increased from 10,000 (low even by medieval standards) to 50,000 by 1600. The city expanded accordingly, although people coming to the city found poverty, disease and squalor in the workers' quarters. Local merchants weren't complaining, however, as the city started to emerge as one of the world's major trading powers.

Amsterdam may have been almost entirely autonomous as a chartered city, but on paper it was still under the thumb of absentee rulers. Through the intricate marriage bureau and shallow genetic pool known as the European aristocracy, the Low Countries (the Netherlands and Belgium) had passed into the hands of the Catholic Austro-Spanish House of Habsburg. The Habsburgs were the mightiest monarchs in Europe, and Amsterdam was still a comparative backwater among their European possessions; nonetheless, events soon brought the city to prominence among its near neighbours.

Amsterdam's new status as a trade centre attracted all kinds of radical religious ideas that were flourishing across northern Europe, encouraged by Martin Luther's condemnation of Catholicism in 1517. When Anabaptists first arrived from Germany in about 1530, the Catholic city fathers tolerated them. But when they started to run around naked and even seized the Town Hall in 1534 during an attempt to establish a 'New Jerusalem' upon the River Amstel, the leaders were arrested, forced to dress, and then executed, signalling an unparalleled period of religious repression: 'heretics' were burned at the stake on the Dam.

After the Anabaptists were culled, Calvinist preachers arrived from Geneva, where the movement had started, and via France. They soon gained followers and, in 1566, the religious discontent erupted into what became known as the Iconoclastic Fury. Churches and monasteries were sacked and stripped of their ornamentation, and Philip II of Spain sent an army to suppress the heresy.

THE EMERGENCE OF ORANGE

The Eighty Years' War (1568-1648) between the Habsburgs and the Dutch is often seen as a struggle for religious freedom, but there was more to it than that. The Dutch were, after all, looking for political autonomy from an absentee king who represented a continual drain on their coffers. By the last quarter of the 16th century, Philip II of Spain was fighting wars against England and France, in the east against the Ottoman Turks, and also in the New World for control of his colonies. The last thing he needed was a revolt in the Low Countries.

Amsterdam toed the Catholic line during the revolt, supporting Philip II until it became clear he was losing. Only in 1578 did the city patricians side with the Calvinist rebels, led by the first William of Orange. The city and William then combined to expel the Catholics and dismantle their institutions in what came to be called the Alteration. A year later, the Protestant states of the Low Countries united in opposition to Philip when the first modern-day European republic was born at the Union of Utrecht. The Republic of Seven United Provinces was made up of Friesland, Gelderland, Groningen, Overijssel, Utrecht, Zeeland and Holland. Though initially lauded as the forerunner of the modern Netherlands, it wasn't the unitary state that William of Orange wanted, but rather a loose federation with an impotent States General assembly.

Each of the seven provinces appointed a Stadhouder (or viceroy), who commanded the Republic's armed forces and had the right to appoint some of the cities' regents or governors. The Stadhouder of each province sent delegates to the assembly, held at the Binnenhof in the Hague. While fitted with clauses set to hinder Catholicism from ever suppressing the Reformed religion again, the Union of Utrecht also enshrined freedom of conscience and religion (at least until the Republic's demise in 1795), thus providing the blueprint that made Amsterdam a safe haven for future political and religious refugees.

The obvious choice for Holland's Stadhouder after the union was William of Orange. After his popular tenure, it became a tradition to elect an Orange as Stadhouder. By 1641, the family had become sufficiently powerful for William II to marry a British princess, Mary Stuart; it was their son, William III, who set sail in 1688 to accept the throne of England in the so-called Glorious Revolution.

A SOCIAL CONSCIENCE WITH CLAWS

From its earliest beginnings, Amsterdam had been governed by four Burgomasters (mayors) and a council representing citizens' interests. By 1500, though, city government had become an incestuous business: the city council's 36 members were

Oude Kerk. *See p89.*

'The refugees brought the skills, the gold and the diamond industry that would make the city one of the world's greatest trading centres.'

appointed for life, 'electing' the mayors from their own ranks. Selective intermarriage meant that the city was, in effect, governed by a handful of families.

When Amsterdam joined the rebels in 1578, the only change in civic administration was that the Catholic elite were replaced by a Calvinist faction of equally wealthy families. The city, now home to 225,000, remained the third city of Europe, after London and Paris. Social welfare, though, was transformed under the Calvinists, and incorporated into government. The Regents, as the Calvinist elite became known, took over the convents and monasteries (one such convent is now home to the Amsterdams Historisch Museum; *see p92. Photo p25*), starting charitable organisations such as orphanages. But they would not tolerate any kind of excess: drunkenness and immorality, like crime, were punishable offences.

In the two centuries before the Eighty Years' War, Amsterdam had developed its own powerful maritime force. Even so, it remained overshadowed by Antwerp until 1589, when that city fell to those darned Spaniards. In Belgium, the Habsburg Spanish had adopted siege tactics, leaving Amsterdam unaffected by the hostilities and free to benefit from the blockades suffered by rival ports. Thousands of refugees fled north, among them some of Antwerp's most prosperous merchants, who were mostly Protestant and Jewish (specifically Sephardic Jews who had earlier fled their original homes in Spain and Portugal to escape the Inquisition). The refugees brought the skills, the gold and, most famously, the diamond industry that would soon help make the city one of the greatest trading centres in the world.

THE GOLDEN AGE

European history seems to be littered with golden ages – but in Amsterdam's case, the first six decades of the 17th century genuinely deserve the label. It is truly remarkable that such a small and isolated city could come to dominate world trade and set up major colonies, resulting in a local population explosion and a frenzy of urban expansion. Its girdle of canals was one of the great engineering feats of the age. This all happened while the country was at war with Spain and presided over not by kings, but businessmen.

The Dutch East India Company, known locally as the VOC (Verenigde Oost Indische Compagnie), was the world's first transnational corporation. Created by the States General charter in 1602 to finance the wildly expensive and fearsomely dangerous voyages to the East, the power of the VOC was far-reaching: it had the capacity to found colonies, establish its own army, declare war and sign treaties. With 1,450 ships, the VOC made over 4,700 highly profitable journeys.

While the VOC concentrated on the spice trade, a new company received its charter from the Dutch Republic in 1621. The Dutch West India Company (West Indische Compagnie), while not as successful as its sister, dominated trade with Spanish and Portuguese territories in Africa and America, and in 1623 began to colonise Manhattan Island. Although the colony flourished at first, New Amsterdam didn't last long. After the Duke of York's invasion in 1664, the peace treaty between England and the Netherlands determined that New Amsterdam would change its name to New York and come under British control. The Dutch got Surinam in return.

Meanwhile, Amsterdam's port had become the major European centre for distribution and trade. Grain from Russia, Poland and Prussia, salt and wine from France, cloth from

Dutch East India Company.

Leiden and tiles from Delft all passed through the port. Whales were hunted by Amsterdam's fleets, generating a thriving soap trade, and sugar and spices from Dutch colonies were distributed throughout Scandinavia and the north of Europe. All this activity was financed by the Bank of Amsterdam, which became the hub of the single most powerful money vault in all Europe, its notes exchangeable throughout the trading world.

PRESENT AND CORRECTED

From 1600 to 1650, the city's population ballooned fourfold, and it was obliged to expand once again. Construction on the most elegant of the major canals circling the city centre, Herengracht (Lords' Canal), began in 1613; this was where many of the ruling assembly had their homes. So that there would be no misunderstanding about status, Herengracht was followed further out by Keizersgracht (Emperors' Canal) and Prinsengracht (Princes' Canal). Immigrants were housed in the Jordaan.

For all its wealth, famine hit Amsterdam with dreary regularity in the 17th century. Guilds had benevolent funds set aside for their members in times of need, but social welfare was primarily in the hands of the ruling merchant class. Amsterdam's elite was noted for its philanthropy, but only the 'deserving poor' were eligible for assistance. Those seen as undeserving were sent to houses of correction. The initial philosophy behind these had been idealistic: hard work would produce useful citizens. Soon, however, the institutions became little more than prisons for those condemned to work there.

Religious freedom wasn't what it might have been, either. As a result of the Alteration of 1578, open Catholic worship was banned in the city during the 17th century, and Catholics were forced to practise in secret. Some started attic churches, which are exactly what their name suggests: of those set up during the 1600s, the Museum Amstelkring has preserved Amsterdam's only surviving example – Our Lord in the Attic – in its entirety (*see p89*).

THE HARDER THEY FALL

Though Amsterdam remained one of the single wealthiest cities in Europe until the early 19th century, its dominant trading position was lost to England and France after

'The Dutch East India Company was the world's first transnational corporation, financing wildly expensive trips to the East.'

1660. The United Provinces then spent a couple of centuries bickering about trade and politics with Britain and the other main powers. Wars were frequent: major sea conflicts included battles against the Swedes and no fewer than four Anglo-Dutch wars, in which the Dutch came off worse. It wasn't that they didn't win any battles; more that they ran out of men and money. The naval officers who led the wars against Britain are Dutch heroes, and the Nieuwe Kerk has monuments to admirals Van Kinsbergen (1735-1819), Bentinck (1745-1831) and, most celebrated of all, Michiel de Ruyter (1607-76).

In the 18th century, the Dutch Republic began to lag behind the major European powers. Amsterdam was nudged out of the shipbuilding market by England, and its lucrative textile industry was lost to other provinces. However, the city managed to exploit its position as the financial centre of the world until the final, devastating Anglo-Dutch War (1780-84). The British hammered the Dutch merchant and naval fleets with unremitting aggression, crippling profitable trade with their Far Eastern colonies in the process.

THE NAPOLEONIC NETHERLANDS

During the 1780s, a Republican movement known as the Patriots managed to shake off the influence of the Stadhouders in many smaller towns. In 1787, though, they were foiled in Amsterdam by the intervention of the Prince of Orange and his brother -in-law, Frederick William II, King of Prussia. Hundreds of Patriots then fled to exile in France, only to return in 1795, backed by a French army of 'advisers'. With massive support from Amsterdam, they celebrated the new Batavian Republic.

It sounded too good to be true, and it was. According to one contemporary, 'the French moved over the land like locusts'. Over ƒ100 million (about €50 million today) was extracted from the Dutch, and the French also sent an army, 25,000 of whom had to be fed, equipped and housed by their Dutch 'hosts'. Republican ideals seemed hollow when Napoleon installed his brother, Louis, as King of the Netherlands in 1806, and so the symbol of Amsterdam's mercantile ascendancy and civic pride, the City Hall of the Dam, was requisitioned as the royal palace. Even Louis was disturbed by the impoverishment of a nation that had been Europe's most prosperous. However, after Louis had allowed Dutch smugglers to break Napoleon's blockade of Britain, he was forced to abdicate in 1810 and the Low Countries were absorbed into the French Empire.

French rule wasn't an unmitigated disaster for the Dutch. The foundations of the modern state were laid in the Napoleonic period, and a civil code introduced – not to mention a huge broadening of culinary possibilities. However, trade with Britain ceased, and the cost of Napoleon's wars prompted the Dutch to join the revolt against France. After Napoleon's defeat, Amsterdam became the capital of a constitutional monarchy, including what is now Belgium; William VI of Orange was crowned King William I in 1815. But while the Oranges still reigned across the north, the United Kingdom of the Netherlands, as it then existed, lasted only until 1830.

A RETURN TO FORM

When the French were finally defeated and left Dutch soil in 1813, Amsterdam emerged as the capital of the new kingdom of the Netherlands but very little else.

ANNO

15 81

92

Amsterdams Historisch Museum. *See p22.*

'The picturesque Jordaan, where regular riots broke out, was occupied by the lowest-paid workers. Its canals were used as cesspits.'

With its coffers depleted and its colonies occupied by the British, the city faced a hard fight for recovery.

The fight was made tougher by two huge obstacles. For a start, Dutch colonial assets had been reduced to present-day Indonesia, Surinam and the odd island in the Caribbean. Just as important, though, was the fact that the Dutch were slow to join the Industrial Revolution. The Netherlands had few natural resources to exploit, and business preferred sail power to steam. Add to this the fact that Amsterdam's opening to the sea, the Zuider Zee, was too shallow for the new steamships, and it's easy to see why the Dutch struggled.

Still, by the late 19th century Amsterdam had begun to modernise production of the luxury goods for which it would eventually become internationally famous: beer, chocolates, cigars and diamonds. The Noordzee Kanaal (North Sea Canal) was opened in 1876, while the city finally got a major rail link in 1889. Amsterdam consolidated its position at the forefront of Europe with the building of a number of impressive landmarks, including Cuypers' Rijksmuseum (1885), the Stadsschouwburg (1894), the Stedelijk Museum (1895) and the Tropeninstituut (1926). The city's international standing soared – to the point where, in 1928, it hosted the Olympics.

MISERY OF THE MASSES

Amsterdam's population had stagnated at 250,000 for two centuries after the Golden Age, but between 1850 and 1900 it more than doubled. Extra labour was needed to meet the demands of a revitalised economy, but the big problem was how to house the new workers.

Today, the old inner-city quarters are desirable addresses, but they used to house Amsterdam's poor. The picturesque Jordaan, where regular riots broke out at the turn of the century, was occupied by the lowest-paid workers. Its canals were used as cesspits, and the mortality rate was high.

Around the centre, new developments – De Pijp, Dapper and Staatslieden quarters – were built: they weren't luxurious, but at least they enjoyed simple lavatory facilities, while the Amsterdam School of architects (*see p48*), inspired by socialist beliefs, designed now-classic housing for the poor. Wealthier city-dwellers, meanwhile, lived in elegant homes constructed near Vondelpark and further south.

The city didn't fare badly during the first two decades of the 20th century, but Dutch neutrality throughout World War I brought problems to parts of the population. While the elite lined their pockets selling arms, the poor faced crippling food shortages and unemployment, and riots broke out in 1917 and 1934.

Many Dutch workers moved to Germany, where National Socialism was creating jobs. The city was just emerging from the Depression when the Nazis invaded in May 1940.

OCCUPATION

Early in the morning of 10 May 1940, German bombers mounted a surprise attack on Dutch airfields and barracks. The government and people had hoped that the Netherlands could remain neutral, as it had in World War I, so the armed forces were unprepared for war. Queen Wilhelmina fled to London to form a government in exile, leaving Supreme Commander Winkelman in charge. After Rotterdam was destroyed by bombing and the Germans threatened other cities with the same treatment, Winkelman surrendered on 14 May.

During the war, Hitler appointed Austrian Nazi Arthur Seyss-Inquart as Rijkskommissaris (State Commissioner) of the Netherlands, and asked him to tie the Dutch economy to the German one and help to Nazify Dutch society. Though it gained less than five per cent of the votes in the 1939 elections, the National Socialist Movement (NSB) was the only Dutch party not prohibited during the occupation. Its doctrine resembled German Nazism, but the NSB wanted to maintain Dutch autonomy under the direction of Germany.

During the first years of the war, the Nazis let most people live relatively unmolested. Rationing, however, made the Dutch vulnerable to the black market, while cinemas and theatres eventually closed because of curfews and censorship. Later, the Nazis adopted more aggressive measures: Dutch men were forced to work in German industry, and economic exploitation assumed appalling forms. In April 1943, all Dutch soldiers were ordered to give themselves up as prisoners of war. Within an atmosphere of deep shock and outrage, strikes broke out, but were violently suppressed.

As Nazi policies became more virulent, people were confronted with the difficult choice of whether to obey German measures or to resist. There were several patterns of collaboration: some people joined the NSB, while others intimidated Jews, got involved in economic collaboration or betrayed people in hiding. The most shocking institutional collaboration involved Dutch police, who dragged Jews out of their houses for deportation, and Dutch Railways, which was paid for transporting Jews to their deaths.

Others resisted. The Resistance was made up chiefly of Communists and, to a lesser extent, Calvinists. Anti-Nazi activities took various forms, including the production and distribution of illegal newspapers, which kept the population informed and urged them to resist the Nazi dictators. Some members of the Resistance spied for the Allies, while some fought an armed struggle against the Germans through assassination and sabotage. There were those who falsified identity cards and food vouchers, while others helped Jews into hiding. By 1945, more than 300,000 people had gone underground in the Netherlands.

THE HUNGER WINTER

In 1944, the Netherlands plunged into the Hongerwinter – the Hunger Winter. Supplies of coal vanished after the liberation of the south, and a railway strike, called by the Dutch government in exile in order to hasten German defeat, was disastrous for the supply of food. In retaliation, the Germans damaged Schiphol Airport and the harbours of Rotterdam and Amsterdam, foiling any attempts to bring in supplies, and grabbed everything they could. Walking became the only means of transport, domestic refuse was no longer collected, sewers overflowed and the population fell to disease.

To survive, people stole fuel: more than 20,000 trees were cut down and 4,600 buildings were demolished. Floors, staircases, joists and rafters were plundered, causing the collapse of many houses, particularly those left by deported Jews. By the end of the winter, 20,000 people had died of starvation and disease, and much of the city was seriously damaged.

But hope was around the corner. The Allies liberated the south of the Netherlands on 5 September 1944, Dolle Dinsdag (Mad Tuesday), and complete liberation came on 5 May 1945, when it became apparent that the Netherlands was the worst-hit country in western Europe.

Amsterdam endured World War II without being flattened by bombs, but nonetheless its buildings, infrastructure, inhabitants and morale were reduced to a terrible state by the occupying Nazi forces. The Holocaust also left an indelible

Begijnhof. *See p91.*

scar on a city whose population in 1940 was ten per cent Jewish. Only 5,000 Jews, out of a pre-war Jewish population of 80,000, remained. When the war was over, 450,000 people were arrested for collaboration, although most were quickly released; mitigating circumstances – NSB members who helped the Resistance, for example – made judgements complicated. Of 14,500 sentenced, only 39 were executed.

THE HOLOCAUST

'I see how the world is slowly becoming a desert, I hear more and more clearly the approaching thunder that will kill us,' wrote Anne Frank in her diary on 15 July 1944. Though her words obviously applied to the Jews, they were relevant to all those who were persecuted during the war. Granted, anti-Semitism in Holland had not been as virulent as in Germany, France or Austria. But even so, most – though not all – of the Dutch population ignored the persecution, and there's still a sense of national guilt as a result.

The Holocaust happened in three stages. First came measures to enforce the isolation of the Jews: the ritual slaughter of animals was prohibited, Jewish government employees were dismissed, Jews were banned from public places and, eventually, all Jews were forced to wear a yellow Star of David. (Some non-Jews wore the badge as a mark of solidarity.) Concentration was the second stage. From early 1942, all Dutch Jews were obliged to move to three areas in Amsterdam, isolated by signs, drawbridges and barbed wire. The final stage was deportation. Between July 1942 and September 1943, most of the 140,000 Dutch Jews were deported via the detention and transit camp Kamp Westerbork. Public outrage at deportations was foreshadowed by the one and only protest, organised by dockworkers, against the anti-Semitic terror, the February Strike of 1941.

The Nazis also wanted to eliminate Gypsies: more than 200,000 European Gypsies, including many Dutch, were exterminated. Homosexuals, too, were threatened with extermination, but their persecution was less systematic: public morality acts prohibited homosexual behaviour, and gay pressure groups ceased their activities. Amsterdam has the world's first memorial to persecuted gays – the Homomonument – which incorporates pink triangles, turning the Nazi badge of persecution into a symbol of pride.

THE DUST SETTLES

Despite intense poverty and drastic shortages of food, fuel and building materials, the Dutch tackled the task of post-war recovery with a strong sense of optimism. Some Dutch flirted briefly with Communism after the war, but in 1948, a compromise was agreed between the Catholic KVP and the newly created Labour party PvdA, and the two proceeded to govern in successive coalitions until 1958. Led by Prime Minister Willem Drees, the government resuscitated social programmes and laid the basis for a welfare state. The Dutch now reverted to the virtues of a conservative society: decency, hard work and thrift.

The country's first priority, however, was economic recovery. The city council concentrated on reviving the two motors of its economy, Schiphol Airport and the Port of Amsterdam, the latter of which was boosted by the opening of the Amsterdam-Rhine Canal in 1952. Joining Belgium and Luxembourg in the Benelux also brought the country trade benefits, and the Netherlands was the first European nation to repay its Marshall Plan loans. The authorities dusted off their pre-war development plans and embarked on a rapid phase of urban expansion. But as people moved into the new suburbs, businesses flowed into the centre, worsening congestion on the already cramped roads.

After the war, the Dutch colonies of New Guinea and Indonesia were liberated from the Japanese and pushed for independence. Immigrants to the Netherlands included

IN CONTEXT

Profile Rembrandt's Amsterdam

The rise and fall of the great Dutch Master.

Rembrandt van Rijn was not born in Amsterdam, though his professional career began and ended here. A transplant to the city from his hometown of Leiden (*see p294*), some 35 kilometres (22 miles) away, saw him become very much the Amsterdammer: broadminded, largely secular, and rather prone to speculating wildly on treasures from abroad.

Rembrandt got his first taste of the city as a teenager, when, in 1623, he took a brief apprenticeship under the painter Pieter Lastman. Lastman's studio was in the artists' quarter of the city, which surrounded Sint Antoniebreestraat from the Nieuwmarkt to Waterlooplein. The area was crammed with art dealers, antiques shops, writers and map-makers, and peopled by recent immigrants, Sephardic Jews and prostitutes – a perfect spot for a young artist to find resources and plenty of models for sketches and biblical paintings.

When Rembrandt officially settled in Amsterdam in 1631, he returned to the same district (today known as the Jodenbuurt), this time to head up a painting academy established by art dealer Hendrick van Uylenburgh. Rembrandt made his own etchings and paintings while teaching pupils, and Van Uylenburgh arranged lucrative commissions of portraits of the city's wealthy merchants and burghers. Among

Rembrandt's early works was *The Anatomy Lesson of Dr Nicolaes Tulp* (1632), now in the Mauritshuis Museum in the Hague, which depicted the famous surgeon's annual dissection in the anatomy theatre in the Waag.

Almost immediately, the young artist became hot property, selling his portraits for hundreds of guilders and running a highly productive studio of his own, with scores of pupils and apprentices. He married his dealer's cousin, Saskia van Uylenburgh, and bought a grand mansion (now the Rembrandthuis; *see p116*), filling it with art and collectibles. High-profile commissions flooded in, including the *Portrait of Jan Six* (a local burgher) and a group portrait of the *Syndics of the Drapers' Guild*.

Rembrandt's *The Night Watch*.

Rembrandt's *Self Portrait.*

Rembrandt's fortunes shifted, though. Three of his four children died in infancy, while Saskia died in 1642. His relationships with his two mistresses ended badly, and commissions dried up as he fell out of favour. He went bankrupt in 1656, and was forced to sell most of his art collections. He died in 1669, a year after his son, Titus, and was buried in an unmarked grave in the Westerkerk (*see p96*).

DARK ARTS

One of Rembrandt's most famous works is the colossal, shadowy painting of the Arquebusiers militia group that now hangs in the Rijksmuseum (*see p108*), *The Night Watch* (1642; *photo left*). A real national treasure, it has twice been vandalised by members of the public, once with a bread knife (look closely and you can see the scars) and once with acid.

"'I see how the world is becoming a desert. I hear the approaching thunder that will kill us," wrote Anne Frank in 15 July 1944.'

colonial natives, and Turkish and Moroccan 'guest workers'. Though poorer jobs and housing have been their lot, racial tensions were notable for being relatively low up until the mid 1990s.

THE PROVOS

The 1960s proved to be one of the most colourful decades in Amsterdam's history. Popular movements very similar to those in other west European cities were formed, but because the Dutch have a habit of keeping things in proportion, popular demonstrations took a playful form.

Discontent gained focus in 1964, when a group of political pranksters called the Provos kickstarted a new radical subculture. Founded by anarchist philosophy student Roel van Duyn and 'anti-smoke magician' Robert Jasper Grootveld, the Provos – their name inspired by their game plan: to provoke – numbered only about two dozen, but were enormously influential. Their style influenced the major anti-Vietnam demos in the US and the Situationist antics in 1969 Paris, and set the tone for Amsterdam's love of liberal politics and absurdist theatre. Their finest hour came in March 1966, when protests about Princess Beatrix's controversial wedding to the German Claus van Amsberg turned nasty after the Provos let off a smoke bomb on the carriage route, and a riot ensued. Some Provos, such as Van Duyn, went on to fight the system from within: five won City seats under the surreal banner of the Kabouter (a mythical race of forest-dwelling dwarves) in 1970.

SQUATTERS

Perhaps the single most significant catalyst for discontent in the 1970s – which exploded into civil conflict by the '80s – was the issue of housing. Amsterdam's small size and historic centre had always been a nightmare for its urban planners. The city's population increased in the '60s, reaching its peak (nearly 870,000) by 1964. Swelling the numbers further were immigrants from the Netherlands' last major colony, Surinam, many of whom were dumped in the Bijlmermeer. It degenerated into a ghetto and, when a 747 crashed there in October 1992, the final number of fatalities was impossible to ascertain: many victims were unregistered.

The Metro link to Bijlmermeer is in itself a landmark to some of Amsterdam's most violent protests. Passionate opposition erupted against the proposed clearance in February 1975 of the Jewish quarter of Nieuwmarkt. Civil unrest culminated in 'Blue Monday' (24 March 1975) when police sparked clashes with residents and supporters. Police fired tear gas into the homes of those who refused to move out, and battered down doors.

Speculators who left property empty caused acute resentment, which soon turned into direct action: vacant buildings were occupied illegally by squatters. In March 1980, police turned against them for the first time and used tanks to evict the squatters from a former office building in Vondelstraat. Riots ensued, but the squatters were victorious. In 1982, as Amsterdam's squatting movement reached its peak, clashes with police escalated: a state of emergency was called after one eviction battle. Soon, though, the City – led by new mayor Ed van Thijn – had gained the upper hand over the movement, and one of the last of the big squats, Wyers, fell amid tear gas in February 1984 to make way for a Holiday Inn. Squatters were

IN CONTEXT

German Occupation: soldiers at Amsterdam's flower market, July 1940. *See p26.*

no longer a force to be reckoned with, though their ideas of small-scale regeneration have since been absorbed into official planning.

THE SHAPE OF THINGS TO COME

Born and bred in Amsterdam, Ed van Thijn embodied a new strand in Dutch politics. Though a socialist, he took tough action against 'unsavoury elements' – petty criminals, squatters, dealers in hard drugs – and upgraded facilities to attract new businesses and tourists. A new national political era also emerged, where the welfare system and government subsidies were trimmed to ease the country's large budget deficit, and aimed to revitalise the economy with more businesslike policies.

The price of Amsterdam's new affluence (among most groups, except the very poorest) has been a swing towards commercialism, with the squatters largely supplanted by well-groomed yuppies. Flashy cafés, galleries and nouvelle cuisine restaurants replaced the alternative scene, and a mood of calm settled on the city. Still, a classic example of Dutch compromise is the development of what the city's minister of culture, Carolien Gehrels, calls 'breathing spaces', which are basically unused buildings that are handed over to artists and other creative types to do with what they will – for a couple of years at a time. One example is the Trouw, a former newspaper office that has been turned into a very successful club, restaurant and cultural events space, with offices and ateliers.

During the recent economic decline, the main advantages of nurturing Amsterdam's long-held reputation as a hotbed for edgy creativity became more apparent – both for business and the general atmosphere, proving the city isn't ready to relinquish its rebel status just yet.

IN CONTEXT

Rioting on the street in the 1980s. See p32.

Key events

EARLY HISTORY
1204 Gijsbrecht van Amstel builds a castle in the area that will eventually become the city of Amsterdam.
1270 Amstel dammed at Dam Square.
1300 Amsterdam is granted city rights by the Bishop of Utrecht.
1306 Work begins on the Oude Kerk.
1313 The Bishop of Utrecht grants Aemstelledamme full municipal rights and leaves it to William III of Holland.
1421 The St Elizabeth's Day Flood; Amsterdam's first great fire.

WAR AND REFORMATION
1534 Anabaptists try to seize City Hall but fail. A sustained and brutal period of anti-Protestant repression begins.
1565 William the Silent organises a Protestant revolt against Spanish rule.
1566 Iconoclastic Fury unleashed. Protestant worship is made legal.
1568 Eighty Years' War with Spain begins.
1577 Prince of Orange annexes city.
1578 Catholic Burgomasters replaced by Protestants in the Alteration.
1579 The Union of Utrecht is signed, allowing freedom of religious belief.

THE GOLDEN AGE
1602 The Dutch East India Company (VOC) is founded.
1606 Rembrandt van Rijn is born.
1611 The Zuiderkerk is completed.
1613 Work starts on the Canal Belt.
1623 The Dutch West India Company colonises Manhattan Island.
1625 Peter Stuyvesant founds New Amsterdam.
1642 Rembrandt finishes *Night Watch*.
1648 The Treaty of Munster is signed, ending Eighty Years' War with Spain.
1654 England begins a bloody drawn-out war against the United Provinces.
1667 England and the Netherlands sign the Peace of Breda.

DECLINE AND FALL
1672 England and the Netherlands go to war; Louis XIV of France invades.

1675 Portuguese Synagogue is built.
1685 French Protestants take refuge after revocation of the Edict of Nantes.
1689 William of Orange becomes King William III of England.
1787 Frederick William II, King of Prussia, occupies Amsterdam.
1795 French Revolutionaries set up the Batavian Republic.
1813 Unification of the Netherlands.
1815 Amsterdam becomes the capital.

BETWEEN THE OCCUPATIONS
1848 City's ramparts are pulled down.
1876 Noordzee Kanaal links Amsterdam with the North Sea.
1885 The Rijksmuseum is completed.
1889 Centraal Station opens.
1922 Women are granted the vote.
1928 Olympics are held in Amsterdam.

WORLD WAR II
1940 German troops invade.
1941 The February Strike, in protest against the deportation of Jews.
1944-45 20,000 die in Hunger Winter.
1945 Canadian soldiers liberate Amsterdam.
1947 Anne Frank's diary is published.

THE POST-WAR ERA
1966 The wedding of Princess Beatrix and Prince Claus ends in riots.
1968 The IJ Tunnel opens.
1976 Cannabis is decriminalised.
1977 First Metro is opened.
1980 Queen Beatrix's coronation.
1997 The Euro approved as European currency in the Treaty of Amsterdam.
1999 Prostitution is made legal after years of decriminalisation.
2002 Dutch politician Pim Fortuyn is murdered.
2004 Filmmaker Theo van Gogh is murdered by an Islamic fundamentalist.
2007: 'Project 1012' clean up begins.
2009: Bystanders killed in assassination attempt on the Dutch Royal Family.
2010: Amsterdam Mayor Job Cohen becomes the Labour Party leader.

IN CONTEXT

Amsterdam Today

*The famously liberal city is being tested
by financial and xenophobic tensions.*

TEXT: NINA SIEGAL

'The most relaxed city in Europe.' 'It really has everything, from the best art and new design to the old sex, drugs and rock 'n' roll.' 'The people are so friendly.' 'It's compact and beautiful, you can bike and walk everywhere and everybody speaks perfect English.'

These are just a few reasons why tourists flock en masse to the Dutch capital. 'Amsterdam has it' was the City's slogan in the mid 1970s. After 40-odd years – and with a new integrationist slogan, 'I amsterdam' – this still rings true, though a lot has changed. Compared to London or Paris, Amsterdam used to be like a kid brother who didn't want to grow up; it was a playground where all involved were guaranteed a good time, bar a few superficial bumps.

That easy ride may be coming to an end, however; in recent years cultural tensions have frequently tested that famously relaxed attitude, and for all the high jinks that still mark Amsterdam out as different, the time may have arrived for the city to come of age.

'Pim Fortuyn, who was flamboyantly gay and vociferously anti-Islamic, gained a huge following among some middle-class Dutch people.'

WAVES OF IMMIGRATION

Until the second half of the 20th century, the Netherlands was a fairly homogeneous country, and the relatively small population of ethnic minorities got along fairly well with the native Dutch. After the country surrendered its colonies in the Dutch East Indies, 300,000 Indonesians came to the former motherland, followed, in the 1960s, by tens of thousands of labour migrants from Turkey and Morocco. The next wave of 300,000 foreigners came in the 1970s, when another colony, Surinam in South America, gained its independence. Dutch passport-holders from the Netherlands Antilles and refugees from all over the world have also contributed to a serious shake-up of the Dutch demographic landscape, which had been white for many centuries but was finally starting to change colour. In the 1960s, Turkish and Moroccan immigrants were hired to help the post-war reconstruction of the Netherlands, most of them in low-paid industrial jobs. Not much attention was given to their language skills, because the idea was that they would go home after a couple of years. However, many of them decided to stay on, brought their families over, and by 2007 about 850,000 Muslims were living in a country with a population of 16.4 million.

BOILING POINT

Until the 1990s, the Netherlands had a great reputation for being a free and tolerant country, where each and everybody, regardless of faith, gender, political beliefs or sexual orientation, could do whatever he or she wanted. At the same time, an ever growing number of non-Western immigrants and their children, often living on social welfare, were occupying dilapidated apartment buildings in and around neighbourhoods like the Bijlmer, where the crime rates were relatively high and there weren't many opportunities for economic or social advancement. From a mixture of indifference and the belief that stigmatising ethnic groups was wrong and would lead to racism, society chose to ignore the problem.

Until Pim Fortuyn, a populist-style right-wing politician arrived on the scene in the 1990s. An unlikely figure who was both flamboyantly gay and vociferously anti-Islamic, he quickly gained a huge following among many middle-class Dutch people who felt he was speaking for them when he argued that the nation should 'close its borders' to Muslims. Xenophobic tensions were building rapidly.

Fortuyn was murdered in 2002 – the first political assassination since the murder of the father of the fatherland, William of Orange, in 1584 – a shock felt throughout the nation. It wasn't a Muslim extremist, however, who pulled the trigger; it was a self-described animal rights activist and environmentalist extremist named Volkert van der Graaf, who said he did it to 'protect weaker groups in society'.

One of Fortuyn's most vocal supporters was filmmaker, media personality and anti-Islamic provocateur Theo van Gogh. Along with MP Ayaan Hirsi Ali, herself a former Muslim and immigrant from Somalia, Van Gogh produced a short film, *Submission*, which featured a woman in a transparent burqa with Koranic script written on her body. It was designed to call attention to violence against women committed in the name of Sharia law, but many people saw it as pure hate-mongering.

On 2 November 2004, Van Gogh was shot to death in an Amsterdam street by Muslim extremist Mohammed Bouyeri, an Amsterdam-born Dutch Moroccan, who then stabbed him in the back with a note threatening the life of Hirsi Ali.

IN CONTEXT

A HERO EMERGES

After the murder of Theo van Gogh, former Amsterdam mayor Job Cohen's speech at the impromptu 'noise' demonstration immediately following the brutal event included the now-famous line '*we moeten de boel bij elkaar houden*' ('we must keep things together'), and that's exactly what he did.

Many Amsterdammers praised his swift and balanced moves, focusing more on dialogue than action to keep the peace in the multicultural city that Amsterdam has become over the years. Others, however, felt he wasn't tough enough and dubbed him 'Mr Pickwick' (after a Dutch tea brand), claiming he spent too much time drinking mint tea in mosques with Muslim delegates instead of setting an example by taking firm measures.

Van Gogh's murder put Amsterdam in international headlines, and Cohen was named one of *Time* magazine's 'Heroes of 2005' because he ensured emotion didn't get the upper hand and turn into rioting, as in France; he was also voted number two in the 2006 World Mayor Awards. In 2008, he was named one of *Time Out Amsterdam*'s local heroes too.

As a politician who could keep the social order in balance and reduce tensions in the capital city, he seemed like a natural choice for a leader on the national stage. In the spring of 2010, Cohen became the new Labour Party leader in the House, though the Labour-led government collapsed shortly thereafter, and was replaced by a far more conservative coalition.

NEW XENOPHOBIA

Although the Fortuynist party managed to hold together for a short while, it ultimately crumbled, through internal conflicts and empty-headedness, and the old political parties picked up where it left off.

However, the right-wing anti-Islamic populist movement found a new spokesman in Geert Wilders, a representative of the Freedom Party, who has antagonised the Muslim community by calling for a ban on the Koran, which he has called a fascist book, akin to *Mein Kampf*.

Although the Dutch media named him 'politician of the year' in 2007 – perhaps because of the sheer volume of news he generates – he was banned from entering the UK in 2009 on the grounds that he was a 'serious threat to one of the fundamental interests of society', when he tried to screen his controversial 17-minute anti-Islamic documentary, *Fitna*, in the House of Lords. In 2010, he was put on trial in Amsterdam for five counts of inciting hatred and discrimination. At press time, the trial was still pending.

In spite of the obvious problems with the emergence of a hate-mongering politician, it's estimated that Wilders has some 1.4 million supporters for his Freedom Party, which went from just nine seats in the 2006 election to 24 in the 2010 elections, beating out the Christian Democrats, previously the nation's leading party. The big winner of the 2010 election was the free-market centre-right VVD (with 31 seats), however, which then formed a new right-wing coalition with the Christian Democrats.

Meanwhile, the Dutch political scene continues to be explosive, with other politicians making other kinds of xenophobic comments. In December 2010, for example, Frits Bolkestein, former leader of the Netherlands ruling rightist VVD party, sparked a heated debate by saying that practising Jews had 'no future here, and should emigrate to the US or Israel'. These kinds of comments would have had no place in Dutch political discourse even two decades ago – this was a country so thoroughly demoralised and ashamed of its action (or rather, inaction) during World War II that it had tended to tread very lightly where any hint of racism might have been perceived. Not so in the new Netherlands.

BUDGET CRUNCHING

One way to understand rising racial and socio-political strains in this once-broadminded nation is to analyse it through the prism of economics.

The Limits of Tolerance

Amsterdam is a city of moral paradoxes.

Amsterdam is famous the world over for being a place where 'anything goes' but most people who spend more than a couple of days here start to notice fairly quickly that the local population itself isn't exactly freewheeling. Those Red Light District attractions that lure millions of visitors to the city are largely designed for tourists, not the locals. It's rare that you'll find a Dutch person hanging out in a coffeeshop, unless they're hosting foreign visitors.

'Tolerance' is a word that gets bandied about a lot in Amsterdam, but the word doesn't necessarily mean 'acceptance' of all kinds of behaviour, and it also doesn't mean encouragement of experimentation and vice. It means, 'we don't mind if you do your thing, as long as it doesn't interfere with the otherwise normal operation of business here... and as long as it doesn't hurt anyone else.'

The city's famed tolerance made it a safe haven for Spanish and Portuguese Jews in the 16th century, the Huguenots in the 1700s, the Belgians during World War I and Hungarians after the 1956 revolution. When the country has been flush, it has received political and war refugees from other countries not only with visas and long-term residency, but also with financial support, housing and a free college education. Its atmosphere of intellectual and artistic freedom has made it a refuge for thinkers and creative types from René Descartes in the 17th century to UK filmmaker and artist Steve McQueen today.

However, it could be argued that the same tolerance that allowed Amsterdam to become known as a Jewish capital of Europe before World War II (engendering the nickname *Mokum* or 'home') was counteracted by the Dutch 'tolerance' of the deportation and extermination of the same Jewish community under Nazi occupation. There may have been a resistance movement here, but in the end, 90 per cent of the Netherlands' Jews were killed during the war – the highest proportion of any western European country, and the second highest in all of Europe after Poland.

On a day-to-day basis, the Dutch character can also be quite a bit more conservative than one might expect. *Gewoon zijn*, or being normal, is considered to be of utmost importance in Dutch culture, and a favourite admonition when someone behaves a little out of the ordinary is '*Doe normaal*' ('Behave normally!') according to the old Dutch saying, '*Doe maar gewoon, dan doe je al gek genoeg*' ('Just behave normally, that's strange enough').

So it's no surprise that although the Netherlands is tolerant of outsiders and people behaving strangely, wandering around high in public places and so on, they're not necessarily thrilled about all of this abnormal behaviour, and don't necessarily welcome newcomers with open arms. Visitors might even be surprised to find that locals will feel free to stop them in the street and lecture them about behaving more appropriately. This is a culture in which, as another Dutch saying goes, the 'nail that sticks up gets knocked down'.

blowverbod
wegens overlast in de buurt
boete € 50,- art. 2.8 lid 4 APV

alcoholverbod
art. 2.8 lid 2 APV
uitgezonderd terras

'"Doe normaal" is from an old Dutch saying, "Doe maar gewoon, dan doe je al gek genoeg" ("Just behave normally, that's strange enough").'

The Netherlands is historically a wealthy country and taxes here are relatively high (about 40 per cent for the average wage-earner). However, since the beginning of the global financial crisis, the state and municipalities have had to face difficult costcutting issues. In 2010, the Dutch finance ministry estimated an annual budget deficit of 6.6 per cent of the GDP. A few months later, the new right-wing coalition government in the Hague announced that it would cut spending by €18 billion over the next four years, starting with €3.6 billion in 2011. Some of the first targets: support for immigration and a range of social benefits, including (perhaps ironically) funding for integration programmes for new immigrants.

It's easy to see how some people might be resentful of the generous social policies and subsidies the state has provided to the disenfranchised in the past. Recent immigrants have certainly benefited from the nation's strong safety net, but as some hard-core nationalists ask, what have they given back? Much to the outrage of some conservatives, many recent arrivals have even refused to learn Dutch, and their religious beliefs prevent them from integrating entirely with Dutch society. Calling attention to these issues first may make it easier for the right-wing parties in power to slash support for social programmes aimed at the poorest citizens, who are often – in a nation that rather blithely 'tolerates' ethnic segregation – also the ones with the darkest skin.

ARTS AND CULTURE IN THE CROSSHAIRS

However, it's not just the ethnic minorities who are likely to see a decline in government support in the immediate future. In the autumn of 2010, the coalition announced that it planned an across-the-board 25 per cent reduction in all government support to the arts and culture. The government pledged to cut €200 million from its arts budget over the next five years, and to simultaneously raise the tax on ticket sales at theatres, cinemas and concerts from 6 per cent to 19 per cent. Law-makers have justified these cuts by arguing that the arts are only for the 'wealthy elite'.

Arts organisations and cultural centres throughout the country, and particularly in Amsterdam, the cultural hub, are scrambling to prepare themselves for the decline in government subsidies. Meanwhile, supporters of culture have gone to the streets to protest these actions. In November 2010, some 20,000 people, including local celebrities, artists and TV presenters, gathered on the Leidseplein to demonstrate against these actions. Other protests took place in the Hague and smaller cities where planned cuts could decimate the small arts communities.

It's unclear how all the cuts will play out during 2011, but it's clear that, if the right-wing coalition government stays in power, the arts and culture will continue to be embattled and there are likely to be larger protests to come.

LEGALISING LICENTIOUSNESS

At the same time, Amsterdam's famous sex and drugs culture has become a different kind of battleground. Back in 2007, the City decided to take a more aggressive stance towards the criminal elements it identified in the Red Light District sex biz (according to the council, about 30 buildings – and therefore 'windows' – were in the hands of criminals who bought the premises with illicit money that was either laundered or gained from selling drugs). The project to clean up the RLD, known as Project 1012 for the zip code of the district (*see p90* **Project 1012**) began with the City buying out many of those

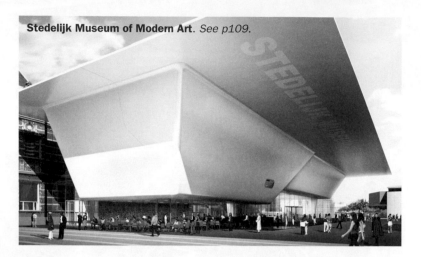

Stedelijk Museum of Modern Art. *See p109.*

buildings from their owners. At the same time, a new law (the 'Bibob') was passed to make it easier to withdraw permits in cases of questionable activities.

The prostitutes' union wasn't pleased, however, since closing windows means that women start working the streets again, with the undesirable effects of invisibility and danger. Though the council would indeed like to see the Red Light District minimised and cleaned up to lessen its magnetism for illegal international sex-trading, it did give permission to the prostitutes' union to erect a statue of a prostitute in the area, honouring the sex workers of the district.

COFFEESHOP CRISIS

Another much-debated issue is that of dope laws. In 2007, the state passed a law that coffeeshops couldn't serve alcohol, so they'd have to choose between dope and booze. Most chose to keep selling marijuana, so now you can mostly only drink tea and soft drinks in coffeeshops. That was followed up by the nation's smoking ban – on tobacco products, that is. So, while it is still legal to smoke marijuana and hash in coffeeshops, joints can't be rolled with tobacco, and cigarette smokers have to head outdoors. Next, the Hague passed a ban on coffeeshops operating within 250 metres (820 feet) of schools. In a compact city like Amsterdam (home to about half the country's coffeeshops), it's estimated that the law could call for the immediate closure of anywhere from about 40 to 200 coffeeshops. At press time, no shops had been shuttered yet because of the law, but coffeeshop owners are anticipating the worst. Meanwhile, additional restrictions have been placed on coffeeshop owners, including a prohibition against advertising their products in newspapers and magazines.

In 2010, the right-wing coalition in the Hague also proposed new rules on coffeeshop customers, as a means of reducing 'drug tourism'. One suggestion is that only people with legal residency in the Netherlands should be allowed to purchase soft drugs, and they must show their ID at the counter. Another would require coffeeshop customers to register with the state for a special pass before they can buy cannabis. Critics of these proposed policy initiatives argue that they would only drive the drug trade further underground, and people would just end up buying hash and marijuana through friends or illegal dealers.

SQUATS OF YEARS GONE BY

During the 1960s, when Amsterdam was facing a housing crisis and yet (paradoxically) had many buildings that were either abandoned or intentionally kept vacant by property speculators, a squatters' movement rose up to make creative use of the empty space. In 1971, a court ruling approved the practice by finding that (to discourage property speculators) squatting should be tolerated if a building had not been used for a period of 12 months and the owner couldn't prove that he or she planned to use it sometime soon.

In spite of the ruling, through the 1970s and '80s, squatters clashed with police repeatedly (with famous riots in 1975 and 1980). Ultimately, the squatters had become a kind of social inevitability and the occupied buildings became hubs of youthful, underground culture and edgy art, which included things like cheap communal restaurants, cutting-edge music venues and locally minded social initiatives. In the heyday of the movement, some 20,000 people lived in squats.

However, with Amsterdam becoming more gentrified and the City's housing market becoming increasingly competitive, fewer property owners were leaving their buildings empty for even a moment, and when they did they employed *anti-kraak* ('anti-squatters' usually poor students) to live in the buildings temporarily so they couldn't be deemed vacant. Meanwhile, many of the former squats were demolished to make way for urban development. By the end of 2009, the 'movement' was only about 2,000 people.

The final blow to the squatters came at the end of 2010, when the state announced that all squatting would be banned, which meant that 300 squats in Amsterdam were slated for immediate closure. If all those squats are closed, some 1,500 of their residents could be put on the street. Protests erupted all over town in response, and squatters have declared that they will not leave their buildings. The fight to save the squats will no doubt be continuing through the coming years, as the City and state attempt to shutter the buildings and drive out the protestors.

Meanwhile, the City council has come up with a different way to endorse Amsterdam's underground creative scene, by developing a new idea of 'breeding spaces' – appointed living and working spaces for artists who are only just starting out. Many of these, including the Volkskrantgebouw and Trouw, both former newspaper offices and printing plants, are temporary office spaces that have been turned into ateliers, performance venues and non profit cultural programme headquarters. While it's true that some things can't be steered from above, particularly not the counterculture, at the same time it's better than nothing at all, and shows that the powers-that-be realise that Amsterdam needs creative souls if it wants to compete with other European cities.

A METRO LINE RUNS THROUGH IT

The most visible manifestation of change – and one that visitors can't miss – is the work on the Noord-Zuidlijn, the new Metro that will connect north Amsterdam to south. Work on the 9.5-kilometre line started in 2003 and will continue until 2013, if not longer; many locals think the new link is unnecessary and far too expensive. Most of the aldermen responsible for initiating this highly unpopular project are now working in other parts of the country, leaving the City with a legacy that's at best merely too expensive, and at worst out of control and irreversible.

The Noord-Zuidlijn is way over its original budget – a staggering €1.8 billion – paid for by the council and the government. The whole thing will, in fact, cost the council well over €600 million, almost double the estimated €314 million. Part of the problem lies in the technical difficulties of digging under a city built on poles; new, time-consuming processes had to be invented to construct tunnels. The area designated for the station in De Pijp, for example, is so small that there's no room for adjacent north- and southbound platforms, so one has to be plopped on top of the other. With the new Metro line on its way, Centraal Station is also undergoing a change. The building needed much renovation anyway, but now even more so, just to be able to contain the extra commuters who will – on top of the current 250,000 a day – use the station once the new Noord-Zuidlijn is in operation. Also, all tram and bus terminals will be removed to a new section, creating a whole new, more user-friendly transport area.

IN CONTEXT

It's hoped that the new Metro line will give the City an economic boost, especially around the south area, which will be more easily accessible once the line is finally up and running. In eager anticipation of the new line – and its hoped-for draw to new companies – many new office blocks were built in the south. Most of them stood empty for a while, and there was even a plan to halt the construction work altogether.

Luckily, thanks to a late blossoming in business, most blocks have now been rented out to big names. The council is not only actively lobbying in Asia, it has also started a campaign to make the City more interesting for foreign businesses and their employees, such as creating a bureau for all aspects of being an expat in the City and offering training to help civil servants and those working in the hotel and catering industries.

As well as its big hopes for the south, the City has been developing the east, notably around Centraal Station. Along with the glamorous Muziekgebouw Amsterdam, it's also home to the Netherlands' newest, biggest and highest library; the Centrale Bibliotheek (Openbare Bibliotheek Amsterdam; see p310), which moved to its new location on the waterfront in the summer of 2007, was designed by Dutch architect Jo Coenen, who created a sleek, open-plan space with lots of room for community activities. At more than 28,000 square metres spread over 10 levels, it may be the largest public library in Europe. Though some complain that its all-white aesthetic, lack of bookshelves, and cutting-edge design furniture make it look more like an Apple showroom, it's won many admirers for its easy checkout and €1 DVD rentals. Its penthouse terrace offers some of the city's most panoramic views. The €88 million tower is part of an ambitious plan to link all the small old 'island' neighbourhoods, such as Kattenburg and Wittenburg, with the newly developed areas that were once part of the harbour but have now become trendy residential zones, like Java- and KNSM-eiland. The idea is to create a lively mix of shops, houses, entertainment and hotels.

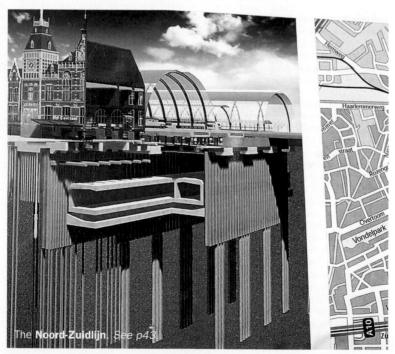

The **Noord-Zuidlijn**. See p43.

Architecture

A 17th-century skyline in transition

TEXT: STEVE KORVER

For the last several years, Amsterdam might have done well by its visitors to post signs reading, 'Please pardon our appearance while we are undergoing renovations.' Construction and renovation seem to be going on wherever you turn, whether it's the Royal Palace on the Dam, the city's two world-class museums, the Rijksmuseum and the Stedelijk, or just the central transit thoroughfares down Damrak and into De Pijp where the new Metro line is currently being installed.

Though it's a pity that the municipal powers-that-be didn't put their heads together to co-ordinate this chaos rather better, the news for visitors isn't all bad. Most of the attractions are open to the public, at least to some extent, and many of the construction projects are due to be completed in the next couple of years.

In spite of what might appear to be a lot of change, the 17th-century skyline in the centre of Amsterdam isn't likely to change any time soon. In 2010 the city's famous Canal district, or *grachtengordel*, was named a UNESCO World Heritage Site, and as such is protected against development.

THE VIEW FROM AFAR

'The colours are strong and sad, the forms symmetric, the façades kept new,' wrote Eugène Fromentin, the noted 19th-century art critic, of Amsterdam. 'We feel that it belongs to a people eager to take possession of the conquered mud.'

The treacherous, blubbery soil on which the merchants' town of Amsterdam is built meant that most attempts at monumental display were destined soon to return to their original element. It's this unforgiving land, combined with the Protestant restraint that characterised the city's early developments and the fact that there were no royals out to project monstrous egos, that ensures Amsterdam's architectural highlights are often practical places like warehouses, homes, the stock exchange and former city hall, rather than overblown palaces and castles.

Amsterdam's architectural epochs have followed the pulse of the city's prosperity. The highly decorative façades of wealthy 17th- and 18th-century merchant houses still line canals. A splurge of public spending in the affluent 1880s gave the city two of its most notable landmarks – **Centraal Station** and the **Rijksmuseum**. Rather conversely, social housing projects in the early 20th century stimulated the innovative work of the Amsterdam School, while Amsterdam's late 1980s resurgence as a financial centre and transport hub led to an economic upturn and to thickets of ambitious modern architecture on the outskirts of town and along the Eastern Docklands.

Prime view time for Amsterdam architecture is late on a summer's afternoon, when the sun gently picks out the varying colours and the patterns of the brickwork. Then, as twilight falls, the canal houses – most of them more window than wall – light up like strings of lanterns, and you get a glimpse of the beautifully preserved, frequently opulent interiors that lie hidden behind the façades.

UNDERNEATH THE PAVING STONES

Amsterdam is built on reclaimed marshland, with a thick, soft layer of clay and peat beneath the topsoil. About 12 metres (39 feet) down is a hard band of sand, deposited 10,000 years ago during the Little Ice Age, and below that, after about five metres of fine sand, there is another firm layer, this one left by melting ice after the Great Ice Age. A further 25 metres (82 feet) down, through shell-filled clay and past the bones of mammoths, is a third hard layer, deposited by glaciers over 180,000 years ago.

The first Amsterdammers built their homes on muddy mounds, making the foundations from tightly packed peat. Later on, they dug trenches, filled them with fascines (thin, upright alder trunks) and built on those. And yet still the fruits of their labours sank slowly into the swamp. By the 17th century, builders were using longer underground posts and were rewarded with more stable structures, but it wasn't until around 1700 that piles were driven deep enough to hit the first hard sand layer.

The method of constructing foundations that subsequently developed has remained more or less the same ever since, though nowadays most piles reach the second sand level and some make the full 50-metre (164-foot) journey to the third hard layer. To begin, a double row of piles is sunk along the line of a proposed wall (since World War II, concrete has been used instead of wood). Then, a crossbeam is laid across each pair of posts, planks are fastened longitudinally on to the beams, and the wall is built on top. Occasionally piles break or rot, which is why Amsterdam is full of old buildings that teeter precariously over the street, tilt lopsidedly or prop each other up in higgledy-piggledy rows.

TRIALS BY FIRE

Early constructions in Amsterdam were timber-framed, built mainly from oak with roofs of rushes or straw. Wooden houses were relatively light and therefore less likely to sink into the mire, but after two devastating fires (in 1421 and 1452), the authorities began stipulating that outer walls be built of brick, though wooden front gables were still

'The first Amsterdammers built their homes on muddy mounds, making the foundations from tightly packed peat.'

permitted. In a bid to blend in, the first brick gables were shaped in imitation of their spout-shaped wooden predecessors.

But regulations were hardly necessary, for Amsterdammers took to their brick with relish. Granted, some grander 17th-century, buildings were built of sandstone, while plastered façades were first seen a century later and reinforced concrete made its inevitable inroads in the 20th century. But Amsterdam is still essentially a city of brick: red brick from Leiden, yellow from Utrecht and grey from Gouda, all laid in curious formations and arranged in complicated patterns. Local architects' attachment to – and flair with – brick reached a zenith in the highly fantastical, billowing façades designed by the Amsterdam School early in the 20th century.

FORCE AND REINFORCEMENT
Only two wooden buildings remain in central Amsterdam: one (built in 1460) in the quiet courtyard of the Begijnhof (no.34, known as the **Houtenhuis**; *see p92*), and the other on Zeedijk. The latter of the two, **In't Aepjen** (Zeedijk 1; *see p85*), was built in the 16th century as a lodging house, getting its name from the monkeys that impecunious sailors used to leave behind as payment. Though the ground floor dates from the 19th century, the upper floors provide a clear example of how, in medieval times, each wooden storey protruded a little beyond the one below it, allowing rainwater to drip on to the street rather than run back into the body of the building. Early brick gables had to be built at an angle over the street for the same reason, though it also allowed objects to be winched to the top floors without crashing against the windows of the lower ones.

Amsterdam's oldest building, however, is the **Oude Kerk** (Old Church, Oude Kerksplein 23; *see p89*). It was begun in 1300, though only the base of the tower dates from then: over the ensuing 300 years the church, once boasting the simplest of forms, developed a barnacle crust of additional buildings, mostly in a Renaissance style with a few Gothic additions. The Gothic building in town is the **Nieuwe Kerk** (at Dam and Nieuwezijds Voorburgwal; *see p81*), still called the 'New Church' even though work on it began at the end of the 14th century.

When gunpowder first arrived in Europe in the 15th century, Amsterdammers realised that the wooden palisade that surrounded their settlement would offer scant defence, and so set about building a new stone wall. Watchtowers and gates left over from it make up a significant proportion of the city's surviving pre-17th-century architecture, though most have been altered over the years. The **Schreierstoren** (Prins Hendrikkade 94-95; *see p85*) of 1480, however, has kept its original shape, with the addition of doors, windows and a pixie-hat roof. The base of the **Munttoren** (Muntplein; *see p92*) originally formed part of the Regulierspoort, a city gate built in 1490. Another city gate from the previous decade, the **St Antoniespoort** (Nieuwmarkt 4), was converted into a public weighhouse (De Waag) in 1617, then further refashioned to become a Guild House and finally a café restaurant. It remains one of Amsterdam's most menacing monuments (*see p86*).

CALL OF THE CLASSICAL
A favourite 16th-century amendment to these somewhat stolid defence towers was the later addition of a sprightly steeple. Hendrick de Keyser (1565-1621) delighted in designing such spires, and it is largely his work that gives Amsterdam's

School of Rock

The influential Amsterdam School movement.

Characterised by its (often rounded) brick constructions and intricate detailing, the Amsterdam School style was applied to creating working-class housing, institutions and schools during the early part of the 20th century.

It was Hendrik Berlage who formed the nexus of the movement. Not only did his work reject all the neo-styles that defined most 19th-century Dutch architecture, he also provided the opportunity to experiment with new forms by coming up with the urban development scheme, **Plan Zuid**.

Although the Amsterdam School was short-lived – it was forced to simplify within a decade when money ran out, and its greatest proponent, Michel de Klerk, died – examples of its work are visible in Spaarndammerbuurt, Rivierenbuurt, Concertgebouwbuurt and the area around Mercantorplein.

Located along the waterfront, the epic **Scheepvaarthuis** (Prins Hendrikkade 108-114, now the Grand Hotel Amrâth Amsterdam; *see p130*) is generally considered to be the school's first work. Completed in 1916, it was created by JM van der Mey, Piet Kramer and De Klerk. Among the hallmarks on show are obsessively complex brickwork, allegorical decorations (reflecting its use as shipping companies' offices), sculptures and seamlessly fused wrought-iron railings.

The **Spaarndammerbuurt** sports the school's most frolicsome work and remains a huge draw for more dedicated architectural tourists. The Ship, as the locals call it, takes up the whole block between Zaanstraat, Hembrugstraat and Oostzaanstraat. Completed in 1919, it was commissioned by the Eigen Haard housing association and includes 102 homes and a school. The grand archway at Oostzaan 1-21 leads to the Ship's courtyard and central meeting hall. A former post office, **Museum Het Schip** (*see p104*), is now an exhibition space devoted to the school that also runs Amsterdam School tours (*see pp75-79* **Tour Amsterdam**).

Located at the border of De Pijp and Rivierenbuurt is **Plan Zuid**. It is here that socialist housing association De Dageraad (the Dawn) allowed Klerk and Kramer (together with their favourite sculptor, Hildo Krop) to do their hallucinatory best. Josef Israelkade, Burg Tellegenstraat and the courtyard of Cooperatiehof are its highlights.

Elsewhere in the city (on Waalstraat and Vrijheidslaan, for example), you'll find later, more restrained examples of the school's work. A window seat at **Café Wildschut** (Roelof Hartplein 1-3, 676 8220) offers rather spectacular views of a whole range of architectural goodies, including **House Lydia** (across the street at no.2), which first served as a home to Catholic girls. Finished in 1927, it stands as one of the very last buildings in which wacky window shapes and odd forms were allowed.

present skyline a faintly oriental appearance. He added a lantern-shaped tower with an openwork orb to the Munttoren, and a spire that resembled the Oude Kerk steeple to the **Montelbaanstoren** (Oudeschans 2), a sea-defence tower that had been built outside the city wall. His **Zuiderkerk** (Zuiderkerkhof 72; *see p114*), built in 1603, sports a spire said to have been much admired by Christopher Wren. The appointment of De Keyser as city mason and sculptor in 1595 had given him free rein, and his buildings represent the pinnacle of the Dutch Renaissance style (also known as Dutch Mannerist) – perhaps the greatest being the **Westerkerk** (Prinsengracht 279; *see p96*), completed in 1631 as the single biggest Protestant church in the world.

Since the very beginning of the 17th century, Dutch architects had been gleaning inspiration from translations of Italian pattern books, adding lavish ornament to the classical system of proportion they found there. Brick façades were decorated with stone strapwork (scrolls and curls derived from picture frames and leatherwork). Walls were built with alternating layers of red brick and white sandstone, a style that came to be called 'bacon coursing'. The old spout-shaped gables were also replaced with cascading step-gables, often embellished with vases, escutcheons and masks. There was also a practical use for these adornments: before house numbers were introduced in Amsterdam in the 18th century, ornate gables and wall plaques were a means of identifying addresses.

The façade of the **Vergulde Dolphijn** (Singel 140-142), designed by De Keyser in 1600 for Captain Banning Cocq (the commander of Rembrandt's *The Night Watch*; *photo p30*), is a lively mix of red brick and sandstone, while the **Gecroonde Raep** (Oudezijds Voorburgwal 57) has a neat step-gable, with riotous decoration featuring busts, escutcheons, shells, scrolls and volutes. De Keyser's magnificent 1617 construction that hugged the canal, the **Huis Bartolotti** (Herengracht 170-72, now a part of the Theater Instituut; *see p118*), is the finest example of the style.

This decorative step-gabled style was to last well into the 17th century. But gradually a stricter use of classical elements came into play; the façade of the Bartolotti house features rows of Ionic pilasters, and it wasn't long before others followed where De Keyser had led. The Italian pattern books that had inspired the Dutch Renaissance were full of the less-ornamented designs of Greek and Roman antiquity. This appealed to many young architects who followed De Keyser, and who were to develop a more restrained, classical style. Many, such as Jacob van Campen (1595-1657), went on study tours of Italy, and returned fired with enthusiasm for the symmetric designs, simple proportions and austerity of Roman architecture. The buildings they constructed during the Golden Age are among the finest Amsterdam has to offer.

THE GOLDEN AGE

The 1600s were a boom time for builders as well as for businessmen. There was no way it could have been otherwise, as Amsterdam's population more than quadrupled during the first half of the century. Grand new canals were constructed, and wealthy merchants lined them with mansions and warehouses. Van Campen, along with fellow architects Philips Vingboons (1607-78) and his younger brother Justus (1620-98), were given the freedom to try out their ideas on a flood of new commissions.

Stately façades constructed of sandstone began to appear around Amsterdam, but brick still remained the most popular material. Philips Vingboons's **Witte Huis** (Herengracht 168, now part of the Theater Instituut) has a white sandstone façade with virtually no decoration: the regular rhythm of the windows is the governing principle of the design. The house he built in 1648 at Oude Turfmarkt 145 has a brick façade adorned with three tiers of classical pilasters – Tuscan, Ionic and Doric – and festoons that were characteristic of the style. However, the crowning achievement of the period was Amsterdam's boast to the world of its mercantile supremacy and civic might: namely, the **Stadhuis** (City Hall) on the Dam, designed by Van Campen in 1648 and now known as the **Koninklijk Paleis**; *see p81*.

There was, however, one fundamental point of conflict between classical architecture and the requirements of northern Europe. For more practical reasons, wet northern climes required steep roofs, yet low Roman pediments and flat cornices looked odd with a steep, pointed roof behind them. The architects solved the problem by adapting the Renaissance gable, with its multiple steps, into a tall, central gable with just two steps. Later, neck-gables were built with just a tall central oblong and no steps. The right angles formed at the base of neck-gables were often filled in with decorative sandstone carvings called claw-pieces.

On very wide houses, it was possible to build a roof parallel to the street rather than end-on, making an attractive backdrop for a classical straight cornice. The giant **Trippenhuis** (Kloveniersburgwal 29, De Wallen), built by Justus Vingboons in 1662, has such a design, with a classical pediment, a frieze of cherubs and arabesques, and eight enormous Corinthian pilasters. It wasn't until the 19th century, when zinc cladding became cheaper, that flat and really low-pitched roofs became feasible.

RESTRAINT VS REFURBISHMENT

Working towards the end of the 17th century, Adriaan Dortsman (1625-82) had been a strong proponent of the straight cornice. His stark designs – such as for the **Van Loon house** at Keizersgracht 672-674 – ushered in a style that came to be known

ARCAM. *See p54.*

'The "Tight Style" was timely. Ornament was costly and, by the beginning of the 18th century, the economic boom was over.'

as Restrained Dutch Classicism (or the 'Tight Style' as it would translate directly from the Dutch description: *Strakke Stijl*). It was a timely entrance. Ornament was costly and, by the beginning of the 18th century, the economic boom was over.

The merchant families were prosperous, but little new building went on. Instead, the families gave their old mansions a facelift or revamped the interiors. A number of 17th-century houses got new sandstone façades (or plastered brick ones, which were cheaper), and French taste – said to have been introduced by Daniel Marot, a French architect based in Amsterdam – became hip. As the century wore on, ornamentation regained popularity. Gables were festooned with scrolls and acanthus leaves (Louis XIV), embellished with asymmetrical rococo fripperies (Louis XV) or strung with disciplined lines of garlands (Louis XVI). The baroque grandeur of Keizersgracht 444-446, for example, is hardly Dutch at all. Straight cornices appeared even on narrow buildings, and became extraordinarily ornate: a distinct advantage, this, as it hid the steep roof that lay behind, with decorative balustrades adding to the deception. The lavish cornice at Oudezijds Voorburgwal 215-217 stands as a prime example of such construction.

REMIXING MASONRY

Fortunes slumped after 1800, and during the first part of the century more buildings were demolished than constructed. When things picked up after 1860, architects raided past eras for inspiration. Neoclassical, neo-Gothic and neo-Renaissance features were sometimes lumped together in mix-and-match style. The **Krijtberg Church** (Singel 446) from 1881 has a soaring neo-Gothic façade and a high, vaulted basilica, while the interior of AL van Gendt's **Hollandsche Manege** (Vondelstraat 140; *see p110*), also 1881, combines the classicism of the Spanish Riding School in Vienna with a state-of-the-art iron and glass roof.

In stark contrast, the **Concertgebouw** (Van Baerlestraat 98; *see p256*), a Van Gendt construction from 1888, borrows from the late Renaissance, with 1892's **City Archive** (Amsteldijk 67) as De Keyser revisited. But the period's most adventurous building is the **Adventskerk** (Keizersgracht 676), which has a classical base, Romanesque arches, Lombardian moulding and fake 17th-century lanterns.

The star architect of the period was PJH Cuypers (1827-1921), who landed commissions for both the **Rijksmuseum** (Stadhouderskade 41; *see p108*) of 1877-85 and what would become its near mirrored twin on the other side of town, **Centraal Station** (Stationsplein; *see p80*), built from 1882 to 1889. Both are in traditional red brick, adorned with Renaissance-style decoration in sandstone and gold leaf. Responding to those who thought his tastes too catholic, Cuypers – while still slipping in some of his excesses later during the construction – decided to organise each building according to a single coherent principle. This became the basis for modern Dutch architecture.

A NEW AGE DAWNS

Brick and wood – good, honest, indigenous materials – appealed to Hendrik Petrus Berlage (1856-1934), as did the possibilities offered by industrial developments in the use of steel and glass. A rationalist, he took Cuypers's ideas a step further in his belief that a building should openly express its basic structure, with a modest amount of ornament in a supportive role. Notable also was the way he collaborated with sculptors, painters and even poets throughout construction. His **Beurs van Berlage** (Beursplein;

see p80), built between 1898 and 1903 – a mix of clean lines and functional shapes, with the mildest patterning in the brickwork – was startling at the time, and earned him the reputation of being the father of modern Dutch architecture.

Apart from the odd shop front and some well-designed café interiors, the art nouveau and art deco movements had little direct impact on Amsterdam, though they did draw a few wild flourishes: HL de Jong's **Tuschinski cinema** (Reguliersbreestraat 26; *see p225*) of 1918-21, for example, is a delightful and seductive piece of high-camp fantasy. Instead, Amsterdam architects developed a style of their own, an idiosyncratic mix of art nouveau and Old Dutch using their favourite materials: wood and brick.

A LOCAL MOVEMENT

This movement, known as the **Amsterdam School** (*see p48* **School of Rock**), reacted against Berlage's sobriety by producing its uniquely whimsical buildings with waving, almost sculptural brickwork. Built over a reinforced concrete frame, the brick outer walls go through a complex series of pleats, bulges, folds and curls that earned them the nickname *Schortjesarchitectuur* ('Apron Architecture'). Windows can be trapezoid or parabolic; doors are carved in strong, angular shapes; brickwork is highly decorative and often polychromatic; and sculptures are abundant.

The driving force behind the school came from two young architects, Michel de Klerk (1884-1923) and Piet Kramer (1881-1961). Two commissions for social housing projects – one for **Dageraad** (constructed around PL Takstraat, 1921-23), one for **Eigen Haard** (located in the Spaarndammerbuurt, 1913-20) – allowed them to treat entire blocks as single units. Just as importantly, the pair's adventurous clients gave them freedom to express their ideas. The school also produced more rural variants suggestive of village life, such as the rather charming BT Boeyinga-designed 'garden village' **Tuindorp Nieuwendam** (Purmerplein, Purmerweg).

ARCHITECTURAL REBELLION

In the early 1920s, a new movement emerged that was the very antithesis of the Amsterdam School – although certain crossover aspects can be observed in JF Staal's 1930-completed **Wolkenkrabber** (Victorieplein), the first ever residential high-rise in the country, whose name appropriately translates as 'cloudscraper'. Developing rather than reacting wildly against Berlage's ideas, the Functionalists believed that new building materials such as concrete and steel should not be concealed, but that the basic structure of a building should be visible. Function was supreme, ornament anathema. Their hard-edged concrete and glass boxes have much in common with the work of Frank Lloyd Wright in the USA, Le Corbusier in France and the Bauhaus in Germany. Perhaps unsurprisingly, such radical views were not shared by everyone, and the period was a turbulent one in Amsterdam's architectural history. Early Functionalist work, such as the 1930s **Openluchtschool** (Open-air School, Cliostraat 40), 1934's striking **Cineac Cinema** (Reguliersbreestraat 31) and the **Het Blauwe Theehuis** (in Vondelpark; *see p110*), has a clean-cut elegance, and the Functionalist garden suburb of **Betondorp** (literally, 'Concrete Village'), built between 1921 and 1926, is much more attractive than the name might suggest. But after World War II, Functionalist ideology became an excuse for more dreary, derivative, prefabricated eyesores. The urgent need for housing, coupled with town-planning theories that favoured residential satellite suburbs, led to the appearance of soulless, high-rise horrors on the edge of town, much the same as those put up elsewhere in Europe.

A change of heart during the 1970s refocused attention on making the city centre a pleasant jumble of residences, shops and offices. At the same time, a quirkier, more imaginative trend began to show itself in building design. The **ING Bank** (Bijlmerplein 888), inspired by anthroposophy and built in 1987 of brick, has hardly a right angle in sight. A use of bright colour, and a return to a human-sized scale, is splendidly evident in Aldo van Eyck's **Hubertushuis** (Plantage Middenlaan 33-35) from 1979, which seems

IN CONTEXT

Bridge at **Eastern Docklands**.

to personify the architect's famed quotation: 'my favourite colour is the rainbow'.
New façades – daringly modern, yet built to scale – began to appear between the
old houses along the canals. The 1980s also saw, amid an enormous amount of
controversy, the construction of what soon became known as the 'Stopera', a combined
City Hall (Stadhuis) and **opera house** on Waterlooplein. The eye-catching brick and
marble of the **Muziektheater** (*see p256*) is more successful than the dull oblongs
that make up the City Hall.

Housing projects of the 1980s and 1990s have provided Amsterdam with some
imaginative modern architecture – especially on the islands of the once-derelict Eastern
Docklands (*see p122* **Walk on the Waterside**). You can get a good view of it from the
roof of Renzo Piano's recognisable **NEMO** building (*see p121*).

EYES FORWARD

At the municipal information centre for planning and housing in **Zuiderkerk** (*see p114*),
visitors can admire scale models of current and future developments set to transform
the city within the near future. Those interested should pay a visit to NEMO's neighbour,
mighty **ARCAM** – the **Architectuurcentrum Amsterdam** (*see p234*) – or pick up a copy
of its excellent publication *25 Buildings You Should Have Seen, Amsterdam*. Bureau
Monumentenzorg Amsterdam, meanwhile, provides an overview of the city's architecture
from its origins to 1940 at www.bmz.amsterdam.nl. Another excellent resource is
www.amsterdamarchitecture.nl.

Architectural travesties of the past have politicised the populace and referendums
are held prior to many developments. Although 130,000 local votes against the
construction of IJburg – a new residential community being built on a series of man-
made islands in the IJ-meer, just east of Amsterdam – was not enough to arrest
development around this ecologically sensitive area, they did inspire the promise
that ƒ15 million (now around €7 million) would be invested in 'nature development'.
Parts of the area will also be a showcase for the recently hyped Dutch concept of *wilde*

'Brad Pitt's favourite architecture firm helped put Dutch architecture back on the map with its "Dutch Big Mac".'

wonen – 'wild living' – where residents get to design and build their own houses, a radical concept in this space-constrained country.

Similarly, the referendum result against the new **Noord-Zuidlijn** (*see p43*) on the Metro network didn't halt the project, but it did establish that the City needed to be considerably more diligent in its thinking. The powers that be apparently overlooked such significant details as financing, loss of revenue for shopkeepers and the potential for all this digging to bring about the speedier sinking of historical buildings above when planning the line, none of which endeared them to voters.

MUSEUMS REVISITED

Now that the facelift of **Museumplein** (*see p107*) has long been completed save for the extension of the Stedelijk Museum, due to be finished at the end of 2011, all eyes are on the **Eastern Docklands** (*see p122* **Walk on the Waterside**). It's hoped redevelopments will turn it into a harbourfront like that of Sydney. Similarly, construction around the ArenA stadium will hopefully pump some life into the nearby architectural prison known as **Bijlmermeer**. This should become home to many businesses and – thanks to the recent leaps and bounds made in building vertically on bog – the single largest residential tower in the country. In 2004, a building called **Living Tomorrow** (www.livingtomorrow.com) also opened as a joint project of companies out to peddle their 'visionary' designs in this 'house and office of the future'.

Another hotspot currently roping in a veritable who's who of architects is **Zuidas** (www.zuidas.nl) in the south. Zuidas is grouped around the World Trade Center, close to the wacky **ING House** (Amstelveenseweg 500); no doubt it caught your eye on the ride in from Schiphol Airport.

Dutch architecture – thanks in part to notable exponents like Rem Koolhaas (who coincidentally has his rather embarrassingly ugly 1991 work, **Byzantium**, viewable at the north entrance to Vondelpark on Stadhouderskade) – is currently very much in vogue. Brad Pitt's own favourite architecture firm, MVRDV, which renovated the Lloyd Hotel (*see p142*), also helped put Dutch architecture back on the map at Hanover World Expo 2000 with its 'Dutch Big Mac', featuring such delicious ingredients as water- and wind-mills for electricity on the roof, a theatre on the fourth floor, an oak forest on the third floor, flowers on the second floor, and cafés, shops and a few dunes on the first floor. Yes, dunes. And in 2007 they began developing the idea of an entirely floating neighbourhood of 35,000 houses called Almere-Pampus.

International periodicals, no longer casting LA and Hong Kong as the primary visionaries, now see the 'Dutch Model' – where boundaries between building, city and landscape planning have blurred beyond recognition – as both pragmatic and futuristic. After all, ecological degradation is now a worldwide phenomenon, and the space-constrained Netherlands has long seen nature as a construct that needs to be nurtured. Expect this principle to define some of the Dutch architecture of the future – although knowing what's gone before, it'll probably be implemented in unexpected fashion. For instance, in 2004, hundreds of old steel containers were reinvented as living spaces for students at both **NDSM** (*see p124*) in the north and **Houthavens** in the west (where they were joined by a cruise ship to house an additional 200 penny-saving students).

Now how's that for pragmatic?

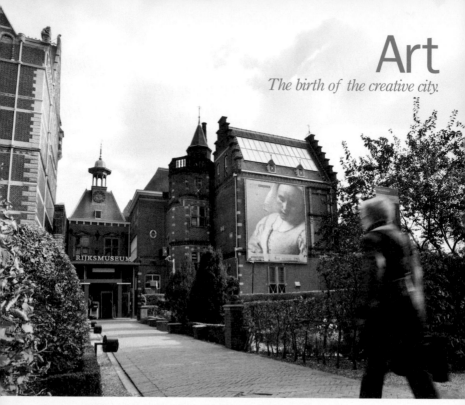

Art
The birth of the creative city.

No statistical analysis has been done to this effect, but it's a fair guess that there are three primary reasons people visit Amsterdam: sex, drugs and art. Sex and drugs come in the next section (*see pp67-71*), so it's safe to start with number three.

Ever since the early 17th century, the city has seen a brisk trade in fine art, both as a form of commerce and as a more ambitious effort to stake a claim in the pantheon of international art. Art, and in particular secular art, has always played a prominent role in Dutch society, from the still life, portrait and genre painters of the 17th century, through the abstract painters of the turn of the 19th century, on into the CoBrA and de Stijl painters and sculptors of the 20th century, and into today's thriving universe of Dutch contemporary art (with its notable emphasis on portrait photography).

If the names of those styles don't register, just think: Rembrandt and Vermeer; Van Gogh and Kees van Dongen; Karel Appel and Piet Mondrian; and today's Erwin Olaf and Rineke Dijkstra.

With so many 'names' coming from such a tiny country, to pass up on Amsterdam's art offerings is like skipping the Guinness on a visit to Dublin.

MEDIEVAL ROOTS

The groundwork for the vital efflorescence of art was laid by a rich medieval artistic tradition sponsored by the Church. Later artists, not content to labour solely *ad majorem dei gloriam*, found more 'individual' masters in the Flemings Bosch and Brueghel. Key among the early artists was **Jacob Cornelisz van Oostsanen** (c1470-1533), also known as Jacob van Amsterdam. He represents the start of the city's artistic tradition, and his observational sharpness became a trademark for all Dutch art that was to follow.

The one painting of his that survived the Iconoclastic Fury, *Saul and the Witch of Endor* (on display at the **Rijksmuseum**; *see p108*), tells the whole biblical story in one panoramic, almost comic book-like swoop; beginning on the left where Saul seeks advice from a strange witch about his impending battle with the Philistines, and ending in the far distance, behind the central witches' sabbath, with his 'poetic justice' of a suicide in the face of certain defeat. And all this, needless to say, at a time when witches could have used some more favourable PR.

The Baker of Eeklo (displayed at **Muiderslot**; *see p283*, another example that seemingly comes from a very much pre-modern time, hangs in the castle built for Count Floris V. Painted in the second half of the 16th century by two rather obscure painters, **Cornelis van Dalem** and **Jan van Wechelen**, the depicted tableaux – of people whose heads have been replaced by cabbages while they await the re-baking of their actual heads – will only make sense to a people weaned on medieval stories of magic windmills that could grind old people up and then churn them out young again. In this related story, bakers are slicing the heads off clients to re-bake them to specification; a cabbage – a symbol for the empty and idle head – was used to keep the spewing of blood to a minimum, although sometimes people's heads came out 'half-baked' or 'misfired'.

THE GOLDEN AGE

The living was certainly sweet during those first six decades of the 17th century, starting with the founding of the East India Company (VOC) and ending when the Brits changed New Amsterdam to New York. Not only did the economic benefits of being the world's leading trading power result in the building of Amsterdam's image-defining ring of canals, but it also led to a flourishing of the arts that continues to this day.

Faking It

When is a Vermeer not a Vermeer? When it's a... Van Meegeren.

The Dutch are as famed for their business acumen as their dykes, which can lead the less scrupulous to a somewhat free and easy attitude towards a work's provenance. An estimated 30 per cent of the world art market consists of forgeries, and it seems even the most famous institutions can be caught out. Back in 1938, the Rijksmuseum, to its eventual relief, lost a bidding war for a Vermeer to Rotterdam's Boijmans Van Beuningen (*see p296*), which bought it for a then astronomical *f*550,000 (€224,000). Proof, if it were needed, that desire has the ability to blind – for how on earth else could Hans van Meegeren's heavy handed *De Emmaüsgangers* be mistaken for a Vermeer?

It was only in 1945, when the forger was facing a traitor's death penalty for selling the Nazis another 'Vermeer', that Van Meegeren admitted both were forgeries, painted to avenge a critic's poor reviews. That self-same critic had fallen for the forgeries, although it's highly unlikely that the satisfaction of making his arch nemesis face his own incompetence was sufficient compensation for Van Meegeren's subsequent jail term: the forger died in 1947 while serving out his sentence.

IN CONTEXT

Vermeer's *Girl with a Pearl Earring. See p60.*

The rise of secular art came to northern Europe much sooner than it arrived in Italy or Spain. Amsterdam's burghers and noblemen, as well as an aspirant middle class and even ordinary working stiffs (especially tavern keepers), became hungry for art to hang on their walls.

Rembrandt van Rijn (1606-69) is, of course, the best known of all those Golden Age painters (*see p30* **Rembrandt's Amsterdam**). However, *The Company of Captain Frans Banning Cocq and Lieutenant Willem van Ruytenburch* (1642) didn't prove the snappiest title for a painting. *The Night Watch* (on display at the Rijksmuseum), though, is far more memorable, and it's by this name that Rembrandt's most famous work is now known. Amsterdam's Civic Guard commissioned this group portrait to decorate their building, but rather than conjure up a neat, unexciting portrait, Rembrandt went for spontaneity, capturing a moment of lively chaos: the captain issuing an order as his men jostle to his rear. It's now the city's most popular work in what is easily its most popular museum.

OLD MASTERS

Rembrandt couldn't decorate Amsterdam on his own, however, and the likes of Johannes Vermeer, Frans Hals, Ferdinand Bol, Jan Steen and Jacob van Ruisdael thrived creatively and economically at this time. Delft-born **Vermeer** (1632-75) painted pictures, such as *The Kitchen Maid* (at the Rijksmuseum), that radiate an extraordinary serenity. In his

Marketing the City

Behind the slogan: the highs and lows of Amsterdam's city image.

It was all much simpler in the 1970s. To entice people to visit Amsterdam, all you had to do was what KLM did: put out some posters cajoling its long-haired American targets to come 'Sleep in Hippie Park'. Word of mouth did the rest. Before that, during the 1960s, there was the tourist board's 'Get In Touch With The Dutch' campaign – surely a slogan from a more innocent period. Compared to that halcyon era, the boom years of the 1990s were surely the most boring of times, if you take their yawn-inducing slogans ('Capital of Inspiration' and 'Business Gateway to Europe') as typical of the mindset.

But now it's the 21st century, and every city needs its own marketing campaign to establish its advantages over every other city on the planet. 'City marketing' is the rather dubious science that might never have been called into existence were it not for the stratospheric success of the ubiquitous 'I♥NY' logo. Now it seems we are all doomed to adopt our own versions of the slogan, whatever we think of our place of residence. So in 2004, the City of Amsterdam paid the usually inspired advertising bureau KesselsKramer to work its glamorous magic and come up with a slogan that would reflect Amsterdam as a 'creative city' – and it came up with 'I amsterdam'.

Unfortunately, a year earlier, the designer Vanessa van Dam had already invented an 'I amsterdammer' logo with a similar accent on 'I am'. This logo even graced 120,000 postcards – it was sort of hard to miss. It thus seemed only fair that Van Dam was awarded a €20,000 settlement from the City. So almost before it got off the mark, the City's 'I amsterdam' campaign had made a big creative oopsie. (Let's hope Van Dam will not get sued in turn by the estate of that other local, René Descartes, who is widely known to have remarked, 'I think, therefore I amsterdam'.)

Like those other inspired plays on the city's name, 'Amsterdamned' and the even better 'Amsterdamaged', 'I amsterdam' is so obvious that we can assume that the slogan has occurred independently in many different minds on many different occasions. The only really annoying thing about the campaign is that it's trying to peddle the idea that the logo will not only attract outside business but also work to unify regular Amsterdammers. This is solidly contradicted whenever a Dutch person tries to say 'I amsterdam' out loud. The accent makes them stutter out something that sounds far more like 'I hamster am', as though they were arrogant rodents rather than a legion of proud Amsterdammers.

OK, so it's easy to mock. We admit that marketing a city can't be easy. There must be more to it than producing a catchy T-shirt slogan. But just what other choices were there? Well, it could be argued that 'Amsterdamned' and 'Amsterdamaged' are, in fact, much better ambassadors for the city. After all, today's visiting army of dopeheads may hold the city's economic future in their rather shaky hands.

It's happened before: sentimental (and rich) ex-hippies, looking for somewhere to recover their lost youths and salve their consciences, were the ones who invested in the place during the booming 1990s. They figured it would be a good excuse to come and visit a few times a year in the hopes of recreating those perfect relaxed coffeeshop moments from decades past.

Thinking of which, isn't being relaxed one of the things that Amsterdam has always been famous for? And neither the campaign nor the brouhaha surrounding it have contributed to this obvious brand benefit. Shame.

Insider Favourites

What to focus on in Amsterdam's multitude of museums?
We asked the city's artistic movers and shakers for their personal picks.

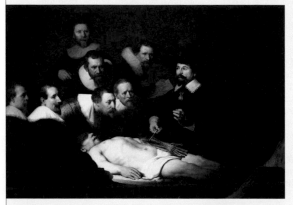 

With more museums per square metre than any other city in the world, Amsterdam has something to suit every taste: from classic to modern, world-famous to obscure. But what about the people behind the scenes? What are their favourite exhibits?

Laura van Hasselt, curator at Amsterdams Historisch Museum (*see p92*), has two, both of which are at her museum. Rembrandt's *The Anatomy Lesson of Dr Jan Deijman* (1656), half of which was destroyed in a fire in 1723, and a Pietà statue (anonymous, c1450) from which the faces of Jesus and Mary were chiselled off by iconoclasts (c1566). For Laura, the damage has added extra depth to the

 works, rather than taking something away.

Colette Olof, curator of Foam (*see p100*), favours the portrait of Thora van Loon-Egidius in the Museum Van Loon (*see p100*). As a lady-in-waiting to Queen Wilhelmina, Van Loon-Egidius travelled to Paris annually to commission new clothes and to be portrayed by the portrait photographer Nadar. Portrait photography was unique for the era and in this picture we see the back of a beautiful woman in her twenties, with only the profile of her face visible. Olof's passion for photography started at a retrospective of Nadar's work.

essential essay, 'Vermeer in Bosnia', Lawrence Weschler suggests that the artist's works are not depictions of actual peace, but rather hopeful invocations of a peace that was yet to come. For Vermeer was painting at a time when Europe was slowly emerging from the ravages of the Thirty Years' War (1618-48), and at the time peace still remained a fervent hope rather than an expectation for the exhausted and war-weary people of Europe.

Leiden's **Jan Steen** (c1625-79) dealt with the chaos of the times in another way – a way that got him a bad rep as a rowdy. While he did run a tavern in his own home, his patchy reputation is more likely based on the drunken folk that inhabit his paintings of everyday life. In fact, if one looks carefully at, for example, *The Merry Family* (at the Rijksmuseum), Steen comes across as highly moralistic.

IN CONTEXT

Thomas Peutz, director of SMART Project Space, chooses *De Stedemaagd* (possibly by De Lairesse) at the Katten Kabinet (*see p100*). Visitors often miss this oil painting because it's on the ceiling. Originally commissioned by Willem van Loon in the 17th century, it portrays a lady who is meant to personify the city of Amsterdam; the tray next to her is filled with treasures that symbolise the city's prosperity. It was painted over in the 19th century, when the Golden Age was history, the city wasn't as rich any more and 17th-century art was out of fashion. It was rediscovered during a renovation in 1996 – perfect timing as Amsterdam was booming again.

Paul Faber, senior curator at the Tropenmuseum (*see p119*), cites the Diorama of Café 't Mandje at Amsterdams Historisch Museum (*see p92*) as his favourite. A great example of a typical Amsterdam 'brown café', this legendary pub on Zeedijk was run by Bet van Beeren from 1927 onwards, and was a safe haven for sailors, pimps, prostitutes, gays and lesbians. Paul feels that the installation, with its counter, beer tap, bar stools, fantastic array of kitsch objects, photographs, paintings, posters, ties hanging from the ceiling, and a jukebox playing the songs of Willy Alberti, captures the café's atmosphere perfectly.

With the inscription over the mantelpiece ('As the Old Sing, So Pipe the Young') putting literally what the painting reflects figuratively (through a plethora of symbols that help to represent the emptiness of a life spent smoking, drinking and talking about nothing), this painting offers a lesson as valid today as the day it was painted. The Alfred Hitchcock of his era, Steen himself cameos as the puffy-cheeked bagpiper.

BEYOND THE GOLDEN ERA

Defying the downturn, art continued to develop after the Golden Age began to tarnish. The Jordaan-born **Jacob de Wit** (1695-1754), long before the invention of sticky glow-in-the-dark stars, brightened up many a local ceiling with cloud-dappled skies, gods and flocks of cherubs. Initially influenced by Rubens's altar work in Antwerp, De Wit

Say Squat?

*From cultural squats to cutting-edge design conventions:
how Amsterdam harnessed its creativity.*

Amsterdam has a lot of nostalgists weeping for those 1980s and '90s salad days when cultural squats like Silo and Vrieshuis Amerika were the coolest, edgiest and most frolicsome places around. But when the powers-that-be closed these cultural beehives in order to make Amsterdam the 'Business Gateway to Europe', it was soon seen to be a monumental blunder in a city defined by its artistic traditions. So the city bureaucrats, in an effort to claw back lost prestige and emigrating artists, did what all such functionaries do in these situations: they threw money at the problem, creating non-squat squats called *broedplaatsen* (or 'breeding grounds').

Don't worry if it all gets confusing: the world of Amstersquats is nothing if not divided into umpteen different categories. In addition to the *broedplaatsen* are proper squats (reappropriated buildings that had been left empty for more than a year); 'anti-squats' (those buildings with temporary residents paying no rent at all so that squatters can't squat in them); and 'bought squats' (old squats that were then sold cheaply by the City to their inhabitants), such as **Vrankrijk** (Spuistraat 216, www.vrankrijk.org), which is still a hotbed of cheap beer and radical politics.

It seems those places that began as bona fide squats are the ones making the crossover most efficiently. The former film academy **OT301** (*see p228*) is totally happening, as is former shipping yard art complex **NDSM** (*see p123 and p124*). And although not actually itself a *broedplaats*, **Westergasfabriek** (*see p278*) is street-smart thanks to its reclaimed industrial cred.

The city's cultural players continue to pump up the image of Amsterdam as

ground zero for creative industries. Not only are there excellent schools and a range of innovative design firms, but its local creative advertising agencies such as KesselsKramer, 180 and Strawberryfrog are kicking ass on a global level. Meanwhile, **Pakhuis de Zwijger** (Piet Heinkade 179, 788 4444, www.zwijger.nl) opened in 2006 as a hub bringing together a range of cutting-edge institutions, complete with an inspiring programme of discussions and exhibitions. That very same year saw the arrival of the 'cross media week' **PICNIC** (www.picnicnetwork.org), an annual congress in September of shows, meetings, readings, seminars and conferences exploring the latest developments in media, technology, art, science and entertainment. It was an immediate success with over 5,000 visitors, and the 2007 edition will feature the esteemed likes of David Silverman, director of *The Simpsons Movie*, and Neil Gershenfeld from MIT's Center for Bits and Atoms.

'Vermeer painted pictures that radiate serenity; not depictions of actual peace, but hopeful invocations of a peace yet to come.'

developed a much more delicate and sympathetic touch that he used to great rococo effect in a number of Amsterdam buildings, among them the **Theater Instituut** (*see p119*), the attic church at the **Museum Amstelkring** (*see p89*), the Rijksmuseum, the **Pintohuis** (now a library; *see p114*) and **Huis Marseille** (*see p95*).

However, his mastery of trompe l'oeil illusion, later named *witjes* after him, is probably best seen at the **Bijbels Museum** (*see p95*). One ceiling was painted for local merchant Jacob Cromhout, while the other, entitled *Apollo and the Four Seasons*, was salvaged in the 1950s from a nearby property on Herengracht. Both paintings have recently been restored to stylish and seriously lively effect.

THE ARRIVAL OF VINCENT

The 18th century produced Monet's inspirer, **Johan Jongkind**, while the 19th century offered George Breitner and Van Gogh – two artists out to reinvent the very relevance of painting in a post-photography world. The career of everyone's favourite earless genius, **Vincent van Gogh** (1853-90), is on full display in Amsterdam, most notably at the popular **Van Gogh Museum** (*see p109*). Here you can marvel at the fact that the creator of the dark shadows of *Skull with Smoking Cigarette* went on to paint, a mere two years later in 1888, the almost kinetic *Bedroom*.

By then he had settled in France's clearer light and abandoned the Vermeer-inspired subdued colouring of his earlier work to embrace the Expressionist style that would make him famous. While the self-portrait clearly reflects his restless nature, *Bedroom* depicts the very bed he would have perhaps been better off sleeping in. Just two months later he had the first of the nervous breakdowns that led finally to his suicide.

Like Van Gogh, **Isaac Israëls** (1865-1934) sought to reinvent the relevance of painting in a post-photographic age. But unlike his buddy George Breitner, who chose to embrace this new technology by using photographs as the basis for his paintings, Israëls chose a more athletic path and achieved the 'snapshot' feel of his paintings by running around like a ninny and painting very fast. And *Two Girls by a Canal* (on display at the Amsterdam Historisch Museum; *see p92*) does successfully reflect an essentially Impressionist view of the city.

DE STIJL AND COBRA

There's a fair case to be made that the 20th century belonged to **Piet Mondrian** (1872-1944), whose career can also be used as a one-man weathervane of modern art. He moved through Realism, Impressionism and Cubism, before embracing the purely abstract and becoming (along with Theo van Doesburg and Gerrit Rietveld) one of the founders of **de Stijl** ('The Style'), an aesthetic approach that represents that part of the Dutch psyche that aspires to order. Mondrian's use of only lines and primary colour blocks inspired accusations of sterility, but actually represented a very personal and subjective quest for essence and harmony. He was also something of a wit, tilting his ultra-minimal canvas *Composition with Two Lines* by 45 degrees.

Karel Appel (1920-2001) once confounded his critics by describing his style thus: 'I just mess around.' Most agree when confronted with his childish forms, bright colours and heavy strokes. But art that chose instinct over intellect is just what was needed after World War II, when CoBrA (*see p112* and **Profile** *p113*) exploded on to the scene. Today, the late New York resident is arguably the best-known modern Dutch artist. His rate

IN CONTEXT

'The 20th century belonged to Piet Mondrian, whose career can also be used as a one-man weathervane of modern art.'

of production was so huge that the Amsterdam ex-forger Geert Jan Jansen claims that Appel had verified several of Jansen's works as his own.

CONTEMPORARY MASTERS

Today's contemporary art scene in Amsterdam is driven by several key non-profit art 'project' spaces, a lively commercial gallery culture (see pp229-236), a prestigious art residency programme, the Rijksacademie, and a fertile breeding ground of artists in the arts masters programme at the Gerrit Rietveld Academy. For several decades, the country has been generous with subsidies towards the fine arts and it shows: big names in contemporary art including photographer Rineke Dijkstra, Erwin Olaf, Anton Corbijn and Marlene Dumas all hail from here.

Emerging talent has no shortage of great showcases for fine art, whether it's during one of the big Dutch fine art fairs, such as the large and fairly mainstream Art Amsterdam, the edgier Art Rotterdam, the more formal PAN Amsterdam, the cheaper Affordable Art Fair, or its fringe fair, Kunstvlaai, not to mention the world's most expensive blue chip art fair featuring Old Masters and modern and contemporary work at TEFAF, which takes place in the southern city of Maastricht each spring.

In addition to all that formal activity, there are enough openings at local galleries and project spaces, open atelier weekends, public art events, and spontaneous countercultural art happenings at squats to keep any art aficionado with a booked social calendar throughout the year.

DESIGN DESTINATIONS

As we move deeper into the 21st century, the focus shifts from painting and over towards design. Marcel Wanders's 1997-produced Knotted Chair could not be more different from that other iconic Dutch chair of the 20th century: the highly geometric Red-Blue Chair (1918-23) by de Stijl guy **Gerrit Rietveld**. But Knotted Chair – which reinvents the frumpy hippie art of macramé with the aid of high-tech epoxy – came to represent the work of a new vanguard of local designers, who seek to encapsulate a uniquely Dutch aesthetic with a fusion of wit, hipness and function – also to be witnessed in **Piet Hein Eek**'s Waste Table. The zanily modern take on design can be experienced still in a number of shops around the city, such as Droog (see p203 **Shop This Street**), Wonen 2000, Wulf Wonen, Moooi, or by simply keeping your eyes open when walking around town.

ONE BIG GALLERY

There's certainly a case to be made that this fine city is one huge gallery. With a long tradition of all-new construction projects having to dedicate a percentage of their costs to public art, one can hardly walk a metre without bumping into some kind of creative endeavour. While not all attempts are successful (please someone start a petition to remove the garishly coloured geometric stacks acting as lighting poles that line the Damrak), one cannot deny the beauty of things like Hans van Houwelingen's bronze iguanas frolicking in the grass around Kleine Gartmanplantsoen; Atelier Van Lieshout's breast-appended houseboat floating in the Langer Vonder in Amsterdam Noord; the stained glass of cartoonist Joost Swarte in the buildings on the east of Marnixstraat's northern end; and Rombout & Droste's insane walking bridges on Java-eiland. All work together to make the urban landscape of Amsterdam a much richer place.

Sex & Drugs

TEXT: NINA SIEGAL

Red light, green light? Here we go. For now at least…

With its open, legal prostitution (in the shape of the window girls) and marijuana-dispensing coffeeshops, Amsterdam's Red Light District is Dutch pragmatism at its most iconic. While other countries outlaw the world's oldest profession and ban soft drugs, legislators in practical-minded Holland have acknowledged that prohibition doesn't necessarily eliminate the sex and drugs trades. Instead, they're doing their best to regulate them.

Sort of, anyway. The Dutch laws governing the buying and selling of marijuana, hash and other soft drugs can be quite paradoxical, and seem to shift on a regular basis. In 2010, for example, the state imposed a ban on magic mushrooms, although the City of Amsterdam announced it wouldn't enforce it. When it comes to the sex trade, on the other hand, the City is questioning its earlier liberalism. In 2008, former mayor Job Cohen questioned the results of the legalisation of prostitution, saying it had contributed to human trafficking, and the City went about closing scores of windows and replacing them with showcases for fashion designers.

At the moment, it's difficult to say anything truly definitive about the future of Amsterdam's famed sex and drugs haven, except that, for at least for the next five years or so, the Red Light District will still be standing, and still attracting millions of visitors a year.

'A former prostitute founded the Prostitute Information Centre, or PIC – which also happens to be slang for 'dick' in Dutch.'

Sex

Yes, prostitution is legal in Amsterdam, and the working girls here register with the City, pay taxes, and have call buttons so they can alert the police if anything goes awry during 'business transactions'. Whether or not visitors are looking for sex, almost everyone who visits the City likes to take a gander at the notorious Red Light District (known as 'De Wallen' by locals), because it really is a sight to behold: scantily clad sex workers promoting their physical virtues the way bakers promote their cakes – right there in the window.

In addition to the more obvious services on offer in the RLD, Amsterdam also has plenty of more discreet ways of scoring (for a fee). There are brothels (or 'private houses'), at least ten major escort services with websites that allow you to select your date based on looks, age and 'skills', and scores of smaller ones or services organised by a solo gal.

For the more sexually adventurous visitor, the City plays host to several very popular fetish parties (about one or two a month), including the twice-annual Wasteland, the biggest fetish fantasy event in Europe. There are also live sex shows, two strip clubs, and plenty of gay sex clubs. The vast majority of the sex on offer here is oriented toward the male consumer, though girls who like to be titillated by girls can get their fill here too.

IN CONTEXT

RED LIGHT MEANS 'GO'
No matter how prepared you think you are, you may still be taken aback the first time you see street after street of huge picture windows, each decorated with red velvet-effect soft furnishings, sparingly lit, and each dominated by a nearly naked woman. But you won't be the only one walking around with mouth agape. The RLD is filled with groups of tourists of all ages from all over the world, stag and hen parties (particularly from the UK), conventioneers who come with company outings, and even some very open-minded families with their kids.

The 'window girls' are used to the gawking, but don't try to take any pictures: that is strictly forbidden. This is, after all, their livelihood, not merely a peep show.

The women come in all shapes, sizes, skin tones and ages, with the slimmest and youngest ones on the prime browsing blocks and the older, heavier, ethnic, and male ones (yes, those are trannies) on the side streets. Not all of them look terribly excited to be there, but neither would you if your job involved standing up for hours and answering a string of stupid questions. Many of the women pass the time between clients by gossiping with colleagues, dancing and cavorting or teasing passers-by.

WHERE THE GIRLS ARE
Amsterdam's best-known Red Light District spreads out around two streets: Oudezijds Voorburgwal and Oudezijds Achterburgwal, and the famous windows alternate with pubs, casinos and fashion design windows (*see p90* **Project 1012**). Two smaller, less heralded Red Light areas sit on the New Side (between Kattengat and Lijnbaanssteeg) and in De Pijp (Ruysdaelkade, from Albert Cuypstraat to 1e Jan Steenstraat).

The most unusual quality about the Red Light District is its integration into the Old Centre neighbourhood (*see p80*). Police patrol the area with just enough visibility to

'You then strut out through the front door, giggly, wasted and – most importantly, for you have done no wrong – paranoia-free.'

dissuade most troublemakers. CCTV cameras keep a close eye on street activity and every window is equipped with an emergency alarm system that the woman behind it can activate if necessary. While the majority of clients, almost half of whom are locals, have no interest at all in harming a prostitute, these safeguards give workers a much-needed feeling of reassurance.

For visitors who want to look but not touch, a visit to a live sex show might inspire an evening of more private and personal fun elsewhere. Two very popular spots are **Casa Rosso** (*see p88*) and the **Bananenbar** (*see p88*).

FOR THE LADIES
In the game of commercial sex, the big losers are female customers. Sorry, girls: your options are limited. There are a few escort services that will supply male or female prostitutes for you, and you may find a window prostitute who is happy to get busy with a woman – though this is more likely to happen if you visit her with your male partner in tow. Another option for the adventurous is to visit a swingers' club; they generally have an overabundance of single men looking for a free frolic. You could also make a point of visiting the female-friendly sex shops in Amsterdam, **Female & Partners** or **Mail & Female** (*see p206*), to pick up a little consolation gift for yourself (though remember, batteries are rarely included).

THE DARKER SIDE OF THE SEX TRADE
In spite of all the regulation and control, prostitution is still prostitution, and even though there are many sex workers who are happy with their profession, there are still plenty of victims of the sex trade here. Luckily there are people like Anita de Wit, a staunch feminist who has spent 'every waking hour' rescuing women from their pimps since she founded her organisation Stoploverboys in 2008. She spends her days speaking at youth centres across Amsterdam, where she believes girls can easily fall prey to the City's sex traders, and has rescued girls as young as nine years old.

On the flip side of the coin, there's Mariska Majoor, a former prostitute who is the City's most vocal advocate for the rights of the working girl. In 1994, she founded the Prostitute Information Centre (Kerksteeg 3, 420 7328, www.pic-amsterdam.com), these days more commonly known as PIC – there's a bawdy joke in there, with pic also being slang for 'dick' in Dutch. 'There were, and still are, many people who are worried about those "pitiful girls" working in window prostitution, but prostitution is not only about misery,' Majoor explained. 'I wanted to create a place for anybody who has questions or problems involving prostitution, be it the prostitutes themselves; their clients; their relatives; tourists; students and so on.'

Right by the Oude Kerk, the centre is open to absolutely everyone who wants to expand his or her understanding of prostitutes and prostitution. Some frequently asked questions include: How do I negotiate a date with a prostitute? (Answer: just speak to them from outside the door, be polite and say what you'd like, for how long, and what you want to pay.) What does it cost? (Answer: the basic plan, about 20 minutes, usually goes for €50, and additional services cost more.) Has legalisation made conditions better for prostitutes? (This one requires a longer answer.) Groups can also arrange for a lecture session or private walking tour. It takes you through the district, and you get a history of the sex industry in Amsterdam while looking at local statues and monuments.

You finally end up in an empty window booth, so you can see exactly what the girls experience from the inside, and how it all works.

Majoor was also the driving force behind the initiative to erect a statue of an anonymous sex worker, 'Belle'. It was installed in March 2007 in the Oudekersplein with the inscription, 'Respect Sex Workers All Over the World'.

ILLEGAL SEX TRADE
In 2000, a number of governmental reforms were aimed at reducing the number of illegal immigrants in prostitution, but this isn't the main problem: only a minority of prostitutes have no legal status. However, there are still exploitative situations involving coercion, parasitic and controlling 'boyfriends', and problems related to substance abuse.

The most positive effect of the legal changes has been to legitimise prostitution as a profession, which means that sex workers have access to social services and can legitimately band together to improve their working conditions. However, the stigma still remains. Even in the most ideal circumstances, it's still difficult for prostitutes to balance work and private lives. Furthermore, prostitutes have problems when trying to get bank accounts, mortgages and insurance, despite being liable for taxes and generating an estimated €450 million a year.

Drugs

It's a uniquely surreal experience from the start. You strut right in through the front door of the coffeeshop, engage in a simple transaction and then smoke the sweet smoke. You then strut out through the front door, giggly, wasted and – most importantly, for you have done no wrong – paranoia-free.

A large part of the country's image has been defined by its apparently lax attitude towards drugs. But this is misleading: soft drugs are still only semi-legal. In 1976, a vaguely worded law was passed to make a distinction between hard and soft drugs, effectively allowing the use and sale of small amounts of soft drugs under 30 grams (one ounce). The 'front door' of the then embryonic 'coffeeshop' was now legal, although the 'back door', where produce arrived by the kilo, looked out on an illegal distribution system.

Legislators and law enforcement have not been entirely pleased with the results of this policy, and suppliers remain in a legal limbo where such clichés as 'Kafkaesque' or 'Catch 22' can seem quite apt. In the past few years, both the nation and the City of Amsterdam have erected new barriers regarding the use of soft drugs, with an eye towards closing some coffeeshops. In 2008, the national government in the Hague passed a ban on the sale of 'magic mushrooms' after a young woman died under their influence. Another law was passed prohibiting the sale of marijuana within 250 metres (820 feet) of a school, and in a densely packed City like Amsterdam, that's a lot of shops indeed.

TOKING TOURISTS

Nevertheless, the easy availability of soft drugs has produced its own brand of tourist: those who come to the City merely to get so stoned they can't remember a thing about it. A full six per cent of visitors cite coffeeshops (*see pp174-180*) as the reason they come here (with 25 per cent of all visitors finding time to visit at least one of them), especially for the annual Cannabis Cup (*see right* **Blunt Opinion**). And it's this six per cent that has led the authorities to look upon their City's most famous law with ambivalence. On the one hand, the coffeeshops attract many visitors to the City. On the other hand, these kinds of visitors are, not to put too fine a point on it, not the type the authorities welcome with open arms. Two thirds of ambulances called for drug problems are for tourists.

Then there's the issue of organised crime, something no one is in a position to ignore. Every country has it in some form, of course, but the gangs in the Netherlands are able to go about their drug-running businesses with more ease than the government would like. Worse still, many Dutch gangs are believed to be freely trafficking drugs, both hard and soft, all over Europe, a fact that hasn't exactly endeared the Netherlands to its neighbours.

Yet, at the same time, the policy works. And before the world has caught up, the Dutch have moved on: in fact, since 1998 the pleasure-seeking public has become less hedonistic, smoking fewer joints (from 28 per cent to 19 per cent), dropping less ecstasy (from 27 per cent to eight per cent) and snorting less coke (ten per cent to three per cent). So you might want to put a bit of that in your pipe and smoke it.

Blunt Opinion

The city's annual cannabis conference.

The Cannabis Cup, an annual debauch centred on the Netherlands' most precious intoxicant, brings together growers, retailers, punters and activists in a blue-grey haze of hash appreciation, weed cultivation and rambling chat. This congregation of sunken eyes and gentle smiles (and what, we wonder, is the collective noun for a group of stoners? A baggie? A bud? A rockery?) is the pinnacle of the planet's puff production, and Amsterdam is its natural home.

The cup has three main parts. There's the expo on Spaklerweg, which is much like other expos in that it has exhibitor booths, breakout seminars and eager networking, but with hairier attendees and fewer shiny suits. There are stoner-friendly gigs at Melkweg, and then there's the competition itself. This is split into seven categories, covering seeds, smoking apparatus, home-grown and imported strains and, of course, the grand prix, the Cannabis Cup itself. Coffeeshops battle it out for top pot by selecting the best weeds they've found over the previous year for the 2,000 or more judges (who have all paid around €250 for the privilege) to try.

'For what it is,' says grower Wernard Bruining, who, in the 1970s, had one of the city's first-ever seed shops, says, 'it's the best thing available in the universe.'

But, for the uninitiated, the difference between one super-strength weed and another might be hard to fathom. Michael Veling, spokesman for the Cannabis Retailers Association, reckons it all comes down to 'the looks, and more importantly the smell, because all grass available in coffeeshops is of excellent quality'.

The legitimacy of being crowned 'best coffeeshop in the world' has sometimes been called into question. There are typically only about 20 Amsterdam shops that participate, when the city itself has more than ten times that number, and the Netherlands as a whole has 700.

Jason den Enting of the coffeeshop Dampkring is unperturbed, however: 'We have 1,000 people come over from America and England, and for them it's a festival – it's a special week, and a good moment in Amsterdam. Don't worry so much about the best coffeeshop, and look at it like a cannabis festival.'

For further information, see http://hightimes.com/public/cancup/.

IN CONTEXT

Sights

De Waag. *See p86.*

Tour Amsterdam

Get to grips with the city's offerings– by bike, on foot or from the water.

Tourists who know Amsterdam primarily through its reputation as the capital of sex, drugs and rock 'n' roll are often stunned by the physical beauty of the city, which is apparent even in its most seedy districts.

Even if your primary intention is to get hammered for the weekend, it's worth escaping the well-trodden tourist centre to have a nose about. You can wander around aimlessly and enjoy all kinds of scenic experiences in this compact city, but the U-shaped canals and winding byways can make it a little tricky for novices to find their way back to the hotel.

To orient yourself and make sure you don't miss the city's highlights, we recommend a tour. There are plenty on offer, employing all modes of transport – walks, bike rides, by bus and, naturally in a city filled with water, by boat.

BY BICYCLE

Joy Ride Tours

Departs from behind the Rijksmuseum, Museum Quarter (06 4361 1798 mobile, www.joyride tours.nl). Tram 2, 5, 7, 10. **Tours** *Apr-Nov* 4pm Mon, Thur-Sun. **Tickets** €18-€20 2-3hrs. **Credit** AmEx, DC, MC, V. **Map** p330 D5.
Hop into the saddle of a *fiets* (bike) and cruise around the major sights and lesser-known land marks of Amsterdam with resident experts guiding you all the way. You can also follow a tailored route, based on your own particular interests, if you book a private tour.

Mac Bike

620 0985, www.macbike.nl. **Tours** 2 4hrs 10am & 2pm daily (City Tour). **Tickets** €15-€29.50. **Credit** AmEx, MC, V.

Offers a wide array of guided tours: windmills, gay Amsterdam, Waterland and the City Tour. You can also opt for Mac Bike's printed routes, including an 'Art on the Edge' guide that takes you past many of the city's outdoor sculptures and art monuments.

Yellow Bike

Nieuwezijds Kolk 29, Old Centre: New Side (620 6940, www.yellowbike.nl). Tram 1, 2, 5, 13, 17. **Open** *Mar-Oct* 9am-5.30pm daily. *Nov-Feb* 9.30am-5pm daily. **Tickets** from €18.50. **No credit cards. Map** p326 C2.
At Yellow Bike, there are two- and three-hour city tours and a four-hour Waterland tour including a visit to a pancake house – among others.

BY BOAT

Unless specified, all the boat companies listed here offer a wide range of cruises, each varying in price, length and departure time. Check individual websites for details.

Amsterdam Canal Cruises

626 5636, www.amsterdamcanalcruises.nl. **Credit** MC, V.
Canal, lunch, dinner, candlelight cruises and charter boats for all occasions. The city canal cruises depart every half hour from opposite the Heineken Brewery, while charter boats will pick you up from an agreed location.

There's nothing like seeing Amsterdam from the water!

What better way could there be of exploring Amsterdam's ancient city centre than by going on a canal tour?

We offer a wide range of regular cruises:

- **100 Highlights Cruise** is the perfect introduction to the city;
- **Ultimate Cruise** shows you also the cutting-edge architecture of the Eastern Docklands;
- Different kinds of evening cruises, from a **Candlelight or Cocktail Cruise** to a luxurious four-course **Dinner Cruise**.

If you want to create your own sightseeing tour, take the **hop on hop off Canal Bus**. Our comfortable boats offer a regular service along four routes. The stops are located near the major museums, tourist attractions and shopping districts. A ticket is valid on all four lines for 24 hours.

www.canal.nl or www.hir.nl

Blue Boat Company

679 1370, www.blueboat.nl. **Credit** AmEx, MC, V.
Take the city cruise from Stadhouderskade 30 (opposite Hard Rock Café) or rent a boat by the hour, with the possibility of booking lunch, dinner and drink arrangements, and entertainment. Each ticket comes with a free entrance ticket to Holland Casino Amsterdam.

Boat trip to Museum Het Schip

Departs from Pier Smith's Koffiehuis, in front of Centraal Station, Old Centre (418 2885, www.hetschip.nl). **Tickets** €42.50. **No credit cards.**
Organised by Museum Het Schip, these tours focus on the architecture around Java and KNSM islands, former wharfs, and renovated warehouses and silos. The boat tour ends at Spaarndammerbuurt's Houthaven (timber docks), but a guided walk ensues along the 'Workers' Palaces' that are found on Spaarndammerplantsoen, and concludes with a visit to the Museum Het Schip.
▶ *For more about the Amsterdam School architectural gem Museum Het Schip, see p104.*

Canal Bus

Departure from Artis, Centraal Station, Keizersgracht, Leidseplein, Rijksmuseum, Scheepvaartmuseum, Tropenmuseum, Westerkerk, NEMO, Rembrandthuis (623 9886, www.canal.nl). **Tickets** €22/24hrs; €33/48hrs; €44/72hrs; 50% discount ages 4-11. **Credit** MC, V.
These fun hop-on, hop-off buses take four different routes through the city: green, red, blue and orange. With your Canal Bus day ticket, you'll receive discounts at museums, tourist attractions and restaurants; book online for a 10% discount.

Canal Rondvaart/Holland International Boat Excursions

625 3035, www.hir.nl. **Credit** MC, V.
Holland International has a variety of boats for rent (including canal boats), with or without catering. The cruises include the '100 Highlights Cruise', focusing on the city's Golden Age heritage, and the 'Ultimate Cruise' that takes you along the Eastern Docklands *(see p121).*

Gondola Tours

686 9868, 06 4746 4545 mobile, http://gondel.nl. **Rates** €100/hr. **No credit cards.**
Amsterdam is often referred to as the Venice of the North, so what better way to explore its waterways than by gondola? Tirza Mol rents out her (own-built) gondola seasonally from May until November to groups of up to six people. Mol or her partner Hans Lentz, the city's only two gondoliers, can take you anywhere: you choose where and when you board, and they do the rest.

Rederij Lovers

530 5412, www.lovers.nl. **Credit** AmEx, MC, V.
Not just for lovers really (the owner's surname is Lover), Lovers offers a wide variety of cruises from museum tours, dinner cruises and winter candlelight cruises to boat-plus-bike trips out of town.

VIP Watertaxi Amsterdam

Stationsplein 8, Centraal Station (535 6363, www.water-taxi.nl). **Open** *Apr-Sept* 10am-10pm daily. *Oct-Mar* 10am-7pm daily. **Rates** €1.75/min. **Credit** AmEx, MC, V. **Map** p326 D1.
Hailed spontaneously or prearranged by phone, these floating cabs can carry up to eight people. It's worth storing the number for next time you and your buddies are caught up Jacob's Creek without a

SIGHTS

paddle. The same company also rents boats, starting at €70 for the first half hour.

Wetlands Safari
Departs from IJ-side bus terminal, Centraal Station (686 3445, 06 5355 2669 mobile, http://wetlandssafari.nl). **Tours** *May-mid Sept* 9.30am Mon-Fri; 10am Sun. **Tickets** (incl public transport & donation to Landschap Noord-Holland) €43; €27 reductions (min age 7). **Map** p326 D1.
These guided canoe trips take you through 17th-century waterside villages and the reed-lands north of Amsterdam. They include short walks in the moorland meadows where possible and a picnic made up of local products. Custom-made tours with bikes and canoes are available too.

Row your own

Canal Bike
Various locations incl Rijksmuseum & Leidsestraat/Keizersgracht (623 9886, www.canal.nl). **Open** *Summer* 10am-8pm daily. *Winter* 10am-5pm daily. **Rates** €8 per person/hr.
The humble pedalo has been repackaged (complete with a snazzy little rain shield) and rebranded for a whole new generation. Choose to pedal aimlessly around the canals or opt for one of the tours, such as the Rembrandt's Amsterdam, the Jordaan or the Mystery tour.

Canal Motorboats
Zandhoek 10a, Westelijke Eilanden, Waterfront (422 7007, www.canalmotorboats.com). **Tram** 3 or bus 18, 21, 22. **Open** 10am-sunset daily. **Rates** €50 1st hr, sliding scale thereafter. **Map** p325 B1.
If we conveniently disregard the fact that in order to generate electricity in the first place one presumably needs to torch some fossil fuels, then the aluminium-hewn electric canal motorboat is an environmentalist's (ahem) wet dream: low on both emissions and noise pollution. With a capacity of six and a maximum speed of 7km/h, it's also the biggest and fastest vessel you'll be allowed to charter without a licence.

ON FOOT

Amsterdam in WWII – History Walks
Departs from Leliegracht 51, Western Canal Belt (337 9733, 06 4098 3208 mobile, www.history walks.eu). **Tram** 13, 14, 17. **Tours** 1.15pm daily (booking essential). **Tickets** €17; €10 reductions. **No credit cards. Map** p326 C3.
Guided by university history students specialising in the period, this informative walking tour teaches you about the Amsterdam of 1940-45, from the beginning of German occupation all the way through to liberation. The tour includes a visit to the Hollandsche Schouwburg (*see p118*) and can be

**INSIDE TRACK
LANGUAGE MATTERS**

All the listed tours are offered in English. However, not every company offers them all of the time or they may have to be specially requested, so it's wise to check in advance.

combined with a visit to the Verzetsmuseum (the Museum of the Dutch Resistance; *see p118*).

Dutch Delicacy Tour
Departs from the Victoria Hotel entrance, Damrak 1-5, Old Centre: New Side (06 4169 1779 mobile, www.dutchdelicacytour.com). **Tram** 1, 2, 4, 5, 9, 13, 16, 17, 24, 25, 26. **Tickets** €49.50 (6-15 people per group). **No credit cards. Map** p326 D2.
A mouth-watering walking and tasting tour highlighting the centuries-old trade in food, coffee and spices that once brought wealth to Amsterdam. Lasting almost five hours, the tour includes tasting sessions at various spots.

Mee in Mokum
Departs from the Amsterdams Historisch Museum (see p92) (625 1390, www.gildeamsterdam.nl/ stadswandelingen/walking-tours/8). **Tours** 11am Tue-Sun. **Tickets** €5; €2.50 reductions. **No credit cards. Map** p326 D3.
Amsterdammers from all walks of life show you around their city, leading you to their personal favourite spots and relating stories along the way. Tour options include the Old Centre, the Jordaan, Amsterdam's seaports or further afield.

Musical Amsterdam – Amsterdamsel Tours
06 2516 1727 mobile, www.amsterdamsel.org. **Tours** by appt. **Tickets** €20 per person (book online). **No credit cards.**
Take a stroll through town to the rhythm of Mozart, Chet Baker and, yup, Eddie van Halen and find out what traces they left behind. You'll also learn about famous local artists and government-funded rock 'n' roll.

Urban Home & Garden Tours
Departs from the Museum Willet-Holthuysen, Herengracht 605, Southern Canal Belt (688 1243, www.uhgt.nl). **Tram** 4, 9, 14, 16, 24, 25 or Metro Waterlooplein. **Tours** *Apr-Oct* 10.30am Fri, 11.30am Sat, 12.30pm Sun. **Tickets** (incl coffee & sweets) €28.50. **No credit cards. Map** p331 E4.
Professional garden designers and art historians give tours of the 17th-, 18th- and 19th-century canal houses. Booking is essential.

Zuiderkerk. *See p114.*

The Old Centre

Hedonism, history and religion converge in the city's beating heart.

Amsterdam's ground zero of vice, consumerism and entertainment is also – by contrast – its compelling historic core. Some key buildings in the city's Old Centre, among them the wooden-roofed Oude Kerk (Old Church), date back to the 14th century, while the castle-like De Waag (the old weighing house) is an impressive 15th-century construction.

Marked off by Centraal Station, Singel and Zwanenburgwal, the area is roughly bisected by Damrak, which turns into Rokin south of Dam Square. Within the Old Centre, the saucier area to the east is the Oude Zijde (Old Side), while the gentler area to the west – where the most notable landmark is the Spui – is the far-from-new Nieuwe Zijde (New Side).

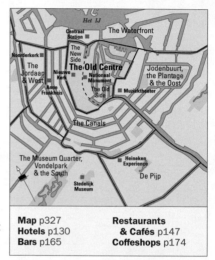

Map p327	Restaurants
Hotels p130	& Cafés p147
Bars p165	Coffeeshops p174

INTRODUCING THE AREA

The Old Centre is the edgiest part of Amsterdam, where window girls practising the world's oldest profession stand beside windows displaying contemporary fashion by the city's up-and-coming designers. The scent of marijuana pours out of overcrowded coffeeshops in narrow byways, and it's not unusual to hear groups of drunken tourists singing at the top of their lungs at 4am.

Along with the city's most unusual asset, the Red Light District (*see pp83-85*), the area is also home to a very small but nonetheless authentic Chinatown on the Zeedijk. It's just a short hop, skip and jump away from the city's central square and meeting point, Dam Square – home to the monumental (by Amsterdam standards) Koninklijk Paleis (Royal Palace).

THE OLD SIDE

Around the Dam

Straight up from **Centraal Station**, just beyond the once watery but now paved and touristy strip named Damrak, lies **Dam Square**, the heart of the city since the first dam was built here back in 1270.

Once a hub of social and political activities and protests, today it's a convenient meeting point for throngs of tourists, the majority of whom convene underneath its mildly phallic centrepiece, the **Nationaal Monument**. The 22-metre (70-foot) white obelisk is dedicated to the Dutch servicemen who died in World War II. Designed by JJP Oud, with sculptures by John Raedecker, it features 12 urns: 11 are filled with earth collected from the (back then) 11 Dutch provinces, while the 12th contains soil taken from war cemeteries in long-time Dutch colony Indonesia.

The west side of Dam Square is flanked by the **Koninklijk Paleis** (Royal Palace; *see below*); next to it is the 600-year-old **Nieuwe Kerk** (New Church, so named as it was built a century after the Oude Kerk, or Old Church, in the Red Light District; *see p89*). In kitsch contrast, over on the south side, is **Madame Tussaud's Scenerama** (*see right*).

Beurs van Berlage

Damrak 277, entrance at Beursplein 1 (530 4141, 620 8112 Artiflex tours, www.beurs vanberlage.nl). Tram 4, 9, 14, 16, 24, 25. **Admission** varies; call for details. **No credit cards. Map** p326 D2.

Designed in 1896 by Hendrik Berlage as the city's stock exchange, the palatial Beurs, while incorporating a broad range of traditional building styles, represents a break from the prevailing tastes of 19th-century architects and, as such, prepared the way for the Amsterdam School. Although critics thought it 'a big block with a cigar box on top', it's now considered the country's most important piece of 20th-century architecture and a powerful socialist statement: much of the artwork warns against capitalism, and each of the nine million bricks was intended to represent the individual, with the building as a whole standing for society.

Having long driven out the moneychangers, the Beurs is now all things to all other people: a conference centre, a café/restaurant, and an exhibition space for shows that range from plastinated human bodies to organic architecture to beer festivals.
▶ *For more on the Amsterdam School's socialist vision and architectural works, see p80*

Koninklijk Paleis (Royal Palace)

Dam (620 4060, 624 8698 tours, www.paleis amsterdam.nl). Tram 1, 2, 4, 5, 9, 13, 14, 16, 17, 24, 25. **Open** *July & Aug* noon-5pm daily. *Other months* varies; call for details. **Admission** €7.50; €6.50 reductions; free under-6s. **No credit cards.** **Map** p326 C3.

Designed along classical lines by Jacob van Campen in the 17th century and built on 13,659 wooden piles that were rammed deep into the sand, the Royal Palace was originally built and used as Amsterdam's city hall. The poet Constantijn Huygens hyped it as 'the world's Eighth Wonder', a monument to the cockiness Amsterdam felt at the dawn of its Golden Age (*see p50*). The palace was intended as a smugly epic 'screw you' gesture to visiting monarchs, a subspecies of humanity that the people of Amsterdam had thus far happily done without.

The exterior (covered in scaffolding as we went to press) is only really impressive when viewed from the rear, where Atlas holds his 1,000kg (2,205lb) copper load at a great height. It's even grander inside than out: the Citizen's Hall, with its baroque decoration in marble and bronze that depicts a miniature universe (with Amsterdam as its obvious centre), is meant to make you feel about as worthy as the rats seen carved in stone over the Bankruptcy Chamber's door. The Palace became state property in 1936 and is still used occasionally by the royal family

INSIDE TRACK BARGAIN BIKES?

If you're planning on cycling during your stay, don't be tempted to buy a cheap *fiets* (bike) from the junkies in the Red Light District; it's most likely to have been stolen. Rent one instead (*see p75*).

Koninklijk Paleis.

SIGHTS

Madame Tussaud's Scenerama

Peek & Cloppenburg, Dam 20 (523 0623, www.madame-tussauds.nl). Tram 4, 9, 14, 16, 24, 25. **Open** 10am-5.30pm daily. **Admission** €19.95; €14.95 reductions; free under-5s, IAmsterdam. **Credit** AmEx, DC, MC, V. **Map** p326 D3.

Craving some queasy kitsch factor? Waxy cheese-textured representations from Holland's own Golden Age of commerce are depicted alongside the Dutch royal family, local celebs and global superstars. Some of the models look like their subjects, some don't. But while there's much campy fun to be had, it comes at a price.

Nieuwe Kerk (New Church)

Dam (626 8168, www.nieuwekerk.nl). Tram 1, 2, 4, 5, 9, 16, 24, 25. **Open** 10am-5pm daily but hrs may vary. **Admission** €15; €11.25-€12 reductions; free under-6s, IAmsterdam; prices may vary with exhibition. **No credit cards.** **Map** p326 C3.

While the 'old' Oude Kerk in the Red Light District was built in the 1300s, the sprightly 'new' Nieuwe Kerk dates from 1408. It is not known how much damage was caused by the fires of 1421 and 1452, or even how much rebuilding took place, but most of the pillars and walls were erected after that time. Iconoclasm in 1566 left the church intact, though statues and altars were removed in the Reformation. The sundial on its tower was used to set the time on all of the city's clocks until 1890. *Photo p85.*

Get the local experience

Over 50 of the world's top destinations available.

TIME OUT GUIDES
WRITTEN BY
LOCAL EXPERTS
visit timeout.com/shop

In 1645, the Nieuwe Kerk was gutted by the Great Fire; the ornate oak pulpit and great organ (the latter designed by Jacob van Campen) are thought to have been constructed shortly after the blaze. Also of interest here is the tomb of naval hero Admiral de Ruyter (1607-76), who initiated the ending of the Second Anglo-Dutch war – wounding British pride in the process – when he sailed up the Medway in 1667, inspiring a witness, Sir William Batten, to observe: 'I think the Devil shits Dutchmen.' Poets and Amsterdam natives PC Hooft and Joost van den Vondel are also buried here. These days, the Nieuwe Kerk hosts organ recitals, state occasions and consistently excellent exhibitions.

The Red Light District

The Red Light District (known as De Wallen; *see p88*), sited in an approximate triangle formed by Centraal Station, Nieuwmarkt and the Dam, is at the very root of Amsterdam's international notoriety. While more overheated imaginations the world over construct images of wild sexual abandon framed in red neon-lit windows, the reality depicted in the postcards on sale locally is a sort of small, cutesy version of Las Vegas. If truth be told, the cheesy joke shop has here been supplanted by the cheesy sex shop: instead of electric palm buzzers and comedy nose glasses, you get multi-orifice inflatables and huge dildos.

Most of the historical significance of the Red Light District – of which there is plenty, this being the oldest part of Amsterdam – has been veneered by another old and very greasy trade: marketing. Although sex is the hook upon which the whole area hangs its reputation, it's actually secondary to window-shopping. People do buy – it's estimated to be a €450-million-per-year trade – but mostly they simply wander around, gawping at the live exhibits.

Most of the window girls are self-employed and, even though prostitution was only defined as a legal and taxable profession in 1988 and bordellos have only been officially legitimate since October 2000 (a tactic intended to make taxation easier), the women have had their own union since 1984.

A new initiative was put into place in 2007 to clean up crime in the area. Armed with new laws enabling the closure of establishments suspected to be involved in criminal activity, the city bought 55 buildings from a former 'prostitution baron'. Needing to breathe new life into these buildings, and the area for that matter, many of

Tiny Chinatown

Small but perfectly formed. Take it away...

Possibly the world's smallest Chinatown can be found on the Zeedijk winding from Centraal Station towards Nieuwmarkt past a string of no-frills restaurants. In many of them, you can eat authentic fare for under a tenner. Among the top local picks are award-winning Chinese eateries **Nam Kee** and **New King** (for both, *see p151*), and the Thai **Bird** (*see p149*), which has a very popular fast food and takeaway location (the 'Snackbar') across the street from its more spacious and elegant restaurant. Culinary travellers who want more Eastern exploration will also be pleased to find Japanese, Malaysian, Vietnamese and even pan-Asian restaurants up and down the street, as well as further east on Koningsstraat past Nieuwmarkt.

If you want to stock up on Asian snacks or plan to cook an Asian meal at home, the pan-Asian **Dun Yong** (Stormsteeg 9, www.dunyong.com) is the perfect culinary destination shop. The shelves, fridges and freezers at this shrine to Eastern cookery are heaving with weird and wonderful Oriental products – frozen dumplings, preserved tofu, handmade noodles, saké,

and exotic fruit and vegetables, just to name a few. In the basement you'll find kitsch and well-priced Asian crockery. The **Oriental Commodities** Chinese food emporium right on the southern edge of the square (Nieuwmarkt 27, www.amazing oriental.com; *see p199*) sells handmade noodles, frozen dumplings and all those special Asian vegetables that you can't find at the Albert Heijn.

Aside from Asian food and tat, the primary attraction on the street is the Chinese **Fo Guang Shan He Hua Buddhist Temple** (*see p85*), which was designed with bluestone steps, roof tiles and ornaments imported directly from China for the prayer centre. Monks and nuns still practise their faith here, but tours are available. You'll be asked to remove your shoes as you're guided through the surprisingly spacious complex, which includes a library, an internet café and a vegetarian restaurant.

Every year, between 21 January and 20 February, Chinatown is where you'll experience street celebrations for **Chinese New Year**, including a traditional Lion Dance performed with live drumming.

The travel apps city lovers have been waiting for...

'Time Out raises the city app bar'–*The Guardian*

**Compiled by resident experts apps and maps
work offline with no roaming charges**

Available now: London, Paris,
Barcelona, Berlin, Buenos Aires and Zagreb

timeout.com/iphonecityguides

Niuewe Kerk. *See p81.*

these cubicles formerly used by prostitutes have been handed over to fashion designers, who can use the space rent-free for the period of one year. For more on the sex trade and the changes afoot in the Red Light District; see pp65-71.

Zeedijk

Before this dyke was built, some time around 1300, Amsterdam was a fishing village with barely enough bog to stand on. But by the 15th and 16th centuries, with the East India Company raking in the imperialist spoils, Zeedijk was the street where sailors came to catch up on their boozing, brawling and also bonking – or 'doing the St Nicolaas', as it was fondly termed in those days (a tribute to their patron saint, an extremely busy chap who watches over children, thieves, prostitutes and the city of Amsterdam).

Sailors who had lost all their money could trade in their pet monkey for a flea-infested bed at Zeedijk 1, which still retains its original name – **In't Aepjen**, meaning 'In the Monkeys' – and is today one of the oldest and most charming wooden houses in the city centre. Just off the street down Oudezijds Kolk, you can spot the **Schreierstoren**, aka the 'Weeping Tower'. Built in 1487, and successfully restored in 1966, it's the most interesting relic of Amsterdam's medieval city wall. It is said that wives would cry there, perhaps with relief, when husbands set off on a voyage, then cry again if the ship

returned with news that said spouse was lost at sea. If the latter happened, then it was but a short walk to Zeedijk, where the bereaved lady would often continue life as a 'merry widow'. Prostitution was often the female equivalent of joining the navy: the last economic option.

During the 20th century, Zeedijk has been sparked by cultural diversity. In the 1930s, the first openly gay establishments appeared, closed, and recently reopened: at **Het Mandje** (no.65), there's a window shrine to flamboyant owner Bet van Beeren (1902-67), who has gone down in local mythology as the original lesbian biker chick. In the '50s, jazz greats Chet Baker and Gerry Mulligan came to jam and hang out in the many after-hours clubs here, among them the still-functioning-as-a-shadow-of-what-it-was **Casablanca** (no.26).

Jazz legend Chet Baker took his final curtain call on this street in 1988, falling on to a cement parking pole from a window (second floor on the left) of the Prins Hendrik Hotel at the entrance of Zeedijk. A brass plaque commemorating the crooning trumpeter has been put up to the left of the hotel's entrance.

You'll also find the city's very small Chinatown here – about half a block long; *see p83* **Tiny Chinatown**. Be sure to visit the Chinese **Fo Guang Shan He Hua Buddhist Temple** (no.106, 420 2357, www.ibps.nl, closed Mon), where monks and nuns provide a library, internet café and vegetarian restaurant.

Oude Kerk. *See p89.*

Nieuwmarkt

At the bottom of Zeedijk, your eyes will be
drawn to the huge, pointy-roofed **De Waag**
(the Weigh House). The Waag, previously called
St Antoniespoort, stands in the centre of
Nieuwmarkt (*see right* **Profile: Nieuwmarkt**)
and dates from 1488, when it was built as a
gatehouse for the city defences. More recently,
in 1980, Nieuwmarkt was the site of riots when
the city demolished housing to make way for
the Metro. In 1991, it was saved by a citizens'
committee from being irrevocably revamped
by designer Philippe Starck.

Today, the Waag is home to the **Society
for Old and New Media** (557 9898,
www.waag.org), which surfs the interface
between technology and culture, and organises
events in the former Anatomical Theatre.

Oudezijds main streets

The two canals Oudezijds Voorburgwal and
Oudezijds Achterburgwal, with their quaint
interconnecting streets, are where carnal sin
screams loudest. So it's ironic that, right in the
middle of Sin City, you'll stumble across a pair
of old churches. The **Oude Kerk** (*see p89*),
Amsterdam's oldest building, is literally in the
centre of the sleazy action, with hookers in
windows ringing the mammoth church like
bullies taunting the class geek. Keep your eyes
peeled for the small brass bosom inlaid by a
mystery artist into the pavement by the front
entrance. The **Museum Amstelkring** (*see
p89*), meanwhile, is tucked away a distance
from the red-lit action, but still shouldn't be
overlooked on your journey around the area.

The **Agnietenkapel** (Oudezijds
Voorburgwal 231) is one of Amsterdam's 17
medieval convents. Built in the 1470s and part
of the University of Amsterdam since its
foundation in 1632, the chapel has an austere,
Calvinistic beauty highlighted by its stained-
glass windows, wooden beams and benches,
not to mention a collection of portraits of
humanist thinkers. The Grote Gehoorzaal (Large
Auditorium), the country's oldest lecture hall,
is where 17th-century scholars Vossius and
Barlaeus first taught; its wooden ceiling is
painted with soberly ornamental Renaissance

INSIDE TRACK
AS SEEN ON SCREEN

The incredibly scenic Staalstraat is the
city's most popular film location, having
appeared in everything from *The Diary of
Anne Frank* to *Amsterdamned*.

SIGHTS

Profile Nieuwmarkt

Take a turn around this historic central square – now a focus for festivities, markets and café culture.

The Nieuwmarkt is one of the city's oldest central squares, dominated by one of its oldest buildings, **De Waag**. Originally part of the medieval city wall, in 1480 it became the weighing hall, where merchants calculated the weight and subsequent value of grains and other goods arriving in Amsterdam by merchant ship. It's easy to see why. Look north down the Geldersekade and you'll see the IJ; this canal used to be an unimpeded thoroughfare directly to the harbour.

De Waag has a fascinating history: while downstairs the busy weighing hall trade was bustling, upstairs the city's medical guild was employed with another kind of business altogether – the cutting up of human bodies. The top tower of De Waag was an Anatomical Theatre, where the city's physicians would perform dissections on executed convicts to describe to an audience of doctors, noblemen and laymen how the body functioned (or, at least, what was known at the time).

Tour guides like to tell visitors that this is where Rembrandt painted his famous group portrait, *The Anatomy Lesson of Dr Nicolaes Tulp* (1632), but that isn't strictly accurate. The tower that houses the Anatomical Theatre wasn't built until 1639, a full seven years after Tulp's commemorated lesson. Though there was probably a more informal dissection chamber in the building before that, Rembrandt would have painted the portrait in his studio on the Sint Antoniesbreestraat (not too far from here). Each guild member who wanted to be featured in the portrait modelled for the painter, paying Rembrandt about 100 guilders (a small fortune). Only the corpse didn't have to pay.

The market around De Waag (built in 1614) has been a bustling farmer's market since the city's Golden Age. It was a particularly popular trading spot for the city's Sephardic Jews, who had been migrating to this neighbourhood since the Spanish Inquisition. During World War II the Nieuwmarkt was the site of far more grim business: rounding up Amsterdam's Jewish residents for deportation to the Nazi concentration camps. A popular fascist magazine, *De Waag*, was also published here.

These days, it's an open market where all kinds of activities take place; on Saturdays a farmers' market offers up freshly baked artisan breads, cheeses and locally grown veg, along with antiques and crafts. There are occasional carnivals here (on Queen's Night) and on New Year's Eve it becomes detonation-central for fireworks displays. But mostly the activity takes place around the square, in two dozen popular cafés and bars.

WEIGHING THE POINT
The roofs of De Waag dominate the Nieuwmarkt.

SIGHTS

motifs including angels and flowers. Rolling exhibitions are only occasional; since 2007 it is used mostly for readings and congresses.

'De Wallen'

The Oudezijds Achterburgwal offers some of the more 'tasteful' choices for the eroto-clubber. The **Casa Rosso** nightclub (Oudezijds Achterburgwal 106-108, 627 8954) is certainly worth a look, even though its famed and peculiar marble cock-and-rotary-ball water fountain at its entrance has been removed.

A short walk away at no.37 is the **Bananenbar** (627 8954), where improbably dexterous female genitalia can be seen performing night after night – and, as the central part of their belief-buggering act, spitting out an average of 15kgs (33lbs) of fruit every evening. A former owner of the Bananenbar once tried to stave off taxmen – and get round the fact that his drinking licence had lapsed – by picking Satan as a deity and registering the Bananenbar as a church. It was a scam that worked for years – until 1988, when the 'Church of Satan' claimed a membership of 40,000 overseen by a council of nine anonymous persons. The tax police were called in to bust the joint, but the bar was tipped off and the 'church' disbanded. Now under the same ownership as the Erotic Museum, the Bananenbar has kept its name and returned to its roots as a purveyor of sleaze.

If your urges are more academic, you can conduct some, ahem, research at the **Erotic Museum** (*see below*), following it in semi-traditional fashion with a smoke at the **Hash Marihuana & Hemp Museum** (which doesn't actually sell dope, but you get the picture; *see below*). Other than that, sleaze and stag parties dominate this strip.

It's all a far cry from the **Spinhuis**, a former convent tucked away at the southern end of the canal (on Spinhuissteeg) that used to set 'wayward women' to work spinning wool. The male equivalent was over on the New Side at Heiligeweg 9 – now an entrance to the Kalvertoren shopping complex – where audiences used to watch the prisoners being branded and beaten with a bull's penis. In a rather curious foreshadowing of Amsterdam's contemporary S&M scene, the entrance gate sports a statue bearing a striking resemblance to a scolding dominatrix.

Erotic Museum
Oudezijds Achterburgwal 54 (624 7303). Tram 4, 9, 16, 24, 25 or Metro Nieuwmarkt. **Open** 11am-1am Mon-Thur, Sun; 11am-2am Fri, Sat. **Admission** €7. **No credit cards**. **Map** p326 D2.
While the Sexmuseum (Damrak 18, www.sexmuseumamsterdam.nl) benefits from its Damrak site in terms of passing trade, the Erotic Museum is in the more appropriate location: slap bang in the Red Light District. That's not to say, though, that it's any more authentic or interesting. Its prize exhibits are a bicycle-powered dildo and a few of John Lennon's erotic drawings, while lovers of Bettie Page (and there are many) will enjoy the original photos of the S&M muse on display. Since 2009, it has put on temporary exhibits in a sexy art gallery on the third floor. In general, however, the museum's name is somewhat inaccurate: despite its best intentions and desperate desire to shock, it's as unsexy as can be. All in all, you're probably best off going to one of the many nearby sex shops for your kicks.

Hash Marihuana & Hemp Museum
Oudezijds Achterburgwal 148 (624 8926 Mon-Fri, www.hashmuseum.com). Tram 4, 9, 14, 16, 24, 25 or Metro Nieuwmarkt. **Open** 10am-11pm daily. **Admission** €9; free under-13s when accompanied by an adult. **Credit** AmEx, MC, V. **Map** p326 D3.
Cannabis connoisseurs will lose themselves ogling larger than life pictures of perfect plants and gleaming balls of hash in this museum in the Red Light District. But this shrine to skunk is not only for smokers. Straight-laced visitors will be entertained by the detailed history of the plant. There's

Zeedijk. *See p89.*

Dam Square. *See p80.*

plenty of pro-cannabis propaganda here, too, including info about its medicinal uses, the environmental benefits of hemp and the cannabis culture of today. Don't miss the indoor grow-op that showcases plants being lovingly cultivated for their seeds, guarded by a guru of ganja who offers advice on using a vaporiser.

★ Museum Amstelkring

Oudezijds Voorburgwal 40 (624 6604, www.museumamstelkring.nl). Tram 4, 9, 14, 16, 24, 25. **Open** 10am-5pm Mon-Sat; 1-5pm Sun. **Admission** €7; €1-€5 reductions; free under-5s, MK, IAmsterdam. **No credit cards. Map** p326 D2.

The Amstelkring takes its name from the group of historians who succeeded in saving it from demolition in the late 1800s. Good job they did save it, too, for what remains is one of Amsterdam's most unusual spots, and one of its best-kept secrets. The lower floors of the house have been wonderfully preserved since the late 17th century, and offer a look at what life might have been like back then.

The main attraction is upstairs, and goes by the name of Ons' Lieve Heer op Solder (Our Sweet Lord in the Attic). Built in 1663, this attic church was used by Catholics during the 17th century when they were banned from worshipping after the Alteration. It's been beautifully preserved, too, the altarpiece featuring a painting by 18th-century artist Jacob de Wit, and was recently entirely renovated. The church is often used for services and a wide variety of other meetings. Don't miss it.

Oude Kerk

Oudekerksplein 1 (625 8284, www.oudekerk.nl). Tram 4, 9, 16, 24, 25, 26. **Open** 11am-5pm Mon-Sat; 1-5pm Sun. **Admission** €5; €4 reductions; free under-12s, MK, IAmsterdam; varies during special exhibitions. **No credit cards. Map** p326 D2.

Originally built in 1306 as a wooden chapel, and constantly renovated and extended between 1330 and 1571, the Oude Kerk is the city's oldest and most interesting church. One can only imagine the Sunday Mass chaos during its heyday of the mid 1500s, when it had 38 altars each with its own guild-sponsored priest. Its original furnishings were removed by iconoclasts during the Reformation, but the church has retained its wooden roof, which was painted in the 15th century with figurative images. Keep your eyes peeled for the mixed Gothic and Renaissance façade above the northern portal, and the stained-glass windows, parts of which date from the 16th and 17th centuries. Rembrandt's wife Saskia, who died in 1642, is buried here. The inscription over the bridal chamber, which translates as 'Marry in haste, mourn at leisure', is in keeping with the church's location in the heart of the Red Light District, though this is more by accident than design. If you want to be semi-shocked, check out the carvings in the choir benches of men evacuating their bowels – apparently they tell a moralistic tale. The church is now as much an exhibition centre as anything else, with shows covering everything from modern art installations to the annual World Press Photo exhibition (*see p209*). *Photo p86.*

Project 1012

Cleaning up the city's most notorious postcode.

Back in 2007, former Amsterdam mayor Job Cohen and his deputy mayor Lodewijk Asscher made international headlines when they announced that the experiment of legalised prostitution in the Netherlands 'wasn't working'.

An investigation of the Red Light District, initiated by a parliamentary inquiry, found that there was a much larger criminal element operating in the city centre than had previously been imagined. The city leaders concluded that there wasn't appropriate legal enforcement in the district, and that the sex and drug trades had given rise to a subculture of money laundering, tax evasion, international sex trafficking and other types of crime.

Enter Project 1012, a multi-part programme designed to address the 'criminal element' in the Red Light District, so named because 1012 is the neighbourhood's postcode. The strategy, adopted in the summer of 2009, focused on five main points: reducing the number of Red Light 'windows' or prostitute booths; reducing the number of coffeeshops in designated streets; limiting the 'Red Light' sprawl to two primary locations (the main area around the Oudezijds Achterburgwal and the area around the Singel canal); working with neighbourhood residents and entrepreneurs to develop other kinds of businesses in the district; and reorganising a number of streets in the area.

Cohen and Asscher were adamant that they had no intention of closing down the Red Light District or initiating a prohibition against prostitution or soft drugs. They merely wanted to get control over the darker elements of the trade and make the district safer for residents and legal workers. Speaking to *Time Out Amsterdam* in March 2010, Asscher said he'd like to see the number of window brothels reduced by half. 'My dream is that, yes, there will be an RLD with legalised prostitution, but there has to be a different kind of prostitution,' he said. 'We'll never have 100 per cent guarantees, but I want it to be something with the maximum number of checks and balances, with regulations and enforcement in place, to make sure that the women working are truly doing it voluntarily.'

Walking through the Red Light District these days, it's impossible not to notice that many of the real women in the windows have been replaced by mannequins sporting haute couture. It's part of 'Red Light Fashion', a co-operative project between the municipality and a group of entrepreneurial local designers, such as Daryl van Wouw, Bas Kosters, ...and Beyond, and CODE Gallery store. Designers say they love it because they get attention from the hordes of international tourists who visit the Red Light District every day – albeit with a different kind of window-shopping in mind.

Warmoesstraat

It's now hard to believe that Warmoesstraat, Amsterdam's oldest street, was once the most beautiful of lanes, providing a sharp contrast to its evil and rowdy twin, Zeedijk. The poet Joost van den Vondel ran a hosiery business at Warmoesstraat 101; Mozart's dad would try to flog tickets at the posh bars for his young son's concerts; and Marx would later come here to write in peace (or so he claimed: he was more likely to have been in town to borrow money from his cousin by marriage, the extremely wealthy Gerard Philips, founder of the globe-dominating Philips corporate machine).

But with the influx of sailors, the laws of supply and demand engineered a heavy fall from grace for Warmoesstraat. Adam and Eve in their salad days can still be seen etched in stone at no.25, but for the most part, this street has fallen to accommodating only the low-end traveller. However, hipper hangouts such as gay/mixed bar **Getto** (see p245), excellent breakfast and lunch spot **De Bakkerswinkel** (located on Zeedijk until end 2012; see p149) and the **Winston Hotel** (see p134), plus shops including the **Condomerie het Guiden Vlies** (see p206) and gallery **W139** (see p231) have ensured that the strip has retained some brighter and less commercial colours, while the council's serial clean-up operation reached the street quite recently and has at least had some of the desired cosmetic effect.

The Nes

Just as Warmoesstraat stretches north from the Nationaal Monument into the Old Side, so Nes leaves the same spot to the south, parallel and to the west of Oudezijds Achterburgwal.

Dating from the Middle Ages, this street was once home to the city's tobacco trade and the Jewish philosopher Benedict Spinoza (1623-77), who saw body and mind as the two aspects of a single substance. Appropriate, then, that you can now witness the alignment of body and mind on the stages of the many theatres that have long graced this street. You can also stop, recharge and realign your own essence at one of the many charming cafés hereabouts. At the end of Nes, either take a turn left to cross a bridge towards **Oudemanhuis Book Market** (where Van Gogh bought prints to decorate his room) on the University of Amsterdam campus; or turn right and end up near the **Allard Pierson Museum**.

Allard Pierson Museum

Oude Turfmarkt 127 (525 2556, www.allard piersonmuseum.nl). Tram 4, 9, 14, 16, 24, 25. **Open** 10am-5pm Mon-Fri; 1-5pm Sat, Sun.

INSIDE TRACK RELIGIOUS ART

While visiting the Begijnhof, be sure to check out the beautiful painted stones on the wall behind the Houtenhuis (see p92), each of which depicts a scene from the Bible. Dating back to the 17th and 18th centuries, these stones, once housed in the Rijksmuseum's vaults, were restored and installed here in 1961.

Admission €6.50; free-€3.25 reductions, MK. **No credit cards**. **Map** p326 D3.
Established in 1934, the Allard Pierson is the University of Amsterdam's archaeological museum – home to one of the world's richest university collections, containing archaeological exhibits from Ancient Egypt, Greece, Rome and the Near East.

THE NEW SIDE

Rhyming (nearly enough) with 'cow', the Spui is the square that caps the three main arteries that start down near the west end of Centraal Station: the middle-of-the-road walking and retail street Kalverstraat (called Nieuwendijk before it crosses the Dam), plus Nieuwezijds Voorburgwal and the Spuistraat.

A quiet backwater accessible via the north side of the Spui square or, when that entrance is closed, via Gedcompte Begijnensloot (the alternating entrances were set up to appease residents), the **Begijnhof** is a group of houses built around a secluded courtyard and garden. Established in the 14th century, it originally provided modest homes for the Beguines, a religious and, as was the way in the Middle Ages with religious establishments for women, rather liberated sisterhood of unmarried ladies from good families who, though not nuns and thus taking no formal vows, lived together in a close community and had to take vows of chastity.

Since they did not have to take vows of poverty, the Beguines were free to dispose of their property as they saw fit, further ensuring their emancipation as a community. They could, however, renounce their vows at any moment and leave, for instance if they wanted to get married. The last sister died in 1971, while one of her predecessors never left, despite dying back in 1654. She was buried in a 'grave in the gutter' under a red granite slab that remains visible – and often still adorned with flowers – on the path. Nowadays, it's one of the best-known of the city's many *hofjes* (almshouses; see p103 **Hidden Hofjes**).

Most of the neat little houses in the courtyard were modernised in the 17th and 18th centuries. In the centre stands the **Engelsekerk** (English

Reformed Church), built as a church around 1400 and given over to Scottish (no, really) Presbyterians living in the city in 1607; many became pilgrims when they decided to travel further to the New World in search of religious freedom. Now one of the principal places of worship for Amsterdam's English community, the church is worth a look primarily to see the pulpit panels, designed by a young Mondrian.

Also in the courtyard is a Catholic church, secretly converted from two houses in 1665 following the complete banning of open Catholic worship after the Reformation. It once held the regurgitated Eucharist host that starred in the Miracle of Amsterdam, a story depicted in the church's beautiful stained-glass windows. The wooden house at no.34, known as the **Houtenhuis**, dates from 1475 and is the oldest house still standing within the city, while **Begijnhof 35** is an information centre. The Begijnhof is also very close to one of the several entrances to the **Amsterdams Historisch Museum** (*see below*), which in turn is the starting point for the highly informal **Mee in Mokum** walking tours (*see p78*).

The Spui square itself plays host to many markets – the most notable being the busy book market on Fridays – and was historically an area where the intelligentsia gathered for some serious browbeating and alcohol abuse after a day's work on the local papers. The *Lieverdje* (Little Darling) statue in front of the **Athenaeum Nieuwscentrum** store (*see p182*), a small, spindly and guano-smeared statue of a boy in goofy knee socks, was the site for wacky Provo 'happenings' that took place in the mid 1960s.

You can leave Spui by going up Kalverstraat, Amsterdam's main shopping street, or Singel past Leidsestraat: both routes lead up to the **Munttoren** (Mint Tower) at Muntplein. Just across from the floating flower market (the **Bloemenmarkt**; *see p200*), this medieval tower was the western corner of Reguliersport, a gate in the city wall in the 1480s; in 1620, a spire was added by Hendrick de Keyser, the foremost architect of the period. The tower takes its name from when it minted coins after Amsterdam was cut off from its money supply during a war with England, Munster and France. There's a shop on the ground floor for fine Dutch porcelain (Holland Gallery de Munt, Muntplein 12, 623 2271), but the rest of the tower is closed to visitors. The Munttoren is prettiest when floodlit at night, though daytime visitors may hear its carillon, which often plays out for 15 minutes at noon.

From here, walk down Nieuwe Doelenstraat past the Hôtel de l'Europe (a mock-up of which featured in Hitchcock's *Foreign Correspondent*). Walk up Staalstraat and you'll end up at **Waterlooplein** (*see p115 & p182*).

★ Amsterdams Historisch Museum
Kalverstraat 92 (523 1822, www.ahm.nl). Tram 1, 2, 4, 5, 9, 14, 16, 24, 25. **Open** 10am-5pm daily. **Admission** €10; €5-€7.50 reductions; free under-6s, MK, IAmsterdam. **No credit cards**. **Map** p326 D3.

A note to all those historical museums around the world that struggle to present their exhibits in an engaging fashion: head here to see how it's done. Amsterdam's Historical Museum is a gem – illuminating, interesting and entertaining. It starts with the very buildings in which it's housed: a lovely, labyrinthine collection of 17th-century constructions built on the site of a 1414 convent. You can enter it down Sint Luciensteeg, just off Kalverstraat, or off Spui, walking past the Begijnhof (*see p91*) and then through the grand Civic Guard Gallery, a small covered street hung with huge 16th- and 17th-century group portraits of wealthy burghers. And it continues with a computer-generated map of the area showing how Amsterdam has grown (and shrunk) throughout the last 800 years or so. It then takes a chronological trip through Amsterdam's past, using archaeological finds, works of art and some far quirkier displays.

Centraal Station. *See p80.*

The Canals

God may have made the water, but you can thank man for the canals.

Keeping the sea and surrounding bog at bay are Amsterdam's 165 *grachten* (canals). Crossed by 1,400 bridges, they stretch for 75.5 kilometres (47 miles) around the city, and are, on average, three metres deep. The major canals and their radial streets are where the real city exists. What they lack in sights, they make up for with places for scenic coffee slurping, quirky shopping, aimless walks and meditative gable-gazing.

Declared a UNESCO World Heritage Site in 2010, the *grachtengordel* (girdle of canals) rings the centre of town, its waterways providing an attractive border between the tourist-laden centre and the gentler, artier, more 'local' outskirts. Here, we've grouped them into the Western Canal Belt and the Southern Canal Belt.

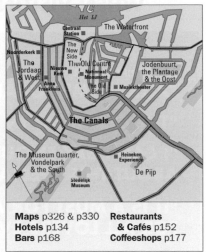

Maps p326 & p330	Restaurants
Hotels p134	& Cafés p152
Bars p168	Coffeeshops p177

SIGHTS

THE WESTERN CANAL BELT

Singel

One of the few clues to Singel's past as the protective moat that surrounds the city's wall is the **Torensluis** (Tower Gate) bridge that crosses it at Oude Leliestraat. It did indeed once have a lookout tower and the space underneath was supposedly used as a lock-up for medieval drunks. A statue of the writer Multatuli depicts his head forming as smoke from a bottle – a reference to the way he let the genie out of the bottle by questioning Dutch imperialism in his novels.

**INSIDE TRACK
TRIPLE X SOUVENIRS**

Amsterdam's 'XXX' logo also emblazons the *amsterdammertjes* (the phallic parking poles scattered throughout the city), which incidentally can be bought for around €105 a piece at the city's material depot (Pieter Braaijweg 10, 561 2111).

While you're wandering this canal, you may wish to contribute to the debate as to whether Singel 7 or Singel 166 is the smallest house in Amsterdam. Always good for a snort is the **House with Noses** at Singel 116, although arty types might be a bit more interested in Singel 140-142. This was once the home of Banning Cocq, the principal figure of Rembrandt's *The Night Watch* (*see p31*). Further south, you'll find the town's poshest old-school sex club, **Yab Yum** (Singel 295, 624 9503, www.yabyum.com), where the country's elite goes for a good old-fashioned servicing.

FREE **Multatuli Museum**

Korsjespoortsteeg 20 (638 1938, www.multatuli-museum.nl). Tram 1, 2, 5, 13, 17. **Open** 10am-5pm Tue; noon-5pm Sat, Sun; also by appt. **Admission** free. **Map** p326 C2.

Just off Singel, this museum is dedicated to the satirical writer Eduard Douwes-Dekker (1820-87), aka Multatuli (meaning 'I have suffered much' in Latin). It is in the house where he was born. The various literary artefacts pay testament to his credo: 'the human calling is to be human'. There's also a small library.

Herengracht

At Herengracht 366, you'll find the Bijbels Museum (Bible Museum; *see below*). A few doors further south is the **Netherlands Institute of War Documentation** (Herengracht 380, 523 3800, www.niod. knaw.nl). This copy of a Loire mansion houses three kilometres of archives that include Anne Frank's diary, donated by her father Otto.

Head north and you'll reach a Vingboons building at no.168, dating from 1638, along with the architectural gem that is De Keyser's **Bartolotti House** (Herengracht 170-172, www.hendrickdekeyser.nl). For a unique look at the history along with some fine examples of handbags and purses, meanwhile, be sure to stop in on the **Tassenmuseum Hendrikje** (Museum of Bags & Purses, *see p101*).

Bijbels Museum

Herengracht 366 (624 2436, www.bijbels museum.nl). Tram 1, 2, 5. **Open** 10am-5pm Mon-Sat; 11am-5pm Sun, public holidays. **Admission** €8; €4 reductions, free under-13s, MK, IAmsterdam. **No credit cards.** **Map** p330 C4.

Housed in a restored 17th-century Vingboons canal house, this museum aims to illustrate life and worship with archaeological finds, models of ancient temples and a splendid collection of Bibles from several centuries (including a rhyming Bible from 1271). You can also admire the splendid Jacob de Wit paintings, and the grand garden with biblical plants and a sculpture entitled *Apocalypse*.

Keizersgracht

Walking down Keizersgracht, you'll soon encounter the **House with the Heads** (no.123), a pure Dutch Renaissance classic. The official story has these finely chiselled heads representing classical gods, but according to local folklore they are the heads of burglars, chopped off by a lusty maidservant. She decapitated six and married the seventh.

Another true classic is at Keizersgracht 174, an art nouveau masterpiece by Gerrit van Arkels. A few paces down are the pink granite triangular slabs of the **Homomonument** (*see p237*), the world's first memorial to persecuted gays and lesbians.

Another key edifice is the **Felix Meritis Building** (Keizersgracht 324, www.felix. meritis.nl), a neoclassical monolith with the motto 'Happiness through merit' chiselled over its door. Nowadays, it's the European Centre for Art & Science. Nearby is the equally epic home of the photography foundation, **Huis Marseille** (*see below*). This whole stretch was also the site of the legendary Slipper Parade, where the posh-footed rich strolled about every Sunday both to see and be seen. These days, those in the fashion know spend their time (and cash) in the surrounding stylish **De 9 Straatjes (Nine Streets)**, *see p99* **Dressed to the Nines.**

Huis Marseille

Keizersgracht 401 (531 8989, www.huis marseille.nl). Tram 1, 2, 5. **Open** 11am-5pm Tue-Sun. **Admission** €5; €3 reductions, free

SIGHTS

Huis Marseille.

under-17s MK, IAmsterdam. **No credit cards**. **Map** p330 C4.

The walls of this photography foundation might host the latest from such hotshots as Hellen van Meene, David Goldblatt or Naoya Hatakeyama; classic work from contemporary photographers, Bernd and Hilla Becher; or landscapes of Amsterdam and perhaps even the moon. Don't miss the videos and mags in the 'media kitchen'. *Photo p95*.

Prinsengracht

Named after William, Prince of Orange, Prinsengracht is the most charming of the canals. Pompous façades have been mellowed with shady trees, cosy cafés and some of Amsterdam's hipper houseboats.

On your way up Prinsengracht, you'll pass the **Anne Frank Huis** and the 375-year-old

Westerkerk.

Westerkerk (for both, *see below*). Mari Andriessen's statue of Frank (1977) stands nearby, at the corner with Westermarkt. Meanwhile, René Descartes fans – and if you think, therefore you probably are – can pay tribute to the great savant by casting an eye on his former house (Westermarkt 6).

If you find yourself at the weekly **Noordermarkt** (*see p182*) or **Boerenmarkt** (*see p199*), then make sure you stop for coffee at the ever-popular **Papeneiland** (*see p172*). According to local legend, a tunnel used to run under the canal from here to a Catholic church located at Prinsengracht 7 at the time of the Protestant uprising.

★ Anne Frank Huis
Prinsengracht 267 (556 7105, www.annefrank.nl). *Tram 13, 14, 17.* **Open** *Jan-Mar, Sept-Dec* 9am-7pm daily. *Apr-Aug* 9am-9pm daily. **Admission** €9; €4.50 reductions, €0.50 under-10s. **Credit** MC, V. **Map** p326 C2.

One of the most visited sights in Amsterdam, Prinsengracht 263 was the canalside house where young Jewish girl Anne Frank and her family hid for two years during World War II. A bookcase marks the entrance to the sober, unfurnished rooms of the annexe they shared with four other Jews until 4 August 1944, when they were arrested and transported to concentration camps.

In the museum's newer wing, there's an exhibition detailing the Jews' persecution during the war, as well as displays charting and exploring the difficulties in fighting discrimination.

Westerkerk
Prinsengracht 277-279 (624 7766, 689 2565 tower, www.westerkerk.nl). Tram 13, 14, 17. **Open** *Apr-Sept* 11am-3pm Mon-Fri. *Services* 10.30am Sun. **Admission** *Tower* €5 (tours only during summer). **No credit cards**. **Map** p326 C3.

Officially opened on Whitsunday in 1631 by Hendrick de Keyser, the Westerkerk is a landmark of the Jordaan. Its painted tower is a great place from which to view the surrounding area, provided you don't suffer from vertigo. Although the last tour up the 186 steps is at 5pm, groups may call to book for other times. The tower is emblazoned with a gaudy red, blue and gold 'XXX' crown; this was granted to the city in 1489 by the Holy Roman Emperor Maximillian in gratitude for treatment he received during a pilgrimage to Amsterdam. The triple-X came to be used by local traders to denote quality, and is now featured on the city's flag and coat of arms.

It's thought that Rembrandt is buried here, though no one is sure exactly where – his burial on 8 October 1669 was recorded in the church register, but the actual spot was not. A plaque inside commemorates the artist, who died a pauper, and it's possible he shares a grave with his son, Titus.

Anne Frank Huis.

Woonbootmuseum

Prinsengracht, opposite no.296 (427 0750,
www.houseboatmuseum.nl). Tram 13, 14, 17.
Open *Mar-Oct* 11am-5pm Tue-Sun. *Nov-Feb*
11am-5pm Fri-Sun. Closed last 2wks Jan.
Admission €3.50; €2.75 reductions, IAmsterdam.
No credit cards. Map p330 C4.

Aside from some discreet explanatory panels, a
small slide show and a ticket clerk, the *Hendrika
Maria* Houseboat Museum is laid out as a houseboat
would be, to help visitors imagine what it's like to
live on the water. It's more spacious than you might
expect and does a good job of selling the lifestyle
afforded by its unique comforts.

THE SOUTHERN CANAL BELT
Around Rembrandtplein

Previously called Reguliersmarkt (Regular
Market), this square was renamed in honour of
Rembrandt in 1876; his statue – the oldest in the
city – stands in the centre of the gardens, gazing
in the direction of the Jewish quarter. Though
there's no longer a market, it's still the centre of
commercial activity, with a wild profusion of
neon lights, and a cacophony of music blaring
out from the cafés, bars and restaurants on all
sides. Unashamedly tacky, the square is home
to a variety of establishments, from the faded
and fake elegance of the traditional striptease
parlours to nondescript cafés, but there are
a few exceptions to the air of tawdriness –
places such as the grand café **De Kroon** (no.17),
the art deco **Schiller** (no.24) and HL de Jong's
crazily colourful dream-as-reality masterpiece,
cinema **Pathé Tuschinski** (*see p225*).

Carry on past here and you'll end up at
Muntplein, by the floating flower market at
the southern tip of Singel (**Bloemenmarkt**;
see p200), also home to miniature art gallery
the **Reflex Miniatuur Museum** (Singel 548,
627 2832, http://reflex-art.nl). Over on the corner
of the Amstel are some lively gay cafés and
bars (*see p241*), and on the façade of Amstel
216, the city's freakiest graffiti. The 'House
with the Bloodstains' was home to former mayor
Coenraad van Beuningen (1622-93), whose
brilliance was eclipsed by insanity. After seeing
visions of fireballs and fluorescent coffins above

Dressed to the Nines

The best boutique booty in Nine Streets.

The affectionately dubbed 'Negens', a
cluster of parallel streets crossing the three
main canals in the heart of Amsterdam,
is the shopping equivalent of Madonna:
hot, happening and a sucker for a pair
of fishnets. First stop has to be vortex
of vintage **Laura Dols** (*see p192*). Loved by
the city's darlings, this fashionable cavern
touts '60s Darcey Bussell-style tutus, '70s
flared trews and '80s tarty tights.

Just a stone's throw away is **Lady Day**
(*see p191*), a somewhat too-cool-for-school
second-hand store that will give you more
for your money than its rivals. Expect to
see the city's creative folk hunting down a
pair of horn-rimmed glasses at the counter,
while gaggles of girls sniff about the bargain
basement in search of a tote for a tenner.

For some bum-hugging denim, stop off
at **Spoiled**'s (*see p188*) denim bar for a cup
of coffee and a chat about your 'problem
areas'. The savvy guys at this bare-brick,
loft-style store know their Levis from their
Citizens of Humanity and won't rest until
your buns are cupped to perfection.

True Dutch style can be cashed in at
Hester van Eeghen (Hartenstraat 37, 626
9212), the shop of the celebrated local shoe
designer. Known for her way with leather,

Hester loves a geometric shape or two
and brash colours (the lime green inlay
is a signature) are his thing. Add a twist
of Mexican flavour at **meCHICas**
(Gasthuismolensteeg 11, 420 3092,
www.mechichas.com), where local talent
Debbie Verhagen designs trinkets 'with Dutch
simplicity and South American flair'.

Exota (Hartenstraat 10, 344 9390,
www.exota.com) – not to be confused with
stores that sell fluffy handcuffs and edible
panties – is one for women and kids. Thick-
knit bright scarves adorn the wooden
shelves in winter, while paisley frocks with
Little House on the Prairie appeal are a big
draw in the summer. Just round the corner
lies **Relaxed at home** (Huidenstraat 19,
320 2001). Despite its bumbling name,
this bright and airy store is the sartorial
equivalent of a cuddle – think thick nude
scarves by Dutch stalwart Scotch & Soda.

Ethnic jewellery store **Parwan** (Herengracht
234, 625 6313), a smörgåsbord of
bohemian glitz, is brimming with chunky
necklaces from the Chinese Miao tribe
vying for attention with Malawian arm cuffs.
Essentially, if the piece hasn't got a story
it's not allowed in the store. Now, that's
definitely something you won't find in H&M.

Golden Bend.

the Reguliersgracht, he scrawled sailing ships, stars, strange symbols, and his and his wife's name with his own blood on the grey stone walls. Subsequent attempts to scrub the stains off have all proved futile. Or so the story goes...

From Rembrandtplein, walk south along the shopping and eating street Utrechtsestraat, or explore Reguliersgracht and Amstelveld.

The canals

As the first canal to be dug in the glory days, Herengracht (named after the man who initially invested in it) attracted the richest of merchants, and this southern stretch is where you'll find the most stately and overblown houses on any of Amsterdam's canals. The **Museum Willet-Holthuysen** (*see p100*) is a classic example of such a 17th-century mansion.

However, it's on the 'Golden Bend' – the stretch between Leidsestraat and Vijzelstraat – that things really get out of hand. By then the rich saw the advantage of buying two adjoining lots so that they could build as wide as they built high. Excess defines the Louis XIV style of Herengracht 475, while tales of pre-rock 'n' roll exuberance are often told about no.527, whose interior was trashed by Peter the Great while he was here learning to be a ship's carpenter and picking up urban ideas for his dream city, St Petersburg.

Canals of Amsterdam.

Home to the Stadsarchief Amsterdam (city archives), the imposing **Gebouw de Bazel** building is round the corner on Vijzelstraat. Mischievous types annoy the mayor by mooring up on his personal dock before the official Herengracht 502 residence. If you're caught, try using the excuse that you're visiting the **Kattenkabinet** (Cat Cabinet, Herengracht 297, 626 5378, www.kattenkabineet.nl).

It's a similarly grand story on this southern section of Keizersgracht (named after Holy Roman Emperor Maximilian I). For evidence, pop into the **Museum van Loon** (*see right*) or photography museum **Foam** (*see right*). But for an alternative view of this area, head to Kerkstraat, parallel to and directly between Keizersgracht and Prinsengracht. The houses here are less grand, but what they lack in swank they more than make up for in funkiness, with their galleries and shops only adding to the community feel. The pleasant oasis of Amstelveld helps, too, with **Amstelkerk** – the white wooden church that once took a break from sacred duties to act as a stable for Napoleon's horses – worth a look.

Head east along Kerkstraat and you'll find the Magerebrug (Skinny Bridge), the most photographed bridge in the city and one said to have been built in the 17th century by two sisters living on opposite sides of the Amstel who wanted an easy way to get together for morning coffee. If you cross it and go down Nieuwe Kerkstraat, you'll get to the **Plantage** (*see p116*). Alternatively, turn right at Amstel and right again down Prinsengracht to see yet more grand canal houses and the 2,000-plus exhibits at the **Pijpenkabinet** (Pipe Cabinet, Prinsengracht 488, 421 1779, www.pijpenkabinet.nl).

★ Foam (Photography Museum Amsterdam)

Keizersgracht 609 (551 6500, www.foam.nl). Tram 4, 16, 24, 25. **Open** 10am-5pm Mon-Wed, Sat, Sun; 10am-9pm Thur, Fri. **Admission** €8; €5.50 reductions; free under-12s, MK, IAmsterdam. **No credit cards. Map** p331 E4.

This excellent photography museum, located in a renovated canal house, holds regular exhibitions of works from shutter-button maestros, and shows covering local themes such as Amsterdam crime scene photos and universal topics. It also organises talks and events for the photographically obsessed.

▶ *For Foam curator's favourite painting; see p60.*

★ Museum van Loon

Keizersgracht 672 (624 5255, www.museum vanloon.nl). Tram 4, 16, 24, 25. **Open** 11am-5pm Mon, Wed-Sun. **Admission** €7; €5 reductions; free under-6s, MK, IAmsterdam. **No credit cards. Map** p331 E4.

Few interiors of Amsterdam's grand canal houses have been preserved in anything approaching their original state, but the former Van Loon residence is one that has. Designed by Adriaan Dortsman, it was originally the home of artist Ferdinand Bol. Hendrik van Loon bought it in 1884 and it was opened as a museum in 1973. The terrifically grand mid 18th-century interior and Louis XIV and XV decor is a delight. So is the art. There's a collection of family portraits from the 17th to the 20th centuries; Ram Katzir's striking sculpture, *There*; and a modern art show every two years.

★ Museum Willet-Holthuysen

Herengracht 605 (523 1822, www.museumwillet holthuysen.nl). Tram 9, 14. **Open** 10am-5pm Mon-Fri; 11am-5pm Sat, Sun. **Admission** €7; €3.50-

€5.25 reductions; free under-6s, MK, IAmsterdam. **Credit** MC, V. **Map** p331 E4.

This 17th-century mansion was purchased in the 1850s by the Willet-Holthuysen family. When Abraham, remembered as 'the Oscar Wilde of Amsterdam', died in 1889, his wife Sandrina Louisa, a hermaphrodite, left the house and its contents to the city on the condition it was preserved and opened as a museum. The family had followed the fashion of the time and decorated it in the neo-Louis XVI style: it's densely furnished, with an impressive collection of rare objets d'art, glassware, silver, fine china and paintings – including a portrait of a rather shocked-looking Abraham (taken on his honeymoon, perhaps?).

► *Urban Home & Garden Tours, guided by professional garden designers and art historians, depart from here; see p78.*

Tassenmuseum Hendrikje (Museum of Bags & Purses)

Herengracht 573 (524 6452, www.tassen museum.nl). Tram 4, 9, 16, 24, 25 or Metro 51, 53, 54. **Open** 10am-5pm daily. **Admission** €7.50, €4-€6 reductions; free under-13s, IAmsterdam. **Credit** AmEx, V, MC. **Map** p331 E4.

This museum is the world's largest collection of its kind, with a total of over 4,000 exhibits: everything from coin purses made of human hair to a Lieber rhinestone collectible named 'Socks' after Hillary Clinton's cat.

Around Leidseplein

Leidseplein lies on the bottom of the 'U' made by the Canal Belt, and runs south from the end of Leidsestraat to the Amsterdam School-style bridge over Singelgracht and east towards the 'pop temple' **Paradiso** (*see p252* and *p264*) to the Max Euweplein (a handy passage to **Vondelpark**; *see p112*) with its **Max Euwe-Centrum** (Max Euweplein 30a, 625 7017, www.maxeuwe.nl) and giant chess set.

Artists and writers used to congregate on Leidseplein in the 1920s and '30s, when it was the scene of clashes between communists and fascists. In the war, protests were ruthlessly broken up by the Nazis and there's a commemorative plaque on nearby Kerkstraat. But thanks to the plethora of tourists drinking in pavement cafés, listening to buskers and soaking up the atmosphere – not to mention the huge variety of booze – Leidseplein's latter-day persona is more jockstrap than political.

The area has more theatres, clubs and restaurants than any other part of town. It's dominated by the **Stadsschouwburg** (the municipal theatre; *see p276*) and by the cafés that take over the pavements during summer. This is when fire-eaters, jugglers, musicians and small-time con artists and pickpockets fill the square.

The café society associated with Leidseplein began with the opening of the city's first terrace bar, the Café du Théâtre, which was sadly demolished in 1877, 20 years before the final completion of Kromhout's **Eden Amsterdam American Hotel** (*see p138*). Opposite the American is a building, dating from 1882, that reflects Leidseplein's dramatic transformation: once grand, it's now illuminated by huge adverts. Just off the square, in the Leidsebos, is the more intriguing **Adamant**, a pyramid-like, hologram-effect sculpture that commemorated 400 years of the city's central diamond trade in 1986.

The Jordaan & West

Gentrification continues apace, but an arty community heart remains.

When Amsterdam was extended in the 17th century, the Jordaan emerged as an area designated for the working classes and smelly industries; it also provided a haven for victims of religious persecution, such as Jews and Huguenots. In keeping with the original residents' modest financial circumstances, the houses are mostly small and densely packed, at least when compared to dwellings along the swankier canals.

These days, the area is a higgledy-piggledy mixture of old buildings, modern social housing and the occasional eyesore. Despite this, property is highly desirable, and though the residents are mainly proud, community-spirited Jordaaners, the nouveaux riches have moved in and the 'hood is gentrifying.

Map p325	Restaurants
Hotels p136	& Cafés p158
Bars p172	Coffeeshops p177

Still, the folk of the Jordaan share a fierce sense of identity, which is known throughout the nation, and a uniquely laid-back lifestyle.

NORTH OF ROZENGRACHT

The area north of Rozengracht is easy to get pleasantly lost in. Little lanes and alleys link the already quiet main streets in a mazy haze, and it's no surprise that such a chilled atmosphere incorporates some of the city's best cafés: 't Smalle (Egelantiersgracht 12; *see p173*), for example, set on a small canal, where Peter

INSIDE TRACK
ART IN THE OPEN

Galleries aside, the area surrounding Haarlemmerdijk offers up a feast for aesthetically sensitive eyes. Cast your gaze upwards and imbibe the stunning façades dotted here and there (in particular nos.39-43); step into Buzhu (no.63) and marvel at the beautiful tiled panels of the store's listed interior; and look out for little gems such as the female torso that's hiding in an alley just before Haarlemmerplein.

Hoppe (of Hoppe & Jenever, the world's first makers of gin) founded his distillery in 1780. (The Japanese have built an exact replica of 't Smalle in Nagasaki's Holland Village.)

Between scenic coffees or decadent daytime beers, check out the specialist shops tucked away on the adorable side streets. Some of the city's best outdoor markets can also be found nearby: Monday morning's bargainous Noordermarkt (*see p182*) and Saturday's paradise of organic produce Boerenmarkt (*see p198*) are held around the Noorderkerk, the city's original Calvinist church, built in 1623. Adjacent to the Noordermarkt is the equally bargain-packed Westermarkt (*see p182*), while another general market fills Lindengracht on Saturdays. For those wishing to add a pinch of culture to their grocery shopping, the Noorderkerk holds concerts every Saturday afternoon at 2pm (mid September to mid June) as well as evening performances (*see p258*).

Between Brouwersgracht and the blisteringly scenic Westelijk Eilanden (*see p120*), more quirky shopping opportunities can be found on Haarlemmerstraat and its westerly extension,

Hidden Hofjes

A stroll around the city's canalside courtyards.

It's widely asserted that the name 'Jordaan' derived from the French *jardin* (garden), most likely introduced by the French Huguenots who migrated to the neighbourhood in the 17th century. Peek behind the grand houses and apartment blocks that flank the nearby canals and you'll see why: there's a multitude of tranquil residential courtyards, known in Dutch as *hofjes* (almshouses).

Originally built by charitable patrons during the Middle Ages for women elders and the vulnerable, these oases now form some of the most desirable spots to live, providing the luxury of verdant seclusion within a busy and vibrant city.

Private tours can be arranged (see http://amsterdam.mokumevents.com), but wandering them on your own helps preserve the tranquil feel. Just remember, while the courtyards may be open to the public, entrances are sometimes locked in deference to the residents. However, as long as you behave well, they don't usually mind people admiring their garden courtyards.

Start your tour at the **Raepenhofje** (Palmgracht 28-38), built in 1648 and considered one of Amsterdam's oldest and most authentic *hofjes*. The 'Dutch Shakespeare', Joost van den Vondel, wrote verse praising its patron, city treasurer Pieter Raepe, as 'bold and compassionate' for founding a courtyard where 'orphans and widows can praise the gods'.

Head south to the idyllic **Karthuizehof** (Karthuizersstraat 21-31). Here, you'll find 50 quaint apartments, two antique pumps, gloriously well-kept gardens and (weather permitting) a bench in the sun. Built originally for widows in 1650, the homes are still owned by the housing council but it's open to the public, so enjoy a moment in this pocket-sized paradise.

Next, visit the **Brienenhofje** (Prinsengracht 133), with its imposing entrance and large clock tower. Commissioned by Arnout Jan van Brienen in his final year of life, this slightly later *hofje* (1804) features a water pump and a beautiful lantern in its courtyard. Current residents have twisted fairy lights around the trees, giving it a sense of dream-like enchantment.

Continue south on Prinsengracht towards Westerkerk, and Tuinstraat on your right will lead you to **Claes Claesz Anslohofje** (Eerste Egelantiersdwarsstraat 1 5). Founded in 1616, it was the home to several *zwaardvege* (knife-makers). It was entirely renovated in 1979 and is now privately owned. As it's officially open to the public, you can wander through its horticultural corridors at ease.

If you have the time and the energy, continue on to the **Rozenhofje** (Rozengracht 147-181) – it's not open to the public unfortunately but its entrance and exterior are a sight in themselves.

Noodermarkt. *See p102.*

Haarlemmerdijk. Though not officially part of the Jordaan, this strip and its alleys share an ambience. Head east towards Centraal Station past **West Indische Huis** (Herenmarkt 93-97). This home to the famous West Indies Trading Company (WIC) stored the silver that Piet Hein took from the Spanish after a sea battle in 1628, and was the setting for such dubious decisions as selling all of Manhattan for 60 guilders, and running the slave trade between Africa and the Caribbean. Today, it's a popular venue for events and wedding receptions. Heading west, Haarlemmerdijk ends at Haarlemmerplein, where you'll see the imposing Haarlemmerpoort city gate, built in 1840.

Behind it is wonderful **Westerpark**, with its happening arts complex **Westergasfabriek** (*see p278*). Back in the 1960s, when the Netherlands switched over to natural gas, a 14.5-hectare coal-gas company site on the western edge of the city became obsolete. It remained a somewhat run-down storage centre until the 1990s, when it was zoned for use as a cultural park.

Designed by American landscape architect Kathryn Gustafson, the Westergasfabriek is a unique example of clever urban reuse. What was once an energy plant is now a thriving park with walking and running trails, a babbling brook, a wading pool for kids, large lawns for football and other sports, tennis courts and outdoor gyms.

The former company buildings have been turned into cultural destinations: an intimate art-house cinema (Het Ketelhuis; *see p227*), large and small performance venues, dance clubs, daycare centres, and a slew of restaurants, bars and cafés. The most surprising reuse of space? A giant former gas tank in the middle of the former factory complex, the Gashouder, has been transformed into a rollerblading rink.

Museum Het Schip

Spaarndammerplantsoen 140 (418 2885, www. hetschip.nl). Bus 22. **Open** 11am-5pm Tue-Fri. *Guided tours every hr. Admission* €7.50; €5 reductions; free MK, IAmsterdam. **No credit cards.** Just outside Westerpark, Spaarndammerplantsoen features three monumental public housing blocks designed by Michel de Klerk, the most expressionist of which is known as Het Schip (The Ship). Museum

INSIDE TRACK LIVING ART

If you want to see the stuff being created rather than simply hanging from a fancy wall, then check out Jordaan's **Open Ateliers** event (www.openateliers jordaan.nl), which every June offers the opportunity to poke your nose into over 70 artists' studios.

Art Throb

Galleries proliferate in the Jordaan, Amsterdam's arty axis.

In a city as eclectic as this, it's never easy to pinpoint a particular cultural scene, but in the last decade, the Amsterdam contemporary art world has crystallised around a handful of streets in the Jordaan, where on certain nights you can find masses of black-clad art aficionados tripping tipsily from one art opening to the next.

Dipping into the Jordaan's numerous galleries – preferably between Thursday and Saturday to ensure the greatest number with open doors – can pleasantly punctuate an afternoon of strolling. Entrance is free and you don't even have to be in the market for buying to strike up a conversation with the gallery owner or director, who is usually on hand (and just dying for an excuse to chat or take a cigarette break).

The hub of the district is a buckle just below the centre of the canal belt, from the Prinsengracht to the Lijnbaansgracht, and from Rozengracht to Leidsegracht. The Jordaan started to emerge as a contemporary art district in the 1980s; the first galleries to open here were **Torch Gallery** (Lauriergracht 94; *see p236*) and **Steendrukkerij Amsterdam** (Lauriergracht 80, 624 1491, www.steendrukkerij.com) – which are both still located right where they started. Another early pioneer was the **Galerie Paul Andriesse**, which has recently moved over to a grand new space on the Westerstraat (no.187; *see p235*) where

Andriesse can continue to showcase favourite and up-and-coming artists.

An enjoyable way to get a good flavour for the art scene is to start by walking down Lauriergracht, where you'll find the two galleries mentioned above, until you hit the Prinsengracht. Turn right and you'll run into **Martin van Zomeren** (no.276, 420 8129, www.gmvz.com), a gallery dedicated primarily to conceptual sculpture and installation art, as well as **Ron Mandos** (no.282; *see p232*), which represents international artists in all mediums.

When you hit Elandsgracht, turn right and pop into **Galerie Gabriel Rolt** (Elandsgracht 34; *see p235*), featuring some of the city's most interesting international contemporary artists. Continue along the street (perhaps stopping in at the shop-cum-denim gallery, **Tenue de Nîmes** (no.60; *see p191*), on the way) and turn right at Hazenstraat.

There are many and various galleries that may tempt you along this street (and equally visually enticing shops), but some good bets are the one-room Amsterdam contemporary art space, **Witzenhausen Gallery** (no.60; *see p236*), which also has an outpost in New York; the **Galerie Wouter van Leeuwen Fotografie** (no.27; *see p236*) with its top-notch photography shows; and **Galerie Diana Stigter** (no.17; *see p234*), a heavy-hitter contemporary art dealer whose space constitutes the district's epicentre. Now, you've arrived.

SIGHTS

Het Schip is one of the finest examples of the Amsterdam School architectural movement, and a must-see for architecture students the world over.

The carefully designed interior is quite an experience to behold, and exhibitions investigate why Amsterdam became a mecca for public housing and the cultural-historical value of the Amsterdam School. Visitors will also learn about the inspiration behind the famous architectural movement and get to see Michel de Klerk's world-famous tower.

ROZENGRACHT & FURTHER SOUTH

Once a canal, the now filled-in Rozengracht scythes through the heart of the Jordaan in unappealing fashion. Rembrandt lived at no.184 from 1659 until his death a decade later – there is a plaque on the first floor. While you're here, look up at the gable of Rozengracht 204 to spy an iron

stickman wall anchor, or consider visiting some of the many galleries (*see above* **Art Throb**).

South of Rozengracht is notable for the **Looier** antiques market (*see p204*). Elandsgracht 71-77 is where the labyrinthine Sjako's Fort was said to have once stood. Sjako is often referred to as the 'Robin Hood of Amsterdam', though while he was happy stealing from the rich, he usually neglected to give to the poor. Still, he had style: not many burglars go about their business dressed in white and accompanied by henchmen clad in black. In 1718, his 24-year-old head ended up spiked on a pole where the Shell Building now stands, but local band Sjako!, anarchist bookstore Fort van Sjako (Jodenbreestraat 24, Jodenbuurt, 625 8979), and a shrine in the window of the building that replaced his fort keep his name alive – even though 2007 saw the release of a study by a local historian that proved the story of Sjako was almost completely myth.

Offset your
flight with
Trees for Cities
and make your
trip mean
something for
years to come

www.treesforcities.org/offset

Trees for Cities
Charity registration number 1032154

The Museum Quarter, Vondelpark & the South

Where Old Masters meet cruising zones and landscaped gardens.

Over a century ago, the area now known as the Museum Quarter was still outside the city limits. Towards the end of the 19th century, the city expanded rapidly and the primarily upper-class city fathers decided to erect a swanky neighbourhood between the working-class areas to the west and south. Most of the beautiful mansions here, with their art deco gateways and stained-glass windows, were built in the late 1890s and early 1900s.

Oud-Zuid, Amsterdam's own golden monument to the good life, is located just a bike ride or stroll through the city's central green space, the Vondelpark. Stretching out in a ring beneath Vondelpark is a fairly indeterminate region known as Nieuw Zuid (New South). Further south is Amstelveen with its beautiful Amsterdamse Bos forest.

The Museum Quarter, Vondelpark & the South

Map p330	Restaurants
Hotels p144	& Cafés p160
Bars p173	Coffeeshops p178

Map p330
Hotels p144
Bars p173
Restaurants & Cafés p160
Coffeeshops p178

SIGHTS

THE MUSEUM QUARTER

The heart of the Museum Quarter is Museumplein, the city's largest square, bordered by the **Rijksmuseum** (*see p108*), the **Stedelijk Museum of Modern Art**, the **Van Gogh Museum** (for both, *see p109*) and the **Concertgebouw** (*see p256*). Developed in 1872, Museumplein served as a location for the World Exhibition of 1883, and was then rented out to the Amsterdam ice-skating club between 1900 and 1936. During the Depression, the field was put to use as a sports ground, and during World War II, the Germans built bunkers on it. In 1953, the country's 'shortest motorway',

Museumstraat, cut it in two. But the more recent additions of grass, a wading pool, a skate ramp, café and a wacky extension to the Van Gogh Museum have helped boost it a bit.

As you might expect in such seriously highfalutin cultural surroundings, property in this area doesn't come cheap, and the affluence is apparent. Van Baerlestraat and, especially, PC Hooftstraat are as close as Amsterdam gets to Rodeo Drive, offering solace to the kind of ladies who would otherwise be lunching.

While you're in the area, it's worth visiting nearby Roemer Visscherstraat. This road, which leads to Vondelpark, is notable not for its labels but rather for its buildings. The houses from

A Fondle in the Vondel

Night-time cruising goes legit.

For decades, Vondelpark has been a notorious midnight meet-up spot for gay men looking for some frisky risk-taking, but it wasn't until March 2008 that the Amsterdam district council proclaimed a new set of rules announcing the official 'toleration' of public sex in the park.

'As long as other people in the park don't feel disturbed then there is no problem with it'. said Paul van Grieken, an alderman in the Oud-Zuid district, which encompasses Vondelpark. 'It's not a law or a formal legislation. We call these our "house rules" for the park.'

According to the 'house rules', enjoying a garden romp is only permitted after dark, and condoms must be discarded carefully or cleared away to keep the surrounds tidy. Police officers cannot interrupt the fun unless participants are causing a public nuisance, such as broadcasting their enjoyment too noisily or appearing too close to a public path.

Unsurprisingly, not everyone is quite so pleased. The Christian Democratic Association, a political party, argues that the policy paints Amsterdam as an anything-goes destination and attracts frisky thrill-seeking tourists. Others, such as 35-year-old Miriam Timas, who lives near Vondelpark and has an eight-year-old son, have more personal concerns: 'It's not something I want to be confronted with. It's not a place I would let my son go by himself.'

Dennis Boutkan, chairman of Cultuur en Ontspannings Centrum or COC, Amsterdam's leading lesbian, gay, bisexual, transgender organisation, which led the campaign to promote tolerance of cruising in Vondelpark, said the number of cruisers hasn't increased since the tolerance policy made international headlines in 2008.

But American Keith Griffith, 51, founder of the website cruisingforsex.com, says he's frequently flown to Amsterdam for a romp in the parks. 'Fresh air, often beautiful settings and of course a variety of men,' he enthuses. He believes Amsterdam's tolerance of sex cruising is 'a wonderful example of rational, logical thinking by the Dutch. See a problem and figure out how best to solve it, rather than approaching it with alarm and fear.' He's convinced, too, that most people are unaware of the sex happening around them.

Walking his dog in Vondelpark on a sunny afternoon, neighbourhood resident Ben Whittle, 31, basically agreed. 'I've only ever noticed drunk people in the park,' he says. 'It's actually quite disappointing – I haven't noticed anything quite that exciting.'

nos.20 to 30 each represent a different country and are all built in the appropriate 'national' architectural style: thus Russia comes with a miniature dome, Italy has been painted pastel pink, and Spain's candy stripes have made it one of the street's favourites.

★ Rijksmuseum

Stadhouderskade 42 (674 7047, www.rijksmuseum.nl). Tram 2, 5, 7, 10. **Open** 9am-6pm daily. **Admission** €12.50; free under-19s, MK, IAmsterdam. **Credit** AmEx, MC, V. **Map** p330 D5.

Designed by PJH Cuypers and opened in 1885, the Rijksmuseum holds the country's largest collection of art and artefacts, including 40 Rembrandts and four Vermeers. The collection was started when William V began to acquire pieces just for the hell of it, and has been growing ever since: it includes Dutch paintings from the 15th century until 1900, as well as decorative and Asian art. While it undergoes a major reconstruction, the Philips Wing remains

Concertgebouw. *See p256.*

open with a sampling of the museum's jewels such as Rembrandt's *The Night Watch* and Vermeer's *Kitchen Maid* and *Woman Reading a Letter*, plus a selection from the likes of Frans Hals, Jacob de Wit and Ferdinand Bol. There's also a wealth of decorative arts on display, including 17th-century furniture, intricate silver and porcelain, and 17th- and early 18th-century dolls' houses. All this plus temporary exhibitions and the museum's freely accessible garden, filled with Golden Age gateways and architectural fragments.
▶ *Visit the Rembrandthuis museum to see the world's largest collection of the Master's sketches, see p116.*

Stedelijk Museum of Modern Art

Paulus Potterstraat 13 (573 2911, www.stedelijk.nl). Tram 2, 3, 5, 12. **Open** 10am-5pm Tue-Sun, Thur until 10pm. **Admission** €10; €5 reductions; free under-12s, MK, IAmsterdam. **Credit** (shop only) AmEx, MC, V. **Map** p330 D6.
The Stedelijk Museum is Amsterdam's go-to institution for modern and contemporary art. It holds an extraordinary pre-war collection that includes works by Cézanne, Picasso, Matisse and Chagall, as well as many paintings and drawings by Malevich. Post-1945 artists represented include De Kooning, Newman, Ryman, Judd, Stella, Lichtenstein, Warhol, Nauman, Middleton, Dibbets, Kiefer, Polke, Merz and Kounellis. While a large-scale renovation of its home on the Museumplein is taking place (scheduled to be completed in the second half of 2011), there has been a popular Temporary Stedelijk presentation of selected sections of the collection, showcasing the museum's art in an innovative way that makes full use of the unfinished building – and this looks set to continue into 2011 (see p111 **What Happened to All the Museums?**).

★ Van Gogh Museum

Paulus Potterstraat 7 (570 5200, www.vangogh museum.nl). Tram 2, 3, 5, 12. **Open** 10am-6pm Mon-Thur, Sat, Sun; 10am-10pm Fri. **Admission** €14; free under-18s, MK, IAmsterdam. *Temporary exhibitions vary.* **Credit** MC, V. **Map** p330 D6.
As well as the bright colours of his palette, Vincent van Gogh is known throughout the world for his productivity, and that's reflected in the 200 paintings and 500 drawings that form part of the permanent

INSIDE TRACK QUEUE HOPPING

Do yourself a favour and get to museums early in the morning: the queues in the afternoon can get frustratingly long, and the galleries unbearably busy. You can avoid the main queues for certain museums altogether if you buy your tickets in advance online or have an IAmsterdam card. Check websites for details.

INSIDE TRACK
KEEPING THE KIDS HAPPY

A visit to a museum with kids doesn't always equal a lingering and peaceful experience. To stop boredom settling in too quickly, ask about any kid-specific activities the museum may offer. Both the Van Gogh and the Rijksmuseum offer treasure hunts and audio tours, while the latter also holds special children's tours.

exhibition based in the Rietveld building. In addition to this collection, there are also examples of his Japanese prints and works by the likes of Toulouse-Lautrec that add perspective to Van Gogh's own artistic efforts.

Temporary exhibitions focus on Van Gogh's contemporaries and his influence on other artists. These shows are assembled from both the museum's own extensive archives and private collections. It's also worth noting that Friday evenings often feature lectures, concerts and films.

▶ *The Van Gogh Museum offers special activities for kids; see p219.*

VONDELPARK

Vondelpark – named after the city's best-known poet, Joost van den Vondel, whose controversial play *Lucifer* caused the religious powers of the 17th century to crack down hard on those who engaged in what was termed 'notorious living' – is the most central of the city's major parks. Its construction was inspired by the large development of the Plantage, which had formerly provided the green background for the leisurely walks of the rich. The original ten acres opened in 1865, and were designed in the 'English style' by Zocher, with the emphasis on natural landscaping. The park has actually sunk some two to three metres since it was first built – some larger trees are in fact 'floating' on blocks of styrofoam or reinforced with underground poles.

There are several ponds and lakes in the park plus a number of play areas and cafés; try **Het Blauwe Theehuis** (Round Blue Teahouse) and the always charming Café Vertigo at the **EYE Film Institute Nederlands** (*see p227*). Keep your eye out for a huge Picasso sculpture in the middle of the park, and the wild parakeets that were mistakenly released in 1976. Around the corner – and providing a unique place for coffee – is the epic **Hollandsche Manege** (*see p52*), a wooden version of the Spanish Riding School in Vienna.

Vondelpark gets insanely busy on sunny days and Sundays, when bongos abound, dope is toked and football games take up any space that happens to be left over. The dicky-tickered

Museumplein. *See p107.*

What Happened to All The Museums?

Major refurbs are under way.

Walking around central Amsterdam these days it's hard not to notice that the city can feel a bit like a construction site, especially in the Museum Quarter, where two of the city's signature museums, the Rijksmuseum and the Stedelijk Museum, are currently undergoing major renovations.

It's a good sign, of course: these cultural temples are going to be expanded and improved with new, glorious space for their impressive collections. We don't blame current visitors for feeling a bit disappointed when they learn that they don't have full access to these treasures, but it's really not as bad as it sounds.

Let's start with the **Rijksmuseum**: Amsterdam's world-class museum, with 1.1 million items of art and history, is under reconstruction, but its Philips Wing is still open with an ongoing exhibition called 'The Masterpieces', and smaller temporary exhibitions. The main exhibition features about 400 items from the 17th century – in other words, the paintings you really want to see – by Johannes Vermeer, Jan Steen, Hendrick Averkamp, Frans Hals and, of course, Rembrandt, including his iconic *The Night Watch*. It's like a 'Greatest Hits' sampler – a way to see the highlights without wearing out the soles of your shoes. The renovated Rijksmuseum is expected to reopen in 2013, when about 7,500 items will be on show.

The **Stedelijk**, Amsterdam's primary destination for modern and contemporary art on the Museumplein, with more than 90,000 works of art in its collection, closed in 2003 and wasn't expected to reopen until late 2011 (although the opening date has been pushed back so many times already that everyone is a bit dubious) but in 2010 a Temporary Stedelijk programme started up, presenting the collection in an innovative way that makes the optimum use of the unfinished space. The programme has been so successful that Temporary Stedelijk 2 kicks off in 2011 with lectures, installations and events running alongside the exhibition.

The older portion of the museum has been restored and a new part will be added, with a futuristic white annexe, which has been dubbed 'the bathtub' (because that's what it looks like), designed by local star architectural firm, Benthem Crouwel. When it's all finished, the basement gallery is expected to be the largest single exhibition space in the city.

Culture vultures can also visit the Stedelijk Museum Bureau Amsterdam (SMBA, Rozenstraat 59, 422 0471, www.smba.nl), which is the museum's project space in the Jordaan, contextualised through lectures, debates and residency programmes and which regularly creates exhibitions of contemporary art.

In any case, visitors need not be concerned about a shortage of opportunities for museuming in the city. Amsterdam is reputed to have more museums per square metre than any other city in the world.

SIGHTS

would do well to look out for rollerbladers, who meet here weekly for the **Friday Night Skate** (www.fridaynightskate.com). Films, plays and musical concerts are also put on, with the **Vondelpark Openluchttheater** festival of free open-air performances that take place throughtout the summer (*see pp 210 & 212*).
▶ *The Groot Melkhuis café hosts a children's creative workshop in its huge playground every Wednesday from 2pm to 5pm; see p218.*

NIEUW ZUID

Nieuw Zuid (New South) is bordered to the north by Vondelpark, to the east by the Amstel and to the west by the Olympisch Stadion (www.olympisch-stadion.net). Built for the 1928 Olympics, it is noted for its original Amsterdam School glory and its highly popular club/restaurant **Vakzuid** (*see p163*). The New South was planned by Berlage and put into action by a variety of Amsterdam School architects, who designed both private and public housing for the area. It's the former that's given the New South what character it has, most notably around Apollolaan and Beethovenstraat (worth visiting simply for the **Oldenburg** bakery at no.17).

The few visitors tend to be here on business, especially around the **World Trade Center** and the steadily rising modern architecture neighbourhood of Zuidas. The controversial Noord-Zuidlijn Metro is set to link this district with the centre of town and Amsterdam Noord. East of here is another staple of Amsterdam business life: the ugly **RAI Exhibition and Congress Centre**, which holds numerous trade fairs, conventions and a range of public exhibitions throughout the year.

However, in between the RAI and the WTC lies one of Amsterdam's most beautiful parks. Extended and renovated in 1994, **Beatrixpark** is a wonderfully peaceful place, very handy if you want to avoid the crowds in town on a summer's day. The Victorian walled garden is worth a visit, as is the pond, complete with geese, black swans and herons. Amenities include a wading pool and play area for kids. Nearby is recently closed arts/design centre **Platform 21** (www.platform21.nl) that was housed in a round former church.

Still further south, **Amstelpark** was created for a garden festival in 1972, and today offers recreation and respite to locals in the suburb of Buitenveldert. A formal rose garden and rhododendron walk are among the seasonal spectacles, and there is also a labyrinth, pony rides and a children's farm, plus tours on a miniature train. The Rosarium Restaurant serves expensive meals, though its outdoor café is less pricey.

AMSTELVEEN

Of all the southern suburbs, Amstelveen is the most welcoming to the casual visitor. Though the **CoBrA Museum** (*see below & **Profile** see right*) helps, the main attraction here is the **Amsterdamse Bos**, a mammoth, artificially built wood that's treasured by locals yet neglected by visitors. Providing work for 20,000 unemployed people during the crisis years, this forestation project started in 1934, and the last tree was planted in 1967. With its 137 kilometres (85 miles) of footpaths, 51 kilometres (32 miles) of cycle paths, 50 bridges, 150 indigenous species of trees and over 200 species of birds, the Amsterdamse Bos is one of the largest city parks in Europe. The eight-square-kilometre site sprawls beautifully, and comes with a great many attractions in case the tranquillity isn't enough. The man-made Bosbaan is used for rowing, fishing and, in freezing winters, a spot of ice-skating. Other attractions include play areas, a horticultural museum, jogging routes, a buffalo and bison reserve, the Fun Forest tree-top climbing park (Apr-Oct), a bike-hire centre (Mar-Oct), a water sports centre, stables and a picnic area. There's also a great goat farm selling cheeses, milk and icecream.

FREE Bezoekerscentrum de Molshoop
Bosbaanweg 5, near Amstelveenseweg, Amsterdamse Bos (545 6100). Bus 170, 171, 172. **Open** noon-5pm daily.
The Amsterdamse Bos visitor centre recounts the history and use of the Amsterdamse Bos. Its mock woodland grotto, which can turn from day to night at the flick of a switch, is wonderful for kids.

★ CoBrA Museum of Modern Art
Sandbergplein 1, Amstelveen (547 5050, www.cobra-museum.nl). Tram 5, Metro 51 or bus 170, 172. **Open** 11am-5pm Tue-Sun. **Admission** €9.50; €6.50 reductions; free under-6s, MK, IAmsterdam. **Credit** (shop only) MC, V.
Taking its name from the Copenhagen-, Brussels- and Amsterdam-based art movement – one of the most influential of the 20th century – this musuem displays the works in a sympathetic environment in which to trace the movement's development.
▶ *For more on CoBrA, see **Profile** right.*

FREE Hortus Botanicus (Vrije Universiteit)
Van de Boechorststraat 8, Zuid (444 9390, www.vu.nl/hortus). Tram 5 or Metro 50, 51 or bus 142, 170, 171, 172. **Open** *Jan-Feb* 8.30am-4.30pm Mon-Fri; *Apr-Oct* 8.30am-4.30pm Mon-Sat.
Though less charming than its city counterpart (*see p118*), this little garden is pleasant for a stroll. The fern collection is one of the best in the world; the Dutch garden next door shows flora native to this country.

SIGHTS

Profile CoBrA Museum of Modern Art

An art destination unto itself.

If there's one reason to visit Amstelveen, it's the marvellous **CoBrA Museum of Modern Art** (*see left*). Its exhibitions include original masterpieces by the avant-garde artists from the CoBrA movement as well as new work by contemporary artists whose aesthetic sensibilities in some way adhere to the values outlined by the CoBrA movement.

Though CoBrA was relatively short-lived, beginning in 1948 and ending in 1951, it produced some of the Netherlands' most enduring names in 20th-century art, such as Constant, Corneille and Karel Appel.

An acronym for Copenhagen, Brussels and Amsterdam – the cities from which the key artists of the movement hailed – it was the Northern European artistic response to the destruction and chaos of World War II. The CoBrA artists created a style unimpeded by academic traditions, marked by vibrant colours and typically created with a sense of spontaneity and freedom from academic convention. The work contains many references to so-called primitive art from Africa and 'naïve' work made by children or untrained artists, using purely emotive imagery and experimental forms.

The museum itself, a beautiful airy space with an abundance of natural light and a view over a swan-dotted canal bordered by weeping willows, was founded 15 years ago with a mission to become the definitive exhibition space and archive for artwork and documentation about the movement. Its permanent collection contains about 300 paintings, sculptures and works on paper as well as archived documents from the CoBrA era, as well as a few works by artists of the later **vrij beelden** ('free images') movement of 1945 and **creatie** (creation) movement that spanned 1950 to 1955.

Jodenbuurt, the Plantage & the Oost

Museums, gardens and galleries in the city's other cultural quarter.

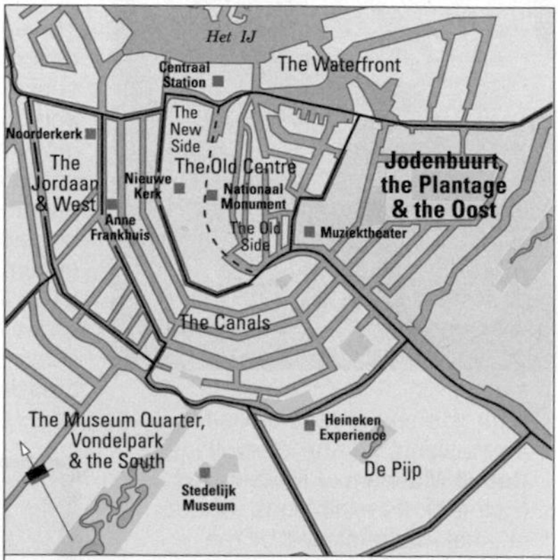

First settled by Sephardic Jewish immigrants who were fleeing from the Spanish Inquisition, the area now known as Jodenbuurt is the city's old Jewish quarter. It was a lively Jewish hub right up to World War II, when the Nazis concentrated the Jewish population of the Netherlands here before deportation. With so many houses left empty after the war, it fell into decay, and was torn down to make way for the new metro and contemporary buildings. It's now a peculiar mix of old and new architectural styles.

The Plantage, by contrast, is positively lush with verdant spaces. The area originally provided wealthy 17th-century Canal Ring residents with gardens and parks to escape to; as the city expanded in the 19th century, it became one of Amsterdam's first suburban developments, with elegant villas bordering its wide, tree-lined streets.

The largely unexplored Amsterdam frontier that is Oost first emerged in the late 19th century with the construction of the Oosterpark and Dapperbuurt, followed closely by the creation of the Indische Buurt, or Indonesian neighbourhood, at the beginning of the 20th century.

Map p327
Hotels p142
Bars p171

Restaurants
& Cafés p156

JODENBUURT

Just off the Nieuwmarkt, **Sint Antoniesbreestraat** is home to assorted shops, bars and cafés, along with the modern yet tasteful council housing designed by local architect Theo Bosch. In contrast, there's the Italian Renaissance-style **Pintohuis** at no.69, which was grandly remodelled in the late 17th century by Isaac de Pinto. A Jewish refugee who had fled the inquisition in Portugal, de Pinto became one of the main investors in the immensely lucrative Dutch East India Company (*see p22*).

Across the street, pop through the bizarre skull-adorned entrance between nos.130 and 132 to enter restful square near the **Zuiderkerk** (South Church), which used to be a graveyard. Designed by master builder Hendrick De Keyser and built between 1603 and 1614, the Zuiderkerk was the first Protestant church to appear after the Reformation. Three of Rembrandt's children were buried here, and the church was painted by Monet during a visit to the Netherlands.

Crossing over the bridge at the end of Sint Antoniesbreestraat, you'll arrive at De Hogeschool voor de Kunsten (the Arts Academy) on the left and the **Rembrandthuis** (*see p116*)

SIGHTS

on the right. Immediately before this, though, a few steps down to the right lead you to **Waterlooplein Market** (*see p182*) – a bargain-hunter's dream if you're a patient shopper.

Nearby you'll find the 19th-century **Mozes en Aäronkerk** (Waterlooplein 205, 622 1305, www.mozeshuis.nl), built on Spinoza's (*see p91*) birthplace. This former clandestine Catholic church is situated above the much chirpier children's playground **TunFun** (*see p219*), which runs below Mr Visserplein square, in a former underpass. Dominating Waterlooplein is the **Muziektheater** (*see p256 & right* Inside Track), an important opera and ballet venue for the city; also nearby are the **Hermitage Amsterdam** and the **Joods Historisch Museum**; for both, *see below*.

By the **Portuguese Synagogue** (*see p116*) on Mr Visserplein, look out for the Jonas Daniël Meijerplein site. Here, Mari Andriessen's bronze *Dockworker* statue, erected in 1952, commemorates the February Strike of 1941 – a protest against Jewish deportations which began among workers in the city's shipyards.

Hermitage Amsterdam

Gebouw Neerlandia, Nieuwe Herengracht 14 (530 8751, www.hermitage.nl). Tram 9, 14 or Metro Waterlooplein. **Open** 10am-5pm daily. **Admission** €15; free under-17s, MK, IAmsterdam. **Credit** AmEx, DC, MC, V. **Map** p327 E3.

Housed in the 17th-century Amstelhof building (originally built as a hospital for elderly women and, from 1817 onwards, men), this outpost of the Hermitage in St Petersburg opened in June 2009 with a star-studded ceremony. It puts on two exhibitions a year, using objects and artworks borrowed from its prestigious Russian parent collection.

Behind the building's grandly classical façade, the architect-remodelled interior is light and airy, with

INSIDE TRACK FROM RUSSIA WITH LOVE

It is only fitting that St Petersburg's Hermitage should have opened an Amsterdam outpost (*see above*). The city has a special connection with Peter the Great, who came here as a young man to study the Dutch shipbuilding industry. He befriended local anatomist Frederik Ruysch, who taught him how to preserve butterflies and pull teeth. The tsar also bought Ruysch's collection of deformed foetuses and anatomical oddities – which are still on display in St Petersburg's Kunstkammer, the first museum in Russia.

INSIDE TRACK THE STOPERA

The **Stadhuis-Muziektheater** (City Hall-Music Theatre; *see p256*) is home to both the Nederlands Opera and the Nationale Ballet. Standing on the site of a former Jewish ghetto, this controversial €136 million civic headquarters-cum-opera house was designed by Wilhelm Holzbauer and Cees Dam. Locals protested against the city's decision to tear down the original 16th- and 17th-century residences, and a riot ensued, causing substantial damage to construction equipment – which is why the theatre is still known as the 'Stopera'.

walls and ceilings stripped away to create two surprisingly modern exhibition spaces; there's also a café and a tranquil central garden. *Photo p116*.

★ Joods Historisch Museum (Jewish Historical Museum)

Nieuwe Amstelstraat 1 (531 0310, www.jhm.nl). Tram 9, 14 or Metro Waterlooplein. **Open** 11am-5pm daily; closed Jewish New Year & Yom Kippur. **Admission** €9; €4.50-€6 reductions; free under-13s, MK, IAmsterdam. **No credit cards**. **Map** p327 E3.

Housed in four former synagogues in the old Jewish quarter, the Jewish Historical Museum is packed

Waterlooplein Market.

SIGHTS

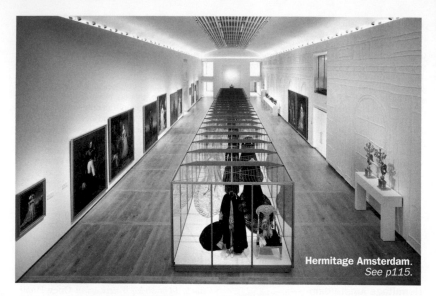

Hermitage Amsterdam.
See p115.

with religious items, photographs and paintings detailing the rich history of Jews and Judaism in the Netherlands throughout the centuries. There's also an excellent children's wing (*see p218*), with interactive exhibits on different aspects of Jewish culture, while temporary exhibitions exploring Jewish life, history and culture often use interviews, film footage and photography to bring their themes to life.

► *For an intimate insight into a Jewish family's life in hiding, visit the Anne Frank Huis; see p96.*

Portuguese Synagogue

Mr Visserplein 3 (624 5351, 531 0380 guided tours, www.esnoga.com). Tram 9, 14 or Metro Waterlooplein. **Open** *Apr-Oct* 10am-4pm Mon-Fri, Sun. *Nov-Mar* 10am-4pm Mon-Thur, Sun; 10am-2pm Fri. Closed Yom Kippur. **Admission** €6.50; €4-€5 reductions, IAmsterdam. **No credit cards**. **Map** p327 E3.

Inaugurated in 1675, architect Elias Bouwman's mammoth synagogue is one of the largest in the world, and was reputedly inspired by the Temple of Solomon. It is built on wooden piles, and surrounded by smaller annexes (including offices, archives and one of the oldest libraries in the world).

Rembrandthuis

Jodenbreestraat 4 (520 0400, www.rembrandt huis.nl). Tram 9, 14 or Metro Waterlooplein. **Open** 10am-5pm daily. **Admission** €9; €2.50-€6 reductions; free under-6s, MK, IAmsterdam. **Credit** AmEx, DC, MC, V. **Map** p327 E3.

Rembrandt bought this house for ƒ13,000 (then a massive sum) in 1639, at the height of his career. Sadly, the free-spending artist went bankrupt in

1656 and was forced to move to a smaller house (Rozengracht 184). It's now a museum, whose faithfully reconstructed interiors were based on the room-by-room inventory of his possessions that was made when he went bankrupt. Knowing it's a mock-up does add a slightly unreal air to proceedings, though. The museum also contains a remarkable collection of Rembrandt's etchings, which show him at his most experimental.

► *If it's Rembrandt's paintings you're interested in, the Rijksmuseum holds one of the largest collections of his work in the world; see p108.*

THE PLANTAGE

South-east of Mr Visserplein lies the largely residential area known as the Plantage. The attractive Plantage Middenlaan winds past the **Hortus Botanicus** (*see p118*), passes close to the **Verzetsmuseum** (*see p118*), runs along the edge of **Artis Royal Zoo** (*see right*) and heads towards the marvellous **Tropenmuseum** (*see p119*).

In the late 19th and early 20th centuries, Amsterdam was a major world diamond centre, and most of the rocks were cut and sold in and around this area. The headquarters of the diamond cutters' union, designed by Berlage as a far more outward expression of socialism than his Stock Exchange (aka **Beurs van Berlage**, *see p80*), still exist on Henri Polaklaan as the **Centrum voor Arbeidsverhoudingen** (Trade Unions Museum). Other extant buildings such as the Gassan, the Saskiahuis and the Coster also act as reminders that the town's most profitable trade was once based here. However, the spectre of World War II reappears at the **Hollandse Schouwburg** (*see p118*), while the **Verzetsmuseum** (*see p118*) documents the Dutch Resistance. Look out, too, for Van Eyck's **Moedershuis** (Plantage Middenlaan 33), built as a refuge for young, pregnant women.

The Plantage is still a wealthy part of town, with graceful buildings and tree-lined streets, although its charm has somewhat faded over the years. The area has seen extensive redevelopment; if you wander down Entrepotdok, you can admire the delicate balancing act between the new and the old, with docked post-hippie houseboats and good

views of Artis providing a charming contrast to the new apartment buildings.

★ Artis Royal Zoo
Plantage Kerklaan 38-40 (0900 27 84 796, €0.25/min, www.artis.nl). Tram 9, 14. **Open** *Summer* 9am-6pm daily. *Winter* 9am-5pm daily. **Admission** €18.50; €15-€17 reductions; free under-3s, IAmsterdam. **No credit cards.** **Map** p327 F3.

The first zoo in mainland Europe (and the third oldest in the world) makes for a great day out for children and adults alike. Along with all the usual birds and beasts, Artis has an indoor 'rainforest' area for nocturnal creatures, and an aquarium that's over 100 years old and includes a simulated

Eastern Promise

The art of reinvention in the Oost.

For the last ten years or so, the City has been trying to encourage artists and creative types to invade Oost, with the funding of artistic incubators like the **Volkskrantgebouw** (Wibautstraat 150, 693 7575, www.volks krantgebouw.nl), home to all sorts of creatives' studios, and **Trouw** (Wibautstraat 131, 463 7788, www.trouwamsterdam.nl), which hosts inventive club nights and gigs and has its own organic restaurant. It's tried and tested urban development logic: artists improve the profile of an area, then the yuppies rush in.

Another example is **Stichting outLINE** (Oetewalerstraat 73, 693 1389, www. outlineamsterdam.nl); once part of the local hospital, this beautiful 19th-century chapel-like structure in a quiet residential *hofje* (almshouse) has now become an artistic hub. The former patients' rooms are artists' ateliers and the main space – an airy, elegant room – hosts six to eight contemporary solo exhibitions a year, curated by artistic director Christina van den Bergh.

This vibrant area is also home to the open-air **Dappermarkt** (Dapperstraat from Eerste van Swindenstraat; *see p181*). Generally speaking, the bundled socks, €5 handbags, cheese and fresh fish stalls here aren't any more exotic than those you'll find at the Westermarkt (*see p181*) or Albertcuypmarkt (*see p127*), but what sets this market apart is the presence of cloth merchants in serious profusion. This colourful fabric haven is a reflection of Oost's extraordinary ethnic diversity, which is also evident in the array of food on offer.

Afterwards, take a break on one of the cafés on the pretty terraces that line the Linnaeusstraat across from Oosterpark – such as Spargo, Boom Eten & Drinken or Café Milo – or at De Ponteneur (Eerste van Swindenstraat 581) with its cheap and excellent daily specials, just seconds from the market. This spacious restaurant, with its raw-wood tables and hippie-inspired elegance, is yet another example of Oost's creative reuse of space.

SIGHTS

INSIDE TRACK NIGHT OWLS

From June to August, **Artis Royal Zoo** (*see p117*) stays open until sunset every Saturday. Known as *ZOOmeravonden*, these extended summer evenings bring a roster of free activities, such as face-painting for kids, live music and zookeeper talks (in Dutch, but worth watching nevertheless). You can even bring a picnic and dine alfresco with the animals.

Amsterdam canal (somewhat less murky than the real thing).

The narration in the planetarium is in Dutch, but an English translation is available. Further extras include a geological museum, a huge butterfly house, a zoological museum, a children's petting zoo and various playgrounds; you could easily spend all day hanging out here.

FREE Hollandse Schouwburg
Plantage Middenlaan 24 (531 0340, www. hollandscheschouwburg.nl). Tram 9, 14 or Metro Waterlooplein. **Open** 11am-4pm daily. **Map** p327 F3.
In 1942, this grand theatre became a main point of assembly for around 80,000 of the city's Jews before they were taken to the transit camp at Westerbork. It is now a monument with a small but impressive exhibition and a memorial hall displaying 6,700 surnames by way of tribute to the 104,000 Dutch Jews who were exterminated.
▶ *For details of guided walks exploring the city's World War II history; see p78.*

★ Hortus Botanicus
Plantage Middenlaan 2A (625 9021, www. dehortus.nl). Tram 9, 14 or Metro Waterlooplein. **Open** 9am-5pm daily (*Dec-Jan* 9am-4pm). **Admission** €7.50; €3 reductions; free under-5s, IAmsterdam. **No credit cards. Map** p332 G3.
This beautiful botanical garden has been at this site since 1682, although it was set up 50 years earlier when East India Company ships brought back tropical plants and seeds to supply doctors with medicinal herbs. Some of these venerable specimens (including a 300-year-old cycad, the oldest potted plant in the world) are still growing in the palm greenhouse, which itself dates from 1912. Three further greenhouses maintain desert, tropical and subtropical climates; in all, some 4,000 different species of plant can be found here. There's also a butterfly house, along with an organic café in the 19th-century Orangery, right at the centre of the gardens.
▶ *Horticulturalists note: there's another garden in Amstelveen (see p112), and many of the city's gardens can be enjoyed for free; see p212.*

Theater Instituut
Sarphatistraat 53 (551 3300, www.tin.nl). Tram 7, 10 or Metro 51, 53, 54 Weesperplein. **Open** 11am-5pm Mon-Fri; 1-5pm Sat, Sun. **Admission** €4.50; €2.25 reductions; free under-6s, MK. **Credit** AmEx, MC, V. **Map** p326 C3.
The ever-changing displays here are largely drawn from the institute's impressive collection of costumes, props, posters, memorabilia and theatrical ephemera. Upstairs is a massive library; call ahead for information on opening hours and prices. Inside there is a ceiling painting by Jacob de Wit, and outside an idyllic garden.

★ Verzetsmuseum (Museum of the Dutch Resistance)
Plantage Kerklaan 61 (620 2535, www.verzets museum.org). Tram 9, 14. **Open** 11am-5pm Mon, Sat, Sun; 10am-5pm Tue-Fri. **Admission** €7.50; €4 reductions; free under-7s, MK, IAmsterdam. **No credit cards. Map** p327 F3.
The Verzetsmuseum is one of Amsterdam's most illuminating museums, and quite possibly its most moving. It tells the story of the Dutch Resistance through a wealth of artefacts: false ID papers, clandestine printing presses, illegal newspapers, spy gadgets and an authentic secret door behind which Jews once hid. The engaging presentation is enhanced by the constant use of personal testimonies. Regularly changing temporary exhibitions explore various wartime themes and modern-day forms of oppression, and there's a small research room as well. All in all, an excellent enterprise.

THE OOST

South of Mauritskade is Amsterdam Oost (East), where the **Arena** hotel complex (*see p142*) is located along the edge of a former graveyard that was long ago transformed into **Oosterpark**. Wild ducks swim on the lake, grey herons nest here, and the park is also home to a Speaker's Corner, for anyone wishing to have a rant. Near the corner of Oosterpark and Linneausstraat is the spot where filmmaker Theo van Gogh was murdered by an Islamic extremist in 2004 after making a film deemed to be offensive to Muslims. A sculpture, *The Scream*, was unveiled in the park in 2007 in his memory.

The **Tropenmuseum** and **Dappermarkt** (*see p181*) are the area's main tourist draws. Here, too, though, the famous **Studio K** (*see p228*) offers hip parties and a terrific café with an expansive terrace, while Javastraat is dotted with ethnic shops and is also home to the wonderful Java Books (no.145, 463 4993, www. javabookshop.nl). Meanwhile, Linnaeusstraat should satisfy all your café-lingering needs.

Further out, the **Brouwerij 't IJ** (*see p171*), a brewery in a windmill in the Indische Buurt (Indonesian neighbourhood), is a good place to

SIGHTS

stop and sip a beer, while the **Eastern Docklands** (*see p122* **Walk on the Waterside**) are well worth a visit.

Tropenmuseum

Linnaeusstraat 2 (568 8200, www.tropenmuseum. nl). *Tram 9, 14 or bus 22.* **Open** 10am-5pm daily. **Admission** €9; €5-€7.50 reductions; free under-6s, MK, IAmsterdam. **Credit** MC, V. **Map** p332 H3.
Originally erected in the 1920s to glorify Dutch colonialism, this vast, handsome building now houses some terrific exhibitions. Through a series of informative and lively displays, the visitor gets a vivid, often interactive glimpse of daily life in tropical and subtropical parts of the world. Arranged according to region, the displays are delightfully eclectic, ranging from weird and wonderful musical instruments to sculptures, masks, paintings, puppets, jewellery, boats and vehicles, everyday utensils and much, much more besides. Children are made welcome here too A special branch of the museum, the Tropenmuseum Junior, is aimed at six- to 13-year-olds and has some inspired exhibitions of its own, and there are also hands-on craft activities at the weekend (in Dutch).

Temporary art and photography exhibitions occupy a large central space on the ground floor, the shop has an excellent selection of books and souvenirs, and the restaurant offers excellent global eats and a terrace with a view.

▶ *The museum's theatrical sibling, Tropentheater, is the city's leading venue for world music; see p228.*

SIGHTS

The Butterfly House at **Artis Royal Zoo**. See *p117*.

The Waterfront
& Noord

Industrial relics, artistic incubators and tranquil waterside walks.

SIGHTS

Amsterdam's historic wealth owes a lot to the city's waterfront, for it was here that all the goods were unloaded, weighed and prepared for storage in the warehouses still found in the area. During Amsterdam's trading heyday in the 17th century, most maritime activity was centred east of Centraal Station, along Prins Hendrikkade and on the artificial islands east of Kattenburgerstraat. At the time, the harbour and its arterial canals formed a whole with the city itself.

A reduction in commerce slowly unbalanced this unity, and the construction of Centraal Station late in the 19th century served as the final psychological cleavage – this neo-Gothic monument to modernity blocked both the city's view of the harbour and its own past.

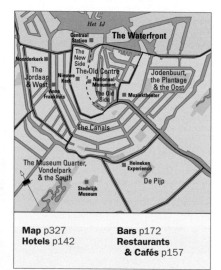

| Map p327 | Bars p172 |
| Hotels p142 | Restaurants & Cafés p157 |

WESTELIJKE EILANDEN (THE WESTERN ISLANDS)

North-west of Centraal Station, and just to the north of the Jordaan, are the Westelijke Eilanden (Western Islands), comprising Realeneiland, Prinseneiland and Bickerseiland. Created in the 17th century for the shipping activities of the WIC (West India Company), these artificial islands were home to shipyards, tar distillers, wine warehouses, the BATCO tobacco industry and fish salters and smokers.

INSIDE TRACK A FREE RIDE

Noord and the Eastern Docklands are easily reached via the free ferries that leave from directly behind Centraal Station. Check www.gvb.nl for times.

Nowadays, the area, with its warehouse flats, artists' studios, traditional 'double-swipe' wooden bridges and a yacht basin, remains the city's best setting for a scenic stroll that harks back to more seafaring times.

CENTRE

If you walk east along the IJ-front, you'll come to the famous **Muziekgebouw** (*see p256*). This epicentre of modern music, also home to the **Bimhuis** (*see p253*), comes appended with studios, rehearsal spaces and exhibition galleries. There's also a grand café and a restaurant complete with a charming terrace overlooking the scenic wateriness of the IJ. Its neighbour is the glass, wave-shaped passenger terminal for luxury cruise ships (check www.pta.nl for docking times should you wish to admire them in their natural watery habitat).

If you head east from Centraal Station, you'll come across the **Schreierstoren** (Weeping Tower; *see p85*), the most interesting relic of Amsterdam's medieval city wall. The nearby Scheepvaarthuis (Maritime House, Prins Hendrikkade 108-114) now houses the Grand Hotel Amrâth Amsterdam (*see p130*). It's a fabulous piece of Dutch modernist design, displaying the signature flowing lines of the Amsterdam School architectural style.

The restaurant on the top floor of Amsterdam's vast central library (**Centrale Bibliotheek** (*see p310*) offers up spectacular views, as does the rooftop of **Science Center NEMO** (*see below*), a science museum whose green building dominates the horizon. Across the water from NEMO is the grand structure of the **Nederlands Scheepvaartmuseum** (Kattenburgerstraat, 523 2222, www.scheep vaartmuseum.nl). One of the world's finest nautical museums, the Scheepvaartmuseum – due to reopen in 2011 after extensive renovation – houses a remarkable collection of models, portraits, boat parts and other naval ephemera.

The museum's large replica VOC (18th-century trading) ship, temporarily docked by NEMO, comes complete with costumed 'sailors'.

Persmuseum (Press Museum)

Zeeburgerkade 10 (692 881, www.persmuseum.nl). *Bus 22, 43.* **Open** 10am-5pm Tue-Fri; noon-5pm Sun. **Admission** €4.50; €3.25 reductions; free under-13s, MK, IAmsterdam. **No credit cards.** This museum covers the 400-year history of magazine and newspaper journalism in Amsterdam and the Netherlands. The temporary exhibitions are usually focused on graphics, cartoons, photography and particular magazines.

★ Science Center NEMO

Oosterdok 2 (531 3233, www.e-nemo.nl). *Bus 22, 42.* **Open** 10am-5pm Tue-Sun. *School holidays* 9am-6pm daily. **Admission** €12.50; free under-4s, MK, IAmsterdam. **Credit** AmEx, DC, MC, V. **Map** p327 F2.
NEMO opened in 1998 and has gone from strength to strength as a truly kid-friendly science museum. It eschews exhibits in favour of hands-on trickery, gadgetry and tomfoolery (in English and Dutch): you can play DNA detective games, blow mega soap bubbles or explode things in a 'wonderlab'.

EASTERN DOCKLANDS

Further east are **Java-eiland** and **KNSM-eiland**, man-made peninsulas originally built as breakwaters for the Eastern Docklands. Java-eiland may, at first glance, look like a dense designer prison, but it's hard not to be charmed while strolling the island's bisecting walking street, which will have you crossing canals on funkily designed bridges and passing beside startling architecture. At Azartplein, Java-eiland meets KNSM-eiland, named after the Royal Dutch Steam Company located here until 1977. Squatters, artists and urban nomads took the area over in the 1980s, but by the '90s, they were ordered to move out.

The entire area was then reshaped into a modern residential area, based on a 1988 blueprint by Jo Coenen. Many of the old buildings were preserved, such as the Loods 6 storage building (*see below*) and the old Rijn Scheepvaart Maatschappij (Rhine Shipping Company) office. While plans initially called for a rather exclusive neighbourhood, the city mandated that a significant portion of the homes were to be built as rentals to attract a more diverse population. Nevertheless, with its many waterside bars and eateries and trendy shops, the area is looked upon as an upmarket neighbourhood.

Loods 6 (KNSM-Laan 143, 418 2020, www.loods6.nl) now contains artists' studios, a shopping arcade, offices, a gallery and an art exchange. The building, a showcase of 1950s design and architecture, also houses an exhibition dedicated to the island's history. *See p122* **Walk on the Waterside.**

Nederlands Scheepvaartmuseum.

Walk on the Waterside

A nautical meander through the Eastern Docklands.

Head east from Centraal Station and follow the route until you reach Sumatrakade on **Java-eiland** (or nip on a no.42 bus), and wander down **Brantasgracht** – the first of four sleepy, parallel canals traversing the island – joining Sumatrakade on the IJ and Javakade on the IJhaven.

Constructed in 1995, these buildings are spanking new by Amsterdam standards. Little rowing boats and motorboats line the waterways, which are worth a look for their signature hump-backed iron bridges, with designs borrowed heavily from Gaudí and the cubists. Turn left into **Imogirituin**, a large communal garden amid residential blocks, for birdsong and no traffic.

Head back the way you came as, with views out on to the IJ, **Sumatrakade** and **Surinamekade** are perfect for boat spotting. Look along the impressive line of tall ships

moored on the IJ and you may well spot one with a skull and crossbones, the VOC Schip Amsterdam, with a viewing platform at the top of its rigging. There's a fixed telescope on the pavement for public use, so you can eye up passing barges and pleasure boats for free. Further down the road, you can admire the former fishing trawlers that have been converted into rusty, bohemian houseboats. Potted plants decorating the quayside hint that these are fixtures, rather than transient trawlers.

Refuel with a scone, laden with cream and a delicious fruit compote of strawberries, blackcurrants, redcurrants and blackberries at **De Kompaszaal** (KNSM-Laan 311). This is no ordinary café; Soviet-style sculptures of shipyard workers outside demonstrate that this place takes its heritage seriously. Downstairs, you'll find models and photos

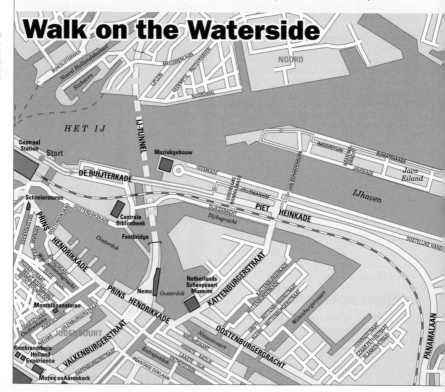

Walk on the Waterside

commemorating historic ships and local architecture. But the highlight is upstairs, a cavernous salon decorated with green-tiled pillars, a jaunty marine mural and frosted-glass windows depicting ships and masts. In the 1950s, this was a grand passenger lounge for cruise ships (you can see where the ship's gangway slotted into the first-floor terrace wall). It's an airy place to listen to jazz, learn tango or idly watch boats passing on the water below.

On the Borneo peninsula, undesirable abodes are rare, but Shipwright Street (**Scheepstimmermanstraat**) is the to-die-for street — a row of lilac-clad dream homes designed in 1999 by owners and their commissioned architects. Each one is different and you'll have to resist temptation to press your nose up against the glass.

© Copyright Time Out Group 2011

AMSTERDAM NOORD

There was a time when Amsterdam Noord was right off the map. Even in centuries past, the land on the other side of that big, watery body called the IJ was known as little more than the spot where the remains of freshly executed criminals were hung on display.

Once that practise stopped, there was really very little of interest to pull short-term visitors northwards – except perhaps the lure of cycling routes towards such scenic fishing villages as Volendam and Marken (*see pp282-302* **Escapes & Excursions**), or the trip on the free ferry from the back of Centraal Station, the latter always good for 20 minutes of seafaring fun. But with the impending Noord-Zuidlijn metro link (*see p44* **A Metro Line Runs Through It**) aiming to unite this once isolated area with the city, plus the various accompanying (and suitably ambitious) redevelopment plans, things are changing very quickly.

Already, the cultural breeding ground of Kinetic Noord, located in the former shipping yard NDSM (*see p124* **Northern Lights**), is by far the largest in the country, with over a hundred artists' studios, a skate hall and a slew of singular spaces. It sports a wonderful and totally unique post-apocalyptic vibe that's ideal for parties, concerts and wacky theatre festivals such as Over het IJ. It's also home to a surrounding neighbourhood of arty student container dwellings, a 'clean energy' exhibition, a great restaurant and café (www.noorderlicht cafe.nl) and the Benelux headquarters of MTV networks. It also boasts regular visits from the highly alternative party boat Stubnitz (www.stubnitz.com), which books bands, DJs and general weirdness for its inspired parties.

The powers-that-be hope to reinvigorate Amsterdam as a culturally-connected 'creative capital' for the 21st century, with major cultural institutions moving across the water. So far, the largest cultural institution to commit to the move is the city's Filmmuseum, which has already been renamed the EYE Film Instituut Nederland (catch that pun on the IJ) in anticipation of its jump to Noord, with an architecturally exciting new home on the banks of the harbour (*see p124* **Northern Lights**).

INSIDE TRACK
OPEN DOOR POLICY

During the Pentecost weekend, the annual **Open Ateliers Westelijke Eilanden** (www.oawe.nl) sees local artists, both starving and successful, throw open their studio doors to the public. See p209.

Northern Lights

From industrial hinterland to arty enclave, the area is changing apace.

The industrial expanse of Noord, once the city's enginehouse, is evolving into one of Amsterdam's hippest enclaves. In the past few years, local arts institutions have been casting their gaze northward: the **EYE Film Institute** (*see p227*) will be relocating here in 2012 and one of the Jordaan's most interesting galleries, **Motive Gallery** (*see p234*), already jumped ship and hopped across the IJ. Together with the **Nieuw Dakota** at 41b (*see p234*), they form the core of what could become the new art district in Amsterdam.

The dimensions of these post-industrial sites in Noord have natural appeal but the transformation of the area hasn't been totally organic: the local municipality provides incentives too, namely cash for converting these metal workshops into gallery spaces.

The truly impressive **NDSM-werf** (tt-Neveritaweg 15, www.ndsm.nl) has been transformed into a *broedplaats*, or cultural incubator. This 82,000-square-metre (882,000-square-foot) former shipyard is now home to workshops and ateliers for artists, theatre companies and other creative professionals. The Motive Gallery is now located in a former metal workshop with high ceilings, bare concrete floors and huge windows. The interior walls of the NDSM-werf, or Kunststad (art city) as it's now known, give

the feeling of an expressionist film set, with parts covered in Banksy-like graffiti and an LED McDonald's sign hanging beside a large-scale chalk drawing of a child crying.

Nearby, you'll find **Skatepark Amsterdam** (tt-Neveritaweg 15a, 337 5954, http://skateparkamsterdam.com); built as a hanging platform, this is where the cool kids come to hang out and practise their jumps. To complete the picture of an alternative area where hippie ideals meet high tech, visit the **Noorderlicht Café** (tt-Neveritaweg 33, 492 2770, www.noorderlichtcafe.nl), which comes into its own during the Over het IJ festival (www.overhetij.nl), a great theatre festival that takes place every July. Hidden behind the NDSM-werf building, Noorderlicht offers a flower-child scene: there's a campfire, lounge music, strings of colourful lights and a sun-bathed terrace.

For retail therapy, visit the local open-air markets on the **Mosplein** (9am-6pm Wed-Sat) and **Buikslotermeerplein** (noon-6pm Mon; 8am-5pm Tue-Sat) for clothes and cheap food. The 'alternative furniture boulevard', **Papaverweg**, has two terrific vintage furniture shops at nos.46-48: mid-century modern furniture dealer **Neef Louis** (486 9354, http://neeflouis.nl) and rustic-inspired vintage shop **Van Dijk en Ko** (684 1524, www.vandijkenko.nl).

SIGHTS

De Pijp

Veer south for boho charm, cheap eats and the home of Heineken.

A trip to the creative and multicultural centre of De Pijp offers a window into one of the city's hippest young urban neighbourhoods, an oft-neglected nugget off the tourist track. While it's hardly a treasure trove of history and sights, De Pijp's time is the present, with more than 150 different nationalities keeping its global village vibe alive – and the economic upturn seeing the opening of more niche eateries and bars than ever before.

Gentrification has begun in earnest in these parts, and De Pijp has become such a popular area that it has even commanded some further residential space, called the 'Nieuwe Pijp', to the south of the city.

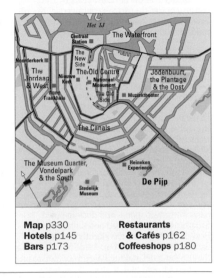

Map p330	Restaurants
Hotels p145	& Cafés p162
Bars p173	Coffeeshops p180

SIGHTS

BOHO ROOTS

De Pijp is the best known of the city's working class quarters built in the late 19th century. Harsh economics saw the building of long, narrow streets, which probably inspired the change in name from the official, double-yawn-inducing 'Area YY' to its appropriate nickname, 'the Pipe'. Because rents were high, many tenants were forced to sublet rooms to students, who then gave the area its bohemian character.

That said, the many Dutch writers who lived here helped add to it. Among the locals were luminaries such as Heijermans, De Haan and Bordewijk, who most famously described World War I Amsterdam as a 'ramshackle bordello, a wooden shoe made of stone'. Many painters had studios here, too – people like Piet Mondrian, who once lived in the attic of Ruysdaelkade 75, where he began formulating de Stijl while enjoying a view of the decidedly old-school Rijksmuseum (*see p108*). It's estimated that over 250 artists currently live in the area, a very healthy crop indeed.

And, of course, the area was packed with brothels and drinking dens. In the basement of Quellijnstraat 64 (now a neighbourhood centre), the Dutch cabaret style – distinguished by witty songs with cutting social commentary for lyrics – was formulated by Eduard Jacobs and continues to live on through the likes of Freek de Jonge, Hans Teeuwen and Najib Amhali.

At the turn of the 20th century, De Pijp was a radical socialist area. The place has lost much of its bite since those days and many families with children have fled to suburbia. Still, the number of cheap one- and two-bedroom places, combined with the reasonably central location, makes the area very attractive to students, young single people and couples, and De Pijp has the densest gay population in Amsterdam.

During the last 40 years, many immigrants have found their way to De Pijp, setting up shop and so inspiring the general economic upswing of the area. De Pijp now houses a mix of nationalities, providing locals with halal butchers, Surinamese, Spanish, Indian and Turkish delicatessens, and restaurants offering authentic Syrian, Moroccan, Thai, Pakistani, Chinese and Indian cuisine.

Thanks to these low-priced exotic eats, De Pijp is easily the best place in town for quality snacking treats, the ingredients for which are mostly bought fresh from the single largest daily market in all the Netherlands: **Albert Cuypmarkt** (*see p127*), the hub around which

Time Out Amsterdam **125**

De Pijp turns. This market attracts thousands of customers every day, and spills merrily into the adjoining roads: the junctions of Sweelinckstraat, Ferdinand Bolstraat and 1e Van der Helststraat, north into the lively Gerard Douplein, and south towards Sarphatipark. The chaos will be heightened over the next few years by the construction of the Metro's controversial Noord-Zuidlijn, whose route will follow a line pretty much directly underneath Ferdinand Bolstraat.

EXPLORING THE AREA

From Albert Cuypstraat, if you cross Ferdinand Bolstraat you'll find a cluster of fine, cheap Chinese-Surinamese-Indonesian restaurants. After passing former Van Moppes & Zoon Diamond Factory, diamond turns to ruby around the corner on Ruysdaelkade, De Pijp's very own mini red light district. Enjoy the sight of steaming, hooter-happy motorists caught in their own traffic gridlock while you lounge casually around an otherwise restful canal.

Head back away from the water (and the red lights) a few blocks along 1e Jan Steenstraat and you'll soon run across De Pijp's little green oasis: the grass-, pond- and duck-dappled **Sarphatipark**, designed and built as a mini Bois de Boulogne by the slightly mad genius Samuel Sarphati (1813-66). Aside from building the Amstel hotel and the Paleis voor Volksvlijt, Sarphati showed philanthropic tendencies as a baker of inexpensive bread for the masses, and as initiator of the city's rubbish collection.

Sarphatipark.

> ### INSIDE TRACK ART ATTACK
>
> Take a look at the street signs in this district, and you'll notice that most of the blocks here are named after famous 17th-century painters. Jan Steen, Ferdinand Bol, Gerard Dou and Frans Hals (whose street, Frans Halsstraat, is very pretty, and rich with cafés and bars) are just a few of the artists honoured.

The centrepiece fountain comes complete with a statue of Sammy himself.

After your stroll in the park, wander north up 1e Van der Helststraat towards Gerard Douplein. This little square, with its cafés, coffeeshops, chip shops and authentic Italian ice-cream parlour, turns into one big terrace during the summer, and is hugely popular with the locals. *See p187* **Shop this Block: Eerste van der Helststraat.**

Heinekenplein, the U-shaped gathering of cafés, Indian restaurants and Irish pubs just by the Heineken Experience (*see below*), is a suntrap in summer months, and often houses one-off cinema screenings and the occasional music festival. It's a good place to be on Queen's Day (*see p209*) for a DJ-fuelled all-day and night party.

Heineken Experience

Stadhouderskade 78 (523 9666, www.heineken experience.com). Tram 7, 10, 16, 24, 25. **Open** 11am-7pm daily (last ticket sale at 5.30pm). **Admission** €15; €1 per year of age under-12s. **Credit** AmEx, MC, V. **Map** p331 E5.
In 1988, Heineken stopped brewing here but kept the building open for tours. The 'experience' is now spread across four levels and 18 attractions, and includes multiple interactive exhibits, a mini brewery and a 'stable walk', where visitors can see Heineken's iconic shire horses, which still deliver beer throughout the city.

Let's be quite frank: this 'experience' begins with a promotional film extolling the virtues of its product and ends with another film about the virtues of its product, and most of the text that accompanies the exhibits would be removed from Wikipedia on the grounds of partiality. One of the interactive 'games' is a completely brazen computerised market research exercise designed to find out just how much we'd be prepared to pay for a Heineken-branded beer tap and whereabouts we'd keep it in our kitchen. And yet, some 8,000 respondents in *Time Out Amsterdam* magazine's 'Best of Amsterdam' 2010 awards declared the Heineken Experience their favourite tourist attraction in the city, so let's not be unnecessarily uppity. Maybe it's the three ice-cold drinks at the end...

Profile Albert Cuypmarkt

Find everything you need (and plenty you don't) at the city's biggest street market.

For those willing to navigate south, Albert Cuypmarkt is a worthy trove of multicultural gems. Just outside Amsterdam's historic centre, this busy market is definitely one for the locals or those keen to break free of the 'grachts'. Once a development for the working class, this 19th-century marketplace is now populated by Dutch, Moroccan, Surinamese, Turkish and Vietnamese shopkeepers. You'll find everything from Turkish flat bread, fresh *stroopwaffels* (the Dutch gooey, syrupy treat) and edam cheese to Vietnamese *loempias* being loudly hawked from stand to stand.

For a taste of raw herring, which is to the Dutch what bratwurst is to the Germans or pork scratchings to the English, head to any one of the fishmongers along Albertcuypstraat and drop one of the omega 3-fuelled fish down your gullet. If this all sounds too much to stomach, why not grab a cone of frites and mayonnaise and park up on a bench in the nearby Sarphatipark?

Aside from its culinary clout, Albert Cuyp is home to the usual market tat, including nylon lingerie that errs on the porno side and those buy-literally-anything-for-a-Euro stalls selling Brillo pads and knock-off perfumes (Guggi Envy, anyone?). The boxes of dodgy Bollywood films and film flops are also worth a perusal for some cringeworthy viewing.

Amid this random mish-mash of wares lies the odd antiques store where it's possible to pick up some one-off pieces, such as military camping chairs and hand-painted vases, and still get change from €10. Perhaps one of the biggest draws to dear old Albert is the slew of florists selling ten white roses for a mere €4 and hefty bunches of tulips for €2.50.

There's also the whole spectrum of textiles, from faux Andy Warhol prints to tan-coloured corduroy and everything in between. While quality is not the name of the game here, quantity certainly is and if you are planning on reupholstering your entire abode for next to nothing, Albert Cuypmarkt is good for the job.

Even if you're just here for the weekend, add a splash of *oranje* (orange) to your stay with a pair of €5 comedy clog slippers. Or, equally, a €20 Turkish rug and a box of baklava.
Albert Cuypstraat (www.albertcuypmarkt.com). Tram 4, 16, 20, 24, 25. **Open** 9am-5pm Mon-Sat.

Discover the city from your back pocket

Essential for your weekend break, over 30 top cities available.

POCKET SIZED *from* £6.99 / $11.95

Consume

Hotels

Budget beds and stylish stays.

With options running from cosy B&Bs and privately owned small hotels to enormous establishments such as the stately Inter-Continental Amstel or the luxurious Grand Hotel Amrâth, Amsterdam does its best to be accommodating. Nonetheless, there is still a shortage of accommodation: the question is, where to put new hotels in this densely packed city?

Because of limited space in the city centre, hotel rooms tend to be on the small side, and you don't get that much bang for your buck. Still, many make up for their somewhat modest dimensions with that most prized commodity: a canal view.

STAYING IN AMSTERDAM

You'll find there is little price difference between a hotel in the thick of things and a hotel way out in the sticks – but the good news is that in a city this compact, nowhere is really that far flung.

Be aware that most rates advertised don't include the five per cent city tax, so don't be surprised when you see it added to your final bill. Breakfast is generally included, though.

Predictably, rates shoot up when there's a conference or a special event in town. Book well in advance, and ask about special package deals.

Hotels cluster around particular districts of Amsterdam: the Museum Quarter and the Canals district have plenty, but there are far fewer places in De Pijp or Jordaan, alas.

THE OLD CENTRE

Deluxe

Grand Hotel Amrâth Amsterdam

Prins Hendrikkade 108-114, 1011 AK (552 0000, www.amrathamsterdam.nl). Tram 1, 2, 4, 5, 9, 13, 14, 16, 17, 24, 25, 26. **Rates** €200-€475 double. **Credit** AmEx, DC, MC, V. **Map** p327 E2 **❶**
The 15th hotel in the Amrâth chain occupies the fine structure known locally as the Scheepvaarthuis (Maritime House). The hotel has the usual range of double rooms, but with supplements for specific views. There's also the prestigious three-storey suite in the front tower. Although there's the usual roster of deluxe frills and fripperies, style-wise, the hotel's unique feeling of timelessness remains.

Bar. Business centre. Concierge. Disabled-adapted room. Gym. Internet (wireless, free). Smoking & no-smoking rooms. Parking (valet, €40/night). Pool (indoor). Restaurant. Room service. Spa. TV: DVD.
► *For a little more on the history behind this monumental building, see p48* School of Rock.

Grand Hotel Krasnapolsky

Dam 9, 1012 JS (554 9111, www.nh-hotels. com). Tram 4, 9, 14, 16, 24, 25. **Rates** €250-€320 double. **Credit** AmEx, DC, MC, V. **Map** p326 D3 **❷**
Slam-dunk in the middle of the action, the Grand Hotel Krasnapolsky – Amsterdam's best-known hotel – is directly opposite the Koninklijk Paleis (Royal Palace; *see p81*), which it can certainly compete with in terms of looks, grace and glamour. Facilities are excellent and the spectacular glass Winter Garden (a listed monument) is open to non-guests for weekend brunch. Accommodation ranges from the untrammelled indulgence of the Tower Suite to cheaper, more compact rooms at the rear, which is where you'll end up if you book one of the bargain deals.

Bars (2). Beauty salon. Business centre. Concierge. Disabled-adapted room. Gym. Internet (wireless, free in lobby, €10.75/24hr in rooms). No-smoking floors. Parking (€4/hr, €50/24hr). Restaurant. Room service. TV: pay movies.

> **❶** Red numbers given in this chapter show the location of each hotel as marked on the street maps. *See pp325-332.*

CONSUME

★ Hotel de l'Europe
Nieuwe Doelenstraat 2-14, 1012 CP (531 1777, www.leurope.nl). Tram 4, 9, 14, 16, 24, 25. **Rates** €539-€609 double. **Credit** AmEx, DC, MC, V. **Map** p326 D4 ❸

A luxury landmark with fabulous views across the Amstel, this is the place to head for an indulgent splurge or a honeymoon hideaway. As should be expected at these prices, every detail is taken care of. The 'provocateur' suite has a round bed and an in-room jacuzzi big enough for two. The hotel is one of the few in Amsterdam to boast a pool, and its restaurant Bord'Eau is highly rated.

Bar. Business centre. Clé d'Or Concierge. Gym. Internet (wireless, free). No-smoking rooms. Parking (€6/hr, €75.50/24hr). Restaurants (3). Room service. Pool (indoor). TV: pay movies.

★ Sofitel Legend The Grand Amsterdam
Oudezijds Voorburgwal 197, 1012 EX (555 3111, www.thegrand.nl). Tram 1, 2, 4, 5, 9, 13, 14, 16, 17, 24, 25. **Rates** €220-€500 double. **Credit** AmEx, DC, MC, V. **Map** p326 D3 ❹

Steeped in centuries of history, this hotel is located near the centre of the Red Light District. Guests nevertheless feel like they've been whisked away a million miles away from the risqué surroundings the moment they step into the luxurious courtyard. Rooms are spacious and airy thanks to huge windows, and the art deco-style bathrooms are embellished with Hermès and L'Occitane smellies. Look out for the hotel's luxury deals and packages.

Bar (3). Bicycle rental. Business centre. Disabled-adapted rooms. Gym. Internet (wireless, €15/3hr, €20/24hr; broadband €18/24hr). Meeting rooms. No-smoking rooms. Parking (€50/24hr). Pool

(indoor). Restaurant. Room service. Spa. TV: pay movies (€15/movie or €29/24hr [unlimited movies & broadband]). Wheelchair access.

Expensive

Barbizon Palace
Prins Hendrikkade 59-72, 1012 AD (556 4564, www.nh-hotels.com). Tram 1, 2, 4, 5, 9, 13, 14, 16, 17, 24, 25. **Rates** from €149-€250 standard double. **Credit** AmEx, DC, MC, V. **Map** p326 D2 ❺

A flash branch of the reliable NH chain, the Barbizon is right opposite Centraal Station. The public parts of the hotel are all decked out in sleek monochrome, which makes the rooms themselves a bit disappointing. The on-site facilities, however, could never be accused of being run-of-the-mill. They include a meeting room in the 15th-century St Olof Chapel and the superb Michelin-starred restaurant Vermeer for the financially limber diner.

CONSUME

Swissotel. See p133.

Whatever your carbon footprint, we can reduce it

For over a decade we've been leading the way in carbon offsetting and carbon management.

In that time we've purchased carbon credits from over 200 projects spread across 6 continents. We work with over 300 major commercial clients and thousands of small and medium sized businesses, which rely upon our market-leading quality assurance programme, our experience and absolute commitment to deliver the right solution for each client.

Why not give us a call?

T: London (020) 7833 6000

*Bar. Business centre. Concierge. Gym. Internet
(wireless, €5.95/hr, €10.70/24hr). No-smoking
& smoking rooms. Parking (€47.50/24hr).
Restaurants (2). Room service.*

Renaissance Amsterdam
*Kattengat 1, 1012 SZ (621 2223,
www.marriott.com). Tram 1, 2, 5, 13, 17.* **Rates**
€189-€294 double. **Credit** AmEx, DC, MC, V.
Map p326 C2 ❻
A smart option for exploring the bohemian charms
of the nearby Haarlemmerstraat and Jordaan areas,
this hotel compensates for its flowery decor with
top-end hotel luxuries like in-house films, interactive videos and even Playstations, making it a good
bet for flush families with recalcitrant kids. There's
also a babysitting service
*Bar. Business centre. Gym (24hr, free). Internet
(wireless, €19.95/24hr). Parking (€5/hr,
€50/24hr). Restaurant. Room service. TV: pay
movies. VIP club/lounge.*

Swissotel
*Damrak 96, 1012 LP (522 3000,
www.amsterdam.swissotel.com). Tram 4, 9, 16,
24, 25.* **Rates** €185-€290 double. **Credit** AmEx,
DC, MC, V. **Map** p326 D3 ❼
Geared firmly towards the business market – some
rooms come with LAN and Wi-Fi internet, and multiple phone lines – the handsome international
Swissotel is also a good choice for holidaymakers.
All rooms are soundproofed against the hullabaloo
outside and come with big beds, on-demand film and
music. Fork out for pricier rooms and you get
espresso machines and some swish design; suites
overlook Dam Square. *Photo p131.*
*Bar. Business centre. Concierge. Disabled-adapted
rooms. Gym. Internet (wireless, €12.50/24hr).
Restaurant. Room service. TV: pay movies.
Valet parking.*
▶ *For some serious retail therapy, pop across to
De Bijenkorf department store; see p181.*

★ Victoria
*Damrak 1-5, 1012 LG (623 4255,
www.parkplaza.com/amsterdamnl_victoria).
Tram 1, 2, 4, 5, 9, 16, 24, 25, 26.* **Rates** €140-
€199 double. **Credit** AmEx, DC, MC, V **Map**
p326 D2 ❽
A reliable stalwart of the city hotel scene, the
Victoria has 300 rooms and is located opposite
Centraal Station. The hotel's public areas, decked
out in browns, creams and reds, are very dapper
indeed. Rooms themselves are of a good size and
come with all the expected trappings. A big plus is
the excellent health club and pool, both open to non-
guests for a fee.
*Bars (2). Business centre. Concierge. Disabled-
adapted rooms. Gym. Internet (wireless,
€9.50/24hr). No-smoking floors. Pool (indoor).
Restaurants (2). Room service. Spa.*

Moderate

Hotel des Arts
*Rokin 154-156, 1012 LE (620 1558, www.hotel
desarts.nl). Tram 4, 9, 14, 16, 24, 25.* **Rates**
€98-€158 double. **Credit** AmEx, DC, MC, V.
Map p326 D4 ❾
A cosy, well-located hotel that exudes a touch of
faded glamour. Rooms – though a tad dark – are
nicely decorated with clunky, polished period
furniture and chandeliers; most of them are spacious and are geared towards use by groups and
families, though there are also a couple of smaller
ones if needed.
Internet (wireless, €12.50 for duration of stay).

Ibis Amsterdam Centre
*Stationsplein 49, 1012 AB (638 9999,
www.ibishotel.com). Tram 1, 2, 5, 9, 13, 17, 24,
25, 26.* **Rates** €89-€184 double. **Credit** AmEx,
DC, MC, V. **Map** p326 C1 ❿
If you're arriving in town late or leaving first thing,
this place is ideal; not only is it as close to the station
as is physically possible without actually being in
it, but the bar is open 24 hours and breakfast begins
at an eyelid-drooping 4am. There's nothing fancy
here – just basic but comfortable rooms and reasonable facilities, plus its 'Fifteen Minute Satisfaction'
promise: if a problem isn't sorted out in 15 minutes,
your stay is free.
Other locations Valkenburgerstraat 68 (531
9135); Transformatorweg 36 (581 1111);
Schipholweg 181 (502 5100).
*Bar. Disabled-adapted rooms. Internet (wireless,
€3.95/24hr). No smoking throughout. Restaurant.*

Nova
*Nieuwezijds Voorburgwal 276, 1012 RD (623
0066, www.novahotel.nl). Tram 1, 2, 5, 13, 14,
17.* **Rates** (incl breakfast) €99-€155 double.
Credit AmEx, DC, MC, V. **Map** p326 D3 ⓫
Arranged across five townhouses, the rooms
at Nova are comfortable, plainly furnished yet
good-looking in an IKEA kind of way. Bathrooms,
though, can be a bit of a tight squeeze. Nova
is handily located for the Nieuwezijds nightlife,
as well as all of the cultural sights. For longer
stays, it rents apartments on Nicolaas Maesstraat
72, near Museumplein.
Internet (wireless, free). No smoking throughout.

★ Residence le Coin
*Nieuwe Doelenstraat 5, 1012 CP (524 6800,
www.lecoin.nl). Tram 4, 9, 14, 16, 24, 25.* **Rates**
€139-€154 double. **Credit** AmEx, DC, MC, V.
Map p326 D3 ⓬
On a quiet, café-lined street between the Old Centre
and the main shopping district, this medium-sized
hotel arranged across seven buildings has spacious, stylish rooms in muted colours with minimal
fussy extras. They are drenched in light thanks to

CONSUME

big windows. Furniture is a classy mix of old and new; attic rooms are particularly full of character. Many rooms come equipped with kitchenettes. *Internet (wireless, €2.50/hr, €5/24hr).*

RHO Hotel
Nes 5-23, 1012 KC (620 7371, www.rhohotel.nl). Tram 1, 2, 4, 5, 9, 13, 14, 16, 17, 24, 25. **Rates** (incl breakfast) €99-€165 double. **Credit** AmEx, MC, V. **Map** p326 D3 **⑬**
If the budget doesn't stretch as far as the swankier hotels on and around Dam Square, this one is the match for them on location, if not on style itself. On an interesting backstreet bustling with lovely bars, restaurants and theatres, the hotel lobby is pure 1930s glam – reflecting the building's past as a gold merchant's offices – though rooms are plain and tidy. Single rooms, it has to be said, are really rather minuscule.
Bar. Concierge. Internet (wireless, free). No-smoking rooms. Parking (€35/night).

Budget

★ Greenhouse Effect
Warmoesstraat 55, 1012 HW (624 4974, www.greenhouse-effect.nl). Tram 1, 2, 4, 5, 9, 17, 24, 25. **Rates** (shared facilities) €95 double/twin; (private facilities) €110-€130 double. **Credit** AmEx, MC, V. **Map** p326 D2 **⑭**
Planning on immersing yourself in cannabis culture? Then this might be just the place to rest your addled head. Some rooms have shared facilities; several are kitted out in suitably trippy style, while others are just plain, old-fashioned sweet, overlooking one of the canals. To take the edge off any sore heads, breakfast is served right up until midday. The bar has an all-day happy hour and even arranges drum 'n' bass, reggae and rare groove nights. The Greenhouse Effect must be truly excellent news if you're young and into smoking weed.
Bar. Internet (wireless in lobby).
▶ *You can toke on some high-quality ganja in its coffeeshop downstairs.*

Winston Hotel
Warmoestraat 129, 1012 JA (623 1380, www.winston.nl). Tram 1, 2, 4, 5, 9, 14, 16, 24, 25. **Rates** (per person, incl breakfast & tax) €45-€60 double; €20-€28 dorm bed. **Credit** AmEx, DC, MC, V. **Map** p326 D2 **⑮**
The legendary Winston is renowned for its youthful, party-loving atmosphere and arty rooms that are decorated in eccentric, eclectic style by local businesses and artists. Dorms of four-, six- or eight-bed rooms are much cheaper – but much less fun. There's a late-opening bar on site, and a good club to boot (*see p261*).
Bar. Disabled-adapted room. Internet (wireless, free). No-smoking rooms.

Hostels

★ Flying Pig Downtown
Nieuwendijk 100, 1012 MR (420 6822, 421 0583 group bookings, www.flyingpig.nl). Tram 1, 2, 3, 5, 13, 16, 17, 24, 25, 26. **Rates** (per person, incl breakfast & tax) €16.90 dorm bed; €40 private room. **Credit** MC, V. **Map** p326 D2 **⑯**
Not so much a hostel, more a way of life. Young backpackers flock here from around the world, as much for the social life as the accommodation; the hostel organises walking tours and in-line skating for free, and there are regular parties and cheap beer. *Bar. Internet (wireless, free). Photo 139.*
See also p139 **Singular Rooms.**
Other locations Flying Pig Uptown, Vossiusstraat 46-47 (400 418).

Shelter City Christian Hostels
Barndesteeg 21, 1012 BV (625 3230, www.shelter.nl). Metro 51, 53, 54 Nieuwmarkt. **Rates** (incl breakfast) €22.50-€28.50 per person. **Credit** AmEx, MC, V. **Map** p326 D2 **⑰**
See p139 **Singular Rooms.**
Bar. Internet (wireless, free). No smoking throughout.

WESTERN CANAL BELT
Deluxe

★ Hotel Pulitzer
Prinsengracht 315-331, 1016 GZ (523 5235, www.pulitzer.nl). Tram 13, 14, 17. **Rates** from €259 double. **Credit** AmEx, DC, MC, V. **Map** p326 C3 **⑱**
Sprawling across 25 canal houses, the Pulitzer is an ideal destination for indulgent getaways. Guests can arrive by boat, there are antiques galore, rooms are big and stylish, and the facilities are top-notch. A lovely garden nestles at the back and, in August, the hotel is host to the city's Grachtenfestival of classical music (*see p213*).
Bar. Concierge. Gym. Internet (wireless, €5/hr, €19/24hr). No-smoking rooms. Restaurant. Room service. TV: pay movies.

Expensive

★ Ambassade Hotel
Herengracht 341, 1016 AZ (555 0222, www.ambassade-hotel.nl). Tram 1, 2, 5. **Rates** €185-€225 double. **Credit** AmEx, DC, MC, V. **Map** p326 C4 **⑲**
Known as the city's 'literary' hotel, where many famous authors check in when visiting, the Ambassade has a library full of books signed by its more illustrious guests, which you're free to peruse. It also has a magnificent collection of art by famous CoBrA artists. Taking up ten canal houses on the Herengracht, it's also a stone's throw

Stylish Stays

Insider tips on the best beds in the city.

Want to stay somewhere the locals love? These two über-stylish hotels are the pick of the crop, according to *Time Out Amsterdam* readers.

Voted 'Best Hotel' by the magazine's readers in a 2010 survey, the **Lloyd Hotel** (*see p142*) is located in the romantic eastern Docklands on the edge of the IJ harbour. Set in a 1920s building, it's a contemporary design hotel that showcases the coolest ideas coming out of Amsterdam's design universe.

Its 117 rooms run the gamut from one- to five-star, with floor space, decor and prices varying accordingly. At the top end of the spectrum, five-star rooms might feature a four-metre-wide bed, a grand piano or a swing suspended from the ceiling. Even the more basic rooms exude a stripped-down sense of style, however (though be prepared for a shared bathroom if you're in a one-star). The hotel also boasts a unique in-house 'cultural

embassy', offering information on events in the city and its own arty goings-on, which guests are welcome to join in for free. Expect the unexpected – in the best possible way, of course. The restaurant is another asset, with its sunny terrace and modishly simple menu.

Meanwhile, 215-room design hotel **CitizenM** (*see p144*) won the accolade of 'Best Budget Hotel'. Housed in a starkly modern building a little way out of town, it's aimed at a savvy, style-conscious clientele. Communal spaces are stuffed full of iconic Vitra furniture, mid-century modern and everything that came after (Eames lounge chairs, the Hella Jongerius Polder Sofa, and so on). Rooms feature power rain showers, free Wi-Fi and enormous beds with Frette linen, while the Philips-designed touch screen MoodPad allows you to control everything in the room, from the TV, music and window blinds to the coloured lighting and wake-up alarm.

CONSUME

Lloyd Hotel. *See p142.*

from Het Spui, where there are plenty of new and second-hand bookshops for furthering your reading, and browsing, pleasure.
Business centre. Concierge. Internet (wireless & high-speed, free). No smoking throughout. Room service. TV: DVD.

Estherea
Singel 303-309, 1012 WJ (624 5146, www.estherea.nl). Tram 1, 2, 5. **Rates** €182-€299 double. **Credit** AmEx, DC, MC, V. **Map** p326 C3 ⑳
Spread over several charming canal houses at the heart of the elegant canal district, this private hotel has been run by the same family for decades. The emphasis in this place is on understated, simple luxury: rooms come equipped with DVDs and marble bathrooms, ensuring that once you're in, you won't want to stray from your front door. There's also a guests' library.
Bar. Concierge. Gym. Internet (wireless, €10/24hr). No smoking throughout. Room service. TV: DVD.

Moderate

★ Belga
Hartenstraat 8, 1016 CB (624 9080, www.hotel belga.nl). Tram 1, 2, 5, 17. **Rates** (incl breakfast) €67-€130 double. **Credit** AmEx, MC, DC, V. **Map** p326 C3 ㉑
Accommodation that is at once family-friendly and cost-conscious is a rare beast in Amsterdam, so thank heavens for cosy Belga. A complete contrast to the stealth wealth of the surrounding Nine Streets, rooms here are functional but clean and tidy, and the downstairs breakfast-lunch room is a kitsch, hugely colourful delight for all-comers.
Bike rentals. Internet (wireless, free).

't Hotel
Leliegracht 18, 1015 DE (422 2741, www.thotel.nl). Tram 1, 2, 5, 13, 14, 17. **Rates** (incl breakfast) €145 double. **Credit** AmEx, MC, V. **Map** p326 C3 ㉒
A stylish bolt hole near some lovely restaurants and bars, and ideally placed for scenic strolls. This prosaically named place is fitted throughout in 1920s-inspired style: Bauhaus prints adorn the walls, the colour scheme is muted, and the armchairs are design classics. The spacious rooms have great views, whether on to the canal in front or the garden behind. The split-level room in the eaves sleeps up to five.
Internet (wireless, free). Stairlift.

Budget

★ Hotel Brouwer
Singel 83, 1012 VE (624 6358, www.hotel brouwer.nl). Tram 1, 2, 4, 5, 9, 13, 16, 17, 24,

25, 26. **Rates** (incl breakfast) €99.75 double. **No credit cards. Map** p326 C2 ㉓
The eight neat, ensuite rooms are named after Dutch painters and all of them look on to the Singel canal. Don't expect rafts of extra touches: it's just honest, reasonably priced accommodation in a long-standing family-run hotel. A traditional Dutch breakfast is included in the price.
Internet (wireless in certain areas, free). No smoking throughout.

Singel Hotel
Singel 13-17, 1012 VC (626 3108, www.singel hotel.nl). Tram 1, 2, 4, 5, 9, 13, 16, 17, 24, 25, 26. **Rates** (incl breakfast) €89-€169 double. **Credit** MC, V. **Map** p326 C2 ㉔
Ideally located for canal and Jordaan strolls, and for arrival and departure by train, the Singel is a five-minute walk from the station, and right next door to the beautiful, domed Koepel church. Inside its 17th-century walls, rooms are plain and furnished in a modern, basic style; they are generally clean and tidy, and all are ensuite. Front-facing rooms have been known to get noisy due to their proximity to the nightlife.
Bar. Internet (wireless, free). No-smoking rooms. TV.

THE JORDAAN
Hostels

Shelter Jordan Christian Hostels
Bloemstraat 179, 1016 LA (624 4717, www.shelter.nl). Tram 13, 17. **Rates** (incl breakfast) €18.50 per bed. **Credit** AmEx, MC, V. **Map** p325 B4 ㉕
See p139 **Singular Rooms.**
Bar. Internet (wireless, €2/hr). No smoking throughout.

SOUTHERN CANAL BELT
Deluxe

★ Amsterdam Marriott Hotel
Stadhouderskade 12, 1054 ES (607 5555, www.marriott.com). Tram 1, 2, 5, 7, 10. **Rates** €140-€395 room (for 1-4 people). **Credit** AmEx, DC, MC, V. **Map** p330 C5 ㉖
Right next to the Vondelpark, the Amsterdam Marriott is decked out in soothing yellows and modern furnishings. All rooms come equipped with Revive beds, six pillows plus luxurious linen and duvets. Bathrooms are similarly upmarket, too, with cherry wood and granite surfaces and lovely cascade showerheads.
Bar. Business centre. Concierge. Disabled-adapted rooms. Gym. Internet (wireless, €19.95/24hr). No smoking throughout. Parking (€4/hr, €30/24hr). Restaurant. Room service. TV: pay movies.

Dylan. *See p138.*

CONSUME

★ Dylan
Keizersgracht 384, 1016 GB (530 2010,
www.dylanamsterdam.com). Tram 1, 2, 5. **Rates**
€435-€540 double. **Credit** AmEx, MC, V. **Map**
p330 C4 **㉗**
Outrageous elegance is the selling point here.
Guests are made to feel like superstars and lodge
in colour-coded chromotherapy rooms designed to
enhance the mood, like zingy raspberry, Zen-like
black or toasty turmeric. Every detail, from chef
Dennis Kuipers' North African-inspired menu to
the careful alignment of the cushions in the public
areas, is well thought through by the owners. The
restaurant, Vinkeles, has earned itself a Michelin
star. *Photo p137.*
Bar. Concierge. Gym. Internet (wireless, free).
Restaurant. Room service. TV: pay movies.

Eden Amsterdam American Hotel
Leidsekade 97, 1017 PN (556 3000,
www.amsterdamamerican.com). Tram 1, 2, 5, 7,
10. **Rates** (season-based) €110-€373 double.
Credit AmEx, DC, MC, V. **Map** p330 C5 **㉘**
The public areas of this dazzling art nouveau monument are all eye-pleasers – especially the magnifi-
cently buttressed Café Americain. Rooms, however,
are pretty cramped and decorated in smart-but-
bland standard hotel fittings. They've all got good
views, though, either on to the canal or the bustling
square below and some have their own balcony.
Meeting facilities are available for those all-impor-
tant business moments.
Bars (2). Concierge. Disabled-adapted rooms. Gym.
Internet (wireless, €17/24hr). No smoking
throughout. Restaurant. Room service. Sauna. TV:
pay movies.

★ Hotel 717
Prinsengracht 717, 1017 JW (427 0717,
www.717hotel.nl). Tram 1, 2, 5. **Rates** €300-
€650 double. **Credit** AmEx, DC, MC, V. **Map**
p330 D4 **㉙**
A rather well-kept secret, this small, flower-filled
boutique hotel only offers suites and is the epitome
of understated glamour. The emphasis is on search-
ing the globe for the best accoutrements – linens
from the USA, bespoke blankets from Wales, box-
spring mattresses from London. There is afternoon
tea every day, and a patio for summer breakfasts or
general lounging. Guests are the type that shed their
Euros on antiques in the Spiegelkwartier. The room
rate includes breakfast, house wines, TV, wireless
internet and a DVD collection. Nice.
Internet (wireless, free). No-smoking rooms.
Room service.

★ Inter-Continental Amstel Amsterdam
Professor Tulpplein 1, 1018 GX (622 6060,
www.interconti.com). Tram 4, 7, 10 or Metro
Weesperplein. **Rates** €316-€600 double. **Credit**
AmEx, DC, MC, V. **Map** p331 F4 **㉚**

They don't come much posher than this. Standing
imperiously over the Amstel river, this is where
movie stars or royalty lay their heads on a super-
soft pillow in one of the huge, soundproofed rooms
when they come to town. Everything here is superlative: arrival by the hotel's own boat is possible; staff
are both liveried and top-hatted; the restaurant is
Michelin-starred; the swimming pool looks out on
the river; even the galleried lobby is breathtaking. If
money is no object or you're after that once-in-a-life-
time splurge, then this is the place to go.
Bar. Concierge. Gym. Internet (wireless & business
centre, prices vary). No-smoking rooms. Parking
(€45/24hr). Pool (indoor). Restaurant. Room
service. Spa. TV: DVD/pay movies.

Expensive

Banks Mansion
Herengracht 519-525, 1017 BV (420 0055,
www.banksmansion.nl). Tram 16, 24, 25. **Rates**
(incl breakfast) €254-€309 double. **Credit** AmEx,
DC, MC, V. **Map** p330 D4 **㉛**
Once you check in to this grand hotel in a former
bank building, everything is yours: drinks and
snacks in the lounge, films and minibar in your room
– they're all free, because the owners want to create
a homely feel. This all-inclusive hotel also encompasses a pillow menu, rain showerheads, plasma
TVs and DVD players in every room.
Bar. Business centre. Concierge. Internet (wireless,
first 50mins free, €16/24hr; business centre, free).
No-smoking rooms. TV: DVD.

Dikker & Thijs Fenice Hotel
Prinsengracht 444, 1017 KE (620 1212,
www.dtfh.nl). Tram 1, 2, 5, 7, 10. **Rates** €115-
€265 double. **Credit** AmEx, DC, MC, V. **Map**
p330 C5 **㉜**
A long-established name on Amsterdam's hotel
scene, this upmarket place often has authors dropping in to stay. In an 18th-century warehouse building near Leidseplein, rooms are plain but smart; the
glamorous penthouse has a wall made of glass for
unsurpassed views over the city rooftops. At breakfast time, guests are bathed in jewel-coloured light
from the stained-glass windows.
Bar. Internet (wireless, €2.50/hr, €10/day). No
smoking throughout. Restaurant. Room service.
TV: pay movies.

Eden Hotel
Amstel 144, 1017 AE (530 7878, www.eden
hotelgroup.com). Tram 4, 9, 14 or Metro
Waterlooplein. **Rates** €135-€350 double.
Credit AmEx, MC, V. **Map** p331 E3 **㉝**
This chain hotel standard has great views over the
Amstel river to the front and is well placed for
crashing after indulging in the fleshpots of
Rembrandtplein behind. It's suited to work and long
stays – there's a business floor, apartments and

Singular Rooms

Accommodation to float everyone's boat.

Amsterdam is, without doubt, a unique city to visit. Its tourist attractions cater for every taste – from the infamous Red Light District, fetish parties, relaxed drugs laws and music festivals, to canals, architecture, history and museums. So it's no surprise that the city also has themed hotels to suit visitors with particular interests. Here are but a few.

If you're on the trail of Spinoza or Descartes, head over to the reasonably priced **Sandton Hotel De Filosoof** ('Hotel of Philosophers'; *see p144*). Each room honours a different great thinker, with decor to match (check out the Henry D Thoreau room, designed to look like 'Walden Pond').

For those of you visiting Amsterdam for one of its more notorious activities, the **Hemp Hotel** (*see p142*) is a specialised five-room hotel where each room has a different international theme (the Tibetan room, the Jamaican room...). Carpets, curtains, mattresses and sheets are made of hemp. So is the soap. There's also the 'Hemple Temple Nightbar', a dingy dive serving hemp beer and other hemp drinks. Every room is a smoking room – you can toke to your heart's content and confirm all those closely guarded Amsterdam stereotypes.

Virtuous visitors who don't want to participate in the vice this city has to offer can enjoy the peace and quiet of the alcohol-, drug- and smoke-free **Shelter Jordan** (*see p136*) or **Shelter City Christian Hostels** (*see p136*). With single-sex dorm rooms, activities like cookie-baking and daily Bible discussion, guests might even be able to counteract the sins they've inadvertently witnessed. Dorm beds are charitably cheap at both locations and you don't even have to be Christian to stay there.

A pool table, chill-out room, DJ nights, 'munchies' for sale: the **Flying Pig Hostels** (*see p134*) are the place for the visitor who giggles when he says the word 'Amsterdam'. It's strictly for the young – they don't accept guests over 40 or under 16 – and our guess is that anyone over 30 will feel like a senior citizen here. With locations in the RLD, on Leidseplein and at the beach in Noordwijk (and free shuttle buses between them), you're sure to find multiple ways to get your party on and make plenty of friends.

Bookworms should check in to the **Ambassade Hotel** (*see p134*), while water babes can dream afloat the **Amstel Botel** (*see p145*) in the Noord.

CONSUME

Flying Pig Downtown. *See p134.*

studios – and disabled travellers are well served with adapted rooms. Café Flo, the on-site restaurant, is highly rated among local gastros.
Bar. Business centre. Concierge. Disabled-adapted room. Internet (wireless in lobby, LAN €15/24hr). No-smoking rooms. Restaurant. TV: pay movies.

★ Mercure Hotel Arthur Frommer

Noorderstraat 46, 1017 TV (622 0328, www.mercure.com). Tram 4, 16, 24, 25.
Rates €99-€259 double. **Credit** AmEx, DC, MC, V. **Map** p331 E5 ㉞
On a charming residential street within walking distance of the sights and the nightlife, this hotel, arranged around a courtyard, is a real oasis of relaxation. A minute or two's stroll from the Amstelkerk, it's also in one of the finest locations in town. Rooms, which occupy a series of attractive townhouses, are both spacious and smart. There's a cosy bar and stylish public areas.
Bar. Internet (wireless €5.95/24hr). Parking (€20/24hr).

> **INSIDE TRACK**
> **SMALL AND BEAUTIFUL**
>
> While bed and breakfasts are often associated with being cheap and cheerful, Amsterdam's B&Bs tend to be chic affairs, kitted out to their stylish owners' exacting specifications. You'll need to book ahead though; restrictions limit the number of people allowed to stay in a house at any one time down to four.

Moderate

Amsterdam Wiechmann

Prinsengracht 328-332, 1016 HX (626 3321, www.hotelwiechmann.nl). Tram 1, 2, 5, 7, 17.
Rates (incl breakfast) €145-€165 double. **Credit** MC, V. **Map** p330 C4 ㉟
From a suit of armour in the reception to 1950s teapots and toasters in the breakfast room, retro touches from every era adorn this rather eccentric, long-established hotel. Room decoration tends towards the chintzy but things are brought up to date with free Wi-Fi. Check the website for plenty of special deals.
Bar. Internet (wireless, free). No smoking throughout.

Bridge Hotel

Amstel 107-111, 1018 EM (623 7068, www.thebridgehotel.nl). Tram 4, 7, 9, 10 or Metro Weesperplein. **Rates** (incl breakfast) €98-€150.
Credit AmEx, DC, MC, V. **Map** p331 F4 ㊱
Feeling gloriously isolated on the eastern banks of the River Amstel, this private hotel in a former stone-mason's workshop is just a few minutes' stroll from the bright lights of Rembrandtplein and the rest of the city centre. It's also well situated for

Mövenpick Hotel Amsterdam City Centre. *See p142.*

CONSUME

exploring the Plantage and Jodenbuurt. Rooms are simple and bright; ones that command a river view cost more, of course. For stays of three days or more, there are two self-catering apartments and a studio sleeping four, which work out at a pretty good price. A planned expansion in summer 2011 brings with it extra apartments.
Bar. Internet (wireless, prices vary; high-speed €2/hr).

Hotel Agora
Singel 462, 1017 AW (627 2200, www.hotelagora.nl). Tram 1, 2, 5. **Rates** (incl breakfast) €70-€100 double. **Credit** AmEx, DC, MC, V. **Map** p330 D4 **㊲**
Ideal for flower-power freaks who want to stock up on bulbs, this homely little place in an 18th-century canal house is right in the thick of it, very close to the floating flower market. The Agora may lacks a few extras, but it does offer a conservatory for break-fast, as well as its own garden. Rooms are plain but neat and all have canal or garden views.
Internet (wireless, free). Room service.

Hotel de Munck
Achtergracht 3, 1017 WL (623 6283, www.hoteldemunck.com). Tram 4, 7, 10, 25 or Metro Weesperplein. **Rates** (incl breakfast) from €79 double. **Credit** AmEx, DC, MC, V. **Map** p331 F4 **㊳**
This higgledy-piggledy place in an old Dutch East India Company sea captain's house is perched on a

secluded little canal near the river. The rooms are basic, clean and neat. The breakfast room is lovely, with a working jukebox and walls plastered with old album covers.
Internet (wireless, free).

Nicolaas Witsen
Nicolaas Witsenstraat 4, 1017 ZH (623 6143, www.hotelnicolaaswitsen.nl). Tram 4, 7, 10, 25 or Metro Weesperplein. **Rates** (incl breakfast) €115-€125 double. **Credit** AmEx, MC, V. **Map** p331 E5 **㊴**
One of the few hotels to fill the gap between the museums and De Pijp, this place, though plain, func-tional and a tad overpriced, is well placed for culture vultures and fun-seekers. There's also an excellent delicatessen on the corner of the street that encour-ages in-room midnight feasting.
Bar. Internet (wireless, free).

★ Seven Bridges
Reguliersgracht 31, 1017 LK (623 1329, www.sevenbridgeshotel.nl). Tram 4, 16, 24, 25. **Rates** €120-€200 double. **Credit** AmEx, MC, V. **Map** p331 E4 **㊵**
Ideal for those who want a luxury hidey-hole far from the madding crowd that's also conveniently located for the museums and city centre. There are no public spaces here, apart from the lobby and gar-den, just eight lovely and largely antique-stuffed rooms. This lack of shared space means all guests must suffer the privation of compulsory breakfast

in bed. One of Amsterdam's best-kept secrets, although we have a strong feeling that it won't remain one for very much longer.
Internet (wireless, free). No-smoking rooms.

Budget

Hemp Hotel
Frederiksplein 15, 1017 XK (625 4425, www.hemp-hotel.com). Tram 4, 7, 10, 25. **Rates** (incl breakfast) €75 double. **Credit** MC, V. **Map** p331 F4 🄴
See p139 **Singular Rooms.**
Bar. Internet (wireless, free). Smoking throughout.

★ Hotel Prinsenhof
Prinsengracht 810, 1017 JL (623 1772, www.hotelprinsenhof.com). Tram 4, 7, 10, 16, 24, 25. **Rates** (incl breakfast) €69-€89 double. **Credit** AmEx, MC, V. **Map** p331 E4 🄵
A good option for budget travellers, this diminutive, ten-roomed hotel with helpful and friendly staff is right near the city's nightlife and foodie Utrechtsestraat. The stairs are positively vertiginous – luggage is hauled up on a pulley. Rooms themselves are simple, clean and tidy, and some have shared facilities. Best of all, rooms with canal views don't attract a premium.
Internet (wireless, €5/stay).

JODENBUURT, THE PLANTAGE & THE OOST
Moderate

Arena
's Gravesandestraat 51, 1092 AA (850 2400, www.hotelarena.nl). Tram 3, 7, 9, 10, 14. **Rates** €99-€189 double. **Credit** AmEx, DC, MC, V. **Map** p332 G3 🄶
A holy trinity of hotel, restaurant and nightclub in a former Catholic orphanage, Arena's ideal for lazy young scenesters after a one-stop-shop of food, booze and boogie. Standard and large rooms are a bit boring from an aesthetic point of view; the extra-large ones and suites, kitted out by leading local designers, look great but come with matching price tags. It's a bit out of the way but trams do whizz you in to the centre in ten minutes and it's a nice walk through an utterly untouristed area.
Bar. Disabled-adapted rooms. Internet (wireless, 1hr free, €10/24hr, €50/7 days). Restaurant. TV: pay movies.

Eden Lancaster
Plantage Middelaan 48, 1018 DH (535 6888, www.edenhotelgroup.com). Tram 9, 14. **Rates** €65-€180 double. **Credit** AmEx, DC, MC, V. **Map** p327 F3 🄸
Even though it's a bit out of the way of the other sights, this hotel is a short tram ride (or a 20-minute

walk) away from Centraal Station, and there are several decent cafés nearby too. Not really a place for a romantic or indulgent getaway; it's quite basic (and bathrooms are cramped), but the rooms are good for business travellers, equipped as they are with Wi-Fi and desks. The hotel's triple and quad rooms are very much aimed at families.
Internet (wireless, free in lobby; €5/hr, €12.50/24hr). No-smoking rooms. TV: pay movies.
▶ *The Artis Royal Zoo, one of the oldest zoos in the world, is across the road; see p117.*

Hostels

Stayokay Amsterdam Zeeburg
Timorplein 21, 1094 CC (551 3190, www.stayokay.com). Tram 7, 10, 14. **Rates** (per person, incl breakfast) €28-€40 twin. **Credit** AmEx, MC, V.
Located in a grand old school building, this branch of the reliable hostel chain is part of Stayokay's designer concept from Edward van Vliet, done out in warm reds, with mosaic floors, sleek but simple furniture and huge photos on the walls. Perfect for families and the more discerning hosteller – HI members get a discount – it offers several special packages; check the website for full details.
Bar. Internet (wireless, €3/hr). Restaurant.

THE WATERFRONT
Expensive

Mövenpick Hotel Amsterdam City Centre
Piet Heinkade 11, 1019 BR (519 1200, www.moevenpick.com). Tram 25, 26. **Rates** €150-€245 double. **Credit** AmEx, DC, MC, V. **Map** p327 F1 🄵
Big, tall and glamorous, this stripy, stone-coloured hotel is a great base for exploring the Waterfront and Noord on the banks opposite. Rooms are decorated in soothing greys and woods; pricier ones grant access to an executive lounge and have great views over the cruise liners ploughing through the waters, or over the city's rooftops. *Photo 140.*
Bar. Business centre. Gym. Internet (wireless, free). No smoking throughout. Restaurant. TV: pay movies.

Moderate

★ Lloyd Hotel
Oostelijke Handelskade 34, 1019BN (561 3604, www.lloydhotel.com). Tram 10, 26. **Rates** €95-€295 double. **Credit** AmEx, DC, MC, V. **Map** p327 F3 🄸
See p135 **Stylish Stays.** *Photo p135.*
Bar. Internet (wireless, free). Meeting rooms. Parking. Restaurant. Room service.

CONSUME

College Hotel. *See p144.*

CitizenM.

CONSUME

THE MUSEUM QUARTER, VONDELPARK & THE SOUTH

Expensive

College Hotel
*Roelof Hartstraat 1, 1071 VE (571 1511,
www.thecollegehotel.com). Tram 3, 5, 12, 25.*
Rates €195-€235 double. **Credit** AmEx, MC ,V.
Map p331 E7 ❼
At the College, a practical outpost of the city's hotel
and catering college, all the staff are students who
are training in situ. The boutique styling and glamorous touches (bathrooms are a strong point)
ensure that prices are far from pocket money, however. Some rooms are small but if you're prepared
to pay top dollar, you get oodles of space. There's
also a bar and ambitious modern Dutch restaurant.
The downside is that service is unpredictable.
*Bar. Bike & scooter rentals. Business centre.
Internet (wireless, free). Massage service.
Restaurant. TV: pay movies.*

Moderate

★ Bilderberg Jan Luyken
*Jan Luykenstraat 58, 1071 CS (573 0730,
www.bilderberg.nl). Tram 2, 5, 7, 10.* **Rates**
€99-€269 double. **Credit** AmEx, MC, V. **Map**
p330 D6 ❹
One of the city's most stylish secrets, this place is
just a kitten-heeled skip away from the designer
shops of PC Hooftstraat. Rooms – slickly done out,
with designer touches and wall-mounted CD players
– are something of a bargain for a place boasting
these looks and facilities. Check for special packages.

*Bar. Internet (wireless, €13/24hr). Room service.
Spa.*

CitizenM
*Prinses Irenestraat 30, 1077 WX (811 7000,
www.citizenm.com). Tram 5, 16.* **Rates** €79-€159
double. **Credit** AmEx, MC, V.
See p135 **Stylish Stays**.
*Bar. Disabled-adapted rooms. Internet (wireless,
free). No smoking throughout.*

Hotel V
*Victorieplein 42, 1078 PH (662 3233,
www.hotelv.nl). Tram 4, 10, 25.* **Rates** (incl
breakfast) €120-€220 double. **Credit** AmEx,
DC, MC, V.
A bit of a hike from the sights and the centre, but
trams stop right outside to whisk you in to town,
and De Pijp is a 15-minute walk away. This boutique
B&B-style hotel is ideal for business travellers sick
of corporate sterility – it's very near the RAI and
business areas of Zuid. There's new-age, sleek decor
in all rooms, but there aren't many extras. The
lounge, with its pebbly fireplace and furry pouffes,
looks lovely.
*Bar. Internet (wireless, free). No smoking
throughout.*

Sandton Hotel De Filosoof
*Anna van den Vondelstraat 6, 1054 GZ (683
3013, www.sandton.eu). Tram 1, 3, 12, 17.*
Rates €110-140 double. **Credit** Amex, MC, V.
Map p329 B6 ❹
See p139 **Singular Rooms**.
*Bar. Internet (wireless, free). No smoking
throughout.*

★ Vondel

*Vondelstraat 28-30, 1054 GE (612 0120,
www.hotelvondel.nl). Tram 1, 2, 3, 5, 7, 10.* **Rates**
from €129 double. **Credit** AmEx, DC, MC, V.
Map p330 C5 ❺

Another hidden gem near museums and upmarket
shopping opportunities, this thoroughly chic place
is covered with art and has a lovely decked garden.
Rooms, ranging from small to huge, are thoroughly
designer driven, with chandeliers and swanky bathrooms. Unusually for such a trendy hotel, families
are positively encouraged, which marks it out from
snootier establishments.
*Bar. Internet (wireless, €10/24hr). Restaurant.
Room service. TV: pay movies.*

DE PIJP

Deluxe

★ Hotel Okura Amsterdam

*Ferdinand Bolstraat 333, 1072 LH (678 7111,
www.okura.nl). Tram 12, 25.* **Rates** €240-€380
double. **Credit** AmEx, DC, MC, V.

This smart stopover has everything captains of
industry need: a top-floor, top-of-the-range French
restaurant, Le Ciel Bleu; a pool and health club (open
to non-guests); state-of-the-art conference facilities;
top-notch sushi bars; and a restaurant with terrace,
Serre. Rooms offer no surprises in terms of facilities
– they've got the lot – or looks. They're done up in
a suitably masculine style, and range from small
standards to the huge (and, as such, hugely expensive) suite on the 21st floor.
*Bars (2). Business centre. Concierge. Disabled-
adapted rooms. Gym. Internet (wireless,
€17/24hr). No-smoking rooms. Parking (€4/hr).
Pool (indoor). Restaurants (5). Room service. TV:
pay movies.*

Expensive

Hotel Savoy

*Ferdinand Bolstraat 194, 1072 LW (644 7445,
www.savoyhotel.nl). Tram 3, 12, 16, 24, 25.*
Rates €175 double. **Credit** AmEx, DC, MC, V.
Map p331 F7 ❺

One of very few accommodation options in the area,
this hotel, in an imposing red-brick Amsterdam
School building, has been styled as a 'concept' hotel,
which suits the gentrified Pijp, and its evolution as
a style centre, down to the ground.
*Bar. Business centre. Internet (wireless, free).
Disabled-adapted rooms. No smoking throughout.
TV: DVD.*

Budget

★ Van Ostade Bicycle Hotel

*Van Ostadestraat 123, 1072 SV (679 3452,
www.bicyclehotel.com). Tram 3, 12, 16, 24, 25.*

Rates (incl breakfast). €50-€115 double.
Credit AmEx, MC, V. **Map** p331 F6 ❺

This beloved, cheap 'n' cheerful staging post for
pedal-pushers was one of the first (and is still one
of the few) places to stay in De Pijp. With good
bicycle access to popular out-of-town routes, the
friendly staff can suggest routes and rent out bikes
– and if you bring your own, you can park it
securely for free. The breakfast room is cute, rooms
are comfy and there are loads of excellent places
nearby to refuel for the energetic day ahead, or
wind down after a long ride.
*Bike rentals. Internet (wireless, free). No smoking
throughout. Parking (€25/24hr).*

Other Options

FLOATING ACCOMMODATION

The Waterfront

Amstel Botel

*NDSM-Pier 3, 1033 RG (626 4247, www.amstel
botel.nl), Ferry NDSM-werfveer.* **Rates** (rear side)
€78-€89; (water side) €83-€94 double. **Credit**
AmEx, DC, MC, V.

A 10-minute cruise from Centraal Station across
the River IJ to Noord, this is a safe bet if you're looking for good, clean accommodation. Unless you are
fooled by the 'luxury' rooms boast and come
expecting the *QEII*, you'll be perfectly satisfied.
The bar has long opening hours, games such as
pinball and pool, and a jukebox. Be warned, the last
ferry leaves Centraal Station at 11.45pm (12.45am
Fri, Sat), but there's a free shuttle bus that runs
between the two during the night.
*Bar. Internet (wireless, €6/hr, €15/3hr). TV: pay
movies.*

The Jordaan

Frederic Rentabike

*Brouwersgracht 78, 1013 GZ (624 5509,
www.frederic.nl). Bus 18, 21, 22.* **Rates** €40-€100
per person per night based on double occupancy.
No credit cards. Map p326 C2 ❺

This bike shop also does a nice little sideline in rent-
ing out nine houseboats all around town, ranging
from the sleek to the downright homely. Houseboat
no.5 on the Prinsengracht is big, stylish and comes
with internet.

BED & BREAKFAST

Southern Canal Belt

★ Kamer01

*Singel 416, 1016 AK (625 6627, www.kamer01.
nl). Tram 1, 2, 5.* **Rates** €188 Mon-Thur, Sun;
€218 Fri, Sat. **Credit** V, MC. **Map** p330 C4 ❺

CONSUME

A very stylish, gay-friendly place designed by Atelier Hertogh. The Red Room is sensually scarlet and comes with a shower big enough for an entire football team; the Blue Room comes with a sexy circular bed. Both share a private roof terrace. Rooms are equipped with an iMac, flat-screen TV and DVD player. The downstairs kitchen area is equipped with help-yourself 'maxi bar' and titbits from nearby bakery Holtkamp. Minimum stay is two nights, with a discount for more than four, booked over a week in advance.

De Pijp

Between Art & Kitsch
Ruysdaelkade 75, 1072 AL (679 0485, www. between-art-and-kitsch.com). Tram 3, 12, 16, 24. **Rates** from €70-€90 double. **No credit cards.** **Map** p331 E6 ⑮
Located on a canal, this two-roomed B&B is well situated for culture and nightlife. Living up to the name's promise, one room is decorated in mock deco with authentic period knick-knacks, the other in faux baroque.

South

City Mundo
Schinkelkade 30, 1075 VK (470 5705, www. citymundo.com). Tram 2 or bus 15, 62. **Open** 10am-6pm Mon-Fri; 11am-6pm Sat. **Credit** AmEx, MC, V.
An agency to match visitors to accommodation, which could be anything from a room in a flat to a traditional Dutch windmill. The website gives a good overview of what's available, but be warned that the minimum stay is three nights.

Xaviera Hollander Bed & Breakfast
Stadionweg 17, 1077 RV (673 3934, www.xavierahollander.com). Tram 5, 24. **Rates** €100-€125 double. **No credit cards.**
Stays in the home of the original Happy Hooker. Rooms, upstairs in Xaviera's own banker-belt villa or in a hut at the bottom of her garden, are fine enough but guests come here mainly for an outrageous anecdote (or several) from the lady herself.

CAMPING

Although none of these campsites are exactly close to the centre, all are well served by good transport links. Zeeburg is a young people's site; Gaasper and Amsterdamse Bos are family campsites (with designated youth fields; Gaasper has water-sporting opportunities on the nearby lake), while everyone is mixed happily together at Vliegenbos. Camping is a national pastime for the Dutch, so all the sites have good facilities, such as laundries and supermarkets, and are well maintained.

Kamer01. *See p145.*

Gaasper Camping Amsterdam
Loosdrechtdreef 7, 1108 AZ (696 7326, www.gaaspercamping.nl). Metro 53 or nightbus 355, 357. **Open** mid Mar-early Nov, sometimes for New Year. **Rates** €5 per person per night; from €6 tent; €5-€10 vehicles. **Credit** MC, V.

★ Het Amsterdamse Bos
Kleine Noorddijk 1, 1187 NZ (641 6868, www.campingamsterdamsebos.nl). Bus 171, 199. **Open** 1 Apr-15 Oct (call for mid Oct-Mar). **Rates** €5 per person per night; from €5.75 tent; €4.50-€9 vehicles. **Credit** AmEx, MC, V.

Vliegenbos
Meeuwenlaan 138, 1022 AM (636 8855, www.vliegenbos.com). Bus 32, 36 or nightbus 73. **Open** *Apr-Sept* 9am-9pm daily. **Rates** from €7.50 per person per night; from €2 tent; €8.50-€29.75 vehicles. **Credit** MC, V. **No pets allowed.**

Zeeburg
Zuider IJdijk 20, 1095 KN (694 4430, www.campingzeeburg.nl). Tram 14 or bus 22, 37. **Open** yr round. **Rates** from €6.50 1 person plus tent; €4-€26 vehicles. **Credit** AmEx, MC, V.

Restaurants & Cafés

Meat-and-mash no more: this city is all about the modern urban gourmet.

Once defined by stodgy veg, meat and gravy, Amsterdam's food scene has come on in leaps and bounds, and is now bolder and more adventurous than ever. Combine the city's rich history with architectural developments and regenerated former dead zones and you get restaurants in quirky locations such as stripped-back warehouses, old greenhouses and disused passenger ferries.

A desire to showcase local products and encourage conscious eating habits has seen many chefs offering menus defined by season and macrobiotic principles. *Gezellig* (cosy) cafés dot the city's charming alleys and canals, while the diverse ethnic make-up of the city means that Michelin-starred restaurants rub shoulders with cheap snack bars and econo-ethnic cuisine from all corners of the world.

THE ESSENTIALS

Dining in Amsterdam is generally a laid-back affair, with dress codes practically unheard of, but it is worth calling ahead if you're in any kind of doubt. Those who keep nocturnal hours should note that the Dutch tend to eat early: many kitchens will close by 10pm (although that's not when they'll kick you out). Making a reservation is advisable for weekend nights, but if you can't get a table at your first choice, take heart: there are so many restaurants and cafés in the city – more than 1,000 – that even locals rarely have to eat at the same place twice.

Note that prices given for main courses in the following listings have been rounded up to the nearest €0.50 and, while accurate at press time, they are of course subject to change. We've used the € symbol to indicate budget eateries, including sandwich shops and takeaways, and ★ denotes a recommendation.

THE OLD CENTRE
The Old Side

1e Klas
Centraal Station, Platform 2B (625 0131, www.restaurant1eklas.nl). Tram 1, 2, 4, 5, 9, 13, 16, 17, 24, 25. **Open** 8.30am-11pm daily. **Main**

courses €16-€22. **Credit** AmEx, DC, MC, V. **Map** p326 D1 ❶ **Café**
This former brasserie for first-class commuters is now open to anyone who wants to kill some time in style – with a full meal or snack – while waiting for a train. The art nouveau interior will whisk you straight back to the 1890s. But if you're running for the train, score something to go from Shakies (west tunnel by stairs to platforms 10/11, 423 4377, www.shakies.nl).

A Fusion
Zeedijk 130 (330 4068, www.a-fusion.nl). Tram 4, 9, 14, 16, 24, 25 or Metro Nieuwmarkt. **Open** noon-11pm daily. **Main courses** €10-€14. **Credit** AmEx, DC, MC, V. **Map** p326 D2 ❷ **Asian**
This loungey restaurant obviously took notes from the hip side of Chinatown in New York City. The dark and inviting interior harbours big screens playing music videos from Hong Kong, and you can drink bubble teas (lychee!) and eat some of the tastiest confusion-free pan-Asian dishes in town. The menu is long but the dim sum and satay dishes are particularly recommended.

> ❶ Blue numbers given in this chapter correspond to the location of each restaurant or café on the street maps. *See pp325-332.*

Blauw aan de Wal.

★ € De Bakkerswinkel
Zeedijk 37 (489 8000, www.debakkerswinkel.nl).
Tram 1, 2, 4, 5, 9, 13, 14, 16, 17, 24, 25. **Open**
8am-6pm Tue-Fri; 8am-5pm Sat; 10am-5pm Sun.
Main courses €3.50-€11. **Credit** AmEx, MC, V.
Map p326 D2 ❸ **Café**
A bakery-tearoom where you can indulge in lovingly
prepared and hearty sandwiches, soups and the
most divine slabs of quiche you've ever had.
Other locations Roelof Hartstraat 68, Museum
Quarter (662 3594); Polonceaukade 1, Westerpark
(688 0632).

Bird
*Zeedijk 77 (snack bar 420 6289, restaurant 620
1442, www.thai-bird.nl). Tram 1, 2, 4, 5, 9, 13,
14, 16, 17, 24, 25.* **Open** *Snack bar* 1-10pm daily.
Restaurant 5-11.30pm daily. **Main courses** €10-
€25. **Credit** (restaurant only) AmEx, DC, MC, V.
Map p326 D2 ❹ **Thai**
The most authentic Thai place in town. No doubt
because of that, it's also the most crowded, but nevertheless it's worth waiting for, whether you drop
by to pick up a pot of *tom yam* soup or go for a full-
blown meal. If you plan to linger, settle into the
restaurant across the street (Zeedijk 72-74).

Blauw aan de Wal
*Oudezijds Achterburgwal 99 (330 2257,
www.blauwaandewal.com). Tram 9, 16, 24 or
Metro Nieuwmarkt.* **Open** 6.30-11.30pm Tue-Sat.
Main courses €29. *Set meal* €55, 3 courses.

Credit AmEx, MC, V. **Map** p326 D2 ❺
Mediterranean
The hallmarks of this culinary mainstay are tempting dishes and a wine list likely to inspire long bouts
of grateful contemplation in visiting oenophiles.

★ Bridges
*Oudezijds Voorburgwal 197 (555 3560,
www.bridgesrestaurant.nl). Tram 4, 9, 14, 16, 24,
25.* **Open** *Lunch* noon-3pm Mon-Fri; 12.30-3pm
Sun. *Dinner* 6-11pm. **Main courses** €21-€55.
Credit AmEx, MC, V. **Map** p326 D3 ❻
Mediterranean
Chef Aurélien Poirot's minimalist style puts an
emphasis on dishes prepared with a limited repertoire of fresh ingredients. The menu features locally
caught, seasonal seafood and five-star ingredients,
such as truffles and foie gras.

Brasserie Harkema
*Nes 67 (428 2222, www.brasserieharkema.nl).
Tram 4, 9, 14, 16, 24, 25.* **Open** 11am-1am daily.
Kitchen noon-11pm. **Main courses** *Lunch* €8-
€17. *Dinner* €13-€17. **Credit** AmEx, MC, V. **Map**
p326 D3 ❼ **Café**
This former tobacco factory titillates the local scene
with its sense of designer space, excellent wines and
a kitchen that stays open late pumping out reasonably priced French classics.

Café Bern
*Nieuwmarkt 9 (622 0034). Tram 4, 9, 14, 16, 24,
25 or Metro Nieuwmarkt.* **Open** 4pm-1am daily.
Kitchen 6-11pm daily. Closed mid July-mid Aug.
Main courses €11-€17.50. **No credit cards**.
Map p327 E2 ❽ **Swiss**
Despite its Swiss origins, the Dutch adopted the
cheese fondue as a 'national dish' long ago. Sample
its culinary conviviality at this suitably cosy brown
bar that was established by the rather unlikely figure
of a nuclear physicist: that the menu be affordable
and the bar stocked with a generous variety of
grease-cutting agents. It's best to book ahead.

Centra
*Lange Niezel 29 (622 3050). Tram 4, 9, 14, 16,
24, 25.* **Open** 2-11pm daily. **Main courses** €7-
€17. **No credit cards**. **Map** p326 D2 ❾ **Spanish**

THE BEST FOOD WITH A VIEW

Greenwoods
For postcard perfection. *See p152.*

Odessa
For waterside wonder. *See p157.*

Wilhelmina-Dok
For Eastern Docklands' delights. *See p158.*

CONSUME

Centra serves decent, wholesome, homely Spanish cooking with a suitably unpretentious atmosphere to match. The seafood paella is especially good.

€ Latei
Zeedijk 143 (625 7485, www.latei.net). Tram 4, 9, 14, 16, 24, 25 or Metro Nieuwmarkt. **Open** 8am-6pm Mon-Wed; 8am-10pm Thur, Fri; 9am-10pm Sat; 11am-6pm Sun. **Main courses** €3-€8. **No credit cards. Map** p326 D2 ⑩ **Café**
Packed with kitsch and bedecked with funky Finnish wallpaper – all of which, including wallpaper, is for sale – this little café serves healthy juices and snacks all day long, plus Indian vegetarian dinners (from 6pm Thur-Sat).

▲ € Nam Kee
Zeedijk 111-113 (624 3470, www.namkee.net). Tram 4, 9, 14, 16, 24, 25 or Metro Nieuwmarkt. **Open** noon-10.30pm daily. **Main courses** €6.50-€19. **No credit cards. Map** p326 D2 ⑪ **Chinese**
Cheap and terrific food has earned this Chinese joint a devoted following: the oysters in black bean sauce have achieved classic status. If it's busy, try massive sister operation and dim sum maestros Nam Tin nearby (Jodenbreestraat 11-13, 428 8508) or equally stellar New King (Zeedijk 115-117, 625 2180). **Other locations** Geldersekade 117 (639 2848); Marie Heinekenplein 4, De Pijp (670 2336).

Oriental City
Oudezijds Voorburgwal 177-179 (626 8352, www.oriental-city.nl). Tram 4, 9, 14, 16, 24, 25. **Open** 11.30am-10.30pm daily. **Main courses** €8-€23. **Credit** AmEx, DC, MC, V. **Map** p326 D3 ⑫ **Chinese**

The location overlooks Damstraat, the Royal Palace and the canals. And that's not even the best bit: Oriental City serves some of city's most authentic dim sum.

The New Side

Gartine
Taksteeg 7 (320 4132, www.gartine.nl). Tram 4, 9, 13, 14, 16, 17, 24, 25. **Open** 8am-6pm daily. **Main courses** €5-€20. **No credit cards. Map** p326 D3 ⑬ **Café**
Open only for breakfast, lunch and a full-blown high tea, Gartine is a testament to slow food served by a friendly couple who grow their own veg and herbs in a greenhouse. Simple but marvellous.

Restaurant De Roode Leeuw
Damrak 93-94 (555 0666, www.restaurantderoodeleeuw.nl). Tram 4, 9, 14, 16, 24, 25. **Open** 10am-10.30pm daily. **Main courses** *Lunch* €6-€29.50. *Dinner* €18-€32. **Credit** AmEx, DC, MC, V. **Map** p326 D2/3 ⑭ **Dutch**
This brasserie is housed in the oldest covered terrace in Amsterdam. As you might guess, it harks back

CONSUME

Gartine.

to classier times, but what's more surprising is its embrace of the digital age, complete with Wi-Fi access. It specialises in rather expensive Dutch fare.

Restaurant Haesje Claes
Spuistraat 273-275 (624 9998, www.haesjeclaes. nl). Tram 1, 2, 5, 13, 17. **Open** noon-10pm daily. **Main courses** €16-€23. **Credit** AmEx, DC, MC, V. **Map** p326 D3 ⑮ **Dutch**
In the heart of the city, between Dam Square and Spui, this beloved Amsterdam landmark is especially popular with tourists, though the locals also come flooding in for traditional Dutch food, including *erwtensoep* (split pea soup) and a great *stamppot* (potato mashed with greens) selection. The service, however, is distinctly un-Dutch: friendly, available and fast.

Supperclub
Jonge Roelensteeg 21 (344 6400, www.supper club.nl). Tram 1, 2, 5, 13, 17. **Open** 7.30pm-1am Mon-Thur, Sun; 7.30pm-3am Fri, Sat. **Set meal** *Mon-Wed, Sun* €65, 5 courses. *Thur-Sat* €70, 5 courses. **Credit** AmEx, DC, MC, V. **Map** p326 D3 ⑯ **Global**
With its white decor, beds for seating, irreverent food combos that change weekly and wacky acts, this arty and unique joint is casual to the point of being narcoleptic. Supperclub also has a cruise ship that trawls the local waters, as well as outposts in Istanbul, San Francisco, London and LA.

Tokyo Café
Spui 15 (489 7918, www.tokyocafe.nl). Tram 1, 2, 4, 5, 9, 14, 16, 24, 25. **Open** 5.30-11pm daily. **Set meal** €22-€25.50. **Credit** AmEx, DC, MC, V. **Map** p326 D4 ⑰ **Japanese**
Thought to be haunted, this art nouveau monument now hosts its umpteenth eaterie in the form of a Japanese café, complete with lovely terrace, teppanyaki pyrotechnics, and sushi and sashimi bar. The high-quality, all-you-can-eat sushi will most likely keep the ghosts at bay.

D'Vijff Vlieghen
Spuistraat 294-302 (530 4060, www.d-vijffvlieghen.com). Tram 1, 2, 5. **Open** 6-10pm

---

THE BEST BLOWOUT MEAL

Beddington's
For modern fusion. *See p154.*

De Kas
For home-grown food in a posh greenhouse. *See p156.*

La Rive
For classic with a twist. *See p156.*

---

daily. **Main courses** €27-€32. **Set meal** €44.50, 4 courses; €50, 5 courses; €54.50, 6 courses. **Credit** AmEx, MC, V. **Map** p326 D3 ⑱ **Dutch**
'The Five Flies' achieves a rich Golden Age vibe – it even has a Rembrandt room, with etchings – but also works as a purveyor of over-the-top kitsch. The food is best described as poshed-up Dutch.

THE CANALS
Western Canal Belt

★ Envy
Prinsengracht 381 (344 6407, www.envy.nl). Tram 13, 14, 17. **Open** noon-3.15pm, 6-10.30pm daily. **Set meal** €45, 4 courses; €52.50, 5 courses. **Credit** AmEx, MC, V. **Map** p326 C3/4 ⑲ **Italian**
A designer deli-cum-restaurant serving an arsenal of delicacies emerging from the streamlined refrigerators that line the walls, and from the able kitchen staff. The perfect place for those times when you want to try a bit of everything.

★ € Greenwoods
Singel 103 (623 7071). Tram 1, 2, 5. **Open** 9.30am-7pm daily. **Main courses** €4.50-€8. **No credit cards.** **Map** p326 C2 ⑳ **Café**
Service at this teashop is friendly but can tend toward the slow. Everything is freshly made, though – cakes, scones and muffins are baked daily on the premises – so it's understandable. In summer, sit on the terrace by the canal for the ultimate alfresco eating experience.

★ € 't Kuyltje
Gasthuismolensteeg 9 (620 1045). Tram 1, 2, 9, 24, 25. **Open** 7am-4pm Mon-Fri. **Sandwich** €2-€4. **No credit cards.** **Map** p326 C3 ㉑ **Sandwiches**
The wonderful and deeply filling world of Dutch *broodjes* (sandwiches) has its greatest champion in this takeaway, one of very few that still features proper home-prepared meat (including excellent roast beef) and fish salads in their buns, as opposed to the hugely unappealing factory-prepared products that have taken over the sandwich market. An awesome lunch every time.
▶ *For more great lunchtime options, check out Loekie (see p154), Koffiehuis de Hoek (see p154) and Bagels & Beans (see p160).*

Lieve
Herengracht 88 (624 9635, www.restaurant lieve.nl). Tram 1, 2, 5, 13, 17. **Open** 5.30-10.30pm daily. **Main courses** €14-€18. **Set meal** €26.50-€32.50, 3 courses. **Credit** MC, V. **Map** p326 C2 ㉒ **Belgian**
Lieve caters to those with an abiding love for Belgium's crowning glory, its beers, by recommending the best choice of beverage to accompany each dish. Menus are available in three degrees:

Open-air Eats

From slow food to Surinamese, the city's markets make for essential nibbling.

CONSUME

Over 100 years old, De Pijp's **Albert Cuypmarkt** (*see p127*) is a fun place to spend an afternoon snacking while sorting through an array of affordable indulgences such as socks and second-hand leather jackets. The Cuyp's diverse ethnic mix – Dutch, Moroccan, Surinamese, Turkish and Vietnamese – is reflected in the huge range of food on offer: everything from local cheeses, herring and fresh *stroopwafels* (an irresistible syrupy cookie), to Turkish flat bread, fish and seafood, mixed nuts and dried fruits.

Every Saturday morning, foodies throughout the city flock to the **Boerenmarkt** (farmers' market; *see p198*) to buy its organic produce. It's certainly one of the more expensive markets in the city, but you'll find an overwhelming selection of unique and delicious products here. Look out for the vibrant green stall covered in freshly cut herbs that are made into big tubs of pesto and salsa; freshly shucked oysters; and a stall selling every conceivable kind of funghi. If you want to be like everyone else, end the day with an apple tart at one of the cafés surrounding the square.

The Saturday farmers' market on **Nieuwmarkt** (9am-5pm every Saturday; *see*

p87 **Profile**) offers freshly baked artisan breads, cheeses and locally grown veg, along with antiques and crafts. Take the time to visit the notable speciality food shops around the market, including Vincent Kaas & Vlees (Nieuwmarkt 6), a deli with exquisite cheeses and meats, just down the street from bakery Kloppenburg (Nieuwmarkt 4), which sells the fresh rolls you might need to wrap them with. At Toko Joyce (Nieuwmarkt 38), you can buy prepared Indonesian dishes, Surinamese roti or ready-made Indonesian ingredients, while the Oriëntal Commodities house (Nieuwmarkt 27) is a fantastic source for frozen prepared dim sum.

Out in Oost, the open-air **Dappermarkt** (*see p181*) makes for a busy multicultural shopping experience. What sets this market apart is its eastern culinary influences – buy fresh Turkish bread and stock up on lentils, chickpeas, beans, and speciality veg and spices from the Middle East and Asia.

A little further south in Park Frankendael, you'll find the **Pure Markt** (http://puremarkt. nl), which has expanded quite rapidly since it was launched in 2008. The market – which takes place on the last Sunday of every month – has between 60 and 80 vendors selling locally grown, sustainable 'slow food'.

hearty living room fare, more formal Belgian baroque and a gut-busting gastronomical line-up for serious eaters.

Southern Canal Belt

An

Weteringschans 76 (624 4672, www.japans restaurantan.nl). Tram 7, 10. **Open** 6-10pm Tue-Sat. **Main courses** €8-€18. **No credit cards. Map** p331 E5 ㉓ Japanese
An serves some of the city's best Japanese cuisine – sushi as well as starters and grilled dishes. The staff are friendly and the place is comfortable.

Beddington's

Utrechtsedwarsstraat 141 (620 7393, www. beddington.nl). Tram 7, 10. **Open** 7-10.30pm Tue-Sat. **Set meal** €48, 3 courses; €55, 4 courses. **Credit** AmEx, MC, V. **Map** p331 F4 ㉔ Global
Proprietor and chef Jean Beddington is doing what she does best: cooking up exquisite creations in which one single dish seems to hint at French haute cuisine, Japanese macrobiotic and English country cooking all at the same time. The restaurant's peaceful interior allows you to concentrate on the delicate flavours.

Blue Pepper

Nassaukade 366 (489 7039, www.restaurant bluepepper.com). Tram 7, 10. **Open** 6pm-midnight Mon, Wed-Sun. *Kitchen* 6-10pm. **Main courses** €25. **Set meal** €53-€70. **Credit** AmEx, DC, MC, V. **Map** p330 C5 ㉕ Indonesian
An Indonesian restaurant near Leidseplein that combines tongue-tantalising food with designer decor. Add a decent bottle of wine and it's the perfect date, fashionable without being fussy and always impressive both in terms of atmosphere and eats.

Bojo

Lange Leidsedwarsstraat 51 (622 7434, www. bojo.nl). Tram 1, 2, 5. **Open** 4pm-2am Mon-Thur; 4pm-4am Fri; noon-4am Sat; noon-2am Sun. **Main courses** €6-€13.50. **Credit** AmEx, MC, V. **Map** p330 D5 ㉖ Indonesian
Bojo is a fine Indonesian eaterie, and one of the few places that stays open into the wee small hours. The price is right and the portions are large enough to glue your insides together before or after an evening of excess. Its sister operation just next door at no.49 compensates for its slightly earlier closing time by serving alcohol.
Other locations Lange Leidsedwarsstraat 49; Cornelis Krusemanstraat 3, Zuid.

Eat at Jo's

Marnixstraat 409 (638 3336). Tram 1, 2, 5, 7, 10. **Open** 5.30-9pm Wed-Sun. **Main courses** €13-€15. **No credit cards. Map** p330 C5 ㉗ Global

Each day brings a different fish, meat and vegetarian dish to the menu of this cheap and tasty international kitchen. Star spotters take note: whichever act is booked to play at the Melkweg across the road (*see p251 and p262*) may very well chow down here beforehand, so keep eyes peeled and autograph books to hand.

€ Hap Hmm

1e Helmerstraat 33 (618 1884, www.hap-hmm.nl). Tram 1, 7, 10. **Open** 4.30-8pm Mon-Fri. **Main courses** €7-€12. **No credit cards. Map** p330 C5 ㉘ Dutch
Hungry but hard up? You need some of the Dutch grandma cooking served in this canteen with a living room feel. 'Yummy Bite', as the name translates, will happily pack your empty insides with meat and potatoes for not much more than €7.

Janvier Proeflokaal

Amstelveld 12 (626 1199, www.proeflokaal janvier.nl). Tram 16, 24, 25. **Open** 11am-1am Tue-Thur, Sun; 11am-3am Fri, Sat. **Main courses** €16.50-€27.50. **Set meal** €39.50, 3 courses; €44.50, 4 courses; €57.50, 6 courses. **Credit** AmEx, DC, MC, V. **Map** p331 E4 ㉙ Global
This place is a bit of a lost opportunity, truth be told. While its modern French 'with a twist' cuisine is reasonable, it remains more about the location than anything else: a wooden church – once the stable for Napoleon's horses – with easily one of the city's greatest terraces.

Japan Inn

Leidsekruisstraat 4 (620 4989). Tram 1, 2, 5, 7, 10. **Open** 6-11pm daily. **Main courses** €10-€35. **Credit** AmEx, DC, MC, V. **Map** p330 D5 ㉚ Japanese
Japan Inn offers both quality and quantity. The fresh sushi and sashimi are served from the open kitchen and are hits with students (who dig the quantity) and Japanese tourists (who come for the quality). Either way, you'll be happy you found it.

€ Koffiehuis de Hoek

Prinsengracht 341 (625 3872, www.koffiehuis amsterdam.nl). Tram 1, 7, 10. **Open** 7.30am-4pm Mon-Fri; 9am-3.30pm Sat. **Sandwich** from €2.50. **No credit cards. Map** p330 C3 ㉛ Café
A traditional Dutch sandwich and lunch (omelettes, pancakes and the like) shop where all walks of life collide – from construction workers to the advertising folk of nearby agency KesselsKramer.

Loekie

Utrechtsestraat 57 (624 3740, www.loekie.net). Tram 1, 2, 5, 7, 10. **Open** 9am-6pm Mon, Tue, Thur-Sat; 9am-1pm Wed. **Sandwich** €5-€8. **No credit cards. Map** p331 E4 ㉜ Sandwiches
Loekie isn't quite as cheap as some other sandwich shops, and you'll have to queue, but a French stick

CONSUME

Dauphine. *See p156*.

with Italian fillings makes for an excellent meal. Fine quiche, cheesecake and tapenade too.

Le Pêcheur

Reguliersdwarsstraat 32 (624 3121, www.le pecheur.nl). Tram 1, 2, 5. **Open** noon-10.30pm Mon-Fri; 6-10.30pm Sat. Sat. **Main courses** €21.50-€40. **Credit** AmEx, MC, V. **Map** p330 D4 ⑬ **Seafood**

Multilingual menus let you choose à la carte or the menu of the day with minimal effort at this popular temple to all things oceanic and edible. The service is friendly but formal; the mussels and oysters are particularly excellent, as is the Golden Age patio.

★ Los Pilones

Kerkstraat 63 (320 4651, www.lospilones.com). Tram 1, 2, 5, 11. **Open** 4pm-1am Mon-Thur; 4pm-3am Fri, Sat; 4pm-midnight Sun. **Main courses** €11-€15. **Credit** AmEx, DC, MC, V. **Map** p330 D4 ⑭ **Mexican**

A splendid Mexican cantina with an anarchic bent, Los Pilones is run by three young and friendly Mexican brothers, one of whom does the cooking, so expect authentic food rather than standard Tex-Mex fare. There are over 180 – yes, 180 – tequilas on offer, so don't be surprised if the evening ends in a blur. **Other locations** 1e Anjeliersdwarsstraat 6, the Jordaan (620 0323).

La Rive

Amstel Hotel, Professor Tulpplein 1 (520 3264, www.restaurantlarive.com). Tram 7, 10 or Metro Weesperplein. **Open** *Lunch* noon-3pm Tue-Fri. *Dinner* 6-10pm Tue-Sat. Closed 2wks Aug. **Main courses** €52-€80. **Set meal** *Lunch* €49, 2 courses. *Dinner* €90, 5 courses; €112, 7 courses. **Credit** AmEx, DC, MC, V. **Map** p331 F4 ⑮ **French**

While Hotel de l'Europe (*see p131*) has the Excelsior, it's Michelin-starred La Rive at the Inter-Continental Amstel Amsterdam (*see p138*) that overshadows the hotel competition, with superb regional French cuisine without the excessive formality that can too often mar such places. For the perfect meal when money is no object.

★ Segugio

Utrechtsestraat 96a (330 1503, www.segugio.nl). Tram 4, 6, 7, 10. **Open** 6-11pm Mon-Sat. **Main courses** €25-€34. **Set meal** €48.50, 4 courses. **Credit** AmEx, MC, V. **Map** p331 E4 ⑯ **Italian**

Best. Risotto. Ever. There are pastas, soups, meat and fish dishes too. In fact, this Italian has all the elements to make the perfect lingering meal for both foodies and romantics. A wide variety of fresh ingredients and flavour combinations embellish and embolden this most luxurious of dishes.

▶ *Can't get a table? There's plenty more great Italian action at Toscanini (see p160) and Yam-Yam (see p160).*

Tempo Doeloe

Utrechtsestraat 75 (625 6718, www.tempodoeloe restaurant.nl). Tram 7, 10. **Open** 6-11.30pm Mon-Sat. **Main courses** €19.50-€42. *Rice table* €27.50-€37.50. **Credit** AmEx, DC, MC, V. **Map** p331 E4 ⑰ **Indonesian**

This cosy and rather classy Indonesian restaurant (heck, it even has white linen) is widely thought to serve the city's best and spiciest rice table, a local speciality, and not without good reason. Book ahead or, if you turn up on the off-chance and find the place full, try neighbour Tujuh Maret (Utrechtsestraat 73, 427 9865, www.tujuh-maret.nl) as a tasty plan B – or the Tibetan next door to that as plan C.

€ Wagamama

Max Euweplein 10 (528 7778, www.wagamama. nl). Tram 1, 2, 5, 7, 10. **Open** noon-10pm Mon-Fri, Sun; noon-11pm Fri, Sat. **Main courses** €9-€15. **Credit** AmEx, MC, V. **Map** p330 D5 ⑱ **Asian**

Amsterdam's branch of the popular London franchise of quick 'n' cheap noodle bars. You may not fancy lingering in the minimalist canteen setting, but you certainly can't fault the speedy service or the tasty noodle dishes and soups.
Other locations Zuidplein 12, Zuid (620 3032).

JODENBUURT, THE PLANTAGE & THE OOST

Dauphine

Prins Bernhardplein 175 (462 1646, www.cafe restaurantdauphine.nl). Tram 9 or bus 59, 69. **Open** 10am-1am Mon-Thur; 9am-1am Fri; 11am-1am Sat, Sun. **Main courses** €17-€23. **Credit** AmEx, MC, V. **Map** p332 H5 ⑲ **Global**

Dauphine is located in a former Renault showroom and oozes old-school modernism. Indulge in French bistro classics – from burgers to lobster – for breakfast, lunch or dinner. *Photo p155.*

★ De Kas

Kamerlingh Onneslaan 3 (462 4562, www. restaurantdekas.nl). Tram 9 or bus 59, 69. **Open** *Lunch* noon-2pm Mon-Fri. *Dinner* 6.30-10pm Mon-Sat. **Set meal** *Lunch* €37.50, 2 courses. *Dinner* €49.50, 5 courses. **Credit** AmEx, DC, MC, V. **Global**

In Park Frankendael, way out east, is a renovated 1926 greenhouse. It's now a posh and peaceful restaurant that inspires fevered talk among local foodies. Its international menu changes daily, based on whatever goodies were harvested that day. *Photo right.*

★ Pompstation Bar & Grill

Zeeburgerdijk 52 (692 2888, www.pompstation. nu). Tram 14. **Open** *Grill* 6-10.30pm Tue-Sat. *Bar* 5pm-1am Tue-Thur; 5pm-3am Fri, Sat. **Main courses** €8.50-€45. **Credit** AmEx, MC, V. **European**

CONSUME

De Kas.

Located in a water-pumping station with lofty 18m (59ft) ceilings and tall, narrow windows (the pumps, now in the cellar, are still in use), this Zeeburg spot combines a bar and spacious restaurant. Its gastronomic USP is its selection of high-quality meat: ribeye, tenderloin, rump steak and hamburgers. There's also a respectable choice of seafood dishes and a smattering of vegetarian options too.

THE WATERFRONT

Blijburg
Bert Haanstrakade 2004, IJburg (416 0330, www.blijburg.nl). Tram 26 or bus 326. **Open** *Summer* 10am-10pm daily. *Winter* 2-10pm Wed-Fri; noon-10pm Sat; 10am-10pm Sun. **Main courses** €8-€22. **No credit cards**. Global
Being 25km (15 miles) from the sea, Amsterdam was hardly anyone's choice for a beach holiday – until sand was tipped on the artificial islands of IJburg. While construction continues (45,000 locals will live here eventually), the vast expanse of sand and surrounding freshwater lake are being exploited for their surreal beach-like properties. The restaurant/bar Blijburg – with barbecues, bands and DJs – is on hand to cater to eating and drinking whims.

Fifteen
Jollemanhof 9 (0900 343 8336 premium rate, www.fifteen.nl). Tram 25, 26. **Open** *Lunch* noon-3pm Mon-Sat. *Dinner* 5.30-10pm Mon-Sat. **Main courses** €16.50-€20. **Credit** AmEx, DC, MC, V. **Map** p327 F1 ㊵ Global
While Jamie Oliver has only found one gap in his hectic TV and cooking schedule to visit the Amsterdam outpost of his culinary empire, this franchise of sorts – complete with TV show that documented the transformation of challenged street kids into a well-oiled kitchen brigade – is inspired by his love of honest and fresh dishes.

★ Hotel de Goudfazant
Aambeeldstraat 10h (636 5170, www.hotelde goudfazant.nl). Ferry from Centraal Station. **Open** 6pm-1am Tue-Sun. **Main courses** €18. **Set meal** €30.50, 3 courses. **Credit** MC, V. Global
Deep in the north and deeper within a warehouse, this is post-industrial dining at its best. Yes, it's about location, but there's also some excellent and affordable cookery, from French cuisine to delicate pizza.

Kilimanjaro
Rapenburgerplein 6 (622 3485). Bus 22, 43. **Open** 5-10pm Tue-Sun. **Main courses** €10-€19.50. **Credit** AmEx, MC, DC, V. **Map** p327 F2 ㊶ African
This relaxed and friendly pan-African eaterie offers an assortment of traditional recipes from Senegal across to the Ivory Coast, Tanzania and Ethiopia. Refreshment comes in the cooling form of the fruitiest of cocktails and the strongest of beers.
▶ *You'll find more home-style African food at Semhar; see p160.*

Odessa
Veemkade 259 (419 3010, www.de-odessa.nl). Tram 10, 26 or bus 26. **Open** 4-10.30pm Wed-Sat. **Main courses** €18.50-€23.50. **Set meal** €34, 3 courses. **Credit** AmEx, MC, V. Global

CONSUME

THE BEST PICNIC FOOD

Foodware
For soups, sandwiches and salads. *See p160.*

Small World Catering
For delicious deli bites. *See p160*

De Taart van m'n Tante
For tooth-achingly sweet treats. *See p164.*

Trendies make the trek to the unlikely environs of a Ukrainian fishing boat for the fusion food and the revamped interior. The vibe is 1970s James Bond filtered through a modern lounge sensibility. On warmer nights, dine on the funkily lit deck, while DJs spin from 10pm at weekends.

★ Pont 13
Stravangerweg 891 (770 2722, www.pont13.nl). Bus 22. **Open** 3-10pm Mon-Sat; noon-10pm Sun. **Main courses** €18.50-€23.50. **Credit** AmEx, MC, V. **Global**
This transformed old ferry in Houthavens in a neighbourhood of students living in revamped shipping containers – is all-round intriguing, if a bit out of the way. The menu includes oysters and antipasti (a vegetarian option is available too) followed by hearty wild hog cassoulet with red cabbage and piccalilli or a root veg and potato 'cake' served with grilled cauliflower. *Photo right.*

Wilhelmina-Dok
Noordwal 1 (632 3701, www.wilhelmina-dok.nl). Ferry from Centraal Station to IJplein-Meeuwenlaan. **Open** 11am-midnight daily. **Main courses** *Lunch* €4.50-€14. *Dinner* €17.50-€19.50. **Credit** AmEx, MC, V. **Map** p326 D1
Mediterranean
Through the large windows of this cubic building you get great views of the Eastern Docklands. Come for soup and sandwiches by day and a daily menu of Mediterranean dishes by night. DJs, terrace and an open-air cinema spice it up in summer.

THE JORDAAN

€ De Aardige Pers
2e Hugo de Grootstraat 13 (400 3107). Tram 10. **Open** 1-11pm daily. **Main courses** €11-€18. **No credit cards. Map** p325 B4 ㊸ **Persian**
'The Nice Persian' sums it up. Iranian cuisine served family style and with family grace. Lovely lamb with *sabzi* greens, plus chicken in walnut and pomegranate sauce. A surprising experience for anyone not yet versed in this rich culinary culture.

€ Balraj
Haarlemmerdijk 28 (625 1428, www.balraj.nl). Tram 3. **Open** 4.30-11.30pm daily. **Main courses** €11-€16. **No credit cards. Map** p325 B1 ㊹ **Indian**
A small, cosy eating house that's been here for several decades. The food is reasonably priced and well prepared, with vegetarians generously catered for, but if you want it hot, you need to ask for it.

Fifteen.

Pont 13.

Balthazar's Keuken

Elandsgracht 108 (420 2114, www.balthazars keuken.nl). Tram 7, 10. **Open** 6-11pm Wed-Fri. **Set meal** €29.50, 3 courses. **Credit** AmEx, DC, MC, V. **Map** p330 C4 ⓯ **Mediterranean**

This tiny restaurant is always packed tight, so you really need to book ahead to make sure of enjoying its excellent set menu of meat or fish dishes.

★ Bordewijk

Noordermarkt 7 (624 3899, http://bordewijk.nl). Tram 3. **Open** 6.30-10.30pm Tue-Sat. **Main courses** €22-€29. **Credit** AmEx, DC, MC, V. **Map** p325 B2 ⓰ **French**

Ideal for sampling some of the city's finest original food and palate-tingling wines in a decent designer interior. The service and atmosphere are both relaxed, and Bordewijk has a very reliable kitchen.

Café Restaurant Amsterdam

Watertorenplein 6 (682 2666, www.cradam.nl). Tram 10. **Open** 11.30am-10.30pm daily. **Main courses** €11.50-€22.50. **Credit** AmEx, DC, MC, V. **Dutch**

This spacious monument to industry just west of the Jordaan pumped water from the coast's dunes for around a century. Now it pumps out honest Dutch and French dishes – from *kroketten* to caviar – under a mammoth ceiling and floodlights rescued from the old Ajax stadium. It's a truly unique – and child-friendly – experience.

Duende

Lindengracht 62 (420 6692, www.cafeduende.nl). Tram 3, 10. **Open** 5-11.30pm Mon-Fri; 4-11.30pm Sat, Sun. **Tapas** €4-€15.50. **Credit** AmEx, MC, V. **Map** p325 B2 ⓱ **Tapas**

Get a real taste of Andalucía with the fine tapas dished up at Duende. Place your order at the bar and be prepared to share your table with an amorous couple or, perhaps, one of the flamenco dancers who might offer you a free lesson before getting up to stamp and strut. There are performances every Saturday night (11pm).

€ Foodware
Looiersgracht 12 (620 8898, www.foodware.nl). *Tram 13, 14, 17.* **Open** noon-9pm daily. **Main courses** €4-€10.50. **No credit cards. Map** p330 C4 ❹ **Global**
A takeaway – with a few chairs – with superlative soups, sandwiches, salads and meals. Ask for a fork and hit a canal-side bench.
Other locations Westerstraat 116, the Jordaan (330 8535).

Semhar
Marnixstraat 259-261 (638 1634, www.semhar. nl). *Tram 10.* **Open** 4-10pm Tue-Sun. **Main courses** €11.50-€17. **Credit** MC, V. **Map** p325 B3 ❹ **Ethiopian**
A great spot to sample the *injera* (a type of sourdough pancake) and the vegetarian-friendly food of Ethiopia (best accompanied by a calabash of beer) after an afternoon spent wandering the Jordaan.

★ € Small World Catering
Binnen Oranjestraat 14 (420 2774, www.small worldcatering.nl). *Bus 18, 22.* **Open** 10.30am-8pm Tue-Sat; noon-8pm Sun. **Main courses** €6-€10. **No credit cards. Map** p325 B1 ❺ **Café**
The home base for this catering company is this tiny deli with a lovely proprietor. Besides superlative coffee and fresh juices, there are salads, lasagnes and excellent sandwiches.

★ Toscanini
Lindengracht 75 (623 2813, www.toscanini.nu). *Tram 3, 10.* **Open** 6-10.30pm Mon-Sat. **Main courses** €18-€22.50. **Set meal** €44.50, 6 courses. **Credit** AmEx, DC, MC, V. **Map** p325 B2 ❺ **Italian**
The authentic, invariably excellent food at this popular spot is prepared in an open kitchen. Expect the

---

INSIDE TRACK
PRIX FIXE TRICKS

If you're travelling on a budget, consider timing your visit so that it coincides with Amsterdam's biannual **Restaurant Week** (www.restaurantweek.nl), when you can dine at the city's best eateries – some with Michelin stars – for a bargainous €20 for a three-course lunch and just €5 more for a three-course dinner.

---

likes of Sardinian sheep's cheese with chestnut honey and black pepper or beef tenderloin with rosemary and *lardo di Colonnata* – and be sure to book early (from 3pm) if you want to get a table.

De Vliegende Schotel
Nieuwe Leliestraat 162 (625 2041, www.vliegende schotel.com). *Tram 13, 14, 17.* **Open** 4-11.30pm daily. **Main courses** €9-€13. **Credit** AmEx, MC, V. **Map** p325 B3 ❷ **Vegetarian**
The venerable 'Flying Saucer' serves a splendid array of dishes, buffet style, for meat-avoiders with meaty appetites. If it's booked up, nearby De Bolhoed (Prinsengracht 60-62, 626 1803) also offers hearty vegan dishes as a consolation prize.

★ Yam-Yam
Frederik Hendrikstraat 90 (681 5097, www. yamyam.nl). *Tram 3.* **Open** 6-10.30pm Tue-Sat; 5.30-10.30pm Sun. **Main courses** €8.50-€18. **No credit cards. Map** p325 A3 ❸ **Italian**
Unparalleled and inexpensive pastas and pizzas (cooked in a wood oven) in a hip and casual atmosphere: no wonder Yam-Yam is a local favourite. It's certainly worth the trip west of the Jordaan, but be sure to book in advance.

THE MUSEUM QUARTER, VONDELPARK & THE SOUTH

€ Bagels & Beans
Van Baerlestraat 40 (675 7050, www.bagels beans.nl). *Tram 3, 5, 12.* **Open** 8.30am-5.30pm Mon-Fri; 9.30am-6pm Sat, Sun. **Main courses** €3-€7. **Credit** AmEx, DC, MC, V. **Map** p330 C/D6 ❺ **Café**
An Amsterdam success story, this branch of B&B has a wonderfully peaceful back patio. Perfect for an economical breakfast, lunch or snack; sun-dried tomatoes are employed with particular skill, elevating the humble sandwich to the status of something far more sublime and satisfying.
Other locations Ferdinand Bolstraat 70, De Pijp (672 1610); Keizersgracht 504, Western Canal Belt (330 5508).

Djago
Scheldeplein 18 (664 2013). Tram 4. **Open** 5-9.30pm Mon-Fri, Sun. **Main courses** €11-€23. **Credit** AmEx, DC, MC, V. **Indonesian**
Djago's West Javanese eats are praised to the hilt by Indo-obsessives. Set near the RAI convention centre, it's a bit out of the way, but worth the trip south.

★ Le Garage
Ruysdaelstraat 54-56 (679 7176, www.restaurant legarage.nl). *Tram 3, 5, 12, 16.* **Open** *Lunch* noon-2pm Mon-Fri. *Dinner* 6-11pm daily. **Main courses** €24.50-€32.50. **Set meal** €49.50, 3 courses. **Credit** AmEx, DC, MC, V. **Map** p330 D6 ❺ **French**

A Bite on the Side

The inside guide to intelligent street snacking.

There's more to Amsterdam's kerbside cuisine than the *vette hap* (greasy snack) that can be acquired with loose change from the fluorescently lit hole-in-the-wall that is FEBO. Look beyond the pallid hot dogs served from carts on Dam Square and mystery meat sweating in kebab shop windows, and you'll find an array of decent street food in Amsterdam.

Probably the most iconic, and most misunderstood, street snack is raw herring. There's a quality fish stall or store (*pictured*) around most corners, selling not only the slimy fish but all manner of smoked, cured and fried fish for the sandwich. The best time to eat raw herring is between May and July when the *nieuw* (new) catch hits the stands and the flesh is at its sweetest. The famous herring can be served on its own with raw onions and pickles or on *broodje* (roll). If you really want to look like a local, forego the toppings and the bread and simply dangle the fillet down your gullet like a pelican.

Fillings for the Dutch *broodje* don't end at seafood. Throughout the city, locals stop at small *eetsalons* (not quite restaurants;

more bars dotted with pots of mustard), where small sandwiches are accompanied by a glass of milk or (if you're brave) buttermilk. You won't find any fancy spreads or artisan breads at these quick pit stops; just white, spongy rolls slathered with butter and topped with paper-thin shaved meats, cheeses or retro classics such as filet américain (raw minced beef) and creamy egg salad.

For an exotic twist on the *broodje*, visit one of De Pijp's Surinamese-Indonesian-Chinese snack bars where meats fragrantly prepared with Surinamese spices are heated and stuffed inside crusty white rolls that have been slathered in a super-spicy paste.

Amsterdam's most palatable street food is probably *Vlaamse frites*, fries cooked to order and served in a paper cone topped with an unhealthy dose of creamy sauce. Some shops offer more than 20 different sauces, such as apple, green pepper and samurai, a spicy mayo flecked with vibrant chilli flakes. For a truly Dutch and highly calorific experience, try the *oorlog* (war), an artery-clogging mélange of mayo, peanut sauce and chopped onions.

CONSUME

Eat at Jo's
For spying pre-performance musicians. *See p154.*

Le Garage
For dining alongside the Dutch elite. *See p160.*

La Rive
For Michelin-starred dining and probably a few extra stars to boot. *See p156.*

Don your glad rags to blend in at this fashionable brasserie, which is great for emptying your wallet while watching a selection of Dutch glitterati do exactly the same. The authentic French regional cuisine – and 'worldly' versions thereof – is pretty good. It also has a more loungey sister establishment, En Pluche (Ruysdaelstraat 48, 471 4695), next door.

I Kriti
Balthasar Floriszstraat 3 (664 1445, www.ikriti.nl). Tram 3, 5, 12, 16. **Open** 5-10pm daily. **Main courses** €15-€24. **Credit** DC, V. **Map** p331 E7 ⑤⑥ **Greek**
Eat and party Greek style in this evocation of Crete, where a standard choice of dishes is lovingly prepared. Bouzouki-picking legends drop in on occasion and pump up the frenzied atmosphere, further boosted by plate-lobbing antics. Nearby, De Greikse Taverna (Hobbemakade 64-65, 671 7923, www.degrieksetaverna.nl) may lack plate-smashing atmosphere but competes on taste.

Paloma Blanca
JP Heijestraat 145 (612 6485, www.paloma blanca.nl). Tram 7. **Open** 6-10pm Tue-Sun. **Main courses** €15-€24. **No credit cards.** **Map** p329 B6 ⑤⑦ **Middle Eastern**
This is *the* place for consumers of couscous. The surroundings are simple and there's no alcohol.

★ € De Peper
Overtoom 301 (412 2954, www.depeper.org). Tram 1. **Open** 6pm-1am Tue, Fri, Sun. *Kitchen* 6-9pm. **Set meal** €6-€10, 2 courses. **No credit cards.** **Map** p329 B6 ⑤⑧ **Vegetarian**
The cheapest and best vegan food in town is to be found in the artistic 'breeding ground' OT301 (*see p228*). De Peper is a collectively organised, non-profit project combining culture with kitchen and there's usually a DJ to aid digestion. But do reserve (call after 4pm) on the day that you plan to visit.
► *Check out the film menu while you're here, for some interesting documentaries or perhaps an old Hollywood classic. See p228.*

€ De Peperwortel
Overtoom 140 (685 1053, www.peperwortel.nl). Tram 1, 7, 10. **Open** 4-9pm Mon-Fri; 3-8pm Sat; 3-9pm Sun. **Main courses** €8.50-€15.50. **No credit cards.** **Map** p329 C5 ⑤⑨ **Global**
One could survive for weeks eating nothing but takeaways from Riaz (*see below*) and this place, the fabulous 'Pepper Root'. It serves a wide range of dishes, embracing Dutch, Mexican, Indian and Spanish cuisines.

€ Riaz
Bilderdijkstraat 193 (683 6453, www.riaz.nl). Tram 3, 7, 12, 17. **Open** noon-9pm Tue-Sat; 3-9pm Sun. **Main courses** €6-€15. **No credit cards.** **Map** p329 B5 ⑥⓪ **Surinamese**
Amsterdam's finest Surinamese restaurant is where Ruud Gullit scores his rotis when he's in town.

Vakzuid
Olympisch Stadion 35 (570 8400, www.vakzuid.nl). Tram 16, 24 or bus 15, 23. **Open** 10am-1am Mon-Fri. **Main courses** *Lunch* €15-€24. *Dinner* €16-€24. **Credit** AmEx, MC, V. **Fusion**
Head chef Andy Tan mixes French and Asian flavours at Vakzuid, with its view over the Olympic Stadium and modish cons making it popular with trendies working nearby.

Vis aan de Schelde
Scheldeplein 4 (675 1583, www.visaandeschelde.nl). Tram 5, 25. **Open** *Lunch* noon-2.30pm Mon-Fri. *Dinner* 5.30-11pm daily. **Main courses** €20-€45. **Credit** AmEx, DC, MC, V. **Seafood**
This eatery out near the RAI convention centre has become a fish temple for the connoisseur. French favourites collide with Thai fish fondue in a menu that travels the waters of the world. *Photo p164.*

DE PIJP

€ Albine
Albert Cuypstraat 69 (675 5135). Tram 16, 24, 25. **Open** 10.30am-10pm Tue-Sun. **Main courses** €5-€14.50. **No credit cards.** **Map** p331 E6 ⑥① **Asian**
One in a whole row of cheap Suri-Chin-Indo spots located in De Pijp, Albine – where a Chinese influence predominates – gets top marks for its lightning service and solid vegetarian or meat meals of roti, rice or noodles.

★ € Bazar
Albert Cuypstraat 182 (675 0544, www.bazar amsterdam.nl). Tram 16, 24, 25. **Open** 11am-midnight Mon-Thur; 11am-1am Fri; 9am-1am Sat; 9am-midnight Sun. **Main courses** *Breakfast/lunch* €4-€10. *Dinner* €8-€15. **Credit** AmEx, DC, MC, V. **Map** p331 F5 ⑥② **North African**
This former church, now an Arabic-kitsch café, is one of the glories of Albert Cuypmarkt. Sticking to

De Taart van m'n Tante. *See p164*.

CONSUME

Vis aan de Scheide. *See p162*.

the winning formula set by its Rotterdam mother-ship, its menu lingers in North Africa.

Burger Meester
Albert Cuypstraat 48 (0900 287 4377 (€0.08/min), www.burgermeester.eu). Tram 16, 24, 25. **Open** noon-11pm daily. **Main courses** €6.50-€8.50. **No credit cards**. **Map** p331 E6 ⑥③ **Burgers**
This designer burger specialist offers a standard choice of beef, lamb, tuna or falafel burgers with toppings such as wild mushrooms, wasabi, grilled peppers or pancetta, as well as changing specials. Spoilt for choice? Opt for the sliders and get three different combinations.
Other locations Elandsgracht 130, Southern Canal Belt; Plantage Kerklaan 37, Oost.

District V
Van der Helstplein 17 (770 0884, www.district5. nl). Tram 3, 25. **Open** 6pm-1am Mon, Wed-Sun. *Kitchen* 6-10.30pm. **Credit** AmEx, MC, V. **Map** p331 F6 ⑥④ **French**
District V not only offers a good and economical daily menu (which draws its inspiration from France), but also sells the locally designed plates, cutlery and tables it's served on. The patio is a lovely spot to sit in summer.

Firma Pekelhaaring
Van Woustraat 127 (679 0460, http://pekel haaring.nl). Tram 16, 24, 25. **Open** 10am-

midnight Mon-Sat. *Kitchen* noon-10pm. **Credit** MC, V. **Map** p331 G5 ⑥⑤ **European**
Meat and fish dominate the menu here – the home-made fennel sausages are divine – although vegetarians will be happy with the creative pasta dishes. Desserts are also exemplary. The whole peach encased in almond cake and served with lavender cream alone would make a trip here worthwhile.

★ Mamouche
Quellijnstraat 104 (673 6361, www.restaurant mamouche.nl). Tram 3, 12, 24, 25. **Open** 6-11pm daily. **Main courses** €14.50-€21.50. **Credit** MC, V. **Map** p331 E5 ⑥⑥ **North African**
In the heart of the multicultural De Pijp, this is a Moroccan restaurant with a difference: it's posh, stylish (in a sexy, minimalist sort of way) and provides groovy background music that can only be described as 'North African lounge'.

Siriphon
1e Jacob van Campenstraat 47 (676 8072). Tram 7, 10. **Open** 4-10pm Mon, Wed-Sun. **Main courses** €10.50-€14. **Credit** MC, V. **Map** p331 E5 ⑥⑦ **Thai**
A small comfortable Thai with a green *kaeng khiaw* curry that's positively to die for, and many other dishes that are worthy of at least a culinary coma.

★ De Taart van m'n Tante
Ferdinand Bolstraat 10 (776 4600, www. detaart.nl). Tram 16, 24, 25. **Open** 10am-6pm daily. **Light meals** €3-€5. **No credit cards**. **Map** p331 E5 ⑥⑧ **Tearoom**
'My Aunt's Cake' started life as a purveyor of over-the-top cakes (which it still makes) before becoming the campest tearoom in town. In a glowing pink space filled with mismatched furniture, it's particularly gay-friendly (note the Tom of Finland cake). A genuine local gem with bags of character. *Photo p163*.

€ Warung Spang-Makandra
Gerard Doustraat 39 (670 5081, www.spang makandra.nl). Tram 7, 10, 16. **Open** 11am-10pm Tue-Sat; 1-10pm Sun. **Main courses** €4.50-€10. **No credit cards**. **Map** p331 E6 ⑥⑨ **Indonesian**
An Indonesian-Surinamese restaurant where the Indonesian influence always comes up trumps with the excellent Javanese *rames*. A relaxed vibe and beautiful dishes encourage long lingering meals.

Yamazato
Okura Hotel, Ferdinand Bolstraat 333 (678 8351, www.yamazato.nl). Tram 12, 25. **Open** *Lunch* noon-2pm daily. *Dinner* 6-9.30pm daily. **Main courses** €25-€68. **Set meals** *Lunch* €50, 5 courses. *Dinner* €62.50-€92.50, 5-8 courses. **Credit** AmEx, DC, MC, V. **Japanese**
If you want class, head out here and surrender to the charming kimono-clad staff, the too-neat-to-eat presentation and the restful views over a fishpond.

Bars

Drink while you think.

Bars come in all shapes and sizes in Amsterdam. From grand cafés to hole-in-the-wall *proeverijen* (tasting houses), the café/bar is central to Dutch life. It acts as home-from-home, off-site office, canteen, debating society and sometimes even nightclub all rolled into one.

The traditional *bruin café* (brown café) is – hurrah! – here to stay, with beer being the main tipple of choice. For something stronger, try *jenever: jong* is like a lighter, more refreshing gin, while *oud* is darker and fuller favoured. Among these no-frills, nicotine-stained boozers, you'll also find speciality wine bars where you can quaff in design-sensitive surrounds, and top-flight cocktails mixed by Holland's finest bartenders. *Proost!*

THE OLD CENTRE
The Old Side

★ De Bekeerde Suster
Kloveniersburgwal 6-8 (423 0112, www.beiaard groep.nl). Tram 4, 9, 14, 16, 24, 25. **Open** 3pm-1am Mon-Thur; noon-2am Fri, Sat; noon-midnight Sun. **Credit** AmEx, DC, MC, V. **Map** p326 D2 ❶
The Amsterdam Steam Beer Brewery has been making beer on-site for more than eight years (though the building's history stretches right back to the Middle Ages, when it was a house for fallen women). A fallen woman these days has most likely over-indulged in the brews. *Photo p167.*
Other locations Spui 30 (622 5110); Marie Heinekenplein 5 (379 0888).
▶ *For a round-up of local breweries, see p169.*

Bubbles & Wines
Nes 37 (422 3318, www.bubblesandwines.com). Tram 4, 9, 14, 16, 24, 25. **Open** 3.30pm-1am Mon-Sat; 2-9pm Sun. **Credit** AmEx, MC, V. **Map** p326 D3 ❷
This long, low-ceilinged room has the feel of a wine cellar, albeit one with mood lighting and banquettes. There are more than 50 wines available by the glass and 180 by the bottle, and accompanying posh nosh (Asetra caviar, truffle cheese, foie gras). Wine flights are also served.

Café Katoen
Oude Turfmarkt 153 (626 2635, www.good foodgroup.nl). Tram 4, 9, 14, 16, 24, 25. **Open** 9am-1am Mon-Thur, Sun; 11am-3am Fri, Sat. **No credit cards. Map** p326 D3 ❸
If shopping on Kalverstraat gets too much, run screaming across Rokin to this oasis of calm on the edge of the Old Centre. It has the stripped-down looks of the 1950s (Formica tables, polished wood), and a decent lunch menu of salads, rolls and wraps. There is no dinner menu but snacks are available.

Freddy's Bar
Nieuwe Doelenstraat 2-14 (531 1777, www.leurope.nl/bars-amsterdam). Tram 4, 9, 16, 24, 25. **Open** 11am-1am daily. **Credit** AmEx, MC, V. **Map** p326 D3 ❹
For details, *see p170* **Profile.**

★ De Jaren
Nieuwe Doelenstraat 20-22 (625 5771, www.cafe-de-jaren.nl). Tram 4, 9, 16, 24, 25. **Open** 9.30am-1am Mon-Thur, Sun; 9.30am-2am Fri, Sat. **Credit** AmEx, DC, MC, V. **Map** p326 D3 ❺
All of Amsterdam – students, tourists, lesbigays, cinemagoers, the fashion pack – comes here for lunch, coffee or something stronger all day long, making it sometimes difficult to bag a seat. Upstairs becomes a restaurant after 5.30pm. Be prepared to fight for a spot on the Amstel-side terrace in summer, with its sweeping views beloved of tourists.

> ❶ Green numbers given in this chapter correspond to the location of each bar on the street maps. *See pp325-332.*

Van Kerkwijk

Nes 41 (620 3316). Tram 4, 9, 14, 16, 24, 25.
Open 11am-1am Mon-Thur, Sun; 11am-3am Fri,
Sat. **No credit cards. Map** p326 D3 ⑥
Far from the bustle of Dam Square, though really
just a few strides away on one of Amsterdam's most
charming streets, Van Kerkwijk is airy by day,
romantic and candlelit by night – and equally good
for group chats or tête-à-têtes. Lunch brings sandwiches and the evening more substantial food,
though the emphasis is as much on genteel drinking.
(Beware the near-vertical stairs leading down to the
bar toilets.)

★ Wynand Fockink

Pijlsteeg 31 (639 2695, www.wynand-fockink.nl).
Tram 4, 9, 14, 16, 24, 25. **Open** 3-9pm daily.
No credit cards. Map p326 D3 ⑦
It's standing room only at this historic tasting house.
Hidden behind the Krasnapolsky hotel, unchanged
since 1679, this has been a meeting place for
Freemasons since the beginning; past visitors
include Churchill and Chagall. The menu of liqueurs
and *jenevers* (many available in take-out bottles)
reads like a list of unwritten novels: Parrot Soup;
The Longer the Better; Rose Without Thorns.

The New Side

Beer Temple

Nieuwezijds Voorburgwal 250 (627 1427). Tram
1, 2, 5, 13, 14, 17. **Open** 4pm-1am Mon-Thur;

De Bekeerde Suster. *See p165.*

4pm-3am Fri, Sat; 2pm-10pm Sun. **Credit** MC V.
Map p326 C3 ⑧
As the name suggests this bar is a place of worship
for serious beer-lovers. With a focus on American
brews, owner Peter van der Arend stocks hard-
to-find, unique beers with15 regular brews and
15 rotating on tap, as well as over 100 bottled varieties. They even have their own special tipple,
Templebier; brewed specifically for the bar.
In addition, there's a food menu and you can surf
the net too.

★ Belgique

Gravenstraat 2 (625 1974, www.cafe-belgique.nl).
Tram 1, 2, 5, 16, 24, 25. **Open** 2pm-1am Mon-
Thur, Sun; 2pm-3am Fri, Sat. **No credit cards.**
Map p326 D2 ⑨
At this goblin's cave hiding behind the palace,
there's barely room for 20 customers, but the atmos-
phere – enhanced by dripping candles – is intimate
rather than cramped and always cheerful.

Café de Dokter

Rozenboomsteeg 4 (626 4427, www.cafe-de-
dokter.nl). Tram 1, 2, 4, 5, 9, 13, 14, 16, 17, 24,
25. **Open** 4pm-1am Tue-Sat. **No credit cards.**
Map p326 D3 ⑩
Definitely the smallest bar in Amsterdam at just a
handful of square metres, the Doctor is also one of
the oldest, dishing out the cure for whatever ails
you since 1798. Centuries of character and all kinds
of gewgaws are packed into the highly compact
space. Whisky figures large (there's a monthly special) and snacks include smoked *osseworst* (cured
sausage) with gherkins.

Café de Koningshut

Spuistraat 269 (624 9998). Tram 1, 2, 5, 13,
17. **Open** 4pm-midnight Mon-Thur, Sun; noon-
2am Fri, Sat. **Credit** AmEx, DC, MC, V. **Map**
p326 D3 ⑪
For details, *see p170* **Profile.**

Café Hoppe

Spui 18-20 (420 4420, www.cafe-hoppe.nl). Tram
1, 2, 5, 16, 24. **Open** 8am-1am Mon-Thur, Sun;
8am-2am Fri, Sat. **Credit** AmEx, DC, MC, V.
Map p326 D4 ⑫
For details, *see p170* **Profile.**

CONSUME

★ Harry's Bar

Spuistraat 285 (624 4384, www.harrysbar amsterdam.com). Tram 1, 2, 5, 13, 14, 17. **Open** 5pm-1am Mon-Thur, Sun; 3pm-3am Fri, Sat. **Credit** MC, V. **Map** p326 D3/4 ⑬
Small, dark and intimate, this is the perfect place to lounge on a leather sofa for a long night of cheerful mixology. There's everything here to suit all kinds of movers and shakers, from Cristal champagne to monumental Montecristo cigars.

THE CANALS
Western Canal Belt

★ 't Arendsnest

Herengracht 90 (421 2057, www.arendsnest.nl). Tram 1, 2, 5, 13, 14. **Open** 4pm-midnight Mon-Thur, Sun; 4pm-2am Fri, Sat. **Credit** MC, V. **Map** p326 C2 ⑭
A temple to the humble hop, the 'Eagle's Nest', in a lovely canal house, sells only Dutch beer. Many of the customers are real-ale types, but even amateurs will enjoy the 350 standard brews and 250 seasonal, from cheeky house ale Herengracht 90 to Texelse Skuumkoppe.

De Twee Zwaantjes

Prinsengracht 114 (625 2729, www.detwee zwaantjes.nl). Tram 1, 2, 5, 13, 14, 17. **Open** 3pm-1am Mon, Thur, Sun; 3pm-3am Fri, Sat. **No credit cards. Map** p326 B3 ⑮
Oom-pah-pah, oom-pah-pah: that's how it goes at this salt-of-the-earth bar. It's relatively quiet during the week, but weekends are real swinging sing-along affairs, with revellers booming out tearjerkers about love, sweat and the Westerkerk. All together now: *'Op de Amster-dam-se grachten…'*

Southern Canal Belt

Café Kale

Weteringschans 267 (622 6363, www.cafekale.nl). Tram 7, 10, 16, 25. **Open** 11am-1am Mon-Thur; 11am-2am Fri, Sat; noon-11pm Sun. **Credit** AmEx, DC, MC, V. **Map** p331 E5 ⑯
If you're burnt out by the Museum District, you can do far worse than recover at this smart locals' café

THE BEST BEER SELECTION

Belgique
For head-splitting Belgian brews. *See p167.*

't Arendsnest
For going Dutch. *See p168.*

Gollem
For everything under one roof. *See p173.*

---

set back from the main road. Although it calls itself a 'real brown bar', styling is colourful and modern. Food is far from old-fashioned, with griddled vegetables and chorizo putting in regular appearances. Rembrandt- and Leidseplein are both within walking distance.

Café Walem

Keizersgracht 449 (625 3544). Tram 1, 2, 5. **Open** 9am-midnight Mon-Thur, Sun; 9am-1am Fri, Sat. **Credit** AmEx, DC, MC, V. **Map** p330 D4 ⑰
One of the city's first designer bars still cuts it after more than 25 years, from the Rietveld-designed exterior to the great international menu that draws folk in for the excellent food as much as for the drinks. The clean lines and flavours attract fashionistas and designer types – plus a good chunk of gays and lesbians – who scope each other on the patio and admire the views.

★ Vyne

Prinsengracht 411 (344 6408, www.vyne. nl). Tram 1, 2, 5, 7, 10, 13, 14, 17. **Open** 6pm-midnight Mon-Thur; 5pm-1am Fri, Sat; 5-10pm Sun. **Credit** AmEx, DC, MC, V. **Map** p330 C4 ⑱
A tasteful – in every sense of the word – bar. The gorgeous, slim-line interior is dominated by an amazing wall of wine, and emphasis is put on pairing drink with good nibbles; for example, Weissburgunder with fine sausage, or smoked eel and Sancerre. It's a streamlined version of sister-restaurant Envy (*see p152*).

Around Leidseplein

Café Eijlders

Korte Leidsedwarsstraat 47 (624 2704, www. eijlders.nl). Tram 1, 2, 5, 7. **Open** noon-1am Mon-Thur, Sun; noon-2am Fri, Sat. **No credit cards. Map** p330 C5 ⑲
Neon tat to one side, trendy Wendys to the other; Eijlders is a cerebral alternative to both. A meeting place for the Resistance during the war, it now has a boho feel, with exhibitions, poetry nights and music – sometimes jazz, sometimes classical. Decor is handsome, with stained glass and dark wood.

★ Kamer 401

Marnixstraat 401 (620 0614, www.kamer 401.nl). Tram 1, 2, 5, 7. **Open** 6pm-1am Wed, Thur; 6pm-3am Fri, Sat. **No credit cards. Map** p330 C5 ⑳
Art students and the terminally hip gather at this red-lacquered temple to pleasure, where there is no food or frippery, just booze and DJ-spun music with a party mood. Nearby Lux (Marnixstraat 403, 422 1412) and Weber (Marnixstraat 397, 622 9910) offer a similar formula and ensure that the party people wear a wavering track between the three.

CONSUME

Brewers' Scoop

The best of the brewhouses.

With Heineken's old brewery now a theme park and Amstel having long since moved elsewhere, the two names most associated with Amsterdam beer aren't made here any more. But the brewers that remain, albeit small by comparison, are well worth seeking out.

A good place to start sampling is the canal-side **De Bekeerde Suster** (*see p165; photo p167*), situated in a building with a long history of beer making. Six brews are produced here, half of them seasonally. The inside of this brewpub, owned by the Amsterdamse Stoombierbrouwerij (Amsterdam Steam Beer Brewery), is lined with shining copper vats and sparkling tubes, part of a brewing system that can create up to 1,000 litres of beer at a time. The truly keen can go for a guided tour to see what all the knobs and levers do while dilettantes sit back amid the beer-related ephemera and sample the house tipples.

Amsterdam's oldest operational brewery, **Brouwerij 't IJ** (*see p171*), opened in 1985, is part of a new wave that has sparked a resurgence in Dutch beer production. Its

output is a drop in the ocean compared to the big boys, but even at 250,000 litres a year, it's by far the largest in the city, with the most widely available product. Those looking to save the planet while punishing their liver could do no better: all ten beers made here are organic. You shouldn't miss the brewery (in fact you can't – the windmill next door gives away its location), as the tasting room is another quirky treat, its tiled walls testament to its past incarnation as a bathhouse. House beers range from a hoppy Plzen to the rich but dangerous IJndejaars, a strong Christmas creation.

Brewery-with-a-conscience **Brouwerij De Prael** is staffed by a dedicated workforce who all have mental disabilities. Its seven beers, all of which are named after famous (all right, some might say tacky) local singers include Mary, a tripel that kicks like a mule at 9.6%, and the lighter Kölsch-style blond Johnny and May bock André. To sample De Prael's beers, head to **'t Arendsnest** (*see p168*) or check out the excellent off-licence **De Bierkoning** (*see p196*) for all these local brews.

Brouwerij 't IJ. *See p171.*

CONSUME

Profile Freddy Heineken

The bon vivant beer magnate's favourite drinking spots.

For Freddy Heineken, life afforded no greater pleasure than watching others enjoy his beer. Especially women. Legend has it that, whenever he overheard a young lady asking for a Heineken at the bar, he'd chime in, 'I'm right here.'

He was a regular at two of Amsterdam's quintessential brown cafés, **Café de Koningshut** (*see p167*) and **Café Hoppe** (*see p167*). He spent so much time in the latter he eventually went ahead and bought it. What appealed to Fred most about this pub is that it catered to everyone from students wanting a cheap *biertje* through tourists enjoying the terrace to 'suits' stopping by after work. Freddy's friend Queen Beatrix has even been known to pop in for a drink. For Freddy, it was the perfect place to mingle with those who made his life's work possible.

But while Mr Heineken may have been touting his beer to the blue-collar everyman, he certainly wasn't one himself. He led a lavish lifestyle, with a St Moritz ski chalet shaped like the Heineken star, counting folk such as Frank Sinatra among his friends and enjoying an extensive art collection.

This jetsetter made sure he had a fitting hangout on home turf, in the imposing form of the Hotel de L'Europe. Still owned by the Heinekens today, the upscale bolt hole not only has a number of Old Master paintings from the family collection, but also features a swanky bar named after the man

himself. When asked about the big guy, the staff of **Freddy's Bar** (*see p165*) smile discreetly, but they don't hesitate to show us Freddy's personal corner table, complete with phone still attached to the wall, as if he might walk in tomorrow. It's a period detail that matches the bar's decor, apparently unchanged since Freddy's heyday in the 1960s and '70s (he died in 2002, aged 78). Staff claim to pour the perfect beer here (Heineken, of course), but they also serve a range of whiskies, which the beer mogul probably had to glug when no one was watching.

CONSUME

INSIDE TRACK MEASURING UP

Draft beer is served in two sizes in the Netherlands: small (a *vaasje*) and miniscule (a *fluitje*), regarded as a 'lady's beer' and no more than a couple of gulps. In true Irish, Antipodean and tourist-oriented bars, you'll be served a half-litre (pint) of beer by default, so order carefully. Specifying 'large' or 'small' is usually enough of an instruction.

Around Rembrandtplein

★ Door 74

Call for location (0877 844 980 mobile; call between 9am and 8pm for reservations; SMS text after 8pm, www.door74.nl). Tram 4, 16, 24, 25. **Open** 8pm-3am Tue-Sun. **Credit** AmEx, MC, V.
'Exclusivity' may be a dirty word in Amsterdam's strenuously egalitarian bar scene, but rather than using inflated prices, long queues or grumpy door-men as its filter, Door 74 employs secrecy – and rewards in-the-know trendies with excellent cocktails mixed by some of the best barmen in the business. This place is one of Amsterdam's hottest drinks commodities. There is a website but it's fair to say that it's as minimalist as they come and definitely not giving anything away.

Onder de Ooievaar

Utrechtsestraat 119 (624 6836, www.onderde ooievaar.nl). Tram 4. **Open** 10am-1am Mon-Thur; 10am-3am Fri, Sat; 10.30am-1am Sun. **No credit cards**. **Map** p331 E4 ㉑
Onder de Ooievaar achieves a great deal by not trying all that hard. What you get is an uncomplicated venue for an evening's carousing among a mixed bunch of trendies, locals and the odd visitor. Highlights include 't IJ beer on tap, the downstairs pool table (which is a genuine rarity in Amsterdam bars) and the lovely Prinsengracht-side terrace for when you fancy an alfresco tipple.

Vooges

Utrechtsestraat 51 (330 5670, www.vooges.nl). Tram 4, 7, 10. **Open** 4pm-midnight Mon-Thur, Sun; 4pm-3am Fri, Sat. **Credit** AmEx, MC, V. **Map** p331 E4 ㉒
A big bow window lets light in to every nook and cranny of this classy, split-level bar. Inside, decor is simple yet self-consciously stylish – a '50s Juliette Greco poster, '70s chairs, '20s chandeliers – rather like Vooges' patrons. The slightly older, moneyed crowd comes for post-work or pre-theatre drinks, food from the mod-European menu, or to while away an evening drinking from the compact, well-priced wine list. There is also a sophisticated seaside version, Vooges Strand, on the beach in Zandvoort.

JODENBUURT, THE PLANTAGE & THE OOST

Amstelhaven

Mauritskade 1 (665 2672, www.amstelhaven.nl). Tram 3 or Metro Weesperplein. **Open** 4pm-1am Thur-Sun. **Credit** AmEx, MC, V. **Map** p331 F4 ㉓
Occupying a prime location on a side-canal of the Amstel, this bar's cavernous interior is usually full of yuppies chowing down posh Dutch food and (at the weekend) grooving to the DJs. But that's not the point. Amstelhaven's raison d'être is summer days spent plopped on the sofas and beanbags set out on the vast deck, watching the boats bob along as staff serve salty dogs in situ.

★ Brouwerij 't IJ

Funenkade 7 (320 1786, www.brouwerijhetij.nl). Tram 10. **Open** 3-8pm daily. **No credit cards**.
The famous tasting house at the base of the Gooyer windmill, where wares from award-winning local brewery 't IJ can be sampled. Inside is bare (still retaining the look of the municipal baths it once was) and seating minimal, so if weather permits, grab a beer and park on the pavement outside. Its standard range includes pale Plzen and darker, stronger Colombus. *Photos p169.*
▶ *For more on local breweries, see p169.*

Café de Sluyswacht

Jodenbreestraat 1 (625 7611, www.sluyswacht.nl). Tram 9, 14 or Metro Waterlooplein. **Open**

Café de Sluyswacht.

11.30am-1am Mon-Thur; 11.30am-3am Fri, Sat; 11.30am-7pm Sun. **Credit** MC, V. **Map** p327 E3 ❷⁴
Listing crazily, this wooden-framed bar has been pleasing drinkers for decades, though the building itself has been around since 1695, when it began life as a lock-keeper's cottage. Suited to both balmy and inclement boozing, Café de Sluyswacht is snug and warm inside, while outside commands great views of Oude Schans. An excellent place for a sneaky sundowner.

Hesp
Weesperzijde 130-131 (665 1202, www.cafe hesp.nl). Tram 12. **Open** 10am-1am Mon-Thur; 10am-2am Fri, Sat; 11am-1am Sun. **Credit** AmEx, DC, MC, V. **Map** p332 H5 ❷⁵
In a nutshell, this is a brown café with knobs on. It has occupied a lovely site on the river near Amstel station for 110 years, and offers all the joys of an old-fashioned boozer, but has moved with the times. The wine list is longer than most bars', the snacks classy and classic (wasabi sits alongside mustard) and entertainment ranges from big bands through Latin to lindy hop. In summer, life-size electric palm trees illuminate the huge terrace on the water.

THE WATERFRONT

Bickers aan de Werf
Bickerswerf 2 (320 2951, www.bickersaande werf.nl). Tram 3. **Open** noon-1am Wed-Fri; 1pm-1am Sat, Sun. **Credit** V. **Map** p325 B1 ❷⁶

Café Soundgarden.

The Western Islands feel like a secluded retreat from the city, and this modern glass cube is great for a break after aimless exploring. Food caters to all pockets, from a slice of cake to caviar, while a cup of coffee here becomes much more of an indulgence when accompanied with a side order of truffles from Jordino. The drinks menu is outstanding: Japanese Iki beer, specialist whiskies and loads of wine by the glass, bottle or half-litre carafe.

THE JORDAAN

★ Café Soundgarden
Marnixstraat 164-166 (620 2853, www.cafe soundgarden.nl). Tram 10, 13, 17. **Open** 3pm-1am Mon-Thur; 3pm-3am Fri-Sun. **No credit cards. Map** p325 B4 ❷⁷
A dirty old rockers' bar where musos, journos and everyone else who refuses to grow up gets smashed in one big, sloppy mêlée. The soundtrack is composed from the entire back catalogue of classic alternative pop, often from DJs and bands, and sometimes accompanied by (inexpert) dancing. Bliss. At the back is a surprisingly restful terrace where boats can moor when it's time for a break from the canal touring. There's also pool, pinball and a good range of beer.

Harlem
Haarlemmerstraat 77 (330 1498). Tram 3 or bus 18, 22. **Open** 10am-1am Mon-Thur; 11am-3am Fri, Sat; 11am-1am Sun. **No credit cards. Map** p325 C2 ❷⁸
Good-looking, very hip bar with friendly staff and a funky soundtrack. The advertised 'soul food' is hit and miss (though it's always filling and reasonable) but drinking is as important here as eating.

Hegeraad
Noordermarkt 34 (624 5565). Tram 1, 2, 5, 13, 17, 20. **Open** 8am-1am Mon-Thur; 8am-3am Fri, Sat; 9am-1am Sun. **No credit cards. Map** p325 B2 ❷⁹
The polar opposite – geographically as well as figuratively – of minimalist Proust (*see below*) and its neighbour, Finch, this gabled building with leaded windows has probably been a café for as long as the Noorderkerk church that it looks on to has been standing.

Papeneiland
Prinsengracht 2 (624 1989, www.papeneiland.nl). Tram 3. **Open** 10am-1am Mon-Thur, Sun; 10am-2am Fri, Sat. **No credit cards. Map** p325 B2 ❸⁰
A wonderful spot for a drink and a chinwag in a beautiful Delft-tiled bar. A definite talking point is the café's fascinating history: apparently, there's a tunnel that runs under the canal that, when Catholicism was outlawed in the 17th century, secretly delivered worshippers to their church opposite, which explains the name: Pope's Island.

THE BEST COCKTAILS

Door 74
For a speakeasy sensation. *See p171.*

Vesper Bar
For trendy tipples. *See below.*

Harry's Bar
For perfect classics. *See p168.*

Proust

*Noordermarkt 4 (623 9145, www.goodfood
group.nl). Tram 1, 2, 5, 13, 17, 20.* **Open** 9am-
1am Mon; 5pm-1am Tue-Fri, Sun; 9am-3am Sat.
Credit AmEx, MC, V. **Map** p325 B2 ③
Still trendy after all these years, and great for a market pit stop or a bar crawl kickstart. Inside is pared
down in style – like the punters. If it's full, try Finch
next door; on warm days, both bars' terraces merge
into one convivial whole to create an atmosphere
that is pure Amsterdam.

★ 't Smalle

*Egelantiersgracht 12 (623 9617). Tram 13, 14,
17, 20.* **Open** 10am-1am Mon-Thur, Sun; 10am-
2am Fri, Sat. **No credit cards. Map** p325 B3 ③
This is one of the most scenic terraces on one of the
prettiest canals, so it's no surprise that waterside seats
are snared early in the day – patience is essential.
Inside it's extremely cute, too, with gleaming brass
fixtures harking back to the heady drinking days of
the 18th century, when it was the Hoppe distillery.

★ Vesper Bar

*Vinkenstraat 57 (846 4458, www.vesperbar.nl).
Bus 18, 22.* **Open** 5pm-1am Tue-Thur; 4pm-3am
Fri, Sat. **Credit** MC, V. **Map** p325 B2 ③
You know you're in the hands of a good bartender
when, instead of offering you a menu, he simply
asks, 'What do you feel like?' Vesper's talented team
serves up old-fashioned classics, modern interpretations or anything you fancy in classy and charming
surroundings. Wine and beer take a back seat to the
hard stuff here, but, like everything at this intimate
bar, both are sourced from small-scale, carefully
selected producers.

THE MUSEUM QUARTER, VONDELPARK & THE SOUTH

Café Wildschut

*Roelof Hartplein 1-3 (676 8220, www.goodfood
group.nl). Tram 3, 5, 12, 24.* **Open** 9am-1am
Mon-Thur; 10am-2am Fri, Sat; 10am-midnight
Sun. **Credit** AmEx, DC, MC, V. **Map** p330 D7 ③
A stunning example of Amsterdam School architecture, this elegant semi-circular place puts the 'grand'
into grand café and drips with nouveau detail. Drink

and food choices mirror the upmarket surroundings,
as does the clientele, which includes flush locals,
loud yuppies and art-weary tourists in desperate
need of refuelling.

Caffe Oslo

*Sloterkade 1a (669 9663, www.caffeoslo.nl). Tram
1.* **Open** 9am-1am Mon-Thur, Sun; 9am-3am Fri,
Sat. **Credit** AmEx, MC, V.
So slick a bar comes as a surprise plonked canal-side
in an unremarkable residential area not far from the
Vondelpark. Inside it's all blond wood, cool, creamy
colours and a beautiful crazy-paving floor. Punters
are slightly older, style-hungry locals who come for
breakfast and stay late for the fashionable menu and
inimitable laid-back atmosphere.

DE PIJP

★ Gollem

*Daniel Stalpertstraat 74 (676 7117, www.cafe
gollem.nl). Tram 16, 24, 25.* **Open** 4pm-1am Mon-
Thur, Sun; 2pm-2am Fri, Sat. **No credit cards.
Map** p331 E6 ③
A simply outstanding place to get sozzled, this dark
and cosy Belgian beer specialist offers more than
150 bottled brews – including 42 abbey beers and 14
trappist – and 14 on tap, from easy drinkers to
demonic head-pounders such as Delirium Tremens.
The helpful menu lists the strengths of the suds for
those erring on the side of caution. There are also
branches at Raamsteeg 4, on the New Side, and at
Overtoom 160-162.

Kingfisher

*Ferdinand Bolstraat 24 (671 2395). Tram 16, 24,
25.* **Open** 11pm-1am Mon-Thur; 11pm-3am Fri,
Sat; noon-1am Sun. **No credit cards. Map** p331
E6 ③
The bar that began the gentrification of De Pijp is
now one of the old guard, but its sleek-with-a-twist-
of-kitsch chic (glossy red walls, American fridges)
still sets the agenda for other young pretenders in
the area, as does its loungey feel, cocktails and
world-fusion snacks menu. The hip clientele has
aged gracefully along with the watering hole, but
makes room for a dash of new blood.

Wijnbar Boelen & Boelen

*1e Van der Helststraat 50 (671 2242, www.
wijnbar.nl). Tram 3, 4, 16, 24, 25.* **Open**
6pm-midnight Tue-Thur, Sun; 6pm-1am Fri,
Sat. **Credit** MC, V. **Map** p331 E6 ③
Many people come here for the Frenchified food but,
as the name implies, the wine is the star at this compact yet airy boozer on the edge of De Pijp's main
nightlife strip. Dozens are available by the glass,
more by the bottle, and prices range from pocket-
friendly to splurge. The emphasis is on Old World,
but there are good selections from the Antipodes and
the Americas.

Coffeeshops

Welcome to the world capital of high culture.

If every drug were removed from the planet, humans would probably grab the nearest hard object and bang themselves on the head to escape reality. Drug wars are seldom won, something the Dutch acknowledged in 1976 when they decriminalised marijuana and hash.

Since then, the laws on cannabis have always been fuzzy, and it has never technically been legal. As for over-the-counter sales, coffeeshops weren't legalised until 1980. Coffeeshops are under continual watch and must regularly dance with the law. They can legally sell to you, but cannot buy from growers – legislators assume ganja magically appears in the storeroom. But fret not: Mary Jane has had a rough ride since the beginning, yet she still enjoys more freedom here than just about anywhere else.

THE COFFEESHOP SCENE

In terms of ambience, every establishment is different. Some offer amazing food, others great couches. Some have a terrible atmosphere but the best hash in town. Others have it all. The following list is our guideline for what a great coffeeshop can be. With roughly 250 in town, you could easily stumble across your own personal favourite just around the next corner.

Coffeeshops are banned from advertising; so many websites listed below do not reveal exact addresses or are 'fan sites'. Thus information is not always strictly accurate, and operational telephone numbers are few and far between.

Since 2007, alcohol has been prohibited in coffeeshops. Since July 2008, it has been illegal to smoke tobacco in a working environment – including, perversely, coffeeshops. You can still smoke 'pure' weed, and many shops have sealed smoking rooms for tobacco. In November 2010, a loophole was written into the ban, exempting owner-operated bars and coffeeshops no larger than 70 square metres (753.5 square feet) with no additional employees. Complicated. A sign in the window should indicate either way, but be cautious and ask before lighting up.

> ⓘ Yellow numbers in this chapter show the location of each coffeeshop as marked on the street maps. *See pp325-332.*

THE OLD CENTRE
Old Side

★ Basjoe
Kloveniersburgwal 62 (627 3858, http://basjoe.com). Metro Nieuwmarkt.
Open 10am-1am daily. **No credit cards.**
Map p326 D3 ①
The canal view alone places Basjoe among our favourite coffeeshops in Amsterdam. The amiable owner, James, greets his visitors with a handshake and manages to remember faces despite being the highest person in the room. Candlelit, with a plain decor of soft vinyl terracotta booths, cream walls and wooden tables, it's all about the weed here – but the coffee is also outstanding.

Greenhouse
Oudezijds Voorburgwal 191 (627 1739). Tram 4, 9, 16, 24, 25. **Open** 9am-1am daily. **No credit cards. Map** p326 D3 ②
This legendary coffeeshop tenders highly potent weed with some fairly strong prices to match. It's won the High Times Cannabis Cup (*see p214*) more than 30 times and, with the Grand Hotel next door, occasional celebrities stop by to get hammered. The vibe inside has grown quite commercial, but it's still worth a peek, if only to see the beautifully handmade interior with sunken floors, mosaic stones and blown-glass lamps.
Other locations Waterlooplein 345, Jodenbuurt; Tolstraat 91, De Pijp.

CONSUME

Hill Street Blues
Nieuwmarkt 14 (427 7878). Metro Nieuwmarkt.
Open 9am-1am daily. **No credit cards. Map**
p326 D2 ❸
With comfortable couches and natural lighting, this
cosy corner shop is ideal for a mellow high.
Delectable milkshakes, smoothies and space cook-
ies are also worth indulging in. But if harder and
louder is more to your liking, head to the sister shop
on De Wallen's Warmoesstraat 52, where the walls
and furniture are covered in barely decipherable
graffiti. The basement has pool tables and arcade
games, and with a police station next door, you can
savour a legal toke right next door to the law. A
favourite of Irvine Welsh.
Other locations Warmoesstraat 52, De Wallen.

New Side

Abraxas
Jonge Roelensteeg 12-14 (625 5763,
www.abraxas.tv). Tram 4, 9, 14, 16, 24, 25.
Open 10am-1am daily. **No credit cards.**
Map p326 D3 ❹
Down a narrow alley, this lively shop is a tourist
hotspot. The staff are friendly, internet is free and
chessboards are plentiful – as are the separate rooms
connected by spiral staircases. It also has a healthy-
sized drug menu, including half a dozen bio weeds
and spacecakes.

★ De Dampkring
Handboogstraat 29 (638 0705). Tram 1, 2,
5. **Open** 10am-1am Mon-Thur; 10am-2am Fri,
Sat; 11am-1am Sun. **No credit cards. Map**
p330 D4 ❺

Known for its unforgettable (even by stoner standards) interior, the visual experience acquired from
Dampkring's decor could make a mushroom trip
look grey. Moulded walls and sculpted ceilings are
painted deep auburn and laced with caramel-
coloured wooden panelling, making a perfect loca
tion for the movie *Ocean's 12.*
▶ *Visit De Dampkring's smaller sister,*
Tweede Kamer (see p177), for a cosy toke
and special spacecakes.

Dutch Flowers
Singel 387 (624 7624). Tram 1, 2, 5. **Open**
11am-11pm Mon; 10am-11pm Tue-Thur, Sun;
10am-2pm Fri, Sat. **No credit cards. Map**
p330 D4 ❻
Squeezed on a little corner near the copious book and
art sales on the Spui, this small shop has its decor
slightly askew – even the CD rack. It's known for
exceptional, high-grade hash, including pre-rolled
joints. The large window up front offers a truly beautiful view of city life on an old sloping street.

CONSUME

De Dampkring.

Grey Area. *See p177.*

▶ *Real Dutch flowers can be found at the Bloemenmarkt (see p200) – a kaleidoscope of an experience for stoned eyes.*

Homegrown Fantasy
Nieuwezijds Voorburgwal 87a (627 5683, www.homegrownfantasy.com). Tram 1, 2, 5, 13, 17, 20. **Open** 10am-midnight Mon-Thur, Sun; 10am-1am Fri, Sat. **No credit cards. Map** p326 C2 ➐
This brightly lit shop has an ever-changing line-up of artwork, tables with chessboards and a UV light in the toilet that makes your pee a trippy colour. The ganja's all organic and Dutch-grown, including its famous Cheese weed, and the (non-alcoholic) drink selection is vast. Glass bongs and a vaporiser are available.

★ Tweede Kamer
Heisteeg 6 (422 2236). Tram 1, 2, 5. **Open** 10am-1am Mon Thur, Sun, 10am-2am Fri, Sat. **No credit cards. Map** p330 D4 ➑
Small and intimate, this sister shop of De Dampkring (*see p175*) embodies the refined look and feel of old-jazz sophistication. Aided by a bakery around the corner, the spacecakes are sweet and lovely. The hash is highly regarded, but seating is extremely limited (it's really rather tiny inside), and the place is notorious for getting very crowded at peak times. If there's no room, walk 12 steps to Dutch Flowers (*see p175*).

THE CANALS
Western Canal Belt

★ Amnesia
Herengracht 133 (no phone). Tram 13, 14, 17. **Open** 9.30am-1am daily. **No credit cards. Map** p326 C2 ➒
You have to wonder at the choice of name but Amnesia is a shop with swank decor, comfortable cushions and deep red walls. Located off the main tourist routes, it's often cool and quiet – though it occasionally fills up with locals. The pre-rolled joints are strong and smokeable. Summertime brings outdoor seating on the large, quiet canal street.

★ Barney's
Haarlemmerstraat 102 (625 9761, www.barneys.biz). Bus 18, 21, 22. **Open** 7am-1am daily. **No credit cards. Map** p326 C2 ➓
Renovated with some lovely old-fashioned apothecary paraphernalia, media screens showing specially filmed information videos and a vaporiser on every table, Barney's serves excellent organic bud worthy of the multiple High Times Cannabis Cup awards bestowed on it. If you're hungry, head a few doors down to Barney's Farm at no.98, which has a truly awesome kitchen. Alcohol is sold there, and you're even welcome to bring your ganja.

Siberië
Brouwersgracht 11 (no phone, www.coffeshop siberie.nl). Tram 1, 2, 4, 5, 13, 17. **Open** 11am-11pm Mon-Thur, Sun; 11am-midnight Fri, Sat. **No credit cards. Map** p326 C2 ⓫
Friendly and mellow, Siberië has internet access and plenty of board games, making it a cool place to while away any rainy day with great coffee or one of its 40 different loose teas (no nasty bags on a string here). The same owners run De Supermarkt (Frederik Hendrikstraat 69, www.coffeeshopdesupermarkt.nl) and well-established neighbourhood coffeeshop De Republiek (2e Nassaustraat 1a, www.coffeeshopderepubliek.nl), both west of the Jordaan.

La Tertulia
Prinsengracht 312 (623 8503, www.coffeeshopamsterdam.com). Tram 7, 10. **Open** 11am-7pm Tue-Sat. **No credit cards. Map** p330 C4 ⓬
This mellow mother-and-daughter-run joint is decorated with plenty of plants, a little waterfall and lots of sunlight, which balances harmoniously with the all-bio buds and scrumptious weed brownies. Two floors provide space for relaxation, quiet reading or gazing at the canal. Look for the seriously stoned Van Gogh painted outside.
▶ *For an eyeful of real-deal Van Gogh, visit the Van Gogh Museum; see p109.*

Southern Canal Belt

★ De Rokerij
Lange Leidsedwarsstraat 41 (622 9442, www.rokerij.net). Tram 1, 2, 5. **Open** 10am-1am daily. **No credit cards. Map** p330 D5 ⓭
A marvellous discovery on an otherwise touristy street by Leidseplein, De Rokerij is an Aladdin's cave. Lit by wall-mounted candles and beautiful metal lanterns, it's decorated with colourful Indian art and a variety of seating (ranging from mats on the floor to decorative 'thrones') – all of which is highly appealing to those feeling the effects. It gets very busy in the evening and on weekends.
Other locations Amstel 8, Old Centre: Old Side; Singel 8, Western Canal Belt; Elandsgracht 53, Southern Canal Belt.

THE JORDAAN

★ Grey Area
Oude Leliestraat 2 (420 4301, www.greyarea.nl). Tram 1, 2, 5, 13, 14, 17. **Open** noon-8pm daily. **No credit cards. Map** p326 C3 ⓮
Run by two blokes living the modern American dream: get the f*@k out of America. They did so by opening this tiny coffeeshop, which offers a selection of quality exclusive strains (try the 4077 or Grey Mist Crystals). Also available are large glass bongs, a Valcano vaporiser and free refills of organic coffee. The owners are highly affable and

Hash Marihuana & Hemp Museum. *See p88.*

often more baked than the patrons: sometimes they stay in bed and miss the noon opening.

Paradox
1e Bloemdwarsstraat 2 (623 5639, www.paradox coffeeshop.com). Tram 10, 13, 14, 17. **Open** 10am-8pm daily. **No credit cards. Map** p325 B3 ⑮

One of the most easygoing coffeeshops around. This down-to-earth joint, with its understated decor and bare wooden tables, feels like a friendly corner café – with the kitchen to match. Substantial foodstuffs include sandwiches, soups, burgers and shakes. A note to late risers: the kitchen closes at 3pm.

★ Sanementereng
2e Laurierdwarsstraat 44 (624 1907). Tram 10, 13, 14, 17. **Open** 11am-1am daily. **No credit cards. Map** p326 C3 ⑯

The only coffeeshop that looks like it's run by a hippie stoner (which it is). It's jammed full of knick-knacks and antiques, all for sale: old kitchenware,

---

INSIDE TRACK HIGH TEA

To save your lungs, consider a spacecake (only available legally from Amsterdam coffeeshops). However, we should advise you to avoid the temptation to eat a whole one first time round. They're as strong as they are delicious, so make sure you're free for the next five hours…

---

vintage lamps, little tables, and even fossils. Sit among the bric-a-brac and smoke the modest weed. Simply a must-see for its uniqueness, the building remains standing thanks to four large tree trunks leaning against the façade.

THE MUSEUM QUARTER, VONDELPARK & THE SOUTH

Kashmir Lounge
Jan Pieter Heijestraat 85-87 (no phone, www. kashmirlounge.com). Tram 1, 7, 11, 17. **Open** 10am-1am Mon-Thur; 10am-3am Fri, Sat; 11am-1am Sun. **No credit cards. Map** p329 A6 ⑰

Lit with little beyond candlelight, Kashmir may seem too dark at first, but once your eyes adjust, it's an opulent cavern of Indian tapestries, ornate tiles, hand-carved walls and cushions swathed in zebra and cheetah prints. With a multitude of obscure corners and enclosed tables, you can feel VIP at no extra charge. Kashmir is also located outside the centre, so prices remain unusually low.

Tweedy
Vondelstraat 104 (618 0344). Tram 1, 2, 3, 5, 12. **Open** 11am-11pm daily. **No credit cards. Map** p330 C6 ⑱

The relocated interior of a Dutch commuter train, circa 1970, is sprawled throughout the shop with fat red vinyl booths, overhead luggage racks, and train tables dotted here and there. Expect prices to slightly outweigh the quality, but the convenience of being able to have a toke just after services at the Vondelkerk next door may be well worth it.

Pot Protocol

The where, the when and the how.

For many, stepping into their first coffeeshop is a moment of lost virginity: the initial encounter might be awkward, but it feels great once you get there. Whether you're new to the smoke or an old-time pro, arriving well versed in coffeeshop etiquette can certainly smooth things out.

When you first walk in, ask to see a menu: it will list the available drugs and their prices, and staff can explain the effects of each. You're welcome to see and smell selections before you buy, though lengthy browsing is discouraged in busier shops. Prices vary: expect to pay around €8 for a gram of decent bud or hash, and more for better quality.

Hash is typically named after its country of origin (Moroccan, Afghan, Lebanese), whereas cannabis usually bears invented names loosely referring to an element of the strain (White Widow, Super Skunk, Silver Haze). These are mostly genetic hybrids developed over the years for supreme effect. Previously, the big rage was for extremely potent weed grown hydroponically under indoor lights. This

is still available, but avoid it if you prefer remaining conscious while getting high. Organic herb is surging in popularity. Various coffeeshops carry a good bio selection; some sell nothing but.

Many coffeeshops also offer bongs, pipes and even vaporisers for use. But if you want to blend in with the locals, roll a (tobacco-free) joint. All shops provide free rolling papers and tips. If you lack the skills, pre-rolled joints are always available, but usually contain low-grade ingredients (though a few shops pride themselves on excellent pre-rolls).

Two numbers can help you through the labyrinth of Dutch cannabis laws: five and 30. You can purchase up to five grams per shop, and you may carry up to 30 grams. Walking outside with all those 30 grams rolled into one smouldering joint hanging from your lips, however, is ill-advised. You could be fined and you'll almost certainly be very ill. Generally, it's considered polite not to toke outside a coffeeshop (some pubs and clubs will allow it, but always ask before lighting up).

CONSUME

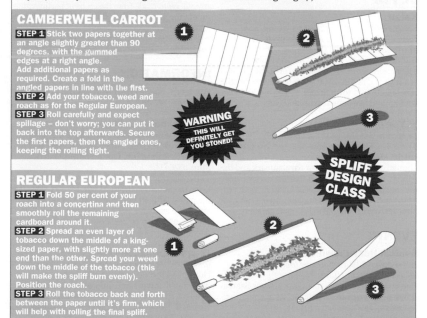

CAMBERWELL CARROT

STEP 1 Stick two papers together at an angle slightly greater than 90 degrees, with the gummed edges at a right angle. Add additional papers as required. Create a fold in the angled papers in line with the first.
STEP 2 Add your tobacco, weed and roach as for the Regular European.
STEP 3 Roll carefully and expect spillage – don't worry; you can put it back into the top afterwards. Secure the first papers, then the angled ones, keeping the rolling tight.

WARNING
THIS WILL DEFINITELY GET YOU STONED!

SPLIFF DESIGN CLASS

REGULAR EUROPEAN

STEP 1 Fold 50 per cent of your roach into a concertina and then smoothly roll the remaining cardboard around it.
STEP 2 Spread an even layer of tobacco down the middle of a king-sized paper, with slightly more at one end than the other. Spread your weed down the middle of the tobacco (this will make the spliff burn evenly). Position the roach.
STEP 3 Roll the tobacco back and forth between the paper until it's firm, which will help with rolling the final spliff.

CONSUME

Cannabis College.

DE PIJP

Katsu

*Eerste van der Helststraat 70 (no phone, www.
katsu.nl). Tram 3, 16, 24, 25.* **No credit cards.**
Map p331 E6 ⑲

A little treasure in De Pijp. This small place packs
a giant selection of various strains of hash and weed
at a wide and fair range of prices. Quite possibly the
best selection in town. Inside is pleasantly green,
with natural live potted plants and older locals.

★ Yo-Yo

*2e Jan van der Heijdenstraat 79 (664 7173).
Tram 3, 4.* **Open** noon-7pm Mon-Sat. **No credit
cards.** **Map** p331 F5 ⑳

Located on a leafy street near Sarphatipark and the
Albert Cuypmarkt (*see p182*), this relaxed spot lacks
the commercialism and crowds found in more central shops. The herb is all-organic and it's run by a
pleasant woman who bakes hot apple pie every day.

EVENTS

Saarein Homegrown Contest

*Elandsstraat 119, the Jordaan (623 4901,
no website). Tram 10, 13, 14, 17.*

One of very few decent lesbian bars in town, Saarein
II (*see p248*) organises a popular home-grown contest every December. On a Friday, usually the second Friday of December, Saarein converts its

smoking room into a pot den where the tokers pass
around joints made from the crops of participating
small-time growers. They then mark favourites on
a small piece of paper.

▶ *For marijuana marking on a grander scale, look
up the High Times Cannabis Cup; see p214.*

INFORMATION

For details on the **Hash Marihuana & Hemp
Museum**, *see p88*.

FREE Cannabis College

*Oudezijds Achterburgwal 124 (423 4420, www.
cannabiscollege.com). Tram 4, 9, 14, 16, 24, 25
or Metro Nieuwmarkt.* **Open** 11am-7pm daily.
Map p326 D3.

The college, occupying two floors in a 17th-century
listed monument in the Red Light District, provides
the public with an impressive array of information
about the cannabis plant (including its medicinal
uses). Admission is free; however, staff request a
donation for a look at the indoor garden.

Drugs Information Line

0900 1995 (€0.10/min). **Open** 1-9pm Mon-Fri;
Dutch recorded message at other times.

A national advice and information line for the
Trimbos Institute (Netherlands Institute of Mental
Health & Addiction). To the relief of drug-addled
tourists, the operators speak excellent English.

Shops & Services

Cutting-edge fashion, fabulous flea markets and plenty more besides.

The beauty of this burg is that, with unique boutiques, eateries, coffeeshops and galleries in most neighbourhoods, there's no need for any ugly scenes over how the day gets spent. Your comrades can do what they need to do, while you start waving the plastic about.

Ramble through the 'Nine Streets', packed to the gills with upmarket boutiques; delve into the Jordaan's many dinky and quirky merchants; or tackle the ritzy glam of PC Hooftstraat, the place you're most likely to rub shoulder pads with a native celebrity in the process of re-wardrobing. Wherever you set foot, you are assured retail treasures of every stripe. For more on shopping areas, *see p195* **Where to Spend It**.

General

DEPARTMENT STORES

★ De Bijenkorf
Dam 1, Old Centre: New Side (0900 0919 (€0.15/min), www.bijenkorf.nl). Tram 1, 2, 4, 5, 9, 13, 14, 16, 17, 24, 25. **Open** 11am-7pm Mon; 10am-7pm Tue, Wed; 10am-9pm Thur, Fri; 9.30am-7pm Sat; 11am-7pm Sun. **Credit** AmEx, DC, MC, V. **Map** p326 D3.
Translated, 'De Bijenkorf' means 'the Beehive' – an apt moniker for this busy department store. Stationed in a grandiose building on Dam Square, this luxe temple to consumerism is arguably on a par with London's Harrods and Berlin's KaDeWe.

Metz & Co
Leidsestraat 34-36, Southern Canal Belt (520 7020, www.metzenco.nl). Tram 1, 2, 5. **Open** 11am-6pm Mon; 9.30am-6pm Tue-Sat; noon-5pm Sun. **Credit** AmEx, DC, MC, V. **Map** p330 D4.
Metz is bang on for upmarket gifts: designer furniture, glass and opulent accessories are all available. For lunch with a view, make for the top-floor restaurant designed by Gerrit Rietveld.

V&D
Kalverstraat 212-220, Old Centre: New Side (622 0171, www.vd.nl). Tram 4, 9, 14, 16, 24, 25. **Open** 11am-6.30pm Mon; 10am-6.30pm Tue-Wed; 10am-9pm Thur; 10am-6.30pm Fri, Sat; noon-6.30pm Sun. **Credit** AmEx, MC, V. **Map** p326 D3.

V&D (short for Vroom & Dreesmann) mirrors the Dutch attitude: unpretentious and to the point. A national stalwart, this affordable chain store offers a little bit of something for everyone, be it a €35 frock or a €2 spatula. Its usually heaving La Place restaurant serves up a whole range of organic treats.

MARKETS

Albert Cuypmarkt
Albert Cuypstraat, De Pijp. Tram 4, 16, 24, 25. **Open** 9am-6pm Mon-Sat. **No credit cards**. **Map** p331 E5.
Amsterdam's largest general market sells everything from pillows to prawns at great prices. The clothes on sale tend to be run-of-the-mill cheapies.
► *For more, see p127* **Profile**.

Dappermarkt
Dapperstraat, Oost. Tram 3, 10, 14. **Open** 9am-6pm Mon-Sat. **No credit cards**. **Map** p332 H3.

**INSIDE TRACK
LATE NIGHT SHOPPING**

Amsterdam's big shopping night is Thursday, when all retailers, big and small, open their doors until 9pm. Whether it's a small boutique in the Nine Streets or the monolithic H&M on Dam Square, your plastic will be welcomed well into the darker hours.

CONSUME

Dappermarkt is a locals' market: prices don't rise to match the number of visitors. It sells all the usual market fodder, and plenty of cheap clothes. *Photo p185.*

★ Noordermarkt
Noordermarkt, the Jordaan. Tram 3, 10 or bus 18, 21. **Open** 7.30am-1pm Mon. **No credit cards. Map** p326 B2.
North of Westermarkt, Noordermarkt is frequented by the serious shopper. The huge stacks of (mainly second-hand) clothes, shoes, jewellery and hats need to be sorted with a grim determination, but there are real bargains to be had. Arrive early or the best stuff will probably have been nabbed.
▶ *Check out the organic farmers' market here on Saturdays; see p198.*

Waterlooplein
Waterlooplein, Jodenbuurt. Tram 9, 14 or Metro Waterlooplein. **Open** 9am-5pm Mon-Sat. **No credit cards. Map** p327 E3.
Amsterdam's top tourist market is basically a huge flea market with the added attraction of loads of new clothes stalls (though gear can be a bit pricey and, at many stalls, a bit naff). Bargains can be found, but they may be hidden under piles of cheap 'n' nasty toasters and down-at-heel (literally) shoes.

Westermarkt
Westerstraat, the Jordaan. Tram 3, 10 or bus 18, 21. **Open** 9am-1pm Mon. **No credit cards. Map** p326 B2.
A Monday market selling all sorts of stuff. The people packing the pavement are proof of the reasonable prices and range of goods, including new watches, pretty (and not so pretty) fabrics and cheap clothes.
▶ *Don't forget to visit the neighbouring (mainly second-hand) Noordermarkt; see above.*

Specialist

BOOKS & MAGAZINES
The best of Dutch literature is celebrated during **Boekenweek** (Book Week) in the third week of March, while the second week of

---

INSIDE TRACK FREE AND EASY

Waterlooplein Market (*see p182*) is a great hunting ground for free trinkets. Head there after 6pm, and usually there are a number of vendors giving away things that didn't sell that day. Expect retro chairs in need of some TLC, scratched vinyl and bizarre porcelain ornaments that are often missing a limb or two.

October sees the focus turn to children's books for the **Kinderboekenweek** (Children's Book Week). For more on Amsterdam's book markets, *see p185.*

General

★ American Book Center
Spui 12, Old Centre: New Side (625 5537, www.abc.nl). Tram 1, 2, 4, 5, 9, 14, 16, 24, 25. **Open** 10am-8pm Mon-Wed, Fri, Sat; 10am-9pm Thur; 11am-6.30pm Sun. **Credit** AmEx, DC, MC, V. **Map** p326 D3.
An Amsterdam institution since 1972, the American Book Center sells English-language books and magazines from the US and UK.

Athenaeum Nieuwscentrum
Spui 14-16, Old Centre: New Side (514 1460 bookshop, 514 1470 news centre, www.athenaeum.nl). Tram 1, 2, 4, 5, 9, 14, 16, 24, 25. **Open** *Bookshop* 11am-6pm Mon; 9.30am-6pm Tue, Wed, Fri, Sat; 9.30am-9pm Thur; noon-5.30pm Sun. *News centre* 8am-8pm Mon-Wed, Fri, Sat; 8am-9pm Thur; 10am-6pm Sun. **Credit** AmEx, MC, V. **Map** p330 D4.
The Athenaeum Nieuwscentrum, as its name might suggest, stocks newspapers from all over the world, as well as a wide choice of magazines, periodicals and tomes in many languages.

Book Exchange
Kloveniersburgwal 58, Old Centre: Old Side (626 6266). Tram 4, 9, 14, 16, 24, 25 or Metro Nieuwmarkt. **Open** 10am-6pm Mon-Fri; 10am-6pm Sat; 11.30am-4pm Sun. **Credit** AmEx, MC, V. **Map** p326 D3.
The owner of this bibliophiles' treasure trove is a shrewd buyer who's willing to do trade deals. Choose from a plethora of second-hand English and American titles (mainly paperbacks), and the biggest science fiction collection in the city.

Waterstone's
Kalverstraat 152, Old Centre: New Side (638 3821, www.waterstones.co.uk). Tram 1, 2, 4, 5, 9, 14, 16, 24, 25. **Open** 10am-6pm Mon; 9.30am-7pm Tue, Wed, Fri; 9.30am-9pm Thur; 10am-6.30pm Sat; 11am-6pm Sun. **Credit** AmEx, MC, V. **Map** p326 D3.
Thousands of books – mainstream and literary – plus newspapers, magazines, audio books, games and DVDs, all in English. The large children's section is delightful.
▶ *For details of book readings for kids, see p218.*

Markets

Head for the year-round book stalls on Spui (9am-6pm Fri) and Oudemanhuispoort (*see p185*), but don't miss out on the four temporary

CONSUME

Athenaeum Nieuwscentrum.

Dappermarkt. *See p181.*

markets in summer. Two of them sit along the Amstel, behind Waterlooplein (art, mid June; religion, mid Aug), and two emerge on Dam (children's, mid May; mysteries, mid July).

Specialist

Architectura & Natura

Leliegracht 22, Western Canal Belt (623 6186, www.architectura.nl). Tram 13, 14, 17. **Open** noon-6pm Mon; 10am-6pm Tue, Sat; 9am-6.30pm Wed-Fri. **Credit** AmEx, MC, V. **Map** p326 C3.

The stock at 'Architecture and Nature', which includes many works in English for monoglots, is exactly what you'd expect from its name: books on architectural history, landscape architecture, plant life, gardens and animal studies. Leliegracht 22 is also home to Antiquariaat Opbouw, which deals in antiquarian books covering architecture and associated topics.

★ Honk Lee

Zeedijk 136, Old Centre: Old Side (421 3688, www.comics.nl). Tram 4, 9, 16, 24, 25 or Metro Nieuwmarkt. **Open** 11am-7pm Mon-Sat; noon-6pm Sun. **Credit** AmEx, DC, MC, V. **Map** p326 D2.

Specialising in American comics and manga, this cosy store usually gets the latest issues as soon as the US does because it does the importing itself. The good stuff arrives on Wednesdays, and that's when

the place turns into an aficionado hangout. Check the website for all the latest news.

Lambiek

Kerkstraat 132, Southern Canal Belt (626 7543, www.lambiek.nl). Tram 4, 16, 24, 25. **Open** 11am-6pm Mon-Fri; 11am-5pm Sat, 1-5pm Sun. **Credit** AmEx, MC, V. **Map** p330 D4.

Lambiek, founded in 1968, claims to be the world's oldest comic shop and has thousands of books from around the world; its on-site cartoonists' gallery hosts regular exhibitions.

Pied-à-Terre

Overtoom 135-137, Museum Quarter (627 4455, www.piedaterre.nl). Tram 1, 3, 12. **Open** 1-6pm Mon; 10am-6pm Tue-Wed, Fri; 10am-9pm Thur; 10am-5pm Sat. **Credit** MC, V. **Map** p330 D4.

Brimming with travel books, international guides and more than 65,000 maps, this place is an absolute must-visit for adventurous types embarking on a trip out of town.

► *If you're thinking of venturing out of town, browse our Escapes & Excursions chapter for inspiration; see pp282-302.*

Used & antiquarian

Oudemanhuis Book Market

Oudemanhuispoort, Old Centre: Old Side. Tram 4, 9, 14, 16, 24, 25. **Open** 10am-4pm Mon-Fri. **No credit cards**. **Map** p326 D3.

People have been buying and selling books, prints and sheet music here since the 18th century.

CHILDREN
Fashion

Funky vintage clothes for kids can be found at **Noordermarkt** (*see p182*); and for plenty of budget garments, try **Albert Cuypmarkt** (*see p181*).

★ Broer & Zus
Rozengracht 104, the Jordaan (772 4229, www.broerenzus.nl). Tram 13, 14, 17. **Open** noon-6pm Mon; 10.30am-6pm Tue-Fri; 10am-6pm Sat. **Credit** AmEx, MC, V. **Map** p325 B3.
Broer & Zus makes gift-giving a cinch with its hand-made toys, adorable T-shirts with goofy slogans and a selection of seriously stylish kit.

Geboortewinkel Amsterdam
Bosboom Toussaintstraat 22-24, Museum Quarter (683 1806, www.geboortewinkel.nl). Tram 3, 7, 10, 12. **Open** 1-6pm Mon; 10am-6pm Tue-Fri; 10am-5pm Sat. **Credit** MC, V. **Map** p330 C5.
A beautiful range of maternity and baby clothes (including premature sizes) in cotton, wool and linen. You'll also find cotton nappies, plus various child-birth DVDs for those still anticipating the big event.

't Klompenhuisje
Nieuwe Hoogstraat 9A, Old Centre: Old Side (622 8100, www.klompenhuisje.nl). Tram 4, 9, 16, 24, 25 or Metro Nieuwmarkt. **Open** 10am-6pm Mon-Sat. **Credit** AmEx, DC, MC, V. **Map** p327 E3.
For delightfully crafted and reasonably priced shoes, traditional clogs and handmade leather and woollen slippers from baby sizes up to size 35, 't Klompenhuisje is the perfect place for turning kids into pint-sized Dutchies for the day.

Toys & games

Joe's Vliegerwinkel
Nieuwe Hoogstraat 19, Old Centre: Old Side (625 0139, www.joesvliegerwinkel.nl). Tram 4, 9, 16, 24, 25 or Metro Nieuwmarkt. **Open** noon-6pm Tue-Fri; noon-5pm Sat. **Credit** AmEx, DC, MC, V. **Map** p327 E3.
Kites, kites and yet more kites – well, you've got to do something with all the Dutch wind. Also a quirky array of boomerangs, yo-yos and kaleidoscopes can be found at this wonderfully colourful shop.

Kramer/Pontifex
Reestraat 18-20, Western Canal Belt (626 5274, htttp://sites.google.com/site/pontifexkramer). Tram 13, 14, 17. **Open** 10am-6pm Mon-Sat. **No credit cards.** **Map** p326 C3.

Broken Barbies and battered bears are carefully restored to health by Mr Kramer, a doctor for old-fashioned dolls and teddies who has practised here for more than 25 years. In the same shop, Pontifex is a traditional Dutch candle seller that seems to ooze old-world atmosphere.

Schaak en Go Het Paard
Haarlemmerdijk 173, the Jordaan (624 1171, www.schaakengo.nl). Tram 3 or bus 18, 21, 22. **Open** 1-5.30pm Mon; 10am-5.30pm Tue, Wed, Fri, Sat; 10am-8pm Thur. **Credit** AmEx MC, V. **Map** p325 B1.
Budding Kasparovs take note: this is the place to come to for a glorious selection of chess sets, from African to ultra-modern examples. And the fun doesn't stop there, as the shop also stocks tons of games, puzzles and books.

Schaal Treinen Huis
Bilderdijkstraat 94, Oud West (612 2670, www.schaaltreinenhuis.nl). Tram 3, 7, 12, 13, 14, 17. **Open** 9.30am-5.30pm Tue-Fri; 9.30am-5pm Sat. **Credit** AmEx, DC, MC, V. **Map** p329 B5.
DIY kits and a ready-made parade that includes electric trains, modern and vintage vehicles, and some truly adorable and intimate dolls' houses.

FASHION
Designer

Azzurro Due
Pieter Cornelisz Hooftstraat 138, Museum Quarter (671 9708, www.azzurrofashiongroup.nl). Tram 2, 3, 5, 12. **Open** 1-6pm Mon; 10am-6pm Tue, Wed, Fri; 10am-9pm Thur; 10am-6pm Sat; noon-5pm Sun. **Credit** AmEx, DC, MC, V. **Map** p330 C6.
If you've got the urge to splurge, this is as good a spot as any, with saucy picks from Anna Sui, Blue Blood, Chloé and Stella McCartney.

★ Blue Blood
Pieter Cornelisz Hooftstraat 142, Museum Quarter (676 6220, www.bluebloodbrand.com).

INSIDE TRACK GO DUTCH

Ready to Fish (*see right*), a gorgeous, airy shopping space on the Prinsengracht, is home to Dutch designer Ilja Visser's whimsical yet wearable clothing line. It has a real *Alice in Wonderland* feel, with weird installation art from Paul Tas (see www.paultas.com), sustainable chocolate that begs 'eat me', and MP3 download stations packed with ethereal tunes. Quite the catch.

CONSUME

Shop This Block
Eerste van der Helststraat, De Pijp

Unearth some of De Pijp's shopping gems on one of the Albert Cuypstraat's busy side streets.

Keeping Amsterdammers on their feet since 1898, Otten & Zn Schoenverzorging (no.31, 662 9724, www.schoenen-gids.org, closed Sun) deals almost exclusively in Birkenstocks, the tree-huggers' footwear of choice. From your basic split toe to the fashion-focused gladiator, these shoes are truly a treat for the feet. The owners are also experts in the repair and maintenance of all manner of footwear, from glittery stilettos to hulking great walking boots.

It's easy to understand why **De Pittenkoning** (no.35, 671 6308, www.depittenkoning.nl, closed Sun) is packed with people clamouring for its kitchen wares. Both knowledgeable and available, the staff can advise you on everything from Tupperware to woks, and the towering floor-to-ceiling stacking system alone is worth a peek. There's an especially ample supply here of Le Creuset cookware – they scream successful dinner party. And they have those gorgeous Global stainless steel knives and genuine Laguiole knives.

Expect Buddhas nestling next to carved African elephants and the odd seashell chandelier at **Interbasics Interieur** (no.41,

662 2371, www.interbasics.nl, closed Sun). This cosy furniture shop, where there's barely room to swing a cat, stocks those nice wooden basics that work in any room, including inexpensive teak and pine bookshelves, side tables and cabinets, but it's dotted with plenty of fun knick-knacks and tchi-crafts to add charm to any room.

This kitsch store, **Loversgiftshop** (no.62, 679 3348, www.loversgiftshop.nl, closed Sun), harbours all manner of silliness – from Jesus-faced clocks to leopard-print toilet seats. There's a Hello Kitty shrine for fans of the Japanese icon and lots of Elvis and Betty Boop tat too. But it's the kooky miniature cow statues that are the real winner in this fun spot.

If your wardrobe is looking a tad drab look no further than **Noor Mode & Schoenen** (corner with Albert Cuypstraat, 670 2916, closed Sun). Here you can build up your basics with a rainbow spectrum of tops, frocks and trews from this boho shop. Add a bright floral-print dress into the mix and job done. On top of sprucing up your aesthetic, Noor's affordable prices will also put a smile on your face.

CONSUME

Tram 2, 3, 5, 12. **Open** 10am-6pm Mon-Wed, Fri; 10am-9pm Thur; 10am-5.30pm Sat; noon-5pm Sun. **Credit** AmEx, DC, MC, V. **Map** p330 C6.
The home of local denim label Blue Blood Jeans has all the lovely aspirational gear any upwardly mobile trendster could ever want, all under one perfectly curated roof. Expect own-brand denim and scooter helmets, as well as make-a-statement Antik Batik frocks.

NL = New Luxury
Jacob Obrechtstraat 20, Oud Zuid (786 4474). Tram 2. **Open** 10am-6pm Tue-Fri; 11am-6pm Sat. **Credit** DC, MC, V. **Map** p330 C6.
Fashion duo Alexander van Slobbe and Francisco van Benthum set up this aptly named boutique to pay homage to classic Dutch design.

★ Puck
Nieuwe Hoogstraat 1A, Old Centre: Old Side (625 4201, www.puckmode.nl). Tram 4, 9, 16, 24, 25 or Metro Nieuwmarkt. **Open** 1-6pm Mon; 11am-6pm Tue-Sat; 1-5pm Sun. **Credit** AmEx, MC, V. **Map** p327 E3.

This Nordic treasure trove is a mid-autumn night's dream come true for women and children, with contemporary fashion's Greatest Danes all present and correct. Bruuns Bazaar, Day Birger et Mikkelsen, Baum and Pferdgarten and Noa Noa bring the attire while the likes of Decadent, Tusnelda Bloch and Pilgrim accessorise.

Ready to Fish
Prinsengracht 581, Southern Canal Belt (330 9332, www.readytofish.nl). Tram 1, 2, 5. **Open** 11am-7pm Mon-Fri; 10am-6pm Sat; noon-6pm Sun. **Credit** AmEx, MC, V. **Map** p330 C4.
See left **Inside Track**.

★ SPRMRKT
Rozengracht 191-193, the Jordaan (330 5601, www.sprmrkt.nl). Tram 13, 14, 17. **Open** noon-6pm Mon; 10am-6pm Tue, Wed, Fri, Sat; 10am-8pm Thur; noon-6pm Sun. **Credit** AmEx, DC, MC, V. **Map** p325 B3.
A whopping 450sq m (4,850sq ft) store (that's pretty big for Amsterdam) of exceptionally cool duds. The prize is the shop-within-the-shop, SPR+, featuring

INSIDE TRACK
FASHION FACTORY

Is it a gallery? Is it a boutique? Modelled on an industrial meat factory (yes, really) and with a keen eye for quirky smaller brands, **Concrete Image Store** (*see right*) offers something a little different. Clothes – it has a penchant for Converse, Levis and Nike – hang from pieces of string and every eight weeks, artists are invited to exhibit their work.

picks from Margiela, Rick Owens, the Acne Jeans collection, Wendy & Jim and more. *Photo p189.*
▶ *To find out what top stylist Bastiaan van Schaik has to say about his favourite store, see p190.*

Studio 91

Elandsgracht 91, the Jordaan (616 5444, www.studio91.nl). Tram 7, 10, 17. **Open** noon-5pm Wed-Sat. **Credit** MC, V. **Map** p329 C4.
Set up by a troupe of Dutch artists and designers, the shelves at this minimalist boutique and gallery buckle with equine-inspired, crocheted clutch bags and avant-garde lingerie (think Ga Ga-esque, flesh-hued see-through bodices).

Van Ravenstein

Keizersgracht 359, Western Canal Belt (639 0067, www.van-ravenstein.nl). Tram 13, 14, 17. **Open** 1-6pm Mon; 11am-6pm Tue, Wed, Fri; 11am-7pm Thur; 10.30am-5.30pm Sat. **Credit** AmEx, DC, MC, V. **Map** p330 C4.
Van Ravenstein is a superb boutique with the best from the Belgian designers: Martin Margiela, AF Vandervorst and Bernhard Willhelm, among others. Viktor & Rolf form the Dutch contingent. Don't miss the itsy-bitsy bargain basement for similarly stylish endeavours with less serious price tags.

General

Be sure to cruise the **Kalverstraat** (*see p195*) as it's high-street heaven.

American Apparel

Westerstraat 59-61, the Jordaan (330 2391, www.americanapparel.net). Tram 3, 10, 13, 14, 17. **Open** 9am-7pm Mon; 10am-7pm Tue-Sat; 10am-9pm Thur; noon-6pm Sun. **Credit** AmEx, MC, V. **Map** p325 B2.
Dov Charney picked Amsterdam for his American Apparel outlets, perhaps because the town has a casual attitude that perfectly suits the sweatshop-free, relaxed style of his cotton T-shirts and other pieces. **Other locations** Utrechtsestraat 85, Southern Canal Belt (624 6635).

★ Charlie + Mary

Gerard Doustraat 84, De Pijp (662 8281, www.charliemary.com). Tram 16, 24. **Open** 1-6pm Mon; 10am-6pm Tue-Fri; 10am-5pm Sat. **Credit** MC. V. **Map** p331 E6.
Along with stocking eco classics such as Alchemist's skinnier than skinny jeans and the aptly named Beyond Skin vegan trainers, this unisex store also doubles up as a tearoom, serving organic cake and fair-trade coffee to pep you up while you browse.

Concrete Image Store

Spuistraat 250, Western Canal Belt (625 2225, www.concrete.nl). Tram 1, 2, 5, 13, 14, 17. **Open** noon-7pm Mon-Wed, Fri, Sat (Thur until 9pm); 1-6pm Sun. **Credit** AmEx, MC, V. **Map** p326 C3.
See left **Inside Track**.

Didi

Kalverstraat 203, Old Centre: New Side (531 0865, www.didi.nl). Tram 1, 2, 4, 5, 9, 13, 14, 16, 17, 24, 25. **Open** 11.30am-7.30pm Mon; 10.30am-7.30pm Tue-Wed; 10.30am-9pm Thur; 10am-8pm Fri, Sat; 11am-8pm Sun. **Credit** AmEx, MC, V. **Map** p326 D4.
While its mannequins seem to take the 'wear everything at once' approach, it's more a case of fishing out a few statement pieces. Aside from offering affordable fashion, Didi has a colourful range of children's wear and maternity togs.

Hema

Kalverstraat 212, Old Centre: New Side (422 8988, www.hema.nl). Tram 1, 2, 4, 5, 9, 13, 14, 16, 17, 24, 25. **Open** 11am-6.30pm Mon; 9.30am-6.30pm Tue-Wed, Fri, Sat; noon-6.30pm Sun. **Credit** AmEx, MC. **Map** p326 D4.
A much-loved Dutch high-street institution, Hema is *the* place to check out when you need just about anything – clothes, towels, notebooks, soap dispensers, ring binders, those little bike lights – you name it.

Spoiled

Wolvenstraat 19, Western Canal Belt (626 3818, www.spoiled.nl). Tram 1, 2, 5, 13, 14, 17. **Open** 1-6pm Mon, Sun; 10am-6pm Tue, Wed, Fri, Sat; 10am-9pm Thur. **Credit** AmEx, MC, V. **Map** p330 D4.
Spoiled ups the ante at its fancy-pants location on the Nine Streets with loads of fashion, art, weird gadgets, designer toys, a hair salon and a jeans concept called DENIMBAR, where one can throw back a drink while the staff relate all the news on the latest denim styles and fashion. Contemporary labels to look out for include Tiger of Sweden, Cycle, Nudie, Freitag and Evisu, plus limited collections from Nike and Levis. *Photo p191.*
▶ *For more on the fabulous Nine Streets, see p195.*

CONSUME

SPRMRKT. *See p187.*

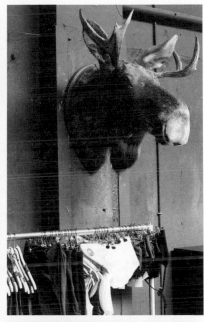

Super new arrivals

April 77

Tenue de Nîmes

Elandsgracht 60, the Jordaan (320 4012, www.tenuedenimes.com). Tram 7, 10. **Open** noon-6pm Mon; 10am-6pm Tue, Wed, Fri, Sat (Thur until 9pm); 1-6pm Sun. **Credit** AmEx, MC, V. **Map** p330 C4.
See p191 **Inside Track**.

2πR

Oude Hoogstraat 10-12, Old Centre: Old Side (421 6329). Tram 4, 9, 16, 24, 25 or Metro Nieuwmarkt. **Open** noon-7pm Mon; 10am-7pm Tue, Wed, Fri, Sat; 10am-9pm Thur; noon-6pm Sun. **Credit** AmEx, DC, MC, V. **Map** p326 D3.
This funky little number's just for the boys (the Gasthuismolensteeg branch does womenswear). Two shops side by side on Oude Hoogstraat offer urban streetwear threads from the likes of Helmut Lang, Psycho Cowboy, D-Squared and Anglomania. **Other locations** Gasthuismolensteeg 12, Western Canal Belt (528 5682).

Specialist

Mateloos

Kwakersplein 1-7, Oud West (683 2384, www.mateloos.nl). Tram 3, 7, 12, 13, 14, 17. **Open** 10am-6pm Mon-Fri; 10am-5pm Sat. **Credit** AmEx, DC, MC, V. **Map** p329 B5.
Mateloos cares for curves, selling its own-brand King Size Babes label for the larger lady. Expect clothes from sizes 44 to 60: evening wear, sportswear, lingerie – the works.

MOOXX

Singel 465, Southern Canal Belt (622 1436, www.highandmighty.co.uk). Tram 1, 2, 4, 5, 9, 14, 16, 24, 25. **Open** 1-6pm Mon; 9am-6pm Tue, Wed, Fri; 9am-9pm Thur; 9am-5pm Sat; noon-5pm 1st Sun of mth. **Credit** AmEx, DC, MC, V. **Map** p330 D4.
Big and tall men are going to love the selection: now they can have the same brands as their buddies. From Ben Sherman through to Yves Saint Laurent, if you wear a 58 or larger, you're in luck.

Streetwear

To look good for less, hunt down streetwear from the market at **Waterlooplein** (*see p182*).

America Today

Magna Plaza, Nieuwezijds Voorburgwal 182 (ground floor), Old Centre: New Side (638 8447, www.americatoday.nl). Tram 1, 2, 5, 13, 14, 17. **Open** 11am-7pm Mon; 10am-7pm Tue, Wed, Fri, Sat; 10am-9pm Thur; noon-7pm Sun. **Credit** AmEx, MC, V. **Map** p326 C2.
This giant started as the tiniest of ventures; today it sells street classics from Converse, Lee, Levis and the like.

Other locations Kalvertoren Singel 457, Southern Canal Belt (638 8812); Sarphatistraat 48, De Pijp (638 9847).

Independent Outlet

Vijzelstraat 77, Southern Canal Belt (421 2096, www.outlet.nl). Tram 4, 16, 24, 25. **Open** 1-6pm Mon; 11am-6pm Tue, Wed, Fri, Sat; 11am-9pm Thur; 1-6pm Sun. **Credit** AmEx, MC, V. **Map** p330 D4.
Independent Outlet is the place for customised skateboards, Vans shoes and labels such as Fred Perry, plus a great selection of punk imports.

Tom's Skate Shop

Oude Hoogstraat 35-37, Old Centre: Old Side (625 4922, www.tomsskateshop.nl). Tram 4, 9, 14, 16, 24, 25 or Metro Nieuwmarkt. **Open** noon-6pm Mon; 10am-6pm Tue-Sat; noon-6pm Sun. **Credit** AmEx, MC, V. **Map** p326 D3.
Dual-gender gear from the likes of Nike SB, Zoo York and London label Addict. Also stocks limited-edition trainers, shades by Electric and skateboards.

Used & vintage

Loads of vintage clothes and accessories can be found (often cheaply) at **Noordermarkt** and also at **Waterlooplein** (for both, *see p182*).

Bij Ons Vintage

Nieuwezijds Voorburgwal 150, Old Centre: New Side (06 1187 1278 mobile, www.bijonsvintage.nl). Tram 1, 2, 5, 13, 14, 17. **Open** 11am-8pm Mon-Wed; 10am-9pm Thur, Fri; 10am-8pm

Shopping with the Stars Bastiaan van Schaik

The celebrity stylist and judge of Benelux's Next Top Model *shares his favourite fashion hit.*

'Vowel-less it may be, but SPRMRKT (*see p187*) is definitively *the* boutique to find those special pieces that, when you enter a party, make everybody curious,' says van Schaik. 'It's good for giving that edgy rock-look to a client.'

The seven-year-old enterprise has its own label, also strictly consonantal (SPRB), and a branch in Oud Zuid, which showcases designers more likely to hail from America (think Rick Owens and Alexander Wang) than Arnhem.

Sat; noon-8pm Sun. **No credit cards**.
Map p326 C3.
Inside the place is rammed to the ceilings with leather jackets, woollen hats, old Polaroid cameras and even some authentic 1960s ottomans. There is so much random gear inside that it instantly fills you with bargain-hunting adrenaline.

Episode
Berenstraat 1, Western Canal Belt (626 4679, www.episode.eu). Tram 13, 14, 17. **Open** 1-6pm Mon; 11am-6pm Tue, Wed; 11am-7pm Thur, Fri; 10am-7pm Sat; 1-6pm Sun. **Credit** AmEx, MC, V. **Map** p330 C4
In a basement on the Nine Streets, Episode's clean, concrete interior is brimming with men's and women's clothes that hail from the 1970s and '80s. There's quite a masculine vibe – its military jackets and Levis are hard to beat – so this may not be the ideal spot for anyone looking for more of a '40s-ladies-tearoom ambience. *Photo p193.*
Other locations Waterlooplein 1, Jodenbuurt (320 3000).

Jutka & Riska
Bilderdijkstraat 194, Oud West (no phone). Tram 3, 7, 12, 17. **Open** 10.30am-7pm daily; Thur until 9pm. **No credit cards**. **Map** p329 B5.
The kooky store – there are Barbie dolls lurking all over the place – that stocks a mix of 'old, new, borrowed and blue' fashion prides itself on its extensive range of reasonably priced 1950s, '60s and '70s frocks (all for around €45). There's also second-hand Sonia Rykiel, vintage Yves Saint Laurent blazers and some colourful one-off pieces from the store's Jutka & Riska label.

INSIDE TRACK JEAN-IUS

Aptly named after the spiritual home of denim (a rustic French town called Nîmes), boutique/photography gallery **Tenue de Nîmes** (*see p190*) ticks all the right boxes. Bare red brick walls are adorned with denim-covered beams, while antiquated Singer sewing machines and limited-edition Raw Cannondale bicycles are scattered about the place. If it's exclusive where-did-you-get-those-from appeal you are after, the store's selection of edgier brands, including Camilla Norrback, Cheap Monday and Minimum is second to none. Oh, and it also sells Swedish wine (made from birch trees, no less). Quirky, cool (and possibly a little tipsy) to the end.

★ I Love Vintage
Prinsengracht 201, the Jordaan (330 1950, www.ilovevintage.nl). Tram 13, 14, 17. **Open** 10am-6pm Mon-Sat. **Credit** AmEx, MC, V. **Map** p325 B2.
There are few vintage stores that combine class (the silk Escada blazers are divine) with affordability (€1.99 for a pair of 1980s pearl earrings) and bang-on service. All in all, it's like stepping into your mum's dressing-up box, but everything fits and you won't resemble a bag lady on exiting.

Lady Day
Hartenstraat 9, Western Canal Belt (623 5820, www.ladydayvintage.com). Tram 1, 2, 5, 13, 14,

CONSUME

Spoiled. *See p188.*

17. **Open** 11am-6pm Mon-Wed, Fri, Sat; 11am-6pm Thur; 12.30-5.30pm Sun. **Credit** AmEx, MC, V. **Map** p326 C3.

Beautifully tailored second-hand and period suits, plus sportswear classics for those rocking the retro aesthetic. Vintage wedge shoes, pumps and accessories complete the stylish ensemble.

★ Laura Dols

Wolvenstraat 6-7, Western Canal Belt (624 9066, www.lauradols.nl). Tram 1, 2, 5, 13, 14, 17. **Open** 11am-6pm Mon-Wed, Fri, Sat; 11am-9pm Thur; 1-6pm Sun. **Credit** MC, V. **Map** p330 C4.

When Jean Paul Gaultier, Viktor & Rolf and Susan Sarandon regularly pop into your store, you know you're on to something. It's jam-packed with Scottish tartan, 1980s taffeta and so many random bits and pieces, including roller skates and flying hats, you just don't know where to start. The boots (a classic leather pair will set you back €40) and shoes stocked here have all been reheeled and generally don't whiff.

Ree-member

Reestraat 26, Western Canal Belt (622 1329). Tram 1, 2, 5, 13, 14, 17. **Open** 1-6pm Mon; 11am-6pm Tue-Sat; 1-6pm Sun. **Credit** AmEx, MC, V. **Map** p326 C3.

Ree-member stocks a terrific collection of vintage clothes and 1960s standards. The shoes are the best in town and priced to match. If you're strapped for cash, then you'll be pleased to learn that the shop sells its less-than-perfect pieces on Noordermarkt by the kilo and at seriously discounted prices.

Rosa Rosas

Rietwijkerstraat 33, Zuid (617 5148, www.rosarosas.nl). Tram 2. **Open** 10am-1pm Tue; 10am-6pm Wed-Sat (Thur until 8pm). **No credit cards.**

If you can manage to ignore the penetrating stares of the retro mannequins, which wouldn't look out of place in *Dawn of the Dead*, new boutique Rosa Rosas is a fruitful stomping ground for vintage lovers. The eclectic mix of clothes – there's a healthy ratio of tea dresses, paisley shawls and granny beads – are carefully chosen by the store's owner, Carien Reugebrink, whose style pedigree is apparent in everything from the lilac walls to the vintage sweet jar at the counter. Thursday is late night for those leaving it right up until the last moment to get their outfit sorted.

Shop This Block Jan Pieter Heijestraat, Oud West

Duck off the bustling Overtoom to discover an abundance of style.

In the time since **Johnny at the Spot** (no. 94, 489 3868, www.johnnyatthespot.com, closed Sun) moved from Centrum to this 'hood, its DNA has switched from decorative and dressy to casual basics with a twist.

Deliberate coffee stains grace the bare plywood walls of **Loenatix** (no.129, www.loenatix.nl, closed Sun), a zany silk-screen T-shirt shop occupying a space that was once a butcher's (check out the large meat hangers still visible on the ceiling). All manner of random, alternative graphics and phrases adorn the shirts that include a single-colour T-shirt to a multicoloured hoodie. Its sister location, Loenatique (no.81), specialises in garments for women and children.

With a luxuriant black loveseat and ottoman bisecting shelving along one pearly white wall, matte-black tiled floors, and a Medusa-style ceiling lamp, **1401 footwear** (nos.153, 616 1734, www.1401footwear. nl, closed Sun) feels like you're in the posh living room of owners Lorraine and Kwong Steinraht. But this space is not just about the feng shui: expect Amsterdam-exclusive trainers from the likes of American standout Supra and Clae.

Once a custom curtain shop, **DOT** (Design On Textile, nos.100 & 108, 320 5738, www.dot-shop.nl, closed Mon & Sun) has now fanned out into furniture, cushions, lampshades and other quirky accessories such as affordable lanterns made of recycled print media. The two Jan Pieter Heijestraat locations (no.108 is the furniture and gifts shop, while no.100 is the slightly smaller shop that sells curtains) allow for a more item-specific shopping focus than their Harlemmerdijk 46 (612 4030) sibling, while their close proximity allows for a breezy transition if you're co-ordinating a full interior makeover.

The combined aroma of shiny new leather, rubber and microfibre at **Accent Sport** (nos.182-184, 683 3937, www.accentsport.com, closed Sun) definitely incites the urge to hit the field, though unfortunately the walls and floors, heaped with sweaters, tracksuits, shin-guards and goal-keeper gloves, restrict the pitch size to a fussball table. Brands include Nike, Adidas, Asics, New Balance and Lacoste. Other location at Keizersgracht 506 (625 6810).

CONSUME

Episode. *See p191.*

CONSUME

Winl

Haarlemmerstraat 29, Old Centre: New Side (427 9393, www.winivintage.nl). Tram 1, 2, 5, 13, 17. **Open** 11am-6pm Mon; 10.30am-6.30pm Tue-Fri; 10.30am-6pm Sat. **Credit** V. **Map** p326 C2.
Nestling comfortably on a popular, eclectic shopping street, this store stocks the usual line-up of 1950s polo shirts, rails of flared jeans and ladies' tea dresses. There's also a collection of vintage fabrics that can be bought by the metre, vintage women's (unused) underwear, '40s petticoats and even '60s all-in-one ski suits.

Zipper

Huidenstraat 7, Southern Canal Belt (623 7302, www.zipperstore.nl). Tram 1, 2, 5, **Open** noon-6pm Mon; 11am-6pm Tue, Wed, Fri, Sat; 11am-9pm Thur; 1-5pm Sun. **Credit** AmEx, MC, V. **Map** p330 C4.
It may not be especially cheap, but the jeans, cowboy shirts, 1980s gear and '70s hipsters are definitely worth a gander; there's real treasure to be found on them there rails.
Other locations Nieuwe Hoogstraat 8, Old Centre: Old Side (627 0353).

FASHION ACCESSORIES & SERVICES

Cleaning & repairs

Gouden Draad Zilveren Naald

Zoutsteeg 8, Old Centre: New Side (622 5416). Tram 4, 9, 16, 24, 25. **Open** 9am-6pm daily (until 9pm Thur). **No credit cards. Map** p326 D2.

Found something you love, but it's damaged? Gouden Draad Zilveren Naald can patch up pretty much any clothing casualty in 24 hours.

Luk's Schoenservice

Prinsengracht 500, Southern Canal Belt (623 1937). Tram 1, 2, 5, 7, 10. **Open** 9am-5.30pm Tue-Fri; 9am-5pm Sat. **No credit cards.**
Map p330 D5.
Reliable and speedy shoe repairs.

Powders

Kerkstraat 56, Southern Canal Belt (0646 27243 mobile). Tram 1, 2, 5. **Open** 7am-11pm daily.
No credit cards. Map p331 E4.
Washing and dry-cleaning at a central location.

Hats & handbags

Many markets have huge selections of hats and bags; try the **Albert Cuypmarkt** (*see p181*).

Cellarrich Connexion

Haarlemmerdijk 98, the Jordaan (626 5526, www.cellarrich.nl). Tram 3 or bus 18, 21, 22. **Open** 1-6pm Mon-Fri; 11am-5pm Sat. **Credit** AmEx, MC, V. **Map** p325 B2.
Nab a sophisticated Dutch handbag in materials from leather to plastic. Many (but not all) of the creations are produced by four local designers. Also expect totes from the likes of Pecard, Abro and Vivienne Westwood.

★ De Hoed van Tijn

Nieuwe Hoogstraat 15, Old Centre: Old Side (623 2759, www.dehoedvantijn.nl). Tram 4, 9, 16, 24,

25 or Metro Nieuwmarkt. **Open** noon-6pm Mon; 11am-6pm Tue-Fri; 11am-5.30pm Sat. Oct-Dec noon-5pm Sun. **Credit** AmEx, DC, MC, V. **Map** p327 E3.
Mad hatters will delight in this vast array of bonnets, homburgs, bowlers, sombreros and caps, plus second-hand and handmade items.

Jewellery

Amsterdam Diamond Center

Rokin 1-5, Old Centre: New Side (624 5787, www.amsterdamdiamondcenter.nl). Tram 4, 9, 14, 16, 24, 25. **Open** 10am-6pm daily (Thur until 8.30pm). **Credit** AmEx, DC, MC, V. **Map** p326 D3.
Amsterdam is famous for its diamond trade and the city's sparkler shops are as much tourist attractions as they are retail outlets. To experience an aspirational brush with luxury, take a tour around any one of them. But beware: falling in love with a piece of crushed carbon is the easy part; paying for it may prove to be a little more tricky.

Galerie Louise Smit

Prinsengracht 615, Western Canal Belt (625 9898, www.louisesmit.nl). Tram 1, 2, 5, 10. **Open** 2-6pm Wed-Fri; 1-5pm Sat. **Credit** AmEx, MC, V. **Map** p330 C4.
'Wet, glittering, dark, shiny, pointy, sharp' is the name of a typical exhibition at this basement gallery-cum-jewellery store, which gives some idea that it ain't your average bling broker. There's an air of respectable yet edgy sophistication, with a faux red carpet painted on to the stairwell, for example, that manages to pull in Amsterdam's well-heeled elite.

Grimm Sieraden

Grimburgwal 9, Old Centre: Old Side (622 0501, www.grimmsieraden.nl). Tram 4, 9, 14, 16, 24, 25. **Open** 11am-6pm Tue-Fri; 11am-5pm Sat. **Credit** AmEx, DC, MC, V. **Map** p326 D3.
While Elize Lutz and Harry Dekkers's shop features the most avant-garde of Dutch jewellery designers, she has the decency – not to mention the sound commercial sense – to concentrate her stock on the most wearable pieces from their various ranges.

Jorge Cohen Edelsmid

Singel 414, Southern Canal Belt (638 0296, www.jorgecohen.nl). Tram 1, 2, 5. **Open** 10.30am-6pm Tue-Fri; 10.30am-5pm Sat. **Credit** AmEx, DC, MC, V. **Map** p330 D4.
This is the kind of art deco-inspired jewellery you'd be proud to pass off as the real thing. Pieces use salvaged jewellery, silver, plus antique and new stones.

MK Jewelry

Reestraat 9, Western Canal Belt (427 0727, www.mk-jewelry.com). Tram 13, 14, 17. **Open** 11am-6pm Tue-Sat. **Credit** AmEx, DC, MC, V. **Map** p326 C3.

Pressing your nose to the immaculate windows you might be afraid of intruding, but you'll be glad you did. Once inside, all is calm and relaxed, allowing the glitter of a million reflected, refracted rays of light to work their mesmeric magic. Prices start low.

Lingerie

Hunkemöller

Kalverstraat 162, Old Centre: New Side (623 6032, www.hunkemoller.com). Tram 1, 2, 4, 5, 9, 14, 16, 17, 24, 25. **Open** noon-6pm Mon; 10am-6pm Tue, Wed, Fri, Sat; 10am-9pm Thur; noon-6pm Sun. **Credit** AmEx, DC, MC, V. **Map** p326 D3.
Female fancy pants fanciers should check out this chain (you can call 035 646 5413 for details of other branches). The undies manage to be feminine and attractive, simply designed and more reasonably priced than at similar enterprises.

Marlies Dekkers

Cornelis Schuytstraat 13, Museum Quarter (471 4146, www.marliesdekkers.nl). Tram 2. **Open** noon-6pm Mon; 10am-6pm Tue-Fri; 10am-5pm Sat. **Credit** AmEx, DC, MC, V. **Map** p330 C5.
Local lingerie designer Marlies Dekkers is already a legend for having given women the world over such stylish, understated underwear, and her wonderful flagship store doesn't disappoint. Besides the lingerie and swimwear lines, there's a variety of treats to help set the mood: scented candles, locally handmade bonbons, and beautifully boxed sets of champagne for slipping lingerie into. Truly dazzling gifts to stir the senses.

★ Salon De Lingerie

Utrechtsestraat 38, Southern Canal Belt (623 9857, www.salondelingerie.nl). Tram 4, 9, 14, 16, 24, 25. **Open** 1-6pm Mon; 10am-6pm Tue-Sat; noon-5pm Sun. **Credit** AmEx, MC, V. **Map** p331 E4.
Find sultry brands such as Lise Charmel (adored by the really quite attractive Dutch supermodel Doutzen Kroes), Eprise, Simone Perele and Freya and the kind of staff who can determine if you've been wearing the wrong sized bra for a decade.

Shoes

For new shoes, try Leidsestraat or Kalverstraat; for second-hand wares there's **Waterlooplein** or **Noordermarkt** (for both, see p182).

Accent Sport

Jan Pieter Heijenstraat 182-184, Museum Quarter (683 3937, www.accentsport.com). Tram 1. **Open** 1-6pm Mon; 9am-6pm Tue-Fri (Thur until 9pm); 9am-5pm Sat. **Credit** V. **Map** p329 B6.
Nike commands half of the store with a rainbow spectrum of boots, hats and sweaters, while Adidas

gets some quality real estate for its wildly popular F50 football boots.

Other locations Keizersgracht 506, Southern Canal Belt (625 6810).

Big Shoe
Leliegracht 12, Western Canal Belt (622 6645, www.bigshoe.nl). Tram 13, 14, 17. **Open** 10am-6pm Wed, Fri; 10am-9pm Thur; 10am-5pm Sat. **Credit** AmEx, DC, MC, V. **Map** p326 C3.
Fashionable footwear for men and women in large sizes only: men's from 47 to 50; women's 42 to 46.

Betsy Palmer
Rokin 9-15, Old Centre: Old Side (422 1040, www.betsypalmer.com). Tram 4, 9, 16, 24, 25. **Open** 10am-6.30pm Mon-Wed, Fri; 10am-9pm Thur; 10am-6pm Sat; 1-6pm Sun. **Credit** MC, V. **Map** p326 D3.

Tired of seeing the same shoes in every store, Dutch fashion buyer Gertie Gerards put her money where her mouth was and set up shop. Betsy Palmer is her in-house label, which sits alongside a huge variety of other labels that change as soon as they sell out.

Other locations Van Woustraat 46, De Pijp (470 9795).

★ Mumu's Shoes
Herengracht 360, Southern Canal Belt (620 4196, www.mumu-shoes.com). Tram 1, 2, 5. **Open** 10am-6pm Tue-Wed; 10am-8pm Thur; 10am-6pm Fri-Sun. **Credit** AmEx, MC, V. **Map** p330 C4.
'I want someone to feel like a princess of the day and queen of the night,' says owner Manuela Sabarez. To this end she shares the ritzy white interior and copper plush carpet of her Herengracht store with the sophisticated haute couture garments of Henk Hendriks.

Where to Spend It

Amsterdam's shopping districts – the cheat sheet.

DAMSTRAAT
A street at war with its former self, Damstraat is fighting to jettison the sleaze and change into a boutique-lined oasis. Alas, its proximity to the Red Light District means that the countless laddish types out on the town can impinge on this otherwise lovely area.

THE JORDAAN
Tiny backstreets laced with twisting canals, cosy boutiques, lush markets, bakeries, galleries, restful, and old-fashioned cafés and bars. The Jordaan captures the spirit of Amsterdam like nowhere else in the city.

LEIDSESTRAAT
Connecting Koningsplein and Leidseplein, Leidsestraat is peppered with fine shoe shops and boutiques, but you'll still have to dodge trams to shop there. Cyclists: note that bikes aren't allowed in this part of town.

MAGNA PLAZA
Right behind Dam Square, this architectural treat was once a post office. Its subsequent reincarnation as a five-floor mall is beloved by tourists, although the locals are less keen.

NINE STREETS
The small streets connecting Prinsengracht, Keizersgracht and Herengracht in between Raadhuisstraat and Leidsegracht offer a

very diverse mix of boutiques, antiques and a good range of quirky speciality stores.

KALVERSTRAAT & NIEUWENDIJK
Kalverstraat and its more scruffy extension Nieuwendijk are where the locals come for their consumer kicks. Shops here are largely unexciting – mainly high-street stores – yet they still get insanely busy on Sundays. Still, it's pedestrian-only, so you can forget the dreaded bikes and focus on the tills; just make sure you follow the unwritten law of keeping left as you cruise up or down the street.

PC HOOFTSTRAAT
Amsterdam's elite shopping strip has had a rocky ride in the last few years, but with a new infusion of designer shops embracing both established and up-and-coming names, things are looking better all the time.

DE PIJP
This bustling district is notable mainly for the Albert Cuypmarkt and its ethnic food shops.

SPIEGELKWARTIER
Across from the Rijksmuseum and centred on Spiegelgracht, this area is packed with antiques shops selling real treasures at accordingly high prices. Dress for success and keep your nose in the air if you want to fit in with the legions of big-spending locals here.

CONSUME

Onitsuka Tiger
Herengracht 356, Western Canal Belt (528 6183,
www.onitsukatiger.com). Tram 4, 9, 14, 16,
24, 25. **Open** 1-6pm Mon; 10am-6pm Tue-Sat.
Credit AmEx, MC, V. **Map** p330 C4.
Small but perfectly formed outlet for the iconic
Japanese trainer brand Onitsuka Tiger, which is
making waves the world over. Should your
favourite pair not be on the shelves, staff will happily order it for you.

Paul Warmer
Leidsestraat 41, Southern Canal Belt (427 8011).
Tram 1, 2, 5. **Open** 1-6pm Mon; 10am-6pm Tue,
Wed, Fri, Sat; 10am-9pm Thur; noon-6pm Sun.
Credit AmEx, DC, MC, V. **Map** p330 D4.
Fashionista heaven: refined footwear for men and
women. Gucci, Roberto Cavalli and Emillio Pucci are
among the upmarket designers represented.

Seventy Five
Nieuwe Hoogstraat 24, Old Centre: Old Side (626
4611, www.seventyfive.com). Tram 4, 9, 16, 24,
25 or Metro Nieuwmarkt. **Open** noon-6pm Mon;
10am-6pm Tue-Sat; noon-6pm Sun. **Credit** AmEx,
MC, V. **Map** p327 E3.
Trainers for folk who have no intention of wearing
them long enough to think of ever having to insert
a pair of Odor Eaters: high fashion styles from Asics,
Nike, Puma, Converse and Diesel.
Other locations Haarlemmerdijk 55C, the Jordaan
(645 5205); Van Woustraat 14, De Pijp (645 5205).

Shoebaloo
Koningsplein 7, Southern Canal Belt (626 7993,
www.shoebaloo.nl). Tram 1, 2, 5. **Open** noon-6pm
Mon; 10am-6pm Tue, Wed, Fri, Sat; 10am-9pm
Thur; 1-6pm Sun. **Credit** AmEx, MC, V. **Map**
p330 C6.
A space age men's and women's shoe shop with a
glowing Barbarella-pod interior. Über cool, but, for
all that, still worth taking the time to cruise for Miu
Miu, Costume Nationale and Patrick Cox.
Other locations Leidsestraat 10, Southern Canal
Belt (330 9147); PC Hooftstraat 80, Museum
Quarter (671 2210).

FOOD & DRINK
Bakeries

For bread, rolls and packaged biscuits, go to a
warmebakker; for pastries and delicious cream
cakes, you need a *banketbakker*.

Runneboom
1e Van der Helststraat 49, De Pijp (673 5941).
Tram 16, 24, 25. **Open** 7am-5pm Mon-Sat.
No credit cards. **Map** p331 E5.
This De Pijp bakery is a staunch favourite with
locals, who queue into the street in all weathers. A

huge selection of French, Russian, Greek and
Turkish loaves is offered, with rye bread being the
house speciality.

Vlaamsch Broodhuys
Haarlemmerstraat 108, the Jordaan (528 6430,
www.vlaamschbroodhuys.nl). Tram 3 or bus 18,
21, 22. **Open** 8.30am-6.30pm Mon-Fri; 8.30am-
5pm Sat. **No credit cards**. **Map** p326 C2.
The name might be something of a mouthful,
but this place is well worth a visit to wrap your gums
round the tasty sourdough breads, fine French pastries and fresh salad greens from restaurant De Kas,
among other treats.
Other locations Vijzelstraat 109, Southern Canal
Belt (626 0654); Cornelis Schuytstraat 26, Museum
Quarter (397 5195).

Drinks

De Bierkoning
Paleisstraat 125, Old Centre: New Side (625
2336, www.bierkoning.nl). Tram 1, 2, 5, 13,
14, 16, 17, 24, 25. **Open** 1-7pm Mon; 11am-7pm
Tue, Wed, Fri; 11am-9pm Thur; 11am-6pm Sat;
1-6pm Sun. **Credit** AmEx, DC, MC, V.
Map p326 C3.
Named in honour of its location behind the Royal
Palace, the 'Beer King' stocks a head-spinning 850
brands of beer from around the world, and a range
of fine glasses to sup from.

Geels & Co
Warmoesstraat 155, Old Centre: Old Side (624
0683, www.geels.nl). Tram 4, 9, 14, 16, 24, 25.
Open *Shop* 9.30am-6pm daily. **Credit** MC, V.
Map p326 D3.
Coffee beans and loose teas, plus a large range of cof-
fee-making contraptions and serving utensils.

Simon Levelt
Prinsengracht 180, Western Canal Belt (624
0823, www.simonlevelt.com). Tram 13, 14,
17. **Open** 10am-6pm Mon-Fri; 10am-5pm Sat;
1-5pm Sun. **Credit** AmEx, DC, MC, V.
Map p325 B3.
Anything and everything to do with brewing and
drinking, stocked in a remarkable old shop. The
premises date from 1839 and the place still has much
of the original tiled decor in situ.
Other locations throughout the city.

De Kaaskamer. *See p199.*

General

Albert Heijn
Nieuwezijds Voorburgwal 226, Old Centre: New Side (421 8344, www.ah.nl). Tram 1, 2, 4, 5, 9, 13, 14, 16, 17, 24, 25. **Open** 8am-10pm daily. **No credit cards. Map** p326 D3.
The Dutch have a uniquely close relationship with this, their biggest of supermarket brands. The monopoly it holds on the city means you're always within a stone's throw of a 'Bertie': be it a regular store, an 'AH XL', or small 'AH To Go'. Be warned, though, branches don't accept credit cards so come wadded up.
Other locations throughout the city.

Dirk van den Broek
Marie Heinekenplein 25, De Pijp (673 9393, www.lekkerdoen.nl). Tram 16, 24, 25. **Open** 9am-9pm Mon-Fri; 9am-8pm Sat. **No credit cards. Map** p331 E5.
Suddenly fashionable – its red bags are now must-haves for the town's designer lemmings and have even been spotted on the arms of the fashion ratpack overseas – Dirk remains cheaper than Albert Heijn, while choice has improved, but it's not the most glam of supermarkets.
Other locations throughout the city.

Organic© Food For You
Cornelis Schuytstraat 26-28, Museum Quarter (379 5195, www.organicfoodforyou.nl). Tram 16. **Open** 9am-7pm Mon-Fri; 9am-6pm Sat; 10am-6pm Sun. **No credit cards. Map** p330 C5.
Top-end organic supermarket with daily staples such as sugar and flour, and more exotic fare like 30-year-old balsamic vinegar, caviar and wild salmon for those with less ordinary shopping lists.

Late-opening

Avondmarkt
De Wittenkade 94-96, West (686 4919, www.deavondmarkt.nl). Tram 10. **Open** 4pm-midnight Mon-Fri; 3pm-midnight Sat; 2pm-midnight Sun. **No credit cards. Map** p325 A2.
The biggest and best of all night shops, this is basically a supermarket, albeit a late-opening one, though it must be said that the selection of wine and beer here puts most standard supermarkets to shame. Worth the trek way out to just west of the Jordaan for the wow factor alone.

Big Bananas
Leidsestraat 73, Southern Canal Belt (627 7040, www.bigbananas.nl). Tram 1, 2, 5. **Open** 9am-1am daily. **No credit cards. Map** p331 D4.
A passable selection of wine, some odd-looking canned cocktails and a variety of sandwiches are stocked here. Big Bananas tends to be a bit more expensive, even for a night shop.

Sterk
Waterlooplein 241, Jodenbuurt (626 5097). Tram 9, 14 or Metro Waterlooplein. **Open** 8am-2am daily. **Credit** MC, V. **Map** p327 E3.
Less of a night shop and more of a delicatessen: quiches, pastries and salads are made on-site, and there's also fruit and veg. Be prepared to ask for what you want here – there's no self-service. This location is known as 'Champagne Corner', which hints at what's on offer.
Other locations De Clercqstraat 1-7, Old West (618 1727).

Markets

Boerenmarkt
Westerstraat/Noorderkerkstraat, the Jordaan. Tram 3, 10 or bus 18, 21. **Open** 9am-4pm Sat. **No credit cards. Map** p326 B2.
Every Saturday, the Noordermarkt turns into an organic farmers' market. Groups of singers or medieval musicians sometimes perform alfresco, making the whole experience feel more like a cultural day trip than a grocery run.
▶ *Serene Saturday concerts take place at nearby Noorderkerk; see p258.*

Marqt
Overtoom 21, Southern Canal Belt (422 6311, www.marqt.com). Tram 1, 2, 3, 5, 7, 12. **Open** 9am-8pm Mon-Sat; 10am-7pm Sun. **Credit cards** AmEx, MC, V. **Map** p330 C5.
Amsterdam's newest organics market focuses on fresh produce, meat and fish sourced from local and regional farmers and independent producers. It also sells great fresh bread from BROOD bakery and pizzas from De Pizza Bakker. Products are predominately fair trade.
Other location Utrechtsestraat 17.

Specialist

BioMarkt
Weteringschans 133, Southern Canal Belt (638 4083, www.biomarkt.nl). Tram 6, 7, 10. **Open** 8am-8pm Mon-Sat; 11am-7pm Sun. **Credit** MC, V. **Map** p331 E5.
The largest health food supermarket in the whole of Amsterdam. You'll find everything here, from organic meat, fruit and vegetables (delivered fresh daily) to really quite surprisingly tasty sugar-free chocolates, and organic wine and beer.

Delicious Food
Westerstraat 24, the Jordaan (320 3070). Tram 3, 10 or bus 18, 21, 22. **Open** 9.30am-6.30pm daily. **No credit cards. Map** p325 B2.
Organic produce has reached the self-contradictory pinnacle of urban rustic chic at what can only be described as a bulk food boutique. Come to Delicious Food to drool over the most enticing

CONSUME

displays of pastas, nuts, exotic spices, along with upmarket oils and vinegars.

Eichholtz
Leidsestraat 48, Southern Canal Belt (622 0305). Tram 1, 2, 5. **Open** 9am-6.30pm Mon-Sat; noon-6pm Sun. **Credit** AmEx, MC, V. **Map** p330 D4.
Beloved of expats, this is the place where Yanks can get their hands on chocolate chips and homesick Brits can source Christmas puddings.

De Kaaskamer
Runstraat 7, Western Canal Belt (623 3483). Tram 1, 2, 5. **Open** noon-6pm Mon; 9am-6pm Tue Fri; 9am-5pm Sat; noon-5pm Sun. **No credit cards. Map** p330 C4.
De Kaaskamer offers over 200 varieties of domestic and imported cheeses, plus pâtés, olives, pastas and wines. Have fun quizzing the staff on the different cheese types and related trivia. *Photo p197.*

Oriental Commodities
Nieuwmarkt 27, Old Centre: Old Side (626 2797, www.orientalgroup.nl). Tram 4, 9, 14, 16, 24, 25 or Metro Nieuwmarkt. **Open** 9am-7pm Mon-Fri; 9am-6pm Sat. **No credit cards. Map** p326 D2.
Visit Amsterdam's largest Chinese food emporium for the full spectrum of Asian foods and ingredients, from shrimp- and scallop-flavoured egg noodles to fried tofu balls and fresh veg. There's also a fine range of Chinese cooking appliances and utensils.

Pâtisserie Pompadour
Huidenstraat 12, Western Canal Belt (623 9554). Tram 1, 2, 5, 7. **Open** 10am-6pm Mon-Fri; 10am-5pm Sat. **Credit** MC, V. **Map** p330 C4.
This fabulous bonbonnerie and tearoom – with an 18th-century interior imported from Antwerp – is likely to bring out the little old lady in anyone. Its sister location (Kerkstraat 148, Southern Canal Belt, 330 0981, open 9am-6pm daily) also sports a decent tearoom serving sublime sarnies.

Puccini Bomboni
Staalstraat 17, Old Centre: Old Side (626 5474, www.puccinibomboni.com). Tram 9, 14 or Metro Waterlooplein. **Open** noon-6pm Mon; 11am-6pm Tue-Sat; noon-6pm Sun. **Credit** MC, V. **Map** p327 E3.
Tamarind, thyme, lemongrass, pepper and gin are just some of the flavours of these delicious hand-made chocolates, which are made completely without artificial ingredients. *Photo p200.*
Other locations Singel 184, Western Canal Belt (427 8341).

Raïnaraï
Prinsengracht 252, Western Canal Belt (624 9791, www.rainarai.nl). Tram 13, 14, 17. **Open** noon-10pm Tue-Sun. **No credit cards. Map** p326 C4.
Mouth-watering North African fodder, from take-away to an assortment of items no pantry should be

Shopping with the Stars Johannes van Damme

Local food writer Johannes van Damme tells us about the city's tastiest shop.

Staying true to his profession, food journalist Johannes van Damme loves to shop at **Caulils** delicatessen (Haarlemmerstraat 115, Western Canal Belt, 412 0027, www.caulils.com, closed Sun). 'It's a small one,' says Van Damme as he browses the fantastic raw-milk cheeses, various meats and unique wines on offer. 'But it's all very good quality, and it's the one I like most.'

Its owner, Maarten van Caulil, is generous with samples: a Gillardeau oyster perhaps; or a spoonful of Seville orange marmalade made by local preserver Elaine Olsthoorn; or maybe a Jersey cheese treated with edible ghee rather than wax.

CONSUME

Puccini Bomboni. *See p199.*

without. A self-proclaimed 'nomadic kitchen', staff will come and cater wherever you please, although most people can't resist eating right on the premises as the food is so damn tasty.

Uliveto
Weteringschans 118, Southern Canal Belt (423 0099). Tram 6, 7, 10. **Open** 11am-8pm Mon-Fri; noon-6pm Sat, Sun. **No credit cards. Map** p331 E5.
Uliveto is a superb Italian deli that – along with the usual wines, pastas and fruity olive oils for dipping bread – has an irresistible takeaway selection of tender roasted seasonal vegetables, grilled fish, rack of lamb and polenta, plus ricotta cheesecake.

Unlimited Delicious
Haarlemmerstraat 122, the Jordaan (622 4829, www.unlimiteddelicious.nl). Tram 3 or bus 18, 21, 22. **Open** 9am-6pm Mon-Sat. **Credit** AmEx, V. **Map** p326 C2.
Known for such twisted treats as tamarind and sambal bonbons, and mango and basil truffles, Unlimited Delicious also offers individual or group courses in bonbon-making so you can devise your own mad combos for dinner parties or simply for stuffing at home.

Wegewijs
Rozengracht 32, the Jordaan (624 4093, www.wegewijs.nl). **Open** 8.30am-6pm Mon-Fri; 9am-5pm Sat. **No credit cards. Map** p325 B3.

The Wegewijs family started running this shop more than a century ago. On offer are around 50 foreign and over 100 different domestic varieties of cheese, including *graskaas*, a grassy-tasting cheese that is available in summer. For those nervous about buying a strange cheese, Wegewijs allows you to try Dutch varieties beforehand.

GIFTS & SOUVENIRS
Flowers

It's tempting to bring home a selection of bulbs from Amsterdam. However, although travellers to the UK and Ireland will be fine, some other countries' import regulations either prohibit the entry of bulbs or, in the case of the US, require them to have a phytosanitary certificate. You'll find that some of the packaging is marked with flags indicating the countries into which the bulbs can be safely carried, but most Dutch wholesalers know the regulations and can ship bulbs all the way to your home.

In terms of cut flowers, travellers to the UK and Ireland can take an unlimited quantity, as long as they're not chrysanthemums or gladioli, while US regulations vary from state to state.

Bloemenmarkt (Flower Market)
Singel, between Muntplein & Koningsplein, Southern Canal Belt. Tram 1, 2, 4, 5, 9, 14, 16, 24, 25. **Open** 9am-6pm Mon-Sat; 11am-5.30pm Sun. **No credit cards. Map** p330 D4.

This fascinating collage of colour is the world's only floating flower market, with 15 florists and garden shops (although many also hawk cheesy souvenirs these days) permanently ensconced on barges along the southern side of Singel. The plants and flowers usually last well and are good value.

Gerda's Bloemen en Planten (Gerda's Flowers & Plants)
Runstraat 16, Southern Canal Belt (624 2912).
Tram 1, 2, 5, 13, 14, 17. **Open** 9am-6pm
Mon-Fri; 9am-5pm Sat. **Credit** DC, MC, V.
Map p330 C4.
Amsterdam's most inspired florist, Gerda's diminutive shop is full of fantastic blooms and sports legendary window displays. If you're lucky, you'll spy sculptural bouquets on their way out the door. Local deliveries from anywhere in the world.

★ Jemi
Warmoesstraat 83A, Old Centre: Old Side (625 6034, www.jemi.nl). Tram 4, 9, 16, 24, 25. **Open** 9am-6pm Mon-Fri. **No credit cards.**
Map p326 D2.
Amsterdam's first stone-built house is now occupied by a delightfully colourful florist. Jemi arranges splendid bouquets, provides tuition in the art of flower arranging, and stocks tons of pots and plants.

Plantenmarkt (Plant Market)
Amstelveld, Southern Canal Belt. Tram 4, 16, 24, 25. **Open** 9.30am-6pm Mon. **No credit cards.**
Map p331 E4.
Despite a general emphasis on plants, pots and vases, the Plantenmarkt also has cut flowers for sale. Each spring, the house plants go on sale, while the later months of the year burst into colour with the transient glory of garden annuals.

General

There are small, weather-dependent open-air arts and crafts markets at **Spui** (Old Centre: New Side, www.artplein-spui.nl) on Sundays and, from March to October, at
Thorbeckeplein (Southern Canal Belt, www.modern-art-market.nl). Both take place on Sundays, from 10am to 6pm. Oil paintings, acrylics, watercolours, graphic arts, sculpture, ceramics and jewellery are among the offerings; it's not the most original art in the world, but either makes for a nice Sunday afternoon stroll.
Check museum shops for prints and postcards.

Art Multiples
Keizersgracht 510, Southern Canal Belt 624 8419). Tram 1, 2, 5. **Open** 1-6pm Mon; 10am-6pm Tue, Wed, Fri, Sat; 10am-7pm Thur; noon-5pm Sun. **Credit** AmEx, MC, V.
Map p330 C4.

The most comprehensive collection of international photographs and posters in the Netherlands, and the largest collection of postcards in Western Europe. The typography posters are good for tourists seeking a unique memento.

Jorrit Heinen
Muntplein 12, Old Centre (623 2271, www.jorritheinen.com). Tram 4, 9, 16, 24, 25. **Open** 9.30am-6pm Mon-Sat; 11am-6pm Sun. **Credit** AmEx, DC, MC, V. **Map** p330 D4.
Souvenirs with provenance. Jorrit Heinen are the official dealers of Royal Delft and Makkum pottery, the bread and butter of the Dutch antiques trade. The stock here includes antiques, too, with some pieces dating from the 17th century – for a price, of course.
Other locations Prinsengracht 440 (627 8299).

Mark Raven
Nieuwezijds Voorburgwal 174, Old Centre: New Side (330 0800, www.markraven.nl). Tram 1, 2, 5, 13, 14, 17. **Open** 10.30am-6pm daily. **Credit** DC, MC, V. **Map** p326 C3.
This eponymously named artistic hub sells Raven's etchings in many guises – from canvases right through to T-shirts.

PGC Hajenius
Rokin 92-96, Old Centre: New Side (623 7494, www.hajenius.com). Tram 4, 9, 14, 16, 24, 25. **Open** noon-6pm Mon; 9.30am-6pm Tue-Sat; noon-5pm Sun. **Credit** AmEx, DC, MC, V. **Map** p326 D3.
A smoker's paradise (tobacco, not dope) for over 250 years, Hajenius offers cigarabilia from traditional Dutch pipes to own-brand cigars. With its art deco interior and inimitable old-world aesthetics, even anti-smokers should pop in for a whiff.

Tesselschade: Arbeid Adelt
Leidseplein 33, Southern Canal Belt (623 6665, www.tesselschade-arbeidadelt.nl). Tram 1, 2, 5, 7, 10. **Open** 11am-5.30pm Tue-Fri; 10am-5pm Sat. **Credit** AmEx, MC, V. **Map** p330 C5.
Absolutely everything at Tesselschade is sold on a non-profit basis by Arbeid Adelt ('Work Ennobles'), an association of Dutch women. There are plenty of toys and decorations, as well as more utilitarian household items such as tea cosies and decorated clothes hangers.

HEALTH & BEAUTY
Opticians

Brilmuseum/Brillenwinkel
Gasthuismolensteeg 7, Western Canal Belt (421 2414, www.brilmuseumamsterdam.nl). Tram 1, 2, 5, 13, 14, 17. **Open** noon-5.30pm Wed-Fri; noon-5pm Sat. **No credit cards. Map** p326 C3.

CONSUME

CONSUME

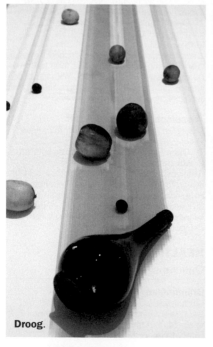

Droog.

Shop This Block Staalstraat, Old Centre: Old Side

Staalstraat's two short blocks are a hub of shopping (and social) activity.

The drawbridge at the Nieuwe Doelenstraat (often used by filmmakers as a cinematic backdrop) is a jaw-droppingly scenic entry point to Staalstraat, and once you cross it, you're in a tiny little retail heaven, containing some of the city's signature shops.

Renny Ramaker's two-room shop, **Droog** (no.7b, 523 5050, www.droog.com, closed Mon. Photo left) is the kind of store-cum-gallery where you might easily bump into a group of students admiring Mario Minale's iconic Red Blue Lego Chair and Tejo Remy's Chest of Drawers while you peruse the new items created by one of Droog's trove of collaborating designers, such as Marcel Wanders, Joris Laarman or Richard Hutten.

Nijhof & Lee (no.13A, 620 3980, www.nijhoflee.nl, closed Mon) is a legendary 40-year-old design and architecture-minded bookshop selling an array of wisely selected tomes, organised in sections that include 'Fine Arts', 'Architecture', 'Graphic Design' and 'Typography'. There's also a nice 50 per cent off section and a terrific selection of art magazines.

Cinephiles will be awed by the collection of movie posters, books, film stills and postcards available at **Cine Qua Non** (no.14, 625 5588, www.cinequanon line.com). Cases of rare and tough-to-find DVDs are organised by categories that include 'Blaxploitation', 'S Loren', 'Trash', 'Avant-Garde' and 'Bra Busting'.

No trip to the Staalstraat would be complete without a stop at the delectable **Puccini Bomboni** chocolatier (no.17, 626 5474, www.puccinibomboni.com). Pepper, thyme, port and rhubarb are just a few of the fillings you can choose from the big metal table laden with chocolates that are twice the size of the normal fare.

The first thing you think when you enter the virtual menagerie of **De Beestenwinkel** (np.26, 623 1805, www.beestenwinkel.nl) is 'Bliss for an eight year old.' But the beasties on sale here aren't just kid's play. Alongside the frog hand-puppets, shark potato-peelers, bumble-bee washcloths, WWF stuffed koalas and ladybird wheelybugs, you'll find unique high-end stuffed animals from brands such as Kösen and Sigikid.

Ladies, listen up: the primary draw at **Biec** (no.28, www.biec.nl) is the gorgeous Italian leather Tadei handbags in assorted colours, wofting the wonderful smell of new leather. Also find pretty Japanese porcelain bowls, an assortment of Pols Potten ceramics, candles and other housewares and inexpensive silver jewellery.

Officially this 'shop' is an opticians' museum, but don't let that put you off. The fascinating exhibits feature glasses through the ages, and most of the pairs you see are also for sale to customers.

Donald E Jongejans
Noorderkerkstraat 18, the Jordaan (624 6888). Tram 3, 10. **Open** 11am-6pm Mon, Sat. **No credit cards. Map** p325 B2.
This vintage frame specialist sells unused frames dating from the mid 1800s to the present day. Most frames are at fabulously low prices and built to last – and the staff are friendly too.

Pharmacies

Dam Apotheek
Damstraat 2, Old Centre: Old Side (624 4331, www.dam-apotheek.nl). Tram 4, 9, 14, 16, 24, 25. **Open** 8.30am-5.30pm Mon-Fri; 10am-5pm Sat. **Credit** AmEx, MC, V. **Map** p326 D3.
This central pharmacy has extended opening hours. Should you need a late pharmacy, *see p309.*

Lairesse Apotheek
Lairessestraat 40, Museum Quarter (662 1022, www.delairesseapotheek.nl). Tram 3, 5, 12, 16, 24. **Open** 8.30am-6pm Mon-Fri; 10am-5pm Sat. **Credit** MC, V. **Map** p330 D6.
One of the largest suppliers of alternative medicines in the country, chemist Marjan Terpstra wanted her shop to reflect her speciality. Designed by Concrete, the shop is out of the way if you're just popping in for haemorrhoid cream, but the interior is so inspiring it should be on any design junkie's must-see list.

Shops

De Witte Tandenwinkel
Runstraat 5, Western Canal Belt (623 3443, www.dewittetandenwinkel.nl). Tram 1, 2, 5, 7, 10. **Open** 1-5.30pm Mon; 10am-5.30pm Tue-Fri; 10am-5pm Sat. **Credit** AmEx, MC, V. **Map** p330 C4.
The store that's armed to the teeth with brushes and toothpastes to ensure that your gnashers are pearly white when you most need them to shine.

CONSUME

Douglas
Kalverstraat 71, Southern Canal Belt (627 6663, www.douglas.nl). Tram 1, 2, 4, 5, 9, 14, 16, 24, 25 or Metro 51, 53, 54. **Open** noon-6pm Mon; 10am-6pm Tue, Wed, Fri, Sat; 10am-9pm Thur; noon-6pm Sun. **Credit** AmEx, MC, V. **Map** p326 D3.
This two-floor superstore sells the usual scents and labels, plus rarer brands like La Prairie, Sisley and Versace. This two-storey superstore also features hair products not normally found outside salons. **Other locations** throughout the city.

Jacob Hooy & Co
Kloveniersburgwal 12, Old Centre: Old Side (624 3041, www.jacob-hooy.nl). Tram 4, 9, 14, 16, 24, 25 or Metro Nieuwmarkt. **Open** 1-6pm Mon; 10am-6pm Tue-Fri; 10am-5pm Sat. **Credit** V. **Map** p326 C3.
Established in 1743, this chemist sells medicinal herbs, teas, homeopathic remedies and cosmetics, many under their own brand. The untouched 18th-century interior is worth a visit in itself.

Lavendula
Westerstraat 45, the Jordaan (420 9140, www.lavendula.nl). Tram 10. **Open** 10am-6pm Mon-Fri; 10am-5.30pm Sat. **Credit** AmEx, MC, V. **Map** p325 B2.
Browse the fancy supplements in this dinky store, or make an appointment with the owner Simone for a consultation about Bach flower remedies and other alternative cures.

Rituals
Kalverstraat 73, Old Centre: New Side (344 9220, www.rituals.com). Tram 4, 9, 14, 16, 24, 25. **Open** noon-6pm Mon; 10am-6pm Tue, Wed, Fri; 10am-9pm Thur; 10am-5pm Sat; noon-5pm Sun. **Credit** AmEx, MC, V. **Map** p326 D3.
A store integrating products for body and home. We all have to brush our teeth and do the dishes, so the shop is full of products to ritualise such daily grinds. **Other locations** Leidsestraat 62, Southern Canal Belt (625 2311).

Skins Cosmetics Lounge
Runstraat 9, Western Canal Belt (528 6922, www.skins.nl). Tram 1, 2, 5, 7, 10. **Open** 1-7pm Mon; 11am-7pm Tue, Wed, Fri; 11am-8pm Thur; 10am-6pm Sat; noon-5pm Sun. **Credit** AmEx, DC, MC, V. **Map** p330 C4.
Sleek, sexy and full of top-of-the-range products you'll have trouble finding anywhere else in town: REN, Creed, organic skincare Kimia and so on.

HOUSE & HOME

Antiques

Visit Spiegelgracht, Nieuwe Spiegelstraat or the markets (*see p181*). At Nieuwmarkt in the Old

Centre, there's a Sunday market (9am-5pm) from April to August; a few streets away from the ladies in the windows, this antiques and bric-a-brac market attracts browsers seeking other kinds of pleasures. There are plenty to be found, too, such as books, furniture and Dutch objets d'art.

For a more rarefied air, head for the auctions at **Sotheby's** (De Boelenlaan 30, 550 2200, www.sothebys.com) and **Christie's** (Cornelis Schuytstraat 57, 575 5255, www.christies.com).

Looier Art & Antique Centre
Elandsgracht 109, the Jordaan (624 9038, www.looier.nl). Tram 7, 10, 17. **Open** 11am-5pm Mon-Thur, Sat, Sun. **Credit** AmEx, DC, MC, V. **Map** p330 C4.
Mainly antiques, with plenty of collectors' items. It's easy to get lost in the quiet premises and find yourself standing alone by a stall crammed with antiquated clocks ticking eerily away.

Postzegelmarkt
Nieuwezijds Voorburgwal, by No.276, Old Centre: New Side. Tram 1, 2, 5, 13, 17, 20. **Open** 10am-4pm Wed, Sat. **No credit cards. Map** p326 D3.
A specialist market for collectors of stamps, coins, postcards and commemorative medals.

General

For intensive browsing of the finest in designer furnishings, don't miss **Overtoom** (map **Oud West**), reinvented as a furniture boulevard.

De Kasstoor
Rozengracht 202-210, the Jordaan (521 8112, www.dekasstoor.nl). Tram 10, 13, 14, 17. **Open** 10am-6pm Tue-Sat. **Credit** AmEx, MC, V. **Map** p325 B3.
De Kasstoor is not your average modern Dutch interior design shop; it also has hand-picked collectors' pieces from the likes of Le Corbusier, Eames and Citterio, and a very extensive upholstery and fabrics library. Plan on excess luggage for the return trip.

Pols Potten
KNSM-laan 39, the Waterfront (419 3541, www.polspotten.nl). Tram 10. **Open** noon-6pm Mon; 10am-6pm Tue-Sat; noon-5pm Sun. **Credit** MC, V.
Stocks innovative furnishings and home accessories, including lots of pots, plus a design team to help you pull off the latest trends.

Specialist

★ Capsicum
Oude Hoogstraat 1, Old Centre: Old Side (623 1016, www.capsicumtextiles.com). Tram 4, 9, 14, 16, 24, 25 or Metro Nieuwmarkt. **Open** 11am-

CONSUME

Mail & Female. *See p206.*

6pm Mon; 10am-6pm Tue, Wed, Fri, Sat; 10am-6pm Thur; 1-5pm Sun. **Credit** AmEx, DC, MC, V. **Map** p326 D3.
All the fabrics on sale here are made from natural fibres, such as cotton woven in India. Staff spin the provenance of each fabric into the sale, and the store has a covetable stash of cushions and shawls. An absolute gem.

HJ van de Kerkhof
Elandsgracht 43, Western Canal Belt (623 4084). Tram 7, 10, 17. **Open** 10am-5pm Tue-Sat. **No credit cards. Map** p330 C4.
Tassel maniacs go wild. A sea of shakeable frilly things, lace and rhinestone banding.

Kitsch Kitchen
Rozengracht 8, the Jordaan (622 8261, www.kitschkitchen.nl). Tram 13, 14, 17. **Open** 10am-6pm Mon-Sat; noon-5pm Sun. **Credit** AmEx, DC, MC, V. **Map** p325 B3.
Mexican Mercado with a twist. Even the hardiest resistors of tat will love the colourful culinary and household objects (including wacky wallpapers).

Stoffen & Fournituren Winkel a Boeken
Nieuwe Hoogstraat 31, Old Centre: Old Side (626 7205). Tram 4, 9, 16, 24, 25 or Metro Nieuwmarkt. **Open** noon-6pm Mon; 10am-6pm Tue, Wed, Fri; 10am-8pm Thur; 10am-5pm Sat. **Credit** MC, V. **Map** p327 E3.

The Boeken family has been hawking fabrics since 1920. Just try to find anywhere else with the range on offer here: latex, Lycra, fake fur and sequins abound.

What's Cooking
Reestraat 16, Western Canal Belt (427 0630, www.whatscooking.nl). Tram 13, 14, 17. **Open** 11am-6pm Tue-Sat. **Credit** AmEx, MC, V. **Map** p326 C3.
Pink salad bowls, green sauces, orange peppermills: culinary gifts don't come any more retina-searing. Due to reopen in the early part of 2011 following renovations.

MUSIC & ENTERTAINMENT
CDs, records & DVDs

Vintage vinyl collectors should also head to the **Noordermarkt** and **Waterlooplein** (for both, *see p182*), or to the Sunday Market at the Westergasfabriek, every first Sunday of the month. The contemporary dance music vinyl junkie/DJ will find a plethora of small independent shops on both Nieuwe Nieuwstraat and its narrower parallel, Sint Nicolaasstraat.

Charles Klassiek en Folklore
Weteringschans 193, Southern Canal Belt (626 5538). Tram 7, 10, 16, 24, 25. **Open** 10am-6pm Mon-Wed, Fri, Sat; 10am 9pm Thur; noon-6pm Sun. **Credit** AmEx, DC, MC, V. **Map** p331 E5.
Literally, 'classical and ethnic'. According to customers, this shop has one of the best collections of contemporary music in the world, as well as an extensive collection of ethnic music. A good place to find classical music from the Middle Ages to contemporary.

Concerto
Utrechtsestraat 52-60, Southern Canal Belt (623 5228, www.concertomania.nl). Tram 9. **Open** 10am-6pm Mon-Wed, Fri, Sat; 10am-9pm Thur; noon-6pm Sun. **Credit** AmEx, DC, MC, V. **Map** p331 E4.
Head here for classic Bach recordings, obscure Beatles items, or that fave Diana Ross album that got nicked from your party. There are also second-hand 45s and new releases at decent prices.
Other locations Utrechsestraat 40 (622 2856); 2e Tuindwarsstraat 53, the Jordaan (421 7110).

Distortion Records
Westerstraat 244, the Jordaan (627 0004, www.distortion.nl). Tram 3, 10. **Open** 11am-6pm Tue, Wed, Fri; 11am-9pm Thur; 10am-6pm Sat. **No credit cards. Map** p325 B2.
Vinyl from 1970s punk rock, jazz, funk, soul, Latin and soundtracks, through lo-fi, indie, noise, garage and industrial, to '80s and '90s indie, electro, hip hop and reggae, ending up in break beats and house for those with more dancefloor-oriented interests.

CONSUME

Fame
Kalverstraat 2-4, Old Centre: New Side (638 2525, www.fame.nl). Tram 1, 2, 4, 5, 9, 13, 14, 16, 17, 24, 25. **Open** noon-7pm Mon, Sun; 10am-7pm Tue, Wed, Fri; 10am-9pm Thur. **Credit** AmEx, MC, V. **Map** p326 D3.
The biggest record store in Amsterdam sits bang on its busiest shopping thoroughfare. Fame offers a vast array of stock in a variety of genres.

Palm Guitars
's Gravelandseveer 5, Old Centre: Old Side (422 0445, www.palmguitars.nl). Tram 4, 9, 14, 16, 24, 25. **Open** noon-6pm Tue-Sat. **Credit** AmEx, DC, MC, V. **Map** p327 E3.
Palm Guitars stocks new, antique, used and rare musical instruments (and their parts). The excellent website features a calendar of upcoming local gigs, all of a worldly and rootsy nature.

SEX & DRUGS
Sex shops

Absolute Danny
Oudezijds Achterburgwal 78, Old Centre: Old Side (421 0915, www.absolutedanny.com). Tram 4, 9, 16, 24, 25 or Metro 51, 53, 54. **Open** 11am-9pm Mon-Thur, Sun; 11am-11pm Fri, Sat. **Credit** AmEx, DC, MC, V. **Map** p326 D2.
A stalwart of the sex scene in a city known for doing the deed, Absolute Danny stocks everything from rubber clothes to erotic toothbrushes.

Condomerie het Gulden Vlies
Warmoesstraat 141, Old Centre: Old Side (627 4174, www.condomerie.com). Tram 4, 9, 14, 16, 24, 25. **Open** 11am-6pm Mon-Sat. **Credit** AmEx, DC, MC, V. **Map** p326 D2.
A variety of rubbers of the non-erasing kind to wrap up trouser snakes of all shapes and sizes in a store that's equal parts amusing and inspiring.

Female & Partners
Spuistraat 100, Old Centre: New Side (620 9152, www.femaleandpartners.nl). Tram 1, 2, 5, 13, 17. **Open** 1-6.30pm Mon, Sun; 11am-6.30pm Tue, Wed, Fri; 11am-9pm Thur; 11am-6pm Sat. **Credit** AmEx, DC, MC, V. **Map** p326 C2.
It's fair to say that, in terms of the sex industry at least, Amsterdam is still predominantly a man's world. The opposite of most enterprises here, Female & Partners bucks the trend by welcoming women (and, yes, their partners) with an array of clothes, videos and toys.

Mail & Female
Nieuwe Vijzelstraat 2, Southern Canal Belt (623 3916, www.mailfemale.com). Tram 7, 10, 16, 24, 25. **Open** 11am-7pm Mon-Sat. **Credit** AmEx, MC, V. **Map** p331 E5.

The Netherlands' oldest mail-order shop for saucy toys and clothes now has a friendly walk-in outlet. *Photo p205.*

Stout
Berenstraat 9, Western Canal Belt (620 1676, www.stoutinternational.com). **Open** noon-7pm Mon-Fri; 11am-6pm Sat; 1-5pm Sun. **Credit** AmEx, DC, MC, V. **Map** p330 C4.
Naughty and nice lingerie and sex toys for the thinking gal: La Fille D'O, Marvel & Malizia, La Perla, Andres Sarda, Chantal Thomass and more.

Drugs

Cannabis College
Oudezijds Achterburgwal 124 I, Old Centre: Old Side (423 4420, http://cannabiscollege.com). Tram 4, 9, 14, 16, 24, 25 or Metro Nieuwmarkt. **Open** 11am-7pm daily. **Map** p326 D3.
Founded by hemp activist Henk Poncin and a group called Green Prisoners Release, Cannabis College is a non-profit organisation and information centre, whose mission is to provide free, accurate and unbiased information concerning all aspects of the Cannabis plant. For €3, you can enjoy a tour of the college's garden.

Conscious Dreams Dreamlounge
Kerkstraat 119, Southern Canal Belt (626 6907, www.consciousdreams.nl). Tram 4, 1, 2, 5, 16, 24, 25. **Open** *Apr-Oct* noon-10pm daily. *Nov-Mar* noon-10pm Wed-Sat. **Credit** AmEx, DC, MC, V. **Map** p330 D4.
Conscious Dreams was the original proponent of the smart drugs wave in Amsterdam. The staff here really know their stuff – the owner worked as a drugs adviser for five years – and you're more or less guaranteed to find whatever you're after.
Other locations Kokopelli Warmoesstraat 12, Old Centre: New Side (421 7000).

Dampkring
Prins Hendrikkade 10-11, Old Centre: Old Side (422 2137, www.dampkringshop.com). Tram 1, 2, 4, 5, 9, 16, 17, 24, 25. **Open** 9am-6pm Mon-Fri; 9am-5pm Sat. **Credit** MC, V. **Map** p326 D2.
The retail member of the legendary Dampkring family, this delightful emporium has everything needed to set up a grow centre at home: from hydroponics and organic equipment to bio-growth books and DVDs.

Hemp Works
Niewendijk 13, Old Centre: New Side (421 1762, www.hempworks.nl). Tram 1, 2, 5, 13, 17. **Open** 11am-7pm Mon-Wed, Sun; 11am-9pm Thur-Sat. **Credit** AmEx, DC, MC, V. **Map** p326 C2.
One of the first shops in Amsterdam to sell hemp clothes and products, and now one of the last, Hemp Works has had to diversify into seed sales and fresh mushrooms, and it's also been a Cannabis Cup-winner for its strain of the stinky weed.

CONSUME

Arts & Entertainment

Stadsschouwburg. *See p258.*

Calendar

Paint the town orange.

Although they're typically a fairly reserved bunch, the Dutch do often shed their inhibitions and dive into a fun-seeking frenzy. On the likes of Oudejaarsavond (New Year's Eve) and Koninginnedag (Queen's Day) – and whenever Ajax win a big game – the city falls into a joyous, orange-tinted psychosis of song, drink and dance.

Not every event is booze-dependent, though, and the city's cultural gems are plentiful, running from Open Monument Days and the ever-popular Museum Night to autumn's Cinekid Amsterdam film festival and the world's largest documentary film festival. Or there's a dedicated cello biennale, a National Windmill Day and – naturally – a National Cycling Day. That said, could the High Times Cannabis Cup really be held anywhere else?

FURTHER INFORMATION

The **AUB** (0900 0191, www.aub.nl) and **Amsterdam Tourism and Convention Board** (201 8800, www.iamsterdam.com) list many upcoming events, as does the monthly *Time Out Amsterdam*, which is available at newsagents and tourist offices across the city.

For the Dutch public holidays, *see p312*. Unless otherwise stated, all events are free.

SPRING

As soon as the sun shows its face after the long, grey winter, terraces are hastily erected and punters move outside en masse. After a season with little going on, spring is also the start of a new buzzing cultural year.

5 Days Off

Various locations (www.5daysoff.nl). **Date** 1st wk Mar. **Tickets** see website for details.
Taking Amsterdam by storm every March, 5 Days Off is a – yep, you guessed it – five-day festival that features a host of international artists and the latest talent in the fields of electronic music, art and media art. What started off in 2001 as a spin-off of the 10 Days Off festival in Ghent, Belgium, Amsterdam's shorter version takes place at the Paradiso (*see p264*), Melkweg (*see p251*) and the Netherlands Institute for Media Art (*see p232*). For full details of the extensive line-up, as well as for booking tickets, see the regularly updated website.

London Calling

Paradiso, Weteringschans 6-8, Southern Canal Belt (626 4521, www.londoncalling.nl, www.paradiso.nl). Tram 1, 2, 5, 7, 10. **Map** p330 D5. **Date** 2 days spring & autumn.
Taking place twice a year, this two-day indie music festival at the Paradiso (*see p252*) is a showcase for new bands, with special focus on the UK and USA. The festival started in 1992, and has since then welcomed names such as Bloc Party, White Lies, Florence & the Machine, Hudson Mohawke and Franz Ferdinand. For details on the latest line-up, see the London Calling website.

★ Amsterdam Restaurant Week

Various locations (www.restaurantweek.nl). **Date** Mar.
A three-course gourmet dinner in a top restaurant for only €25? Possibly only during Amsterdam Restaurant Week. Just as in New York, where the idea originated, local restaurant owners think this is a great way to promote their businesses. The food isn't fast, but your reservation really needs to be, especially for the high-end restaurants: bookings start as early as mid February.

National Museum Weekend

Throughout the Netherlands (www.museumweekend.nl). **Date** early-mid Apr.
Around a million visitors flock to one or more of the 500 state-funded museums, which offer free or discounted admission and special activities during National Museum Weekend.

★ World Press Photo

Oude Kerk, Oudekerksplein 23, Old Centre: Old Side (625 8284, www.worldpressphoto.nl). Tram 4, 9, 16, 24, 25. **Map** p326 D2. **Date** mid Apr.
Running since 1955, this is the world's largest photography competition, and includes exhibits from thousands of photojournalists. The exhibition is held in the Oude Kerk (*see p89*); after kicking off in Amsterdam, it goes on tour to another 70 locations around the world.

Koninginnedag (Queen's Day)

Throughout the city. **Date** 30 Apr.
The most popular event in the city actually kicks off the night before, with street parties and late-night drinking sessions in cafés. The date in question was the late Queen Juliana's birthday and not that of Beatrix, but it doesn't matter: locals and tourists still crowd the streets in search of a bargain (everyone is permitted to sell their household junk out on the streets), and to sing and dance. The best areas to experience the festivities are around the canals in the Jordaan, Rembrandtplein and the centre; Vondelpark is for the kids. *See also p210* **A Right Royal Party**. *Photo p211*.

Herdenkingsdag & Bevrijdingsdag (Remembrance Day & Liberation Day)

Remembrance Day *Nationaal Monument, Dam, Old Centre: Old Side. Tram 1, 2, 4, 5, 9, 13, 14, 16, 17, 24, 25.* **Map** p326 D3. **Date** 4 May; 7.30pm.
Liberation Day *Vondelpark, Museum Quarter. Tram 1, 2, 3, 5, 12.* **Date** 5 May. **Map** p330 C6.
Ooosterpark Festival *Oosterpark Oost (www.oosterparkfestival.nl). Tram 3, 9, 14.* **Map** p332 H3. **Date** 5 May.
In the presence of the Queen and many dignitaries, those who lost their lives during World War II are remembered at the Nationaal Monument on Dam Square (*see p80*). Gays and lesbians have their own ceremony with a remembrance service held at the Homomonument (*see p237*) and there are also other ceremonies in various quarters around the city.

Liberation Day is celebrated on 5 May with music and a variety of speeches. The best areas for visitors to enjoy it from are Museumplein, Leidseplein and Westermarkt (the focal point of the gay commemorations). The Oosterparkfestival is all about emphasising community between different nationalities through the shared mediums of music, sports, cultural customs and food.

National Windmill Day

Around the Netherlands (0900 400 4040, www.visitamsterdam.nl). **Date** 2nd Sat May.
Got a windmill on your mind? On this day, about 600 state-subsidised windmills open to the public and spin their sails. Most have demonstrations and activities; you can even buy products such as flour and mill bread made the traditional way.

Open Ateliers (Open Studios): Kunstroute de Westelijke Eilanden

Prinseneiland, Bickerseiland & Realeneiland, West (330 4842, www.oawe.nl). Tram 3 or bus 18, 21, 22. **Date** mid May.
Neighbourhoods with populations of artists and artists' studio complexes, among them the Jordaan and De Pijp, hold open days in spring and autumn, when dozens of artists open their doors to the public over the course of a weekend. The annual Westelijke Eilanden is the most popular: situated on the picturesque and peaceful islands around Prinseneiland.
▶ *The Jordaan also hosts an Open Ateliers day (www.openateliersjordaan.nl).*

Art Amsterdam

RAI Congresgebouw, Europaplein, Zuid (549 1212, www.kunstrai.nl). Tram 4, 25 or NS rail RAI station. **Date** mid May-early June.
A hundred or so galleries, both national and international, present their artists' work at this huge commercial five-day exhibition (formerly known as KunstRAI). Expect everything from ceramics and jewellery to paintings and sculptures.

National Cycling Day

Around the Netherlands (0900 400 4040, www.visitamsterdam.nl). **Date** late May.
On your marks, get set, go! Roughly 200,000 cyclists spin their wheels around 200 special cycle routes of varying lengths and difficulty, making this a day for both *fiets* (bike) fanatics and families.

Kunstvlaai

Westergasfabriek, Westerpark (588 2400, www.sandberg.nl, www.kunstvlaai.nl). Tram 3, 10 or bus 18, 21, 22. **Date** see website for details.
This edgy art market works in collaboration with the more commercial Art Amsterdam (*see above*), focusing on new and more original artists, groups and galleries.
▶ *The Affordable Art Fair is also well worth a visit; see p214.*

ARTS & ENTERTAINMENT

A Right Royal Party

Queen's Day in Amsterdam turns the town orange.

Don't say it in front of Beatrix, but the annual royal birthday party that attracts more than 700,000 visitors to the city isn't really about the Queen. It's a huge street party with a very strict dress code: the colour orange. And as there's no one that actually looks good in orange, the colour becomes a camouflage for some really silly behaviour. Of course you can just walk around the canal district and enjoy the street performances and massive yard sale (the 'free market'), but it's also an especially great day for outdoor clubbing, with public stages set up at various squares around town, where a variety of live acts and DJs spin all day long and into the night.

WETERINGPLANTSOEN: TWISTED TECHNO PARTY

The infamous Queen's Night and Day programme, hosted by DJ café TWSTd on the Weteringplantsoe, is known for its diverse array of DJ performances. Locals Bart Skils, Melon, Carlos Valdes, Lauhaus and Steve Rachmad, plus international names such as Matthias Kaden, Vince Watson, Audio Bullys and Sebo K, have all played the extremely crowded park on the Weteringcircuit, right opposite the Heineken Experience, in the past. The events are generally laid-back affairs, but be aware that a fair share of attendees will be popping pills and partaking in class As for all to see. A kerfuffle is always looming.

MUSEUMPLEIN: MUSIC FOR THE MASSES

Probably the largest and most schizophrenic party of the day is the Museumplein rave-up hosted by every teen's fave radio station. Although Radio 538 is always very hush-hush about the line-up beforehand, it's a good bet that trance über-god Tiësto, once the number-one DJ in the world according to *DJ* mag, will end up spinning for the crowd on the massive lawn behind the Rijksmuseum. Besides the big guy, expect a load of Dutch *X Factor* winners (and losers), cheesy Dutch pop stars, urban and hip hop DJs, and throwback retro acts to keep Mum and Dad happy.

WESTERSTRAAT: OLD-SCHOOL TRADITIONS AND ROCK

Nothing says Queen's Day like café Blaffende Vis's enormous mural mounted at the café's front each year, which will be revealed during Koninginnenacht (the night before the big day). It's the same idea every year (members of the Royal Family depicted in comic fashion), but it gets folk waiting for it, and drinking beer like they're training for the Oktoberfest in Munich. Several Amsterdam bands play throughout the night and day, and the vibe is friendly and fun.

SUMMER

Locals love the sun, and drfop everything to move outdoors. Hot spots for sunbathing include the nearby beaches at Bloemendaal, Zandfoort and Wijk aan Zee, along with the city's urban beaches; IJburg, a short tram ride from Centraal Station, is the favourite as it allows swimming. Both Vondelpark and Westerpark get jammed with sun-worshippers, bongo players, artists and barbecues.

★ Vondelpark Openluchttheater
Vondelpark (www.openluchttheater.nl). Tram 1, 2, 5, 3, 12. **Date** early June-mid Aug.
Each summer, the big open-air stage in this popular park is used to the max, with a programme that ranges from classical music to stand-up to pop. There are dance nights, and kids afternoons too. Few places capture the laid-back vibe of Amsterdam in the summer with quite such conviction.

Amsterdam Roots Festival
Various venues (www.amsterdamroots.nl).
Date June.
World music acts from around the globe flock to Amsterdam for this four-day annual shindig, which was voted 'Best Music Festival' by *Time Out Amsterdam* readers. Staff Benda Bilili – the Congolese street band – were highlights of the 2010 line-up. It culminates in a free open-air extravaganza in Oosterpark, starting at noon and going on until late. *See p254.*

Holland Festival
Various venues (788 2100, www.hollandfestivall.nl). **Date** June.
This hugely popular event is the Netherlands' leading arts festival, with a genuinely adventurous programme that includes (both mainstream and oddball) art, dance, opera, theatre, literature and a whole lot more. Tickets go on sale months before the event, so check the online reservation service.

ARTS & ENTERTAINMENT

Queen's Day. *See p209.*

ARTS & ENTERTAINMENT

Dam tot Damloop.

ARTS & ENTERTAINMENT

Canal Gardens in Bloom
Various locations (www.opentuinendagen.nl).
Date 3rd wknd June.
This event sees owners of the beautiful, hidden gardens behind posh canal houses open their doors, giving the public a chance to have a peek at these stunning secret gems. Dogs and prams are sadly not allowed and wheelchair access is almost impossible.
▶ *If you're not in town at this time, you can still admire the Jordaan's hidden courtyards; see p103* Hidden Hofjes.

Vondelpark Openluchttheater
Westerstraat 187 (428 3360, www.openlucht theater.nl). Tram 1, 2, 3. **Date** late June-Aug.
Vondelpark has played host to theatrical events since the late 19th century, and the tradition endures to this day. Each summer brings a series of free shows, running from concerts at the bandstand to Saturday workshops and Sunday afternoon pop concerts. *See p278.*

Julidans
Various locations (www.julidans.nl). **Date** July.
This international contemporary dance festival provides a taster of what's going on – and what's to come – in the field of dance theatre. Over the years, the festival has included internationally renowned dance artists as well as new names that now rank among the greatest in their fields, such as Akram Khan, Dave St Pierre and Sidi Larbi Cherkaoui.
At Julidans' sister event, Julidans Next, the main festival's headlining guests present a young,

unknown artist of their choice who in their opinion has something remarkable to show the world.

Live at Westerpark
www.liveatwesterpark.nl. **Date** July
Big name international acts perform alfresco in the park at this summer series of concerts; Faithless were the openers for 2010. *See p254.*

De Parade
Martin Luther Kingpark, Zuid (033 465 4555, www.deparade.nl). Tram 25 or Metro Amstel.
Date Aug.
When this travelling show (Rotterdam, the Hague and Utrecht are also on their route) lands in the city, locals flock en masse to eat, drink and be merry; oh and to catch an act (cabaret, music, comedy, drama) in one of the many kitschly decorated tents that give the whole thing a vibe of ancient carnivals. Afternoons are child-friendly.
▶ *For more on the Parade's unique mix of art, theatre, music and cabaret, see p278.*

★ Amsterdam Gay Pride
Prinsengracht, Canal Belt (620 880, www. amsterdampride.nl). **Date** 1st Sat Aug.
Though Gay Pride is always surrounded by drama and controversy, whether around money, politics or big egos, the atmosphere during this spectacular boat parade is just fabulous. Around 250,000 spectators line the Prinsengracht to watch the boats, all with garish decorations, loud sound systems and a crew of bare-chested sailors. It's the climax to a

ARTS & ENTERTAINMENT

INSIDE TRACK DAM TO DAM

The annual **Dam tot Damloop** (Dam to Dam Run, www.damloop.nl) takes place on the third Sunday in September and stretches 16.1 kilometres (ten miles) from Amsterdam to Zaandam. Up to 200,000 people gather to watch the 30,000 participants trying to finish in the two-hour limit. There's also a 6.5-kilometre mini marathon, bands lining the main route and a circus in Zaandam to keep the little ones amused.

whole weekend of activities from drag queen fashion shows to political debates on gay issues.

Appelsap
Oosterpark, Oost (www.appelsap.net). Tram 3, 9, 14. **Date** mid Aug.
Organised by Appelsap, which also runs club nights and parties, the atmosphere at this outdoor hip hop festival is always hot. Attracting some 5,000 visitors every year, the programme takes hip hop back to its roots and includes up-and-coming artists as well as some local favourites.

Grachtenfestival
Various venues (421 4542, www.grachtenfestival.nl). **Date** mid Aug.
Founded in 1997, the week-long 'Canal Festival' involves almost 100 classical music concerts, which take place in unusual locations across the city. For details, *see p258.*

Het Theaterfestival
Around Amsterdam (624 2311, www.theater festival.be). **Date** end Aug-early Sept.
The Theaterfestival showcases an edited selection of the best Dutch and Belgian theatre of the previous year. As at the Edinburgh Festival, the accompanying Amsterdam Fringe event is uncurated, and brings a heady mix of more experimental productions. *See p278.*

Uitmarkt
Various locations (www.uitmarkt.nl).
Date last wknd Aug.
From Friday to Sunday, the chaotic Uitmarkt previews the coming cultural season with foretastes of theatre, opera, dance and music events. It's all free, and as such it gets very crowded.

AUTUMN

Weather-wise, autumn might not be the best season for outdoor activities (notwithstanding the occasional Indian summer), but don't let that put you off. Come September, the droves of tourists slowly disappear, and the true spirit of the city comes bubbling back to the surface. Just be sure to bring a brolly and be prepared to duck into a bar to avoid the elements.

Open Monument Days
Various locations (552 4888, www.open monumentendag.nl). **Date** 2nd wknd Sept.
'Heritage Days', as it's officially called, gives you the chance to visit buildings that are normally closed to the public. Some are breathtaking historic buildings from the Golden Age; others, though, are schools,

Amsterdam Dance Event. *See p214.*

former industrial buildings or even farms. The event is defined by a different theme each year; for 2011, it's 'Reuse' and looks at the new uses of old buildings. Look out for the Open Monumentendag flag, check the website or pick up a brochure at the VVV.
▶ *Architecture fans take note: the must-see Museum Het Schip also runs boat tours exploring the architecture around the waterfront; see p77.*

Affordable Art Fair
Gashouder, Klonneplein 1, Westerpark (622 7728, www.affordableartfair.nl). Tram 3, 10 or bus 18, 21, 22. **Date** Oct.
For one weekend in October, the Westergasfabriek (*see p278*) is all about affordable art. Launched in Amsterdam in 2006, this international art phenomenon presents work from local and international galleries. The wide range of art on sale – from figurative to abstract, traditional to avant-garde – ranges from around €100 to €5,000. Perfect for starting your own contemporary art collection.
▶ *If you're in the market for buying art, or you simply want to browse, find out the best places to go in the Galleries chapter; see pp229-236.*

★ Cinekid Amsterdam
Westergasfabriek, Westerpark & the Movies cinema, Haarlemerdijk 161 (531 7890, www.cinekid.nl). Tram 3, 10 or bus 18, 21, 22. **Date** Oct.
This week-long film festival takes place during the Dutch autumn half-term and offers quality films from around the globe, including many in English. Its brilliant MediaLab lets four- to 14-year-olds experience the ins and outs of movie-making through interactive playtime, workshops and media installations, all guided by industry professionals.
▶ *For more about kids' specific activities, check out the Children section of this guide; see pp216-220.*

Amsterdam Dance Event
Various locations (035 621 8748, www.amsterdam-dance-event.nl). **Date** mid Oct.
The organisers claim that this festival, which draws 30,000 each year, is the world's biggest festival of clubbing. It combines business with pleasure: during the day, there are conferences and workshops, while at night, roughly 400 international acts and DJs make sure your feet keep moving. *Photo p213.*

Amsterdamse Cello Biennale
Het Muziekgebouw aan 't Ij, Piet Heinkade 5, Waterfront (519 1808, http://amsterdamse cellobiennale.nl). Tram 25, 26. **Date** Nov 2012 & 2014.
This biennial, nine-day festival of daytime and evening concerts, master classes and presentations has given listeners plenty of reasons to love the cello since 2006. Spanning both generations and genres, it shows off the cello as an artistic, a virtuosic and a

---

INSIDE TRACK FILM FESTIVALS

Whether you want to submerge yourself fully in the film experience or simply dip your toe in the celluloid pool, take a look at what Amsterdam's film festivals have to offer on page 226.

---

versatile element in its own right. Musicians and ensembles the world over attend, giving the Biennale immense international character.

★ Museum Night
Various locations (621 1311, www.n8.nl). **Date** Nov.
The success of this night (tickets sell fast) shows that the locals like to mix art with entertainment. Almost every museum and gallery in town opens late and organises something special to complement the regular exhibits. You might see a take on Rembrandt's *Night Watch* made out of Chupa Chups lollies, or dance the night away in the Anne Frank Huis.

High Times Cannabis Cup
Around the city (http://hightimes.com/public/cancup). **Date** end Nov.
See p71 **Blunt Opinion.**

Sinterklaas
By boat: Amstel, Nieuwe Herengracht. Then city route: Prins Hendrikkade, Damrak, Dam, Raadhuisstraat, Rozengracht, Marnixstraat, Leidseplein. **Date** mid Nov-5 Dec.
Sinterklaas (St Nicholas) marks the start of three weeks of Christmassy festivities by sailing into town on his steamboat mid November. In his white beard, red robe and mitre, he parades around the centre of town on his horse while his staff, dozens of blacked-up Zwarte Pieten (Black Peters), hand out sweets. The celebrations continue, with little gifts being left in children's shoes at night, until Pakjesavond on 5 December, when families celebrate by exchanging presents and poems.

The tradition started when the Church decided to tame the riot and disorder that had always accompanied the end of the slaughter season. It ruled that the traditional celebration should be based around the birthday of St Nicholas, the patron saint of children (and prostitutes, thieves and Amsterdam itself, for that matter); a once-violent tradition was reborn as a Christian family feast. Some believe Black Peter was originally the devil; the colour and appetite for mischief are the only leftovers of an evil vanquished by Sinterklaas; others say he got his dark skin from climbing down chimneys to deliver sweets. Either way, he still manages to divide opinion on whether his swarthy complexion is innocent or utterly racist. But the kids don't care.

★ IDFA

Various locations (www.idfa.nl). **Date** Nov.
The 11-day epic that is International Documentary Film Festival Amsterdam is the largest festival of its kind in the world. Some 280 titles on a multitude of themes, including social issues, politics, art and culture, history, nature and science, educate audiences at various locations around the city.

WINTER

Winter is relatively quiet in Amsterdam, and people generally stay in and prepare for the family festivals: **St Nicholas's Day** (*see above*), which is as important to the Dutch as Christmas, and **New Year's Eve**. You might even be lucky enough to catch a cold snap, and find many locals skating along the Amstel and smaller waterways nearby.

Cinedans

Various locations (www.cinedans.nl). **Date** Dec.
Tickets call for details.
The only one of its kind in the Netherlands, this international dance and movie festival blurs the boundaries between film and dance. The artistic programme includes short and feature-length dance films, documentaries, installations, readings, debates and workshops.

Winterparade

Westergasfabriek, Haaarlemmerweg 8-10, West (www.winterparade.nl). Tram 10 or bus 18, 22.
Tickets €27.50. **Date** Dec.

Much like the medieval feasts of centuries gone by, Winterparade at the Westergasfabriek (*see p278*) offers banquet-style dining with table-top entertainment. While the majority of it is in Dutch, the vats of mulled wine and hordes of poets, musicians, circus acts and the like will get you in the festive mood irrespective of any language barriers.

Oudejaarsavond (New Year's Eve)

Various locations. **Date** 31 Dec.
No, you haven't got off the wrong train or plane, and you're not in a war zone: New Year's Eve – and seeing out the *oud* and welcoming in the new – is a riot of champagne, *oliebollen* (greasy deep-fried blobs of dough, apple and raisins), and tons and tons of scary fireworks that officially only go on sale the day before. Come midnight, people take to the streets (and bars, many of which only open at midnight) to celebrate. The best areas to visit are Nieuwmarkt and Dam Square; the latter often stages a big council-sponsored concert, with Dutch acts and DJs to help keep things moving. Not for the faint-hearted.

Chinese New Year

Nieuwmarkt, Old Centre: Old Side (06 2476 0060, www.zeedijk.nl). **Map** p326 D2. **Date** late Jan/early Feb.
The Nieuwmarkt is a focal point for Amsterdam's Chinatown, complete with restaurants, a temple and a fantastic supermarket selling all things Asian. Chinese New Year is welcomed during the daytime with lion dances, firecrackers, and Chinese drums and gongs.

Christmas market at **Sinterklaas**.

ARTS & ENTERTAINMENT

Children

Nature, film, artistic pursuits – and some brilliant places to play.

Amsterdammers love to hang out with their kids and the amount of activities on offer is staggering. Schools finish at midday every Wednesday, so there's particularly plenty going on. Check out the *Jeugd* (youth) or *Kind* (child) sections in Amsterdam's free magazines.

Amsterdam's scale and numerous sites make it a pleasure to walk around, even for those with smaller legs. Changing facilities, however, are few and far between: the best bets are department stores or the public library. A trip on the canals is a must for all ages (see **Tour Amsterdam**, *pp75-79*).

Alternatively, head Noord on one of the free IJ ferries from behind Centraal Station. And if you're thinking about hiring bikes, the *bakfiets* (box bike) is great for loading in your pre-pedalling offspring.

ANIMAL FUN

Viewing the horses at Amsterdam's riding school, the **Hollandsche Manege** (*see p52* **Horsing Around**) is free but the daily lessons are worth the money; parents can relax in the beautiful café while their offspring trot around in the yard below.

Small animal-lovers will love one of the 17 or so **children's farms** that are dotted around the city; check www.goudengids.nl under '*Kinderboerderijen*' for one near you. Further afield is the **Ridammerhoeve Goat Farm** (Nieuwe Meerlaan 4, Amsterdamse Bos, 645 5034, www.geitenboerderij.nl, free), where kids can pet and feed the goats, pigs, hens and horses while parents purchase some excellent quality cheese. For something a little larger, head to **Artis Royal Zoo** (*see p117*) – enjoyable even on a wet day.

INSIDE TRACK SHIP AHOY

For a proper pirate experience, visit the **VOC Schip Amsterdam**. This replica of an 18th-century East India Company cargo ship, with 'real' sailors, is docked by the Science Center NEMO (*see p218*) until 2011. It then moves back to its original spot by the newly renovated **Scheepvaartmuseum** (*see p121*).

BABY SITTING

Oppascentrale Kriterion

(624 5848, www.kriterionoppas.org). **Rates** €5-€6/hr; additional charge Fri, Sat. *Administration charge* €3 per booking. *Annual membership fee* €13. **No credit cards**.

This service uses students who are all aged over 18, and all of whom have been carefully vetted both before and during service. Advance booking advised, register first online or by phone.

CREATIVE ARTS

Keramiekstudio Color Me Mine

Roelof Hartstraat 22, Museum Quarter (675 2987, www.amsterdam.colormemine.nl). Tram 3, 5, 12, 24. **Open** 11am-7pm Tue-Sat; noon-6pm Sun. **Rates** (excl cost of ceramic item) €15; €10 reductions. **Credit** MC, V.

Choose a ceramic from a huge selection and then decorate it, or design and make your own mosaic. Staff are happy to advise little ones suffering an early onset of artist's block. Tots under six must be accompanied by an adult.

Het Kinderkookkafe

Vondelpark 6b, Museum Quarter (625 3257, www.kinderkookkafe.nl). Tram 1, 2, 3, 5, 12. **Open** *Help Yourself Bar* 10am-5pm daily. **Rates** vary. **No credit cards**. **Map** p330 C6.

Kids can make pizza, sausage animals and decorate cupcakes under expert guidance at the DIY bar, while

216 **Time Out** Amsterdam

TunFun. *See p219.*

INSIDE TRACK
MINI MAD SCIENTISTS

A truly kid-friendly science museum, the
Science Center NEMO *(see below)*
eschews exhibits in favour of hands-on
trickery, gadgetry and tomfoolery: play DNA
detective games, blow mega soap bubbles
and explode things in a 'wonderlab'.

---

parents relax and enjoy the fruits of their offspring's
labour. Additional courses run during school holidays; check the website for events and to register.

★Groot Melkhuis

*Vondelpark 2, Museum Quarter (612 9674,
www.groot-melkhuis.nl). Tram 2, 3, 5, 12.* **Open**
10am-6pm daily. **No credit cards. Map** p330 C6.
A great play area within the grounds of a self-service
café in Vondelpark, with free Wi-Fi to boot. The
Wednesday afternoon *kinderatelier* (children's studio, 2-5pm, €5) invites kids to play in an artistic way.

FILMS

Most kids films are dubbed, but an 'OV' after the
title means it's showing in its original language.
The children's bookshop **Helden en Boeven**
(Bosboom Toussaintstraat 27, 427 4407, www.
heldenboeven.nl) has regular screenings in the
impressive old Waag (*see p86*).
During autumn, the **Cinekid** film festival
(531 7890, www.cinekid.nl) offers quality films
from around the globe. Its MediaLab also lets
four- to 14-year-olds experience movie-making
through play, workshops and installations, all
guided by industry professionals.

LIBRARIES

★ Openbare Bibliotheek Amsterdam

*Oosterdokskade 143, Waterfront (523 0900,
www.oba.nl). Tram 1, 2, 4, 5, 9, 13, 16, 17, 24,
25, 26.* **Open** 10am-10pm daily. **Map** p327 E1.
As well as having English-language books, a play
area, changing rooms and a great roof-top restaurant, Amsterdam's spectacular central library hosts
a multitude of events for kids, including story-
reading sessions in English on Tuesdays at 11am.
▶ *English bookshop Waterstone's (see p182) also
holds regular readings for kids.*

MUSEUMS

Amsterdam's museums are either highly
interactive, extraordinarily life-like or the real
thing. Experience life on a houseboat at the
Woonbootmuseum (*see p98*); watch pianos
play themselves at the **Pianola Museum**

(Westerstraat 106, the Jordaan, 627 9624,
www.pianola.nl); or catch a ride on the antique
Electrische Museumtramlijn (www.museu
mtramlijn.org) in the Amsterdamse Bos.
Information listed details child-specific
activities at major museums. Also, check for kids'
audio tours, treasure hunt leaflets and the like.

CoBrA Museum

For listings, see p113.
Every Sunday at 11am, the CoBrA hosts its *kinderatelier* (children's studio), where children can paint
and draw under the guidance of a teacher. At 1pm,
there's a children's tour of the museum.

Joods Historisch Museum

For listings, see p115.
Guided kids' tours take place in the main museum,
while the special kids' museum allows children to follow the life of a Jewish family, partake in Hebrew
workshops and get creative with special activities.
▶ *The Anne Frank Huis is one of the city's most
evocative sites; see p96.*

Science Center NEMO

*Oosterdok 2 (531 3233, www.e-nemo.nl). Bus 22,
42.* **Open** 10am-5pm Tue-Sun. School holidays
10am-5pm daily. **Admission** €11.50; €6.50
students; free under-3s. **Map** p327 F2.
For review, see p121.

Van Gogh Museum

For listings, see p109.
This popular museum hosts children's sessions at weekends. They begin with a full tour of the museum and end in the kids' studio where the children make their own paintings, themed to the current exhibition. English tours are available with advance group bookings. There's also a free *Treasure Hunt* guide and children's audio tour (€1.25).

PARKS

Vondelpark (*see p110*) is a very popular spot but you'll find at least one good park per district. With its city farm, water adventure park and swimming area (summer only), **Westerpark** (*see p104*) entertains the young and young-at-heart. **Amstelpark** (*see p112*) promises hours of fun with a miniature train and a maze. Take the whole day to explore the **Amsterdamse Bos** (*see p112*); the goat farm and pancake house are sure to be a hit.

PLAY

★ Toy Libraries

Various locations (www.dse.nl/~splot/splotladr.htm or look up 'Speel-o-theek' at www.goudengids.nl).
A visit to the local *speel-o-theek* (toy library) could be the move that saves the (rainy) day.

★ TunFun

Mr Visserplein 7, Jodenbuurt (689 4300, www.tunfun.nl). Tram 9, 14 or Metro Waterlooplein. **Open** 10am-6pm daily. **Admission** €7.50 ages 1-12; free adults. **No credit cards. Map** p327 E1.
An urban recycling success, this cavernous indoor playground used to be an underpass. Huge soft-play constructions provide endless joy for those under 12, with ball pools for tiny tots and full-on jungle gyms for more adventurous older kids. *Photo p217.*

SWIMMING & SPORTS

De Mirandabad and **Zuiderbad** indoor pools, and the **Brediusbad** and **Flevoparkbad** outdoor pools are good for kids (*see p271*). The **Vondelpark** (*see p110*) and **Westerpark** (*see p104*) offer outdoor water areas in the summer.

Drier activities include the massive Klimhal Amsterdam, which is the biggest indoor climbing centre in the Netherlands, featuring different walls and 'mountains' to suit kids from six years up. With two pistes and real snow, Snowplanet is almost like the real thing, and there are even introductory sessions for three- to four-year-olds. For something a little closer to the ground, kids will go crazy for the indoor carting track at Race Planet for Kids, where they can play with pedal cars, electric F1 cars and more.

ARTS & ENTERTAINMENT

Science Center NEMO.

★ Klimhal Amsterdam
Naritaweg 48, Sloterdijk (681 0121, www.klimhal amsterdam.nl). Tram 12 or Station Amsterdam Sloterdijk. **Open** 5-10.30pm Mon, Tue, Thur; 2-10.30pm Wed; 11am-10.30pm Sat; 9.30am-10.30pm Sun. **Admission** €12; €5-€9 reductions; €6 equipment hire. **No credit cards**.

Race Planet for Kids
Herwijk 10, Sloterdijk (611 1120, www.race planet.com). Tram 17 then bus 82. **Open** times vary. **Admission** from €15.75. **Credit** MC, V.

★ Snowplanet
Recreatieschap Spaarnwoude, Heuvelweg 6-8, Velsen-Zuid (025 554 5848, www.snowplanet.nl). Tram 17 then bus 82. **Open** 9am-11pm daily. **Admission** from €10/hr; €7.50 equipment hire. **Credit** MC, V.

THEATRE & MUSIC

Both the **Jeugdtheater De Krakeling** (Nieuwe Passeerdersstraat 1, Western Canal Belt, 624 5123 reservations, www.krakeling.nl) and **Het Nederlands Marionettentheater** (Jacob Obrechtstraat 28, Museum Quarter, 692 8031, www.nederlandsmarionetten theater.nl) offer language-no-problem puppet and mime performances for kids; check websites for programmes. Amsterdam's pre-eminent venue for classical music, the **Concertgebouw** (*see p256*) regularly programmes children's concerts, featuring multidisciplinary elements such as film to engage all the senses.

OUTSIDE AMSTERDAM

Set in a forest, the enormous **Efteling** amusement park is packed with state-of-the-art thrills, traditional rides, fairy-tale characters, and even talking rubbish bins. The miniature city of **Madurodam** (*see p294*) is a wonderland (especially when they're lit up from within on summer evenings) of over 700 scale models of the Netherlands' most famous sights.

In the beautiful nature reserve of Berg en Bos, the expansive **Apenhaul** is home to all manner of primates that are free to roam the grounds, as visitors do likewise.

★ Apenheul
JC Wilslaan 21, Apeldoorn (055 357 5757, www.apenheul.com). **Open** *Aug-July* 9.30am-5pm daily. *July-Aug* 9.30am-6pm daily. **Admission** €16; €12 reductions; free under-3s. **Credit** AmEx, MC, V.
► *For other attractions out of town, see pp281-302* **Escapes & Excursions**.

Efteling
Europalaan 1, Kaatsheuvel, Noord Brabant (0900 0161, www.efteling.nl). **Open** *July, Aug* 10am-6pm Mon-Fri, Sun; 10am-midnight Sat. *Apr-Oct* 10am-6pm daily. **Admission** €27-€29; €24-€27 reductions; free under-4s. **Credit** AmEx, MC, V

State of Play

A primer of fun for the little ones.

PLAY! AMSTERDAM is an ingenious guidebook listing Amsterdam's best playgrounds, from lone pieces of climbing equipment to large-scale playgrounds. Written and published by Becky Russell, the book came about when Russell found herself at the start of the summer break one year with two young children and no plans. Bored of their usual playgrounds, they decided to seek out some new spots.

Consequently, Russell decided to create a book of her findings. Exploring every street in the city, she noted all types of play areas; the main criterion for inclusion was that the playground has to be free of charge. When rating the playgrounds, Russell opted against placing any age recommendations as she feels this says nothing about a child's ability; instead, she chose to use 'small explorers', 'medium adventurers' and 'big adventurers'.

Turns out that there are 414 ways for kids to have gratis fun in Amsterdam. Becky's top three are **Het Woeste Westen** (Westerpark, tram 3, 10 or bus 18, 21, 22), which, with its combination of space, high grass, wild flowers, canals and tunnels, recaptures what it's like to grow up in the country. **Willem de Zwijgerlaan** (Bos en Lommer, tram 12, 14) includes challenging equipment that's suitable for all, including a rope bridge, wobbly bridge and high tube slide down a large hill. A green oasis in an otherwise concrete neighbourhood, **Speeltuin Wittenburg** (Fortuinstraat, Waterfront, bus 22, 43) also appeals to all, but the high climbing frame with balance beams and bridges is particularly good for 'big adventurers'.

• PLAY! AMSTERDAM is available via www.playamsterdam.nl.

Dance

A spicy and experimental scene, decently funded.

Schizophrenic is the best way to describe Dutch dance. On the one hand it has a boutique, experimental feel with screaming domestic creations that are hard on both eye and ear. On the other hand its two headline companies, Dutch National Ballet and Netherlands Dance Theatre, are the envy of the classical and contemporary dance worlds.

International choreographers such as Jirí Kylián, William Forsythe, Sidi Larbi Cherkaoui and Lightfoot León have seen their works flourish with regular premières at the Stadsschouwburg and Muziektheater. Commercial fare passes through the RAI Theatre care of the Kirov and Bolshoi Russian ballet companies, while the less classically minded should visit in July when the Leidseplein theatres host Julidans, a festival for the newest styles making waves around the world.

TICKETS AND INFORMATION

Tickets for the majority of performances can be bought at the venues themselves, or from any of the various phone, online or drop-in AUB operations (*see p208*).

VENUES

Dance in all its forms is performed at a variety of venues in Amsterdam, the biggest of which are detailed below. Other local venues that stage occasional events include **Theater Bellevue** (*see p276*), the **Stadsschouwburg** (*see p276*), the **Frascati** (*see p274*), **De Brakke Grond** (*see p274*), **NDSM** (*see p124*), **OT301** (*see p228*) and **Het Rozentheater** (*see p275*).

DWA-Studio Theatre

Arie Biemondstraat 107b, Museum Quarter (689 1789, www.danswerkplaats.nl). Tram 1, 17. **Box office** *Phone* 10am-6pm Mon-Thur. *In person* 7.45pm until start of performance. **Tickets** free €15. **No credit cards. Map** p329 B6.

Danswerkplaats is a podium that allows young recently graduated students to develop their choreographic talents. Performances have been staged at least once a month, both here and elsewhere in the city or the Netherlands, since 1993.

hetveem Theater

Van Diemenstraat 410, Western Docklands (626 9291, www.hetveemtheater.nl). Tram 3 or bus

18, 21, 22. **Box office** *Phone* 10am-4pm performance days. *In person* from 1hr before performance. **Tickets** €8-€10; €5 reductions. **No credit cards.**

A homophone for 'fame', hetveem Theater occupies the third floor of a renovated warehouse and hosts modern dance and multimedia productions from home and abroad. Performances usually take place at 8.30pm; between October and March there's also a Sunday slot at 4pm.

KIT Tropentheater

Kleine Zaal Linnaeusstraat 2, Oost; Grote Zaal Mauritskade 63, Oost (568 8500, www.tropentheater.nl). Tram 7, 9, 10, 14 or bus 22. **Box office** *Phone* 10am-6pm Mon-Fri; 2-6pm Sat. *In person* noon-6pm, & from 1hr before start of performance Mon-Sat. **Tickets** €12-€20. **Credit** MC, V. **Map** p332 H3.

The Tropeninstituut organises performances in music and dance that are related to or drawn from various non-Western cultures. The dance programme varies from classical Indian styles to South African, Indonesian to Argentinian. The flamenco programme is quite a draw-card. The meal-and-performance packages that are popular.

★ Melkweg

Lijnbaansgracht 234a, Western Canal Belt (531 8181, www.melkweg.nl). Tram 1, 2, 5, 7, 10. **Box office** from 4.30pm daily. **Performances** usually 8.30pm. **Tickets** €5-€45. **No credit cards. Map** p330 C5.

ARTS & ENTERTAINMENT

This venerated multidisciplinary venue opened its doors to national and international dance and theatre groups in 1973. For many years, the small stage hosted dancers and choreographers at the start of their careers. Its renovated theatre lives up to tradition: many of the country's hottest new project groups perform between the higher-profile mainstays. Sharing a roof with a live-music venue means that all shows have a rock edge.

▶ *See p251 and p262 for more about the Melkweg's music and club offerings.*

★ Muziektheater
Waterlooplein 22 (625 5455, www.muziek theater.nl). Tram 9, 14 or Metro Waterlooplein. **Box office** noon-6pm or until start of performance daily. **Tickets** €20-€100. **Credit** AmEx, DC, MC, V. **Map** p327 E3.

The Muziektheater is Amsterdam at its most ambitious. Its plush, crescent-shaped interior has room for 1,596 people and was for many years the largest stage in Europe. It is home to both Dutch National Ballet (*see p223*) and De Nederlandse Opera, but the stage is also used by visiting companies such as Nederlands Dans Theater (*see p223*). The panoramic glass walls of the foyer offer impressive views over the River Amstel, but don't be too distracted: the venue has a strict lock-out policy for late arrivals – no entry until intermission.

Out of town venues

Lucent Danstheater
Spuiplein 150, The Hague (070 880 0333, www.ldt.nl). NS rail Den Haag Centraal Station.

Box office *Phone* 10am-6pm Mon-Fri; noon-6pm Sat. *In person* noon-6pm Mon-Sat, & from 1hr before performance. **Tickets** €14-€35. **Credit** AmEx, DC, MC, V.

The Lucent Danstheater, located in the centre of the Hague, is the fabulous home of the world-famous Nederlands Dans Theater (*see p223*) and boasts a stage facility built especially for dance. As well as mounting high-quality Dutch productions in both dance and opera, it's also become one of the country's foremost venues in which to see touring international dance companies.

Rotterdamse Schouwburg
Schouwburgplein 25, Rotterdam (010 411 8110, www.schouwburg.rotterdam.nl). NS rail Rotterdam Centraal Station. **Box office** 11am-7pm Mon-Sat. Closed July-mid Aug. **Tickets** €12-€42.50. **Credit** AmEx, DC, MC, V.

This large, square theatre opened in 1988 and soon became known by the waggish nickname *Kist van Quist* ('Quist's Coffin'; Wim Quist was the architect). The building hosts a generous variety of classical ballet and modern dance from both Dutch and international troupes in its two auditoria: one has 900 seats, while the other seats a mere 150.

Toneelschuur
Lange Begijnestraat 9, Haarlem (023 517 3910, www.toneelschuur.nl). NS rail Haarlem Centraal Station. **Box office** 1.30-9.45pm daily. **Tickets** €13-€20. **No credit cards.**

With two stages and two cinemas housed within its hypermodern home designed by cartoonist Joost Swarte, Haarlem's Toneelschuur has every reason

Stadsschouwburg. *See p221.*

to be proud of its addition to the nation's cultural heritage. Its nationally renowned programme of theatre and modern dance has many Amsterdam culture vultures swooping in especially.

COMPANIES

Dansgroep Amsterdam
669 5755, www.dansgroepamsterdam.nl.
Dansgroep Amsterdam is the city's foremost contemporary dance company. Helmed by two artistic directors, Krisztina de Châtel and Itzik Galili, it specialises in high-energy proscenium choreographies as well as sophisticated site-specific projects. The group regularly performs at the Stadsschouwburg, but has also appeared in the corridors of important galleries and museums.

★ Dutch National Ballet
Muziektheater box office 625 5455, www.het-nationale-ballet.nl.
Amsterdam's premier classical dance company is based at the Muziektheater and ranks alongside the Royal Ballet and New York City Ballet as one of the largest ensembles either side of the Atlantic; indeed it has the most comprehensive Balanchine repertoire of any European company. Under artistic director Ted Brandsen, the company now attracts guest dancers and choreographers from around the world.

ICK Amsterdam
616 7240, www.ickamsterdam.com.
The Internationaal Choreografisch Kunstencentrum (ICK) Amsterdam was founded by Emio Greco and Pieter C. Scholten. Together, the choreographer-director team produce high-quality contemporary dance works with moody lighting and an unmatched sense of mise-en-scène. Works tour internationally, but can be seen locally at the Stadsschouwburg (*see p276*) and Frascati (*see p274*).

Out of town

★ Netherlands Dance Theater
Lucent Danstheater box office 070 880 0333, www.ndt.nl.
Netherlands Dance Theater, founded in 1959, has transcended the Dutch dance scene and become a company of the world. Thanks to its former artistic director Jirí Kylián, whose choreographies are desired by almost every high-profile company on the planet, NDT is met with open arms wherever it tours. In Amsterdam, performances usually take place at the Muziektheater (*see p222*), but NDTII (a second company of aspirant dancers) can be seen at the Stadsschouwburg (*see p276*) and other venues.

Scapino Ballet Rotterdam
010 414 2414, www.scapinoballet.nl.
The oldest dance company in the country, Scapino used to be a little on the stuffy side. But in the 1990s,

attention shifted from convention to innovation; once again, they're now a force to be reckoned with, under the tutelage of Ed Wubbe and his breathtaking group of professional dancers.

Courses & training

Henny Jurriëns Foundation
Bellamystraat 49, Oud West (412 1510, www.hjs.nl). Tram 7, 17. **Classes** 9.30am, 11am, 12.45pm Mon-Fri; 11am Sat. **Cost** €7.50 per class; €60 10 classes. **No credit cards. Map** p329 A5.
The Henny Jurriëns Foundation provides open training for professional dancers in both classical and modern dance techniques throughout the year. The studio is at the top of the Olympia Building (an old cinema) and has a New York loft atmosphere. Instructors are a mixture of locals and visiting master teachers from abroad. The foundation also offers workshops, for which pre-registration is necessary. Give them a call to book your place or to get more information about the programme.

Festivals

Holland Dance Festival
Nobelstraat 21, 2513 BC The Hague (070 361 6142, 070 356 1176 information, www.hollanddancefestival.com). **Date** biennial, Nov (2011, 2013).
Held every two years in November, the Holland Dance Festival takes place at three venues (including the Hague's Lucent Danstheater; *see p222*), and is one of the biggest and most important festivals on the Dutch dance calendar. Many of the world's larger companies are attracted to the event thanks to its reputation, and the quality of the work is consistently high. Clips of previous work can be watched with the website's YouTube link.

Julidans
www.julidans.nl
July festival that attracts many of the world's finest choreographers and companies, who showcase work around the city. Past programmes have included premieres from Kathak master Akram Khan and an unexpected collaboration between Belgian dancer-choreographer Sidi Larbi Cherkaoui and flamenco star María Pagés.

★ Nederlandse Dansdagen
Various locations in Maastricht (www.nederlandse dansdagen.nl). **Date** first week Oct.
During October, the Nederlandse Dansdagen (Dutch Dance Days) in Maastricht form the official start of the national Dansweek (www.dansweek-brabant.nl, www.dansweekgelderland.nl) held in theatres all over the country to promote Dutch dance to a larger audience. During the festival, the season's best performances are repeated and the main Dutch dance prizes are granted.

ARTS & ENTERTAINMENT

Film

Keeping it reel with champion fests and charming cinemas.

One of the world's celebrated beauties, Amsterdam itself has of course starred in movies including blockbuster *Ocean's Twelve*, and you'll probably recognise Dutch household names like Tom Cruise's *Valkyrie* co-star Carice van Houten and *Control* director Anton Corbijn. Still, chances are you won't get the best out of Dutch-origin films without mastering the language or at least waiting for the DVD version with subtitles.

That said, language restrictions are no impediment to enjoying Amsterdam's diverse and outward-looking celluloid culture. The city is home to some of Europe's most beautiful mainstream cinemas, like deco delight Pathé Tuschinski, a fine crop of arthouse institutions, and an annual roundabout of film festivals, ranging from the world-class to the plain weird. The 2011 relocation of the EYE Film Institute Netherlands (formerly the **Film Museum**; *see p227*) to a massive building across the waters of the IJ means this hive of restoration and research will be able to achieve so much more without its former space restraints.

CINEMAS
First run

Movies
Haarlemmerdijk 161, the Jordaan (624 5790, www.themovies.nl). Tram 3 or bus 18, 21, 22. **Tickets** €8-€9; €65 10-visit card. **Screens** 4. **No credit cards. Map** p325 B1.
The oldest cinema in Amsterdam to remain in regular use, the Movies has been circulating celluloid since way back in 1912, and it still exudes a genteel atmosphere of sophisticated elegance to this day. The excellent adjoining restaurant serves decent set dinners, and the cost – between €28 and €36 depending on the number of courses – includes your admission to the film. *Photo p227.*
▶ *The Movies also plays host to the brilliant annual Cinekid Amsterdam film festival, see also p214 and p216.*

Pathé ArenA
ArenA Boulevard 600, Bijlmermeer (0900 1458 premium rate, www.pathe.nl). Metro Bijlmer. **Tickets** €5-€12. **Screens** 14. **Credit** MC, V.
This multi-screen complex is one of the best places to enjoy those guilty-pleasure blockbusters with little or no chance of bumping into someone you know, because of its peripheral location way out by

the Ajax stadium. Styled with all the finesse of a big brick house, it nonetheless has comfortable seating and the only IMAX screen in Amsterdam, unquestionably the best place to catch 3D movies.

Pathé City
Kleine-Gartmanplantsoen 15-19, Southern Canal Belt (0900 1458 premium rate, www.pathe.nl). Tram 1, 2, 57, 10. **Tickets** €5-€11. **Screens** 7. **Credit** MC, V. **Map** p330 D5.
Once the cinematic equivalent of a used-car salesman, this former multiplex received a long-overdue reinvention in late 2010 as an arthouse/mainstream hybrid, with the emphasis firmly on quality programming. It's perfect for date night, with a grown-up theatrical vibe (think velvet curtains) and a wine bar. Tickets are priced slightly higher than at the other Pathés, to keep students and the under-30s at bay.

INSIDE TRACK THE REEL DEAL

If you come across an 'OV' at the end of a film title when looking at cinema listings (especially with animated/kids' flicks), it means the film is showing in its original version (read: language).

Film Clubbing

Vexed by the multiplex? Try these…

The desire to show films any place but in buildings specifically designed for that purpose is nearing criticial mass in Amsterdam, but it wasn't always so. 'About five years ago, I decided Amsterdam was in dire need of an underground film scene,' says American long-time Amsterdam resident Jeffrey Babcock. These days, the cinema connoisseur – hundreds of DVDs line the walls of his apartment – curates several indie nights around the West, including the packed weekly Cinemanita gatherings in the cavernous space at the back of hipster hangout **De Nieuwe Anita** (*see p228*).

Hardly any of his choices have been screened in the Netherlands before. Notions like profit or star power are of no concern, and other non-commercial criteria can prevail. 'Every film I show has something unique and valuable,' explains Babcock. 'To me, cinema is about ideas and creativity, about life.'

Kindred spirit Bas Jacobs regularly invites Babcock and others to programme both films and music at his **Delicatessen** (www.delicatessenzeeburg.com), an artsy meeting space in a tiny former deli in the Indische Buurt, to the east of the city.

'I want to bring people together in an intimate setting,' says Jacobs. He also serves themed food with the flick: 'Thai curry with a Thai film, and so on,' Delicatessen has quickly established a faithful audience keen on the sociable experience, almost irrespective of the film, just like the Cinemanita.

Same goes for Italian restaurant l'Ozio (www.ozioamsterdam.com) in De Pijp, which may not be your typical alternative venue,

perhaps, but it's got its own underground cinema: in the small basement exhibition space, mostly Italian classics are shown for free. Dinner upstairs is optional, but what kind of Italian views on an empty stomach?

'It proves people are interested in seeing something different from Pathé blockbusters,' Babcock says. It also shows that you don't need an expensive marketing scheme; all three venues rely solely on emailing lists. Subscribe on their websites to receive email updates yourself.

ARTS & ENTERTAINMENT

Pathé de Munt
Vijzelstraat 15, Southern Canal Belt (0900 1458 premium rate, www.pathe.nl). Tram 4, 9, 14, 16, 24, 25. **Tickets** €5-€9.50. **Screens** 13. **Credit** MC, V. **Map** p330 D4.
This is central Amsterdam's monster-sized multiplex. In its favour are huge screens and comfortable, spacious seating, and now that the City (*see p224*) has gone upmarket, this is the place to go for big-budget Hollywood kicks.

★ Pathé Tuschinski
Reguliersbreestraat 26-34, Southern Canal Belt (0900 1458 premium rate, www.pathe.nl). Tram 4, 9, 14, 16, 24, 25. **Tickets** €5-€10. **Screens** 6. **Credit** MC, V. **Map** p331 E4.

This extraordinary cinema is named after Abraham Tuschinski, Amsterdam's most illustrious cinematic entrepreneur. Built in 1921 as a 'world theatre palace', the decor is an arresting clash of rococo, art deco and Jugendstil, which can make it hard to keep your eyes on the silver screen. Glittering premières take place to road-blocking effect. If you're more 'in the red' than red-carpet-ready, check out the morning screenings.

Arthouses

Cinecenter
Lijnbaansgracht 236, Southern Canal Belt (623 6615, www.cinecenter.nl). Tram 1, 2, 5, 7, 10. **Tickets** €6-€9. **Screens** 4. **No credit cards.** **Map** p325 A3.

Film Festivals

If you screen it, they will come.

Discover Amsterdam's cornucopia of film festivals and a plethora of exotic alternatives to the regular fare suddenly appear. Whether you want to submerge yourself in the film experience or just take a little dip in the celluloid pool, here is a selection of festivals worth checking out.

The festival season kicks into gear at the end of January with the annual **International Film Festival Rotterdam** (www.filmfestivalrotterdam.com), which is the largest film festival as well as one of the largest cultural events in the country. Lasting 12 days and taking over venues all over the city, IFFR specialises in art-house fare and exotic films from all over, with a traditionally strong helping of esoteric Asian flicks, and large numbers of directors show up for Q&As and talk shows. Befriend a volunteer for access to the best after-parties.

Something of a moveable fest this one, in terms of venue and time year, is the **Roze Filmdagen** (www.rozefilmdagen.nl; *see p246*), literally Amsterdam's 'pink film days'. For the time being, the festival seems to have settled in the wonderful Westerpark venue **Het Ketelhuis** (*see right*), showing queer-minded flicks from around the world in mid March. Look out for the promo posters around town – they're typically wonderfully witty.

Filling up four days at the end of March, the **Unheard Film Festival** (www.unheard film.nl), at Kriterion (*see right*), is a smaller festival focused on the use of sound in films. Some films get a soundtrack makeover by a famous Benelux band, some are selected for their exceptional soundtracks, while clips from others are given wholly new audio.

The end of April heralds **Imagine: Amsterdam Fantastic Film Festival** (www.imaginefilmfestival.nl), also held at the Kriterion, which caters to gore-hounds and kids alike, via screenings of films inspired by fantasy, sci-fi and horror. Gory and ghoulish appearances notwithstanding, the crowds and crew are a good-natured bunch and the festival has grown large enough to offer up some intriguing flicks while maintaining a cosy atmosphere for all-comers.

Even Amsterdam nights can get sultry in August, so get comfortable in front of

one of the many open-air screens that litter the city, with the one at the Stenen Hoofd, Westerdoksdijk, even devoting several nights to screening the unreleased gems of that year at the free after-dark festival **Pluk de Nacht** (www.plukdenacht.nl).

For five fun-packed days in September, Amsterdam becomes the animated capital of Europe, courtesy of the brilliant **KLIK! Amsterdam Animation Festival** (www.klik amsterdam.nl), geared towards the young, the old, and every cartoon-lover in between.

The kids are all right during October's autumn break when **Cinekid** (*see p214 and p216*), the largest kid-oriented film festival on the planet, has its annual play date, with animation-happy adults often just as giddy as the tots at the centre of proceedings, at the Westergasfabriek culture park and the Movies.

November's **Africa in the Picture** festival (www.africainthepicture.nl) focuses on the many overlooked films coming from the continent, giving the emerging African Nouvelle Vague a much-needed platform by organising a host of screenings, discussions and parties.

The biggest documentary festival in the world also happens to touch down in Amsterdam at the end of November in the form of the **International Documentary Filmfestival Amsterdam** (www.idfa.nl). IDFA's massive quantity of titles is geared towards neophyte and die-hard alike, with intimate Q&As and cinematic workshops from the best in the biz.

Tucked discreetly away from the madding bustle of the nearby Leidseplein, this snug, artsy and student-friendly cinema is home to a cosmopolitan array of films and even has a trendy yet welcoming bar that's the perfect arena for a little post-film debate, should you emerge from the screening to find it's raining. That's if you even need an excuse.

★ EYE Film Institute Nederlands

www.eyefilm.nl. Due to relocate in 2011. Address details and ticket information were unavailable at time of press, so please check website for details.
The most important centre of cinematography in the Netherlands by a country mile, the EYE Film Institute specialises in major retrospectives and edgier contemporary fare. The annual summer programme typically features an exhaustive array of screenings, talks and exhibits dedicated to the celebration and reassessment of showbiz lynchpins, with past examples including the astonishingly adaptable Ingrid Bergman. A lesser-known function of the place is its loving programme of celluloid restorations.

Filmhuis Cavia

Van Hallstraat 51-52, West (681 1419, www.filmhuiscavia.nl). Tram 3, 10. **Tickets** €4. **Screens** 1. **No credit cards. Map** p325 A3.
Blink and you'll miss this one. Housed in the amiable seclusion of a once-squatted school above a gym, the left-of-mainstream Cavia specialises in obscure, queer and/or political pictures. You can also rent it for film-themed parties of your own; ideal if you consider yourself something of an armchair revolutionary.

Het Ketelhuis

Haarlemmerweg 8-10, Westerpark (684 0090, www.ketelhuis.nl). Tram 10 or bus 18, 22. **Tickets** €8-€9. **Screens** 3. **No credit cards. Map** p325 A1.
What once was of little interest to non-Dutch-speaking film fans (it used to specialise in unsubtitled home-grown movies), the Ketelhuis now screens interesting international art films alongside the Netherland's finest flicks. The revival of the Westergas area and regular festivals haven't hurt its popularity among cinematically minded Amsterdammers, and the staff here are among the friendliest in town.
▶ *For more on the Westerpark and all the goodies it has to offer, see p104.*

Kriterion

Roetersstraat 170, Oost (623 1708, www. kriterion.nl). Tram 7, 10 or Metro Weesperplein. **Tickets** €5.50-€8. **Screens** 2. **No credit cards. Map** p332 G3.
Founded in 1945 by a group of Resistance-fighter undergraduates, this cinema continues to be run by a bunch of students – to great success. Their unbeatable formula is to show quality films, first run as well as contemporary classics, while the *CinemaDiscutabel* programme of films plus debate

guarantees thought-provoking discussions. The Kriterion's sneak previews are almost always sold out, while the convivial bar usually facilitates much after-film analysis. *Photo p228.*
▶ *The Kriterion is also host to some great film festivals; see left.*

Rialto

Ceintuurbaan 338, De Pijp (676 8700, www.rialto film.nl). Tram 3, 12, 24, 25. **Tickets** €7.50-€9. **Screens** 3. **No credit cards. Map** p331 F6.
The neighbourhood cinema of Oud-Zuid and De Pijp, the Rialto offers an eclectic mix of arty features, documentaries, classics, festivals and kids' fare. It broadens the mix with frequent avant-garde film premières, as well as regularly holding introductory talks to films chosen by guest speakers. The Rialto also has good disabled access. Be warned, though, as the foreign films here rarely have subtitles other than Dutch ones.

De Uitkijk

Prinsengracht 452, Southern Canal Belt (623 7460, www.uitkijk.nl). Tram 1, 2, 5, 7, 10. **Tickets** €7.50-€8.50. **Screens** 1. **No credit cards. Map** p330 D5.
This charming little hole-in-the-wall place shows select art house flicks for a discerning audience, plus a smattering of mainstream and foreign-language gems that may have escaped your attention first time around, even if they do tend to stick around here for a little longer than normal.

Movies. *See p224.*

Multimedia centres

De Balie

Kleine-Gartmanplantsoen 10, Southern Canal Belt (553 5100, www.debalie.nl). Tram 1, 2, 5, 7, 10, 20. **Tickets €5-€7. Screens 2. No credit cards. Map** p330 D5.

A temple to high culture, De Balie is a bar, theatre, debating ground and host to several leftfield film festivals and expertly curated cinematic curiosities. Look out for Cineville Talkshow, often your first chance to see an upcoming release, with a little heated (quite often Dutch) debate thrown in for good measure.

Filmhuis Griffioen

Uilenstede 106, Amstelveen (598 5100, www.filmhuisgriffioen.nl). Tram 5. **Tickets €5-€76. Screens 1. No credit cards.**

A small student-run cinema on the campus of the Free University, the Filmhuis Griffioen is a cheap and eminently enjoyable way to check out the films you missed in their first run, even if you've missed them by a decade or so (think turn-of-the-20th-century awards magnets like *Magnolia*).

Melkweg

Lijnbaansgracht 234a, Southern Canal Belt (531 8181, www.melkweg.nl). Tram 1, 2, 5, 7, 10, 20. **Tickets €5-€7 (incl membership). Screens 1. Credit MC. Map** p330 C5.

For a venue primarily famed for its musical appeal, the Melkweg hosts a surprisingly broad array of quality cinema, from foreign-language festival fodder to music-video nights, although the racket that comes through the floor when there's a band playing elsewhere in the building might distract you from your flick. Rather than plain old noise pollution, it helps if you go with the flow and consider this a free sample.
▶ *The Melkweg is also the place to go for great club nights (see p262) and gigs (see p251).*

De Nieuwe Anita

Frederik Hendrikstraat 111, West (no phone, www.denieuweanita.nl). Tram 3, 10, 14. **Tickets €2. Screens 1. No credit cards. Map** p325 A3.

This former squat is a buzzing hive of hipster activity for the kind of people sporting directional hairdos. Aside from the live performances, laid-back lounging nights and (but of course!) impromptu hair salons that crowd the eclectic schedule here, Monday evenings feature staggeringly obscure but highly enjoyable films (*see p225* **Film Clubbing**) often with a lengthy intro from the Anita's voluble curator.

OT301

Overtoom 301, Oud West (779 4913, www.ot301.nl). Tram 1. **Tickets** from €4. **Screens** 1. **No credit cards. Map** p329 B6.

A former Dutch film academy transformed by squatters into a cultural 'breeding ground', OT301 has a radio station, a vegan restaurant and a charming

Kriterion. *See p227.*

80-seat art house cinema that shows unusual films ranging from activist documentary to double and even triple bills of art house classics. Screenings typically happen on Tuesdays and Sundays, and the ragtag bunch of volunteers who work here is generally happy to hear programme suggestions.

SMART Cinema

Arie Biemondstraat 101-111 (427 5951, http://smartprojectspace.net). Tram 1, 17. **Tickets €6-€7. Screens 2. No credit cards. Map** p329 B6.

Part of the gigantic SMART Project Space, showing an eclectic mix of art-house and experimental independent films, all of which, somewhat unusually, have English-language subtitles. A recent welcome innovation, ideal for those who hate having to wolf down their dinner before catching a flick, is the programme of 'Film & Dinner' themed nights held in association with local distributor A-Film. Triumphs include an aristo-themed screening of *Gosford Park*. Spiffing.

Studio/K

Timorplein 62, Indische Buurt (692 0422, www.studio-k.nu). Tram 7, 14. **Tickets €6-€7.50. Screens 2. No credit cards.**

The 'K' here might stand for 'kooky', sometimes veering into the realms of the pleasantly 'kitsch'. Screening mostly alternative and non-commercial films, the venue also has a theatre, art gallery and a café, which makes it the ideal venue for festivals; in 2010, it played host to the inaugural Turkish Film Festival, a diverse programme demonstrating much Eastern promise.

Tropentheater

Kleine Zaal Linnaeusstraat 2, Oost; Grote Zaal Mauritskade 63, Oost (568 8500, www.tropentheater.nl). Tram 9, 10, 14. **Tickets €8-€9. Screens 2. Credit MC, V. Map** p332 H3.

Next door to the Tropenmuseum, this superlative cultural venue sporadically shows documentaries and feature films from developing countries far and wide. Programming typically chimes with the current theme of the museum proper, so check ahead and make a day of your virtual globetrotting.
▶ *Visit next door's Tropenmuseum (see p119) or one of the musical performances; see p252.*

Galleries

Famed for its Old Masters, the city also has plenty of new talent.

Amsterdam is known for heavy-hitters of art history – Rembrandt, Vermeer, Van Gogh – but visitors might be less familiar with its modern art stars. Contemporary photographers Rineke Dijkstra, Erwin Olaf and Anton Corbijn may not be household names, but they rank high on the international art charts, and Dutch architects, including Rotterdam-born Rem Koolhaas and Amsterdammer Herman Hertzberger, have made a not-insignificant mark on 20th- and 21st-century architecture.

Amsterdam is also an exciting design destination, and product designers including Marcel Wanders, Richard Hutten and Tejo Remy, acolytes of design universe Droog, all come from here. At the same time, the creativity-inducing atmosphere in the city has lured many an expat (one such is UK artist and filmmaker Steve McQueen) to set up canalside studios.

ARTS & ENTERTAINMENT

THE LOCAL SCENE

What makes Amsterdam a hotbed for creative types? One simple answer might be, 'there's money'. Historically, the Dutch government has been incredibly generous with subsidies for artists (for a while, every art-school grad got financial assistance for their first five years out of school).

The government is less keen to splash the cash these days and in late 2010, the right-wing coalition in the Hague announced plans to cut cultural subsidies by 25 per cent in 2011. Still, as home to the prestigious international art residency the Rijksakademie and the fecund graduate programme in art at the Rietveld Academie, this city is teeming with young and up-and-coming artists from all over the world who are producing work, in all mediums, like crazy. You don't have to look very hard to find it.

FINE ART HUNTING

Galleries, mini museums, art ateliers and non-traditional art spaces abound in Amsterdam, in just about every quarter of the city. The Jordaan is still the central congregating point for the more established and internationally minded contemporary art galleries (*see p105* **Art Throb**), and the Spiegelkwartier (literally, 'mirror quarter') in the Southern Canal Belt is

where you'll find anything pre-dating 1945, including Old Master paintings, CoBrA art, antiques and genuine Delftware. In recent years, urban art pioneers have headed over to Noord, where the massive warehouse-turned-studio-complex NDSM is a breeding ground of creative production (*see p124* **Northern Lights**), while others have migrated to De Pijp, West and Oost (*see p117* **Full of Eastern Promise**) for cheaper or funkier art digs.

Amsterdam's art spaces can be divided into two categories: commercial art galleries devoted to selling work by more established artists; and non-profit project spaces where emerging and non-traditional artists have more opportunities to 'play'. Among the first group, Annet Gelink Gallery, Grimm, Torch Gallery, Galerie Gabriel Rolt and Galerie Fons Welters are always good bets. For art project spaces, Smart and Mediamatic are not to be missed, and if you're

Bags packed, milk cancelled, house raised on stilts.

You've packed the suntan lotion, the snorkel set, the stay-pressed shirts. Just one more thing left to do – your bit for climate change. In some of the world's poorest countries, changing weather patterns are destroying lives.

You can help people to deal with the extreme effects of climate change. Raising houses in flood-prone regions is just one life-saving solution.

Climate change costs lives.
Give £5 and let's sort it *Here & Now*

www.oxfam.org.uk/climate-change

Be Humankind Ⓧ Oxfam

Chiellerie.

looking for younger, fresher, edgier work, head over to W139 (*see right*) in the Old Centre or Studio/K (*see p232*) in Oost.

Meantime, Amsterdam continues its rich tradition of nourishing a street-art culture (in spite of the police's efforts to curb graffiti), so you can also find plenty of eye candy pretty much anywhere you look (*see p233* **Walls of Fame**).

THE OLD CENTRE
The Old Side

Chiellerie
Raamgracht 58 (320 9448, www.chiellerie.nl). Metro Nieuwmarkt. **Open** 2-6pm daily. *Openings* 5-10pm Fri. **Map** p327 E3.
Chiellerie was originally created by Amsterdam's former *nachtburgemeester* (night mayor) Chiel van Zelst (*see p263* **Profile**), and with a new exhibition

---

INSIDE TRACK FAIR'S FAIR

Although the Netherlands' best art fairs are in Rotterdam (Art Rotterdam, for contemporary art) and Maastricht (TEFAF, for Old Masters and modern art), this city has plenty of fairs of its own. Check out the **Affordable Art Fair**, **PAN Amsterdam**, **Art Amsterdam** art fair, and its edgier sidebar, **Kunstvlaai**; *see pp208-215*.

---

of local art every week or two, this is more hangout than mere art hangar.

Oude Kerk
Oudekerksplein 23 (625 8284, www.oudekerk.nl). Tram 4, 9, 14, 16, 24, 25 or Metro Nieuwmarkt. **Open** 11am-5pm Mon-Sat; 1-5pm Sun. *During World Press Photo exhibition* 10am-6pm Mon-Sat; 1 6pm Sun. **Admission** €7, €6 reductions; €2 under-12s. **Map** p326 D2.
The 'Old Church' exhibits everything from contemporary Aboriginal art to photographs documenting the life of albinos in Africa. *Photo p232.*
▶ *Oude Kerk also launches the annual World Press Photo exhibition before it starts its worldwide tour; see p209.*

Sexy Art Gallery
Oudezijds Achterburgwal 54 (06 4359 6234 mobile, www.sexyartgallery.com). Bus 35 or Metro Nieuwmarkt. **Open** 11am-1am Mon-Thur, Sun; 11am-2am Fri, Sat. **Map** p326 D2.
Located on the third floor of the Erotic Museum (*see p88*), this gallery showcases art that fits right into the Red Light District, in which it's situated. That is, contemporary art with suggestive, erotic or sometimes downright raunchy content.

★ W139
Warmoesstraat 139 (622 9434, www.w139.nl). Tram 4, 9, 14, 16, 24, 25. **Open** noon-6pm daily during exhibitions. **Map** p326 D2.
In its two decades of existence, W139 has never lost its squat aesthetic, nor its occasionally overly

conceptual edge. It's a big hangout for Rietveld graduates, with legendary openings that typically spill out into the street. *Photo p234.*

THE CANALS
Western Canal Belt

★ Grimm
Keizersgracht 82 (422 7227, www.grimmfine art.com). Tram 13, 14, 17. **Open** noon-6pm Wed-Sat. **Map** p326 C2.
Grimm is an internationally minded gallery just off the main drag of the Jordaan art scene. Its stable includes trendy visual artists such as German painter Daniel Richter and mixed media artist Matthew Day Jackson. **Other locations** 1e Jacob van Campenstraat 23-25.

Netherlands Institute for Media Art
Keizersgracht 264 (623 7101, www.nimk.nl). Tram 13, 14, 17 or bus 170, 171, 172. **Open** 11am-6pm Tue-Fri; 1-6pm Sat & 1st Sun of mth. **Map** p326 C3.
The Netherlands Institute for Media Art is dedicated to applying new techniques to visual arts, alongside photography and installations. Admire tech in an old-world space, or read up on an assortment of topics in the reference room. There's usually a token entry fee for exhibitions.

Southern Canal Belt

Galerie Akinci
Lijnbaansgracht 317 (638 0480, www.akinci.nl). Tram 7, 10, 16, 24, 25. **Open** 1-6pm Tue-Sat. **Map** p326 E5.
Part of a row of connected galleries, Akinci thrives on surprising its visitors, hosting exhibitions that employ every contemporary art medium, with a slightly political aesthetic and a bent towards feminist interpretations.

Galerie Alex Daniëls – Reflex Amsterdam
Weteringschans 83 (423 5423, www.reflex amsterdam.com). Tram 7, 10. **Open** varies by location. **Map** p330 D5.
Alex Daniëls is a second-generation gallerist from Amsterdam who now has three spaces in and around the Spiegelkwartier. The art he presents is contemporary, accessible and often linked to the world of fashion. **Other locations** Weteringschans 79a (627 2832); Lijnbaansgracht 318 (422 9020).

★ Mediamatic
Vijzelstraat 68 (638 9901, www.mediamatic.net). Tram 7, 10, 16, 24, 25. **Open** 1-7pm Mon-Fri; 1-6pm Sat, Sun. **Map** p331 E4.

This art-based media lab is based in the centre of town but is responsible for creating projects all over the place, not just inside its space. It is known for presenting all kinds of fascinating multidisciplinary projects, such as an Arabic Guide to Noord. Its openings are excellent.

Melkweg
Marnixstraat 409 (531 8181, www.melkweg.nl). Tram 1, 2, 5, 7, 10. **Open** 1-8pm Wed-Sun. **Map** p330 D5.
The quality shows of contemporary photography held at the Melkweg reflect the broad interests of its director, Suzanne Dechart. Expect anything from portraits of the descendents of runaway slaves to quirky pop photography.
▶ *The Melkweg is also home to music (see p251) dance events (see p221), film screenings (see p228) and great club nights (see p262).*

Ron Mandos
Prinsengracht 282 (320 7036, www.ronmandos. nl). Tram 9, 13, 16, 17 or bus 170. **Open** noon-6pm Wed-Sat. **Map** p326 C4.
In a spacious gallery, Mandos presents local and international contemporary artists, often with a slightly sentimental edge, and frequently with a few exhibitions running concurrently.

Oude Kerk. *See p231.*

Walls of Fame

The writing's on the walls.

'Low art' is highly visible in Amsterdam. The city's street-art culture dates back to the punk era of the early 1980s, when squatters and politicos took their message to the walls. The city's early legends – Delta, Shoe, Again – are still making marks locally, but these days they've been joined by a whole range of artists who aren't just working with spray cans.

Maybe you've seen the philosophical sidewalk ramblings of Laser 3.14 ('sometimes hope delays a lot'), the giant abstract pieces by Zedz or the cheerful black-and-white bubble-headed lads by the London Police, who started painting in Amsterdam in the 1980s?

'Amsterdam produced the first names in Europe for graffiti,' says Henk Kramer, who's now been selling spray cans in Waterlooplein for 20 years and is also the owner of Henxs graffiti supply and urbanwear shop on Sint Antoniesbreestraat (638 9478, www.henxs.com). 'I still get little kids coming who are amazed by the magic of the spray can; their heads barely come above the counter.'

Although it's as illegal here as anywhere else to mark public and private buildings, the city's famous liberalism still makes it a place writers (as they're called in common graff parlance) love to visit and

tag. And even though the City spends approximately €350,000 a year on cleaning up monuments and municipal buildings, and fines street vandals, according to Stadsdeel Centrum spokesman Edwin Oppedijk, that's just a pittance compared to other cities (New York City, for example, spends about $25 million annually).

Still, there are plenty of legal walls around, known as 'Halls of Fame', which become the sites of painting jams where artists come together to collaborate on a single stretch of concrete, or even an entire building. 'Every weekend there's nice weather there are painting sessions, people popping out of the woodwork, eating, and lots of music,' says Melissa Scholten, who started making street art as MLSS, member of Xstreets Collective.

Under the heading AllTourNative, locals Shona Cottan and Pia de la Maza organise tours to reveal the 'real side' of Amsterdam, and they'll guide you to some of the city's best sites for graffiti viewing – most of them legal. They've got walking tours of two to three hours and biking tours that go further afield for three to four hours, after which they'll introduce you to some of the famous locals, including Ives and Faith71 (prices from €10 per person; check http://alltournative-amsterdam.com).

Jodenbuurt, the Plantage & the Oost

★ Studio/K

Timorplein 62 (692 0422, www.studio-k.nu). Bus 22, 43. **Open** *varies.*

This youthful project space also has a theatre, a café and a cinema screening mostly alternative films. Previous exhibitions have included painting-photography artworks by Jack Vissers and cityscape-inspired pieces by Lisette Alblas.

The Waterfront & Noord

ARCAM

Prins Hendrikkade 600 (620 4878, www.arcam. nl). Bus 22, 42, 43 or Metro Waterlooplein. **Open** 1-5pm Tue-Sat. **Map** p327 E3.

Architecture Centrum Amsterdam (better known as ARCAM) is concerned with the promotion of Dutch contemporary architecture, both at home and abroad, and organises tours, forums, lectures and exhibits. *Photo p51.*

Motive Gallery

Ms van Riemsdijkweg 41a (330 3668, www. motivegallery.nl). Bus 35, 91 or ferry NDSM-werf. **Open** 11am-6pm Wed-Sat.

One of the escapees from the Jordaan, Motive Gallery is now housed in a former metal workshop, where it exhibits contemporary art to perfectly suit its enormous open-plan space.

▶ *Home to the Motive Gallery and Nieuw Dakota, Amsterdam's industrial expanse in Noord has become one of the city's hippest enclaves; see p124* **Northern Lights**.

Nieuw Dakota

Ms van Riemsdijksweg 41b (331 8311, www. nieuwdakota.nl). Bus 35, 91 or ferry NDSM-werf. **Open** 11am-7pm Thur, Fri; 11am-5pm Sat, Sun.

Part of a mini gallery row including Motive (*see above*), this post-industrial space presents contemporary work from international artists such as Tom Tlalim, and established Dutch names including Pieter Lemmens.

The Jordaan

★ Annet Gelink Gallery

Laurierstraat 187-189 (330 2066, www.annet gelink.com). Tram 13, 14, 17. **Open** 10am-6pm Tue-Fri; 1-6pm Sat. **Map** p329 B4.

Opened in 2000, the Annet Gelink Gallery is seen by many artists as the most desired contemporary art dealer of the moment. Why? Simple: her stable of hot, young international up-and-comers, including David Maljkovic, Barbara Visser, Carlos Amorales and Ryan Gander. And she has plenty of space and light to lavish on them. Exhibitions have also combined old and new artists, featuring works by the likes of Matisse and Van Gogh.

W139. *See p231.*

Foam. *See p100.*

Galerie Diana Stigter
Hazenstraat 17 (624 2361, www.dianastigter.nl).
Tram 7, 10, 13, 14, 17. **Open** 11am-6pm Wed-
Fri; 1-6pm Sat and by appt. **Map** p330 C4.
Stigter is at the epicentre of the Jordaan contemporary art gallery scene, both physically and metaphorically. Her impressive roster of artists includes Tjebbe Beekman, Irene Fortuyn and Prix de Rome winner Thomas Manneke.

★ Galerie Fons Welters
Bloemstraat 140 (423 3046, www.fonswelters.nl).
Tram 13, 14, 17. **Open** 1-6pm Tue-Sat. **Map** p325 B3.
Fons Welters likes to 'discover' the latest new (and often local) talent, and has shown remarkable taste in both sculpture and installation, having provided a home to Magali Reus, Matthew Monahan and Jennifer Tee.

★ Galerie Gabriel Rolt
Elandsgracht 34 (785 5146, www.gabrielrolt.com).
Tram 10, 17. **Open** noon-6pm Wed-Sat and by appt. **Map** p330 C4.
Housed in one of the more elegant gallery spaces in the district, Rolt is on top of the newest trends in contemporary art, representing artists who are fun, edgy and (mostly) pretty well established. Look for photographer Desiree Dolron, American performance/installation artist Abner Price and British painter Paul Haworth.

Galerie Paul Andriesse
Westerstraat 187 (623 6237, www.paulandriesse.nl).
Tram 13, 14, 17. **Open** 11am-6pm Tue-Fri; 2-6pm Sat; 2-5pm 1st Sun of mth. **Map** p325 B2.

One of the original gallerists in the Jordaan district, Andriesse moved to an enormous space on the Westerstraat, with plenty of room to show his top-tier artists Marlene Dumas and Thomas Struth, along with up-and-comers.

Gallery KochxBos
1e Anjeliersdwarsstraat 3-5 (681 4567, www.kochxbos.nl).
Tram 13, 14, 17. **Open** 1-6pm Wed-Sat. **Map** p325 B3.
The roster includes luminary 'lowbrow' artists Ray Caesar, Mark Ryden, Tim Biskup, Joe Sorren and Glenn Barr. Art for those who like their hot rods ablaze, their punk snotty and their films in the Lynchian tradition.

Go Gallery
Prinsengracht 64 (422 9580, www.gogallery.nl).
Tram 13, 14, 17. **Open** noon-6pm Wed-Sat; 1-5pm Sun (call to confirm) and by appt. **Map** p325 B2.
Owner Oscar van den Voorn is an energetic supporter of street-art culture and many of the artists he represents reside in that middle ground between graffiti and canvas. His local stars are Fake, Sit and the London Police (see their mural on the wall outside the gallery too).

Serieuze Zaken Studioos
Lauriergracht 96 (427 5770, www.serieuzezaken studioos.com).
Tram 7, 10. **Open** noon-6pm Wed-Sat; noon-5pm 1st Sun of mth. **Map** p329 D4.
Rob Malasch was already known as a quirky theatre type and journalist before opening this gallery in the Jordaan. Shows here might feature Brit art or works by contemporary Chinese painters. *Photo p236.*

ARTS & ENTERTAINMENT

INSIDE TRACK ART ESCAPES

Make a daytrip out of museuming.
For contemporary art, head just south
of Amsterdam to Amstelveen and the
terrific **CoBrA Museum** (*see p112*)
or go even further south to the Hague
for the **Gemeentemuseum Den Haag**
(Stadhouderslaan 41, 070 338 1111,
www.gemeentemuseum.nl). In good
weather, you might want to make a trip
to the **Kröller-Müller Museum**, with its
outdoor sculpture park (in the centre of
national park Hoge Veluwe, 0318 591
241, www.kmm.nl).

Stedelijk Museum Bureau Amsterdam

*Rozenstraat 59 (422 0471, www.smba.nl). Tram 13,
14, 17.* **Open** *11am-5pm Tue-Sun.* **Map** *p329 B4.*
While the Stedelijk is closed, its Rozenstraat outpost
continues to present exhibitions and events, though
curiously not from the mothership's collections. Still,
curators maintain the same high standards.
▶ *To find out what's happening with two of
Amsterdam's major museums, the Stedelijk
and Rijksmuseum, see p111.*

★ Torch Gallery

*Lauriergracht 94 (626 0284, www.torchgallery.
com). Tram 7, 10.* **Open** *2-6pm Thur-Sat and
by appt.* **Map** *p329 D4.*
Founded by Amsterdam art pioneer Adriaan van
der Have, Torch has always attracted artists who
court a little controversy; his son, Mo van der Have,
who's now running the gallery, continues that edgy
tradition with international artists such as Tinkebell,
Terry Rodgers and Susan Anderson.

Witzenhausen Gallery

*Hazenstraat 60 (644 9898, www.witzenhausen
gallery.nl). Tram 7, 10, 13, 14, 17.* **Open** *noon-
6pm Thur-Sat and by appt.* **Map** *p325 C2.*
An internationally minded gallery that now has an
outpost in New York, Witzenhausen is a one-room
white box that often features surprisingly terrific new
work by acclaimed artists such as Alvaro Barrios and
Hendrik Kerstens, as well as emerging artists.

Galerie Wouter van Leeuwen

*Hazenstraat 27 (06 5203 1540 mobile). Tram 7,
10, 13, 14, 17.* **Open** *noon-6pm Thur-Sat.* **Map**
p330 C4.
A small space presenting excellent contemporary
and historic photography: Elliott Erwitt, William
Wegman and Paul Huf. Van Leeuwen is, incidentally,
also probably the most amiable dealer in the district.

The Museum Quarter, Vondelpark & the South

★ Smart Project Space

*Arie Biemondstraat 105-113 (427 5951, www.
smartprojectspace.net). Tram 1, 3, 12.* **Open**
noon-5pm Tue-Sat. **Map** *p329 B6.*
Located in a former pathology lab, this large arts
complex houses artist studios, a cinema, a café/
restaurant (Lab111), a lecture hall and museum-
style exhibition space. The shows are intelligently
curated around themes, rather than mediums, featuring a mixture of local and international artists.

Serieuze Zaken Studioos. *See p235.*

Gay & Lesbian

Get out and proud in the epicentre of queer rights.

Everyone's gay in Amsterdam, according to a 2010 international advertising campaign. This is a city that's keen to broadcast its credentials as a haven for liberalism and open-mindedness.

Sure enough, it has an impressive track record when it comes to gay rights. Homosexuality was decriminalised here in 1811, the first gay bar opened in 1927 (Café 't Mandje, still open today at Zeedijk 63), and one of the first gay rights organisations, the COC Nederland, was founded in Amsterdam in 1946, at a time when much of the rest of the world considered homosexuality an illness.

THE SCENE TODAY

Still, there are those who say that the city has lost ground since it hosted the world's first legal gay wedding in 2001. The COC had to sell its premises in 2010 due to lack of funding; newspaper headlines claim that gaybashing is on the rise; and an epidemic of venue closures has left some wondering whether the one-time 'gay capital of Europe' remains such a great place for those who think pink.

So is Amsterdam Gay Pride now something that comes but once a year, or is Amsterdam simply the world's first integrated, post-gay city, where anything goes? Whatever conclusions you draw, you'll certainly have fun getting there.

INFORMATION

Gay & Lesbian Switchboard
623 6565, www.switchboard.nl.
Now affiliated with the umbrella outreach organisation Schorer, this band of sympathetic and knowledgeable volunteers has been giving advice for years. You can ask them about anything, from HIV risk factors to the best new bars, and they speak perfect English.

Homomonument
Westermarkt, Western Canal Belt. Tram 13, 14, 17. **Map** p326 C3.
Unveiled in 1987, Karin Daan's three-sectioned pink triangle – symbolising past, present and future – was a world first. It's also a place to celebrate and to be proud: on Queen's Day and Pride it gets annexed to the open-air disco and market.

★ IHLIA
6th floor, Oosterdokskade 143, Waterfront (523 0837, www.ihlia.nl). **Open** 10am-6pm daily. **Map** p327 E1.
The spectacular view alone is reason enough for journeying up to the sixth floor of Amsterdam's amazing public library, but this archive of LGBT-related materials, from biographies to condom packets, is Europe's largest. The airy space is often used for topical exhibitions.

★ Pink Point
Westermarkt, Western Canal Belt (428 1070, www.pinkpoint.org). Tram 13, 14, 17. **Open** 10am-6pm daily. **Map** p326 C3.
Queer queries? Need to know which party to go to? Looking for political pamphlets? Or just a gay postcard or a street map? Head to this year-round information kiosk near the Homomonument (*see left*) with friendly and chatty staff. Pink Point also publishes the *Bent Guide To Amsterdam* (€13.95).
▶ *For information about gay and lesbian matters, and HIV, see pp308-309.*

MEDIA
Print

With the exception of English-language *Time Out Amsterdam* magazine's Gay & Lesbian pages (*see p238* **Who, What, Where?**), most other lesbigay printed matter available is in Dutch, but it's good to know that a fair chunk is bilingual. Falling into the latter camp are *Gay & Night* (www.gay-night.nl) and *Gay News* (www.gay-news.com), which are published

ARTS & ENTERTAINMENT

monthly, as is the Amsterdam Gay Map. The standard of English can be decidedly dodgy, and they're quite often waving the rainbow flag solely for advertisers, but they are at least free, and can be picked up in bars around the city.

Amsterdam-published *Butt* looks like a low-rent porn mag (and there are plenty of sexy pictures) but pulls off some of the most interesting interviews of any gay publication, anywhere; Edmund White, Rufus Wainwright and Marc Jacobs are just three of the names to appear between its pink sheets. From the same stable comes *Fantastic Man*, a 'gentleman's style journal' that, if not strictly gay, is at the very least doused in homosexual sensibility.

If you can read some Dutch, check out the local edition of *Winq* (www.winq.com), the

global gay glossy with brains that is published from a canal house in the Red Light District. The magazine may rely heavily on boys in pants for its newsstand appeal, but its think pieces deal with more uncomfortable subjects such as racism in online dating. *PS, Het Parool*'s glossy Saturday supplement, also has pink listings, while the lifestyle/news digest *De Gay Krant*, in print since 1980, is in Dutch but has an integrated translate-to-English option (www.gk.nl) and even some lesbian content.

Also in Dutch is *Zij aan Zij*, a general lesbian glossy covering the usual celebrity interviews plus articles about emotional issues and the like. Back copies of the mag are available online (www.zijaanzij.nl). Online-only *La Vita* (www.la-vita.nl) offers a similarly bland diet, and both have national listings, although these are in Dutch only.

Radio & TV

Run by a rag tag collection of volunteers and nightlife notables, **Pinq Radio** has been streaming online (www.pinqradio.nl) since April 2008. Broadcast from Amsterdam's best gay parties, it's a way of sharing in the fun, even if you can't be there in person. For a relatively small player, the station has attracted some impressive celebrity guests, including Gossip's Beth Ditto.

Aside from this, the gay community gets two regular broadcast outlets on Dutch TV (two hours a week on Tuesdays and Saturdays) and radio (every night).

MVS Radio
106.8 FM or 88.1 or 103.3 on cable (638 6386, www.mvs.nl). **Times** 7-8pm Mon-Sat; 6-8pm Sun. Daily news, features, interviews and music with a gay twist. The shows are in Dutch, but with a Sunday programme in English.

MVS TV
Through Salto TV: channels 39+/616MHz (638 6386, www.mvs.nl). **Times** 9-10pm Tue (except 1st Tue of mth); 10-11pm Sun.
The lesbian and gay community media company broadcasts shows on all aspects of gay life, from visiting porn stars to retired hairdressers to lesbian movers and shakers, and all points in between. Usually in Dutch but with occasional English-language items; some programmes are also online.

WHERE TO STAY

The hotels listed below are mostly gay-run. The Gay & Lesbian Switchboard (*see p308*) has more details of gay- and lesbian-friendly hotels. For more hotels, *see pp130-146.*

The Queer Year

Your seasonal guide to gay and lesbian festivals and events.

The Amsterdam calendar is stacked with gay and lesbian-oriented celebrations and shindigs. For a full guide to festivals and events, *see pp208-215* **Calendar**.

SPRING

It's been something of a moveable feast for a while, but the **Roze Filmdagen** – a week-long celebration of LGBT film, both international and home-grown – seems to have settled into March for the time being. The opening and closing night parties are especially popular.

While most of the town turns bright orange during **Koninginnedag** (Queen's Day, 30 April, *see p210* **A Right Royal Party**), pockets of Amsterdam are shocking pink as queers and dykes celebrate the late Queen Juliana's birthday – festivities focus on the memorial Homomonument (*see p237*) and the Amstel.

The Homomonument itself is at the centre of a more sombre commemoration on **Remembrance Day** (4 May), when victims of Nazi persecution are remembered with flowers and speeches. The following day is **Liberation Day**, a huge party with plenty of dancing at the monument.

AIDS Memorial Day in late May remembers victims around the world with songs, music, candles and speeches. It takes place at the Dominicus Church in Spuistraat.

Every second May, De Balie (*see p228*) plays host to the **Transgender Film Festival** (www.transgenderfilmfestival.com).

SUMMER

The biggest event of the summer is, of course, **Amsterdam Gay Pride**, the largest visitor attraction after Queen's Day. Gradually taking over the entire first week of August, this all-encompassing event includes cultural and sports activities, but at its heart it's really just a big party. The main attraction is the canal parade on Saturday, with around 70 floats, boats and thousands of spectators. *See also p212.*

AUTUMN

In October, a darker and more intimate party takes place. **Leather Pride** is celebrated with FF, rubber and other men-only parties in the main leather bars. To top it off, there's a huge Get Ruff! party where, as the name suggests, guys come to have all kinds of unfeasibly pervy fun behind closed doors.

WINTER

World AIDS Day on 1 December is marked with Paradiso's **Love Dance**, a massive and hugely popular AIDS-benefit party with DJs, performances and fashion shows. The fundraising festivities are now spilling out over other gay and gay-friendly venues (see www.worldaidsnight.com for details).

The year ends with **Pink Christmas**. Organised by ProGay, the folks behind summer's Gay Pride, it has been criticised in the past for being too commercial, but additions to the programme have featured community outreach initiatives and drag Winter Olympics on the Leidseplein.

ARTS & ENTERTAINMENT

Amistad

Kerkstraat 42, 1017 GM, Southern Canal Belt (624 8074, www.amistad.nl). Tram 1, 2, 5. **Rates** €79-€158 double. **Credit** AmEx, DC, MC, V. **Map** p330 D4.

Run by owners – and hubbies – Johan and Joost, this hip hotel shines like the pages of a trendy magazine. The rooms are cosy, and the breakfast area on the ground floor doubles as a gay internet lounge every day after 1pm. The lounge is also open to non-residents.

Anco Hotel

Oudezijds Voorburgwal 55, 1012EJ, Old Centre: New Side (624 1126, www.ancohotel.nl). Tram 4, 9, 14, 16, 24. **Rates** incl breakfast €99 double; €45 dorm bed. **Credit** AmEx, DC, MC, V. **Map** p326 D2.

Minutes away from the Zeedijk and Warmoesstraat, the Anco has double, single and 3-4 bed dorm rooms, and a studio. All come with TV, free gay adult channel and free wireless internet access.

Golden Bear

Kerkstraat 37, 1017 GB, Southern Canal Belt (624 4785, www.goldenbear.nl). Tram 1, 2, 5. **Rates** €97-€118 double. **Credit** AmEx, MC, V. **Map** p330 D4.

The first gay hotel in town, the Golden Bear has spacious and comfortable rooms, though not all have private bathrooms. Single rooms have double beds.

★ ITC Hotel

Prinsengracht 1051, 1017 JE, Southern Canal Belt (623 0230, www.itc-hotel.com). Tram 4. **Rates** €90-€135 double. **Credit** AmEx, MC, V. **Map** p331 E4.

Situated in a listed building on a quiet stretch of Prinsengracht convenient for the gay hotspots, the ITC Hotel has 20 charming rooms. The free internet access and friendly staff also go towards ensuring a pleasant stay.

BARS & CLUBS

The gay scene is concentrated in a handful of areas in the **Old Centre**. Getting between them is easy and quick, though each has its own identity. Clubs and bars are listed by area below, with specialist establishments – restaurants, cafés, coffeeshops and lesbian bars – and the pick of one-off club nights and sex parties listed separately. Entry to bars and clubs listed here is free unless stated otherwise.

Warmoesstraat

The long and narrow **Warmoesstraat** (Old Centre: Old Side) is the oldest street in town. Although nothing to do with 'warm', it is just around the corner from the red-lit headquarters of the oldest profession. Packed in the tourist season, it's full of cheap hostels and eateries, coffeeshops, bars and sex shops aimed at backpackers. **Getto** (*see p245*) provides a warm haven to rest and eat. It's also the street with leather/sex bars, a gay porn cinema/shop and a gay hotel, the **Anco** (*see above*) just minutes away. Be aware that junkies and drug sellers think tourists are easy prey, so act streetwise.

Argos

Warmoesstraat 95 (622 6595, www.argosbar.com). Tram 4, 9, 16, 24, 25. **Open** 10pm-3am Mon-Thur, Sun; 10pm-4am Fri, Sat. **No credit cards**. **Map** p326 D2.

'No perfume' it says at the door. Argos, the most venerable and most famous leather bar in town, likes men to smell like men. Friendly staff, porn on a big screen, and hot clientele of all ages, some of whom just come for the basement darkroom with cabins and a sling for less sedate entertainment.

Eagle

Warmoesstraat 90 (627 8634). Tram 4, 9, 16, 24, 25. **Open** 10pm-4am Mon-Thur, Sun; 10pm-5am Fri, Sat. **No credit cards**. **Map** p326 B2.

Known for its reputation – sexy and friendly punters, but dirty toilets and unfriendly staff – this menonly cruise bar can get absolutely packed. The downstairs darkroom is always action-filled and so is the upstairs area late at night; it has some cosy benches should you want to get intimate and a pool table complete with adjustable sling above it.

Zeedijk

Once full of junkies, this notorious street (Old Centre) just off Nieuwmarkt and running all the way to Centraal Station has been cleaned up, and is full of Asian eateries, bars and restaurants. Still, stay on guard, as it's no country lane.

De Barderij

Zeedijk 14 (420 5132). Tram 4, 9, 16, 24, 25 or Metro Centraal Station. **Open** 4pm-1am Mon-Thur, Sun; 4pm-3am Fri, Sat. **No credit cards**. **Map** p326 D2.

This no-frills bar attracts older gays and straight locals who all enjoy the living room-like atmosphere. Before you know it, you're chatting and boozing with the unpretentious guys until the early hours.

★ Queen's Head

Zeedijk 20 (420 2475, www.queenshead.nl). Tram 4, 9, 16, 24, 25 or Metro Centraal Station. **Open** 4pm-1am Mon-Thur, Sun; 4pm-3am Fri, Sat. **No credit cards**. **Map** p326 D2.

Fun, attitude-free bar and clientele, with a great view over a canal at the back. Tuesdays is Show Night with drag acts and Thursdays is ArtLaunch café. It also hosts special parties on – not surprisingly –

Queen's Day, plus skin nights, football nights (most usually during the World Cup season), Eurovision Song Contest night and so on.

Rembrandtplein

Not just the main drag for commercial nightlife and tourist hotspots, Rembrandtplein is also home to many of Amsterdam's gay and lesbian bars. Although just a few minutes' stroll from the Reguliersdwarsstraat, the scene here is much more light-hearted and camp. There's also a couple of reasons for lesbians to visit: the bar **Vive la Vie** (*see p249* and windowless dance cupboard **Club Roque** (Amstel 178, www.clubroque.nl), which is a funny old mix of sweat and karaoke, though it can be a laugh if you're in the right frame of mind.

Halvemaansteeg is a short lane of brash, loud bars full of male punters of all ages (with the odd lesbian and straight girl to leaven the mix). They're attitude-free, and will burst into a Eurovision singalong at the drop of a feather boa. Round the corner on the Amstel are a few more bars that blast out cheesy hits.

Amstel 54
*Amstel 54 (623 4254, www.amstelfiftyfour.nl).
Tram 4, 9, 14, 24, 25.* **Open** 4pm-1am Mon-Thur; 4pm-3am Fri, Sat. **No credit cards.**
Map p331 E4.
Previously known on the scene as Amstel Taveerne, this place was totally renovated in 2007, to mixed feedback. Some are complaining that the old-fashioned friendliness is gone and that the place is becoming straighter. Regardless, it continues to tout itself as Amsterdam's only 'gay video bar', whatever that means.

Entre Nous
Halvemaansteeg 14 (623 1700). Tram 1, 2, 4, 5, 9, 14, 16, 24, 25. **Open** 9pm-3am Mon-Thur; 9pm-4am Fri-Sun. **No credit cards.**
Map p331 E4.
Although it looks slightly terrifying from the outside – put that down to the blacked-out windows – on the inside, Entre Nous is actually pretty fluffy, full of younger gay guys with a thirst for cheap music and good fun. Many local gay folk flit between this place and the Montmartre, opposite.

**INSIDE TRACK
TIDBITS AND TICKETS**

At gay shopping haven **Dom** (*see p246*), you'll find all sorts of things you never knew you needed. More importantly, though, the staff will sell you tickets to the hottest gay circuit parties in town.

★ Lellebel
*Utrechtsestraat 4 (427 5139, www.lellebel.nl).
Tram 9, 14, 20.* **Open** 8pm-3am Mon-Thur; 8pm-4am Fri, Sat; 8pm-3am Sun. **No credit cards.**
Map p331 E4.
Lellebel is a tiny drag bar where the cross-dressing clientele provide all the entertainment themselves. Though most people will be found in drag, admirers and friends are welcome, and the atmosphere is friendly. Entertainment runs all week: Tuesday is karaoke night, Thursday is salsa and Monday is Whatever You Want, You Get, when the punters themselves are responsible for providing the music.

't Mixcafé
Amstel 50 (420 3388, www.mixcafe.nl). Tram 4, 9, 14, 20. **Open** 9pm-3am Fri, Sat; 3pm-midnight Sun. **No credit cards. Map** p331 E4.
A total cheesefest of a bar that attracts attitude-free lesbian and gay customers, who get down and dance to the music of Kylie and the like. The alarmingly strong house drink is a *heugemeug*, a B52-style booze bomb that should be downed in one. Nearby bars Hotspot (Amstel 102) and Rouge (Amstel 60) are similarly jaunty joints if you're out for a night on the razzle with your gang.

Reguliersdwarsstraat

Once unquestionably the gayest stretch of street in Amsterdam, Reguliersdwarsstraat had its heyday in the 1990s, when practically every other bar on the miniature strip between Koningsplein and Vijzelstraat was broadly painted with the pink brush. Following the demise of its most iconic venues (*see p249* **Gay Scene Investigation**), there's much talk of a City-aided renaissance, but in tough economic times, it remains to be seen what form that will take. In the meantime, there are enough independent stalwarts and small-scale new initiatives to keep the place ticking over.

Coffeeshop Downtown
Reguliersdwarsstraat 31 (622 9958, www.coffeeshopdowntown.nl). Tram 1, 9, 16, 24, 25. **Open** 10am-8pm daily. **No credit cards. Map** p331 D4.
There is no cannabis available in this coffeeshop, but there are sandwiches, cakes, drinks and international mags. You might need the latter – as service can be slow when the place is busy. Ah well, there's always the hunky, dressed-to-a-T guys to look at in this tiny multi-level hangout. In summer, the lovely and popular terrace sometimes attracts straight couples from the nearby Flowermarket, who suddenly realise their mistake.

★ House of Rising
Reguliersdwarsstraat 41 (320 2244, www.thehouseofrising.com). Tram 1, 2, 4, 5, 9, 16, 24, 25.

ARTS & ENTERTAINMENT

ARTS & ENTERTAINMENT

Prik.

Open noon-1am Tue-Thur; noon-3am Fri, Sat; 4pm-1am Sun. **Map** p331 D4.
Although way too millennial to bother with boring old labels such as 'gay' and 'straight', this five-in-one bar, hairdressing salon, art space, shop and live music venue is right in the heart of the 'Reguliers' strip, and features a pair of sparkly 'Dorothy' shoes as its decorative centrepiece. The Sunday night jam sessions are extremely popular with the city's more bohemian queers.

't Leeuwtje
Reguliersdwarsstraat 105 (639 3012, www.cafe hetleeuwtje.nl). Tram 1, 2, 4, 5, 9, 16, 24, 25. **Open** 5pm-1am Mon-Thur, Sun; 5pm-3am Fri, Sat. **No credit cards. Map** p329 E4.
A gay bar with a typical Dutch interior blasting home-made and international pop hits. The bar is popular with gays of all ages, but straight folk and tourists often swing by as well.

Reality Bar
Reguliersdwarsstraat 129 (639 3012, www.reality bar.nl). Tram 1, 2, 4, 5, 9, 16, 24, 25. **Open** 8pm-3am Mon-Thur, Sun; 8pm-4am Fri, Sat. **No credit cards. Map** p329 E4.
One of the few bars in town where black and white gay guys regularly meet and mingle, Reality Bar is always popular during the happy hour, which runs from 8.30pm to 10pm. Things really get going later on, however, when ferociously uptempo Latin music gets pumped out of the speakers to get the crowd moving and grooving.

Taboo
Reguliersdwarsstraat 45 (775 3963, www.taboo bar.nl). Tram 1, 2, 4, 5, 9, 16, 24, 25. **Open** 6pm-3am Mon-Thur; 4pm-4am Fri, Sat; 4pm-3am Sun. **Map** p331 D4.
The latest venture from Brendan van de Ruit, formerly the manager of Reguliersdwarsstraat stalwart Exit, Taboo is hoping to breathe a little life back into an ailing district. In some ways, it's just another gay bar – it plays Cher, and is festooned in rainbows – but what the place lacks in mould-breaking sparkle, it makes up for in decent prices.

Kerkstraat

Home to pioneering cradle of filth Club Church and the Bronx sexshop (*see*), this quiet street off the busy Leidsestraat sure is gay. It even has a few gay hotels. Yet it is less posing pink than other areas. Nearby you'll find the Netherlands' only Arabian gay bar, **Habibi Ana** (Lange Leidsedwarsstraat 93, no phone), with a strict Arabian-music-only policy, but a mixed, young and handsome international crowd.

★ Club Church
Kerkstraat 52 (www.clubchurch.nl). Tram 1, 2, 5. **Open** 8pm-midnight Tue, Wed; 10pm-3am Thur; 10pm-4am Fri, Sat; 7pm-1am Sun. **Map** p330 D4.
This deceptively cavernous venue is more than a little progressive, and it's been a long time since Amsterdam has seen the opening of a gay venue

where sex is so unambiguously on the agenda. Erotic theme nights here run the full gamut of (mostly male) pervy possibility, from naked parties to fisting to the women-friendly Horenbal, where those 'dressed for trade' are offered free bubbly. Several of the city's fetish parties (for example, *see p239* **Leather Pride**) have migrated here from smaller venues in the Red Light District.

De Spijker

Kerkstraat 4 (620 5919). Tram 1, 2, 5. **Open** 4pm-1am Mon-Thur, Sun; 4pm-3am Fri, Sat. **No credit cards. Map** p330 C4.
This small boozer used to be a theatre in its previous life. Punters still liven things up and it can become rather crowded, rowdy and smoky. Its diverse clientele covers the waterfront – from cute young guys to older muscle men and a few women – and all mingle happily. On the downside, the pool table always seems to be occupied.

Other areas

★ Cozy Bar

Sint Jacobsstraat 8, Old Centre: New Side (320 0002, www.cozybar.nl). Tram 1, 2, 3, 5. **Open** 4pm-1am Mon-Thur, Sun; 4pm-3am Fri, Sat. **Map** p326 D2.
They say that size doesn't matter, but it's the diminutive scale of this brown café-style newcomer off Nieuwendijk that gives the place its charm. Gorgeously decked out with fresh flowers and sympathetic lighting, and with a tiny fireside snug at the

back, it's the perfect place to retreat from an otherwise hectic part of town. Fun regular events include the monthly gay expat mixer, with live piano music and snacks.

Mankind

Weteringstraat 60, Southern Canal Belt (638 4755, www.mankind.nl). Tram 7, 10, 16, 24, 25. **Open** noon-11pm Mon-Sat. **No credit cards. Map** p329 D5.
Mankind is a quiet locals' place tucked down a side street near the Rijksmuseum, and the antiques shops and art galleries of Spiegelstraat. Not just an excellent stop for culture cruisers, this bar also provides delicious sandwiches and a cheap dish of the day. In summer the canalside patio is perfect to catch some sun, read the international magazines or simply watch the world go by.

★ Prik

Spuistraat 109, Old Centre: New Side (320 0002, www.prikamsterdam.nl). Tram 1, 2, 5, 13, 17. **Open** 4pm-1am Tue-Thur, Sun; 4pm-3am Fri, Sat. **No credit cards.**
Queer or not – Prik is certainly hot. Indeed, true to the bar's slogan, this popular meeting point succeeds in attracting a diverse crowd who enjoy its movie nights, delicious snacks and groovy sounds. The sporadic speed-dating events held here are a particularly fun way to infiltrate the local scene. After a night here you might even be tempted to squeeze yourself into one of those saucy T-shirts. *Photo p242.*

Web
Sint Jacobsstraat 6, Old Centre: New Side (623 6758). Tram 1, 2, 3, 5. **Open** 1pm-1am Mon-Thur; 1pm-3am Fri, Sat; 7pm-1am Sun. **No credit cards. Map** p326 D2.

The cheap booze and sexy bartenders, the cheesy/classic dance tracks, the sex shop vouchers lottery on Wednesdays, the Sunday 5pm snack afternoon – these ingredients make this men-only leather/cruise bar heave with a crowd from all ages. The upstairs darkroom is hygienic and the numerous cubicles almost resemble those at a gym/swimming pool: great to act out that locker room porn fantasy that you've always dreamed of.

ONE-OFF CLUB NIGHTS

For lesbian club nights, *see p248.*

Danserette
Akhnaton, Nieuwezijds Kolk 25, Old Centre: New Side (624 3396, www.akhnaton.nl). Tram 1, 2, 5, 13, 17. **Open** Sat; check website for dates. **Admission** see website. **Map** p326 D2.

This occasional Saturday-nighter at Akhnaton is for those who aren't afraid to mouth the words to Madonna hits. Also on the decks are classic disco hits and recent chart tunes.

De Trut
Bilderdijkstraat 165, Oud West (612 3524). Tram 3, 7, 12, 17. **Open** 11pm-4am Sun. **Admission** €1.50. **No credit cards. Map** p329 B5.

If you don't want the weekend to end, head to this alternative dance night in a former squat on Sundays. It's cheap, it's crowded, it's fun and it's

been going on for about 20 years. Arrive early, certainly before 11pm, or you might find you have to queue for a long time.

Fresh
Club Roses, Rozengracht 133, the Jordaan (www.clubrapido.com). Tram 13, 14, 17. **Open** 11pm-5am; 2nd Sat of mth. **Admission** €7.50 before midnight; €13.50. **Map** p325 B3.

Little brother to Rapido (*see p245*), this more intimate club night attracts the same bodies beautiful. It touches down every second Saturday of the month at Club Roses.

★ F*cking POP Queers
Jimmy Woo, Korte Leidsedwarsstraat 18, Southern Canal Belt (www.ultrasexi.com). Tram 1, 2, 5, 7, 10. **Open** varies; see website. **Admission** varies; see website. **Map** p330 C5.

This monthly night at glam Jimmy Woo is where the young fashion gays go to dance around their designer bags. Practise your pout beforehand – this party's Facebook page is as much of an event as the night itself.

▶ *If you're not in town for this night, you can always schmooze at Jimmy Woo or sister cocktail bar, Suzy Wong, any other time of the month; see p262.*

Furball
www.furball.nl.

This hirsute heaven for hairy men and their smooth admirers has been held at various venues around town, but seems to have settled at the WesterUnie (www.westerunie.nl). It's a great dance night, sometimes with a theme. There's no dress code, no dark-

Vrolijk. *See p246.*

INSIDE TRACK TAKING PRIDE

Don't miss out on **Amsterdam Gay Pride**'s fantastic canal parade in August. Find yourself a spot on the Prinsengracht and watch a stream of packed boats, flamboyant costumes and writhing bodies float past you. It's a sight to behold. *See p212 and p239.*

room, just plenty of sweaty hairy guys, in all shapes, sizes and ages, having a furry old time.

★ MULTISEXI

Studio 80, Rembrandtplein 17, Southern Canal Belt (www.studio-80.nl). Tram 4, 9, 14. **Open/admission** varies; see website for details. **Map** p331 E4.

Taking over Studio 80, this fashionable monthly night offers a blast of electro in an alternative atmosphere that welcomes one and all. If this description sounds like a tangle of contradictions, it's probably pretty accurate.

▶ *Studio 80 has plenty to offer the other days of the month too; see p264.*

Rapido

Paradiso, Weteringschans 6-8, Southern Canal Belt (www.clubrapido.com). Tram 1, 2, 5, 7, 10. **Open/admission** varies; see website for details. **Map** p330 D5.

Super-popular – but irregular – club night that sells out quickly at Paradiso where shirtless muscle marys dance and flirt to pumping house. Check out the website for up-to-date nights, and a peek at the online magazine.

▶ *Gigs, club nights and host to a variety of music festivals, Paradiso does it all; see also p200, p252 and p264.*

Spellbound

OCCII, Amstelveenseweg 134, Museum Quarter (www.spellbound-amsterdam.nl). Tram 1, 2. **Open/admission** varies; see website for details.

Held at OCCII, this is a cheap and alternative club night, which is popular with a non-scene crowd. Whether 'Disco Hospital' or 'Queer Underground', its success is easily explained by the heavy beats, performances and the snug bar.

★ UNK

Club 8, Admiraal de Ruiterweg 56, Oud West (www.club-8.nl). Tram 7, 12, 13, 14. **Open/admission** varies; see website for details.

An alternative mixed gay-straight night of bouncy electro from DJ Lupe, hosted every fourth Saturday of the month at the pleasantly grungey, graffiti-sprayed Club 8, on top of a pool hall, and a short cycle ride out west.

(Z)onderbroek

Club Church, Kerkstraat 52, Southern Canal Belt (www.clubchurch.nl). Tram 1, 2, 5. **Open** 10pm-4am Fri. **Admission** €6. **Map** p330 C4.

Weekly, men-only dance party that takes place at Club Church (*see p242*), with an underwear-only dress code. Tank tops are tolerated, but only just.

Sex parties

Apart from the lesbian leather and S&M group Wild Side (www.wildside.dds.nl), which organises events, parties and workshops in different venues, there are no women-only sex parties in Amsterdam; just occasional, mixed fetish parties.

Despite the controversial closure in summer 2010 of sleaze behemoth Cockring, gay visitors will have no difficulty finding relief. That's largely thanks to the opening of Club Church (*see p242*), a multi-level perve paradise hosting everything from regular FF parties to its occasional Twink Sex Orgy. Meanwhile 'erotic café' **Same Place** (Nassaukade 120, 475 1981, www.sameplace.nl) goes gay every Monday night between 8pm and 1am.

RESTAURANTS

Plenty of restaurants in Amsterdam have more than their fair share of gay diners, even if they are not specifically gay. A good rule of thumb: if a place is brand spanking new or has rather spectacular decor, it's sure to attract the homo herds. The eateries listed below are gay-run, or have significant numbers of gay diners. For details of more restaurants across the city, *see* chapter **Restaurants** *pp147-164.*

Garlic Queen

Reguliersdwarsstraat 27, Southern Canal Belt (422 6426, www.garlicqueen.nl). Tram 1, 2, 5. **Open** 5pm-midnight Wed-Sun. *Kitchen* 5-11pm Wed-Sun. **Main courses** €17-€22. **Credit** AmEx DC, MC, V. **Map** p330 D4.

Portraits of the real queen, Beatrix, smile on to the metaphorical queens – as well as a wide range of other diners – chowing down in this campy temple to the stinking rose. Every dish contains at least one clove of the stuff – one contains 60 – though spoilsports can order any dish garlic-free.

★ Getto

Warmoesstraat 51, Old Centre: Old Side (421 5151, www.getto.nl). Tram 4, 9, 16, 24, 25. **Open** 4pm-1am Tue-Thur; 4pm-2am Fri, Sat; 4pm-midnight Sun. *Kitchen* 6-11pm Tue-Sun. **Main courses** €10-€15. **Credit** AmEx, DC, MC, V. **Map** p326 D2.

Cheap, cheerful, tasty and filling. That's what the food is like at this sparkly diner at the back of the

ARTS & ENTERTAINMENT

thoroughly mixed lesbian and gay lounge. On Wednesday night, all burger dinners (a house speciality) cost just €10. Combined with the weekday, two-for-the-price-of-one cocktail happy hour, this is the ideal place to take a cheap date.

Kitsch
Utrechtsestraat 42, Southern Canal Belt (625 9251, www.restaurant-kitsch.nl). Tram 4, 9, 14. **Open** 6pm-2am daily. *Kitchen* 6-11pm. **Main courses** €17-€32. **Credit** AmEx, DC, MC, V. **Map** p331 E4.
There's Abba on the stereo, there's sassy service, and it's all set off with glitter balls and faux fur. The wine list honours Betty Ford (she of celebrity rehab clinic fame), and dishes also carry cheeky names. Despite Kitsch's playful nature, food is taken seriously here (foie gras, caviar…) and there's plenty to satisfy the most discerning palate, albeit with a similarly impressive price tag.

FILM & THEATRE

Most of the independent cinemas in Amsterdam screen gay and lesbian flicks when they're released, and even the mainstream Pathé chain has caught on. The first Wednesday of the month is **Gay Classics** night at Pathé de Munt (*see p225*), where you get a drink – pink champagne – at the cinema thrown in with your ticket, plus a two-for-one voucher for a local watering hole after the show. Though films shown here can often stretch the definition of what constitutes a 'classic', it's usually a fun night out.

Wednesday night is **Camp Film Night** at Cozy Bar (*see p243*); it's free and the choice of movies is invariably sound. Het Ketelhuis (*see p227*) hosts March's queer film festival **Roze Filmdagen** (Pink Film Days, www.rozefilmdagen.nl), a five-to-ten-day event of features, shorts and international documentaries, while De Balie (*see p228*) plays host to the biennial **Nederlands Transgender Film Festival** (www.transgenderfilmfestival.com) in May. Yet another two-yearly festival, spring's **Cinemasia** (www.cinemasia.nl), first started as the Queer & Asian Film Festival, and remains lesbian-run to this day.

The **Queen's English Theatre Company** (www.qetc.nl) gives the queer eye to classic English-language plays a couple of times a year; its production of Alan Bennett's *The History Boys* was particularly well received, both at the CREA theatre and at the Edinburgh Festival. The excellent **Gay & Lesbian Switchboard** (*see p308*) can tell you which cinemas and theatres are running gay and lesbian programmes.

For our **Film** chapter, *see pp225-228*.

SHOPS & SERVICES
Bookshops

The stores below all have dedicated gay stock, though you'll find gay books and magazines on sale in most of Amsterdam's bookshops. The **American Book Center** (*see p182*) has a well-stocked gay section, and while **Waterstone's** (*see p182*) doesn't have a dedicated gay section, it does carry the major British gay titles.

Intermale
Spuistraat 251, Old Centre: New Side (625 0009, www.intermale.nl). Tram 1, 2, 5, 13, 14, 17. **Open** 11am-6pm Mon; 10am-6pm Tue, Wed, Fri, Sat; 10am-9pm Thur; noon-5pm Sun. **Credit** AmEx, MC, V. **Map** p326 C3.
Apart from a wide selection of new and recently published gay men's books, this shop also has some rare and out-of-print books, plus books in Spanish.

★ Vrolijk
Paleisstraat 135, Old Centre: New Side (623 5142, www.vrolijk.nu). Tram 1, 2, 5, 13, 14, 17. **Open** 11am-6pm Mon-Fri; 10am-5pm Sat; 1-5pm Sun. **Credit** AmEx, DC, MC, V. **Map** p326 C3.
The best international selection of rose-tinted reading, whether fiction or fact – plus CDs, DVDs, guides and the best gifts you'll find in town. It also has a second-hand section, and sells a good range of gay T-shirts, condoms and cheeky gifts. *Photo p244.*

Gift shops

★ Dom
Spuistraat 281, Old Centre: New Side (428 5544, www.dom-ck.com). Tram 1, 2, 5, 13, 14, 17. **Open** 11am-8pm Mon-Sat; 11am-9pm Fri; 1-8pm Sun. **Credit** AmEx, DC, MC, V. **Map** p330 D3.
Established back in 1998, Dom is a pleasing riot of cheap camp frippery (gun-shaped ketchup shooters, for example) combined with deadly serious fashion statements. The first on the high street to embrace that difficult harem pants (nappy) look, the staff are prone to broadcasting their – admittedly entertaining – personal woes across the shop floor.

Gays&Gadgets
Spuistraat 44, Southern Canal Belt, Old Centre: New Side (330 1461, www.gaysandgadgets.com). Tram 1, 2, 5, 13, 14, 17. **Open** 11am-7pm Mon-Sat; noon-7pm Sun. **Credit** AmEx, DC, MC, V. **Map** p326 C2.
A dazzling and demented array of camp nonsense and household objects, most of it manufactured in China. If a willy or boobs can't be incorporated into the design proper, you can bet your bottom dollar it can be dipped in pink paint or accessorised with a sparkly boa, which is why sections of Gays&Gadgets look like Paris Hilton has chucked her guts there.

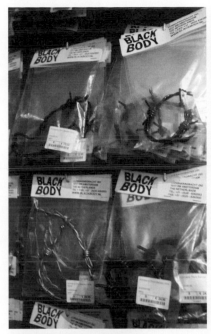

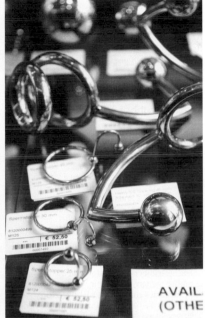

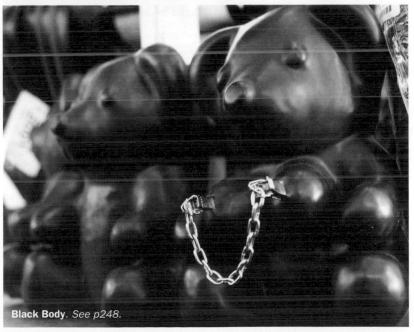

Black Body. *See p248*.

Hairdressers

★ Cuts 'n' Curls

Korte Leidsedwarsstraat 74, Southern Canal Belt (624 6881, www.cutsandcurls.nl). Tram 1, 2, 5, 7, 10. **Open** 10am-8pm Tue-Fri; 10am-4pm Sat. **Credit** AmEx, DC, MC, V. **Map** p330 D5.

Butch and basic haircuts with a sensitive side: many of its shampoos and conditioners are vegan-friendly.

Leather/rubber/sex

Whether just in need of a tattoo, a piercing, some kinky toys or a complete leather outfit, Amsterdam's Leather Lane is where to find it all. **Mr B** (Warmoesstraat 89, 420 8548, www.mrb.nl) sells anything from a simple and cheap cockring to expensive chaps. It also does tattoos and piercings (there's a female piercer too), plus DVDs and tickets for all the big gay events.

The street's **RoB Amsterdam** branch (Warmoesstraat 71, 422 3000, www.rob.nl) is more for accessories; here you can pick up a wristband, or indeed a full complement of leather/rubber gear, before hitting the bars. If rubber is more your thing, you can make your fantasies come true at **Black Body** (Spuistraat 44, 626 2553, www.blackbody.nl). Two sex shops with porn cinemas are **Bronx** (Kerkstraat 53-55, 623 1548, www.thebronx.nl) and **Drakes** (Damrak 61, 627 9544). Women with a dirty mind should head to **Female & Partners** or **Stout** (for both, *see p206*). **Demask** (Zeedijk 64, 620 5603, www.demask.com) is fun for all. For erotic and fetish shops, *see p206*.

SAUNAS

Fenomeen

1e Schinkelstraat 14, Zuid (671 6780, http://saunafenomeen.nl). Tram 1, 2. **Open** 1-11pm daily. Women only Mon; closed Aug. **Admission** €8 before 6pm; €3 after 10pm. **No credit cards.**

A relaxed, legalised squat sauna, housed in old horses' stalls, that's popular with lesbians on women-only Mondays. It has a sauna, steam bath, cold bath, chill-out room with mattresses, plus showers in the courtyard. Massages are also available. The café is ecologically minded, with vegetarian dishes and vegan soup always on the menu.

Thermos

Raamstraat 33, Southern Canal Belt (623 9158, www.thermos.nl). Tram 1, 2, 5, 7, 10. **Open** noon-8am daily. **Admission** €19; €14 reductions. **Credit** AmEx, DC, MC, V. **Map** p330 C4.

Quite busy during the week and absolutely packed at weekends, this four-level sauna offers it all: a tiny steam room, large dry-heat room, darkroom, porn cinema, private cubicles, bar, hairdresser, masseur, gym and small roof terrace. And for those who want to heat, meet and 'greet', then eat, there's a restaurant too.

LESBIAN SCENE

The lesbian scene isn't brilliant, but it's not as bad as it has been in the past, and at the moment there's a fair variety of bars and one-off club nights to satisfy most tastes.

That said, there's less variety than on the men's scene and, given the lack of any genuinely mixed bars (apart from Getto, *see p245*), that's reason enough for lesbians to gird their loins and go to the men's bars. Apart from a few strictly men-only places (generally sex clubs), women are welcome everywhere around the city – though they will, of course, be in the minority.

Flirtation

www.flirtation.nl.

As the biggest lesbian night in the country – currently housed in Panama (*see p265*) – this extravaganza claims to attract more than 1,000 women a pop. The secret of its success? Themed parties – angels & devils or cowgirls & showgirls – where dressing up is encouraged, a playlist of house and a keep-'em-hungry-for-more policy.

Garbo an de Amstel

Miranda Paviljoen, Amsteldijk 223, Zuid (www.garboforwomen.nl). Metro Amsterdam Rai. **Open** 5pm-midnight 1st Sat of mth. **Admission** see website.

A space for gay and bisexual ladies to socialise and strut their stuff to tunes by DJ Promiss. This laidback meet occasionally incorporates free tango workshops, and takes place every first Saturday in the month.

★ Girlesque

www.girlesque.nl.

Perhaps the most invigorating development on the lesbian scene of late has been the rise of girl-orientated burlesque. Formed in 2007 by Bianca Morel, the Girlesque collective hops between the city's queer-minded club nights (BOOM! at Boom Chicago, Dirty Disco Dykes) delivering high-end titillation and a refreshing dose of glamour to a mixed crowd. It's worth noting that seasoned Girlesque performer Kris Alexanderson (aka Pepper Minsky) writes a monthly fetish column in *Time Out Amsterdam* magazine.

★ Saarein II

Elandsstraat 119, the Jordaan (623 4901, www.saarein.nl). Tram 7, 10. **Open** 4pm-1am Tue-Thur; 4pm-2am Fri; noon-2am Sat; noon-1am Sun. **No credit cards.** **Map** p330 C4.

Never in fashion, so never out of it, this hardy perennial of the lesbian scene is particularly popular at weekends. The women it attracts tend to be slightly older, but young bucks certainly make an appearance. The only lesbian pool table in town resides in the basement.

★ Vive la Vie

Amstelstraat 7, Southern Canal Belt (624 0114, www.vivelavie.net). Tram 4, 9, 14. **Open** 4pm-3am Mon-Fri; 4pm-4am Sat, Sun. **Credit** AmEx, DC, MC, V. **Map** p330 E4.

In business for over 30 years, this place is run by Mieke Martelhoff and partner Rosemary. The walls of this small and basic bar just off Rembrandtplein are lined with pictures of female Hollywood icons. Under the watchful gaze of Elizabeth Taylor, a varied bunch of lesbians (and their friends) drink and dance to mainstream and Dutch hits. It gets packed late on Saturdays, so arrive early if you want a seat.

Gay Scene Investigation

Is Amsterdam over the rainbow?

To anyone revisiting Amsterdam in the second decade of the 21st century, 'What gay scene?' might be a logical rejoinder. The Reguliersdwarsstraat, once synonymous with the city's gay culture, is a shadow of its 1990s heyday, characterised by boarded-up windows, empty shop units and a distinct absence of punters under the age of 30.

In an essay for joop.nl, University of Amsterdam sociologist Laurens Buijs coined the term *Homorecessie* (gay recession) to describe the street's decline after the closure of stalwart venues Arc, Exit, April and Pub Soho.

Those who thought things couldn't get any worse were proved wrong by the demise of the iconic Warmoesstraat sex club the Cockring, which was raided back in July 2010 for drugs and subsequently shut down by city hall.

Co-owner of Club Church Richard Keldoulis makes no secret of his suspicion that gay venues – both existing and proposed – are particularly susceptible to the council's clean-up drive. 'Applications to establish gay saunas and kinky hotels are routinely rejected,' says Keldoulis. 'It's a joke. By cracking down on sexual freedom, we're eroding Amsterdam's unique selling point as a destination. By comparison, Singapore has five saunas, and it's not even legal to have gay sex there.'

Away from the tumbleweed of the Reguliersdwarsstraat, it's not all doom and gloom, however. Business at Church (established in late 2008) is booming, and there are rumours that the owners of the routinely stuffed 'hetero-friendly' Prik on Spuistraat (*see p243*) are looking into starting another venture. A cursory glance at *Time Out Amsterdam* magazine's Gay & Lesbian listings hints that, far from staying at home, Amsterdam's queers are availing themselves of a host of new nightlife options, albeit away from the designated 'gays-only' districts and venues.

Increasingly, they're joined at the bar by legions of open-minded 'straights' looking for a fashionably edgy night on the tiles. Standard bearer for this trend is the aptly named **MULTISEXI** at Studio 80, which sells out to a hip, 'poly-sexual' crowd of revellers on a monthly basis, but there's also **F*cking Pop Queers** at Jimmy Woo, **Zonde!** at Paradiso, and **Cowboys 'n' Angels** at super-club AIR, a glamorous, multi-million-euro venue that, according to its website, 'represents tolerance, diversity and freedom'. In other words, you're more likely to be turned away for wearing the wrong sneakers than for anything as irrelevant as whom you sleep with.

ARTS & ENTERTAINMENT

Music

A democratic scene, refreshingly free of tribalism.

There's no denying it; a list of Dutch musical icons fails to trip easily off the tongues of many visitors. But that's not to say that they don't exist. From the electronically generated beats delivered by Tiësto and Junkie XL to the globally renowned Royal Concertgebouw Orchestra, Amsterdam's native music scene shouldn't be underestimated.

In addition to all the acts emanating from the city, Amsterdam has long been established as one of the world's most important ports of call for international musicians, and major acts in virtually every imaginable genre are constantly passing through town. Whatever you're seeking, it'll be readily available within close proximity to the Canal ring.

TICKETS AND INFORMATION

For full event listings, head to the **AUB Ticketshop** (621 1311, www.amsterdam suitburo.nl), or check **Ticketmaster** (www. ticketmaster.nl), free Dutch-language monthly *Uitkrant*, or national music magazine *Oor* (www.oor.nl). For updated listings, check the Time Out website (www.timeout.com/ amsterdam) or try finding a bargain at the **Last Minute Ticket Shop** (www.lastminute ticketshop.nl). Discounts on tickets are often available for students and over-65s on production of ID. Book in advance.

ROCK & POP

ArenA

ArenA Boulevard 1, Bijlmermeer (311 1333, www.amsterdamarena.nl). Metro Bijlmer. **Open** times vary. **Admission** from €40.
When the football season ends, Ajax's stadium is reborn as a musical amphitheatre, hosting tours by the likes of U2, Madonna and the Rolling Stones, outdoor raves, and even a few Dutch stars. Bring your lighter, and don't forget binoculars if you're stuck in those garishly cheap seats.

Bitterzoet

Spuistraat 2, Old Centre: New Side (421 2318, www.bitterzoet.nl). Tram 1, 2, 5. **Open** 8pm-3am Mon-Thur, Sun; 8pm-4am Fri, Sat. **Admission** from €5. **No credit cards**. Map p326 C2.
This busy, comfy and casual bar triples as a venue for theatre and music. Both bands and DJs tend to embrace the jazzy, world and urban side of sound, as demonstrated by once-a-monther Crime Jazz: words, poetry, live jam sessions and beyond.

De Brakke Grond

Nes 45, Old Centre: Old Side (622 9014, www.debrakkegrond.nl). Tram 4, 9, 14, 16. **Open** times vary. **Admission** €5-€12. **No credit cards**. Map p326 D3.
Belgian culture does stretch beyond beer, and De Brakke Grond is here to prove it. This Flemish cultural centre and general artists' hangout presents a variety of contemporary music, visual art and stage productions from Flanders. If you're really lucky you might find a musician or two joining you for a drink at the adjoining restaurant.

Café Pakhuis Wilhelmina

Veemkade 576, Docklands (419 3368, www.cafe pakhuiswilhelmina.nl). Tram 26 or bus 42. **Open** times vary, Wed-Sun. **Admission** €5-€8. **Credit** MC, V.
Part of the Pakhuis Wilhelmina 'breeding ground' for underground young artists in the Docklands, this café aims to host challenging dance nights and interesting live acts. That said, regular events such as Hardrock Karaoke and themed tribute nights are also great fun if you're looking for more familiar sounds or fancy getting out the leather trousers and treading the boards.

Heineken Music Hall

ArenA Boulevard 590, Bijlmermeer (0900 687 4242 premium rate, www.heinekenmusichall.nl).

Metro Bijlmer. **Open** *Box office* from 6.30pm, concert days only. **Admission** from €27.50. **Credit** AmEx, MC, V.

A surprisingly cosy musical arena in the ArenA complex, the Heineken Music Hall regularly plays host to pop, rock and dance acts that are too big for the more central venues. Its modern design lacks character but makes up for it in acoustics. It isn't hard to get close up to your musical heroes.

Melkweg
Lijnbaansgracht 234a, Southern Canal Belt (531 8181, www.melkweg.nl). Tram 1, 2, 5, 7, 10, 20. **Open** *Box office* from 4.30pm daily. *Club times vary.* **Admission** €5-€32. *Membership* (compulsory) €3/mth; €15/yr. **No credit cards**. **Map** p330 D5.

A former dairy (the name translates as 'Milky Way'), the Melkweg acts as a home away from home for music of all styles, and thus draws a suitably eclectic crowd. Its two decent-sized concert halls offer a full programme year round; after a refit in 2007, which brought the capacity of the Max room up to 1,500, you've got an even better chance of getting tickets for the big shows. *Photos p252 & p253.*

FREE Mulligans
Amstel 100, Southern Canal Belt (622 1330, www.mulligans.nl). Tram 4, 9, 14, 16, 24, 25. **Open** *Bar* 4pm-1am Mon-Thur; 4pm-2am Fri; 2pm-3am Sat; 2pm-1am Sun. Music starts at 10pm, sessions at 7pm. **No credit cards**. **Map** p327 E3.

You'll find Irish pubs in every major European city, but only a handful are as much fun as Mulligans. The formula will be familiar to anyone who has frequented Irish pubs in the past: the music on offer ranges from traditional Celtic acts to modern-day rock and pop singers and songwriters. There's even an open session on Sundays, great for musicians and onlookers alike.

De Nieuwe Anita
Frederik Hendrikstraat 111, West (www.de nieuweanita.nl). Tram 3, 12. **Open** times vary. **Admission** varies. **No credit cards**. **Map** p329 A4.

A fixture in Amsterdam's subculture, DNA has become a sparkling promoter of fresh talents in the world of independent rock and electronica. It may keep itself to itself, but for those in the know it's the place to be. Programming is sporadic and based on good relations with understanding neighbours; check the website first before heading out.

OCCII
Amstelveenseweg 134, Museum Quarter (671 7778, www.occii.org). Tram 1, 2. **Open** 9pm-2am Mon-Thur, Sun; 10pm-3am Fri, Sat. **Admission** €3-€7. **No credit cards**.

Formerly a squat, this friendly bar and concert hall is tucked away at one end of Vondelpark. While its squat-scene days may be over, the legacy remains: the roster offers touring underground rock, experimental and reggae acts, plus adventurous local bands.

OT301
Overtoom 301, Museum Quarter (no phone, http://ot301.nl). Tram 1. **Open** times vary. **Admission** from €4. **No credit cards**. **Map** p329 B6.

A former Dutch film academy transformed by squatters into a cultural 'breeding ground'. Music

De Nieuwe Anita.

ARTS & ENTERTAINMENT

varies from underground acts to estalished names, but tends to be on the less commercial side of things. If you don't like the music, it also has a radio station, vegan restaurant and arthouse cinema to keep you entertained.

★ Paradiso

Weteringschans 6-8, Southern Canal Belt (626 4521, www.paradiso.nl). Tram 1, 2, 5, 7, 10. **Open** times vary. **Admission** from €5. *Membership* €3/mth; €18/yr. **No credit cards.** **Map** p330 D5.

A cornerstone of the Amsterdam scene, this former church is in such high demand that it often hosts several events in one day. The main hall has a rare sense of grandeur, with multiple balconies and stained-glass windows peering down upon the performers. The smaller venue upstairs is a great place to catch new talent before the big time. Both are wonderfully intimate; bands feed off the surroundings, making for some special nights.

▶ *Not content with holding intimate yet brilliant concerts and regular club nights, Paradiso is also host to the two-day indie music festival, London Calling; see p208.*

★ 'Skek

Zeedijk 4-8, Old Centre: Old Side (427 0551, www.skek.nl). Tram 4, 9, 14, 16, 24, 25 or Metro Nieuwmarkt. **Open** noon-1am Mon-Thur, Sun; noon-3am Fri, Sat. **No credit cards.** **Map** p326 D2.

Run by the same student organisation as is in charge of Filmtheater Kriterion (*see p227*), 'Skek's focus is on value and quality. While students lap up the discounts, music-lovers will appreciate regular singer-songwriter and jazz gigs, which are both entertaining and great for the wallet.

Sugar Factory

Lijnbaansgracht 238, Southern Canal Belt. (627 0008, www.sugarfactory.nl). Tram 1, 2, 5, 7. **Open** 9pm-4am Thur, Sun; 9pm-5am Fri, Sat. **Admission** from €5. **No credit cards.** **Map** p330 C5.

Sugar Factory has found its niche as a place where performance meets clubbing by hosting late-night gigs in the atmospheric surrounds of the 'night theatre'. WickedJazzSounds hosts Sunday evenings, and the cutting-edge Electronation brings top acts from the worlds of '80s synthesiser electro to current day minimal techno. Sweet it most certainly is.

Tropentheater

Mauritskade 63, Oost (568 8500, www.tropentheater.nl). Tram 7, 9, 10, 14 or bus 22. **Open** Box office noon-6pm Mon-Fri; 2-6pm Sat. **Tickets** from €18. **Credit** MC, V. **Map** p332 H3.

Falling under the umbrella of the Royal Tropical Institute (KIT), an independent non-profit organisation that specialises in the areas of international and intercultural co-operation, the Tropentheater is the number one place to catch acts from every faraway corner of the world.

▶ *For a vivid and interactive glimpse into the daily life of tropical and subtropical parts of the world, visit the Tropenmuseum; see p119.*

Winston Kingdom

Warmoesstraat 125-129, Old Centre: Old Side (623 1380, www.winston.nl). Tram 4, 9, 16, 24, 25. **Open** 9pm-3am Mon-Thur, Sun; 9pm-4am Fri,

OCCII. See p251.

Melkweg. *See p251.*

Sat. **Admission** €5-€10. **No credit cards.**
Map p326 D3.
Part of a weird and wonderful hotel complex, the
Winston is where artistic decadence collides with
rock 'n' roll grime. Evenings offer new talent, both
local and international followed by a club night
(included in the entry price).
▶ *After a long night of partying, collapse for a kip
upstairs in the hotel; see p134.*

JAZZ & BLUES

★ FREE Alto

*Korte Leidsedwarsstraat 115, Southern Canal
Belt (626 3249, www.jazz-cafe-alto.nl). Tram 1,
2, 5, 7, 10.* **Open** 9pm-3am Mon-Thur, Sun;
9pm-4am Fri, Sat. **No credit cards.**
Map p330 D5.
The widely renowned Alto club is one of the city's
older and better jazz venues. The famous Dutch
saxophonist Hans Dulfer has a long-running
Wednesday evening slot at this intimate venue, but
the quality isn't generally much lower on the other
six nights of the week.

Badcuyp

*1e Sweelinckstraat 10, De Pijp (675 9669,
www.badcuyp.nl). Tram 4, 16, 24, 25.* **Open**
11am-1am Tue-Thur, Sun; 11am-3am Fri, Sat.
Admission varies. **Credit** MC, V. **Map** p331 F5.
The focus at this small and friendly venue is on
world and jazz. Besides the intriguing range of international talents that play the main hall, the cute café
plays host to regular open jam sessions. The
Brazilian jazz sessions on Wednesday nights always
feature a diverse range of talented musicians.

Bimhuis

*Piet Heinkade 3, Waterfront (788 2188,
www.bimhuis.nl). Tram 25, 26.* **Open**
Telephone reservations noon-7pm Mon-Fri.
Box office 7-11pm show nights; most shows
9pm. **Admission** from €14. **Credit** AmEx,
MC, V. **Map** p327 F1.
Jazz musicians from far and wide queue up for
a chance to grace the stage at the Bimhuis, even
after its transplant to the Muziekgebouw aan 't IJ
complex. It may no longer be a smoky jazz joint but
the eye-catching building and familiar interior lay-
out have more or less guaranteed the Bimhuis a
healthy future.

Bourbon Street

*Leidsekruisstraat 6-8, Southern Canal Belt (623
3440, www.bourbonstreet.nl). Tram 1, 2, 5, 7, 10.*
Open 10pm-4am Mon-Thur, Sun; 10pm-5am Fri,
Sat. **Admission** usually free before 11pm, then
€5-€8. **Credit** AmEx, MC, VC. **Map** p330 D5.

**INSIDE TRACK
CULTURAL BEACON**

Music isn't the sole remit at the Melkweg
(*see p251*): the complex is also home to
a cinema, an art gallery and a café, and
stages weekend club nights to boot. It's
also opened a state-of-the-art theatre hall
together with neighbours Stadsschouwburg
Amsterdam. Music fans would be mad to
miss this key cultural beacon in the centre
of the city.

In the heart of the tourist area, this blues club has a spacious bar and a late liquor licence. Musicians are welcome at regular jam sessions and international acts drop by at least a couple of times a week. It's by no means a glamorous venue, but if late-night music played live is your thing then you won't be disappointed.

Maloe Melo
Lijnbaansgracht 163, Western Canal Belt (420 4592, www.maloemelo.com). Tram 7, 10, 13, 14, 17. **Open** 9pm-3am Mon-Thur, Sun; 9pm-4am Fri, Sat. **Admission** free-€5. **No credit cards. Map** p331 E5.
'Well, I woke up this morning, feeling Maloe Melowed…'. This small, fun juke joint on Lijnbaansgracht is Amsterdam's native house of the blues. Quality rockabilly and roots acts also play here on a regular basis, so shed your gloom and enjoy the boogie.

Zaal 100
De Wittenstraat 100, the Jordaan (www.zaal 100.nl). Tram 3, 10 or bus 18, 21, 22. **Open** times vary. **Admission** from €3. **No credit cards. Map** p325 A2.
While Zaal 100 has its roots in the squatting scene, it's tastefully decorated, unlike some of its more grungy counterparts. The weekly jazz workshops every Tuesday are a highlight and feature some of Amsterdam's best-known musicians. It's also a gallery space and is frequently rented out by local artists, so if you're lucky you might get a glimpse of some art while you enjoy the music.

FESTIVALS

The Dutch club scene slows in summer, but it's really more of a sideways step. Purpose-built beaches such as Blijburg, Strand West and NEMO Beach (on the roof of the science museum) spring up to host shows and mad parties throughout the week. Major musical events are scattered throughout the country from April to September, and many are completely free; check www.festivalinfo.nl for locations and line-ups.

Amsterdam Roots Festival
www.amsterdamroots.nl. **Date** June.
This festival brings some of the best world music acts to Amsterdam every year. Artists and musicians from all over the world perform in venues throughout the city over four days, with the festival culminating in a free open-air extravaganza in Oosterpark. *See also p211.*

Crossing Border
www.crossingborder.nl. **Date** Nov.
Based in the Hague, this gathering puts words before melody. Crossing Border offers a stimulating

mix of literature and music, with many well-known international authors and artists arriving in town for spoken-word and musical performances. Impromptu collaborations are not uncommon and the festival's laid-back atmosphere makes for an enjoyable all-round experience.

Live at Westerpark
www.liveatwesterpark.nl. **Date** July.
Held in collaboration with Mojo Concerts, this series of outdoor concerts is held in one of the city's parks and attracts acts of serious clout. Those who can't (or don't want to) get tickets can lay out a blanket anywhere in the surrounding park and enjoy the concert audibly over a picnic and some beer. Sweet.

London Calling
www.londoncalling.nl. **Date** late Mar, mid Nov.
The twice-yearly London Calling concerts are often the first opportunity for Dutch audiences to catch the hottest new rock and pop talents from the UK. Thanks to its increasing popularity, a number of big-name acts from outside the UK have been added to the festival line-up in recent years.

Lowlands
www.lowlands.nl. **Date** late Aug.
Holland's largest alternative music festival takes place over three days, attracting up to 60,000 young hipsters on each. The music, theatre acts and street performers create a lively atmosphere, and weather is largely unimportant – all the important stages are inside huge tents.

Noorderslag Weekend
www.eurosonic-noorderslag.nl. **Date** mid Jan.
A rare midwinter fest stretched over three days in Groningen, Noorderslag Weekend is for those seriously into the rock and pop scenes. An international industry showcase, the first two days fall under the name Eurosonic and are all about acts expected to make an impact across Europe in the coming year.

North Sea Jazz
0900 300 1250 premium rate, www.northsea jazz.nl. **Date** mid July.
This three-day mega-event is a favourite among Dutch jazz fans and outsiders. Staging marvellous

> ### INSIDE TRACK
> ### FESTIVAL AMUSEMENTS
>
> Those seeking extra adventure at the Lowlands festival (*see above*) can buy a ticket that includes entry to the Walibi World amusement park, which sits next to the festival site. All told, it's the closest thing Amsterdam has to a Glastonbury of its own.

Take the Mic

Release your inner performer.

For all you rambling troubadours eager to find a stage to strum a guitar, read a poem or try out your voice in public for the first time, Amsterdam is bursting with open-mic nights.

An evening of listening to budding, often untalented, singer-songwriters can often be trying on the ears. Nonetheless there is still something to love about those welcoming stages, whether getting the first glimpses of promising new talent or beering up and taking to the stage yourself for an impromptu performance. Luckily, there is no shortage of these intimate venues and you can find a place to stretch your vocal chords all the workweek long.

On Mondays, you can hop on board **The Tricky Theatre** (Oosterdokskade 10, Waterfront, www.trickytheatre.nl), a small boat that hosts an open music stage run by highly energetic New Yorker Cindy Peress. An open-mic veteran of sorts, she's been on the scene here since 1976, welcoming over three generations of singer-songwriters to her water-bound sessions.

If you're looking for something a bit more experimental, you can sing, steam and even get stoned at the **Sauna Fenomeen** (Eerste Schinkelstraat 14, Zuid, www.sauna fenomeen.nl) on Tuesday nights. Here, it's strictly music and not necessarily of the songwriter sort; that is, from *hang* (a Swiss instrument) to opera, anything

goes when stoners are in charge. As an additional bonus, the day's sauna fee is waived for participants.

The slightly more glamorous **Paleis van de Weemoed** (Oudezijds Voorburgwal 15-17, Old Centre: Old Side, www.schreierstoren.nl/paleis) caters to a different crowd every Wednesday. The burlesque theatre and restaurant opens its red-velvet curtains to a mixed bag of musicians that usually veer towards the jazzy side of things. Though there's no official dress code, you may want to consider a zoot suit and fedora as opposed to a pair of tattered Levis.

Taking place at **Molly Malones** (Oudezijds Kolk 9, Old Centre: Old Side, www.mollyin amsterdam.com), an Irish pub in the Red Light District, 'Monty Pagan's Third Thursday Thing' bridges the gap between disparate pub and poet types. Expect anything from poetic odes through crowd-pleasers to cheesy cover songs.

To round off your week, the **American Book Center** (Voetboogstraat 11, Old Centre: New Side, www.treehouse.abc.nl) runs a quaint open-podium session on Friday evenings. There's usually an eclectic mix of songwriters, poets, comedians and storytellers, which makes for a diverse evening. It's also a good start for the first-timer as the audience is quiet, polite, supportive and attentive for every act, good or bad.

ARTS & ENTERTAINMENT

big-name line-ups (around 180 acts) and drawing 23,000 visitors per day, the festival has settled into the Ahoy complex in the south of Rotterdam. It's hardly the most attractive of locations, but it has allowed breathing space for further growth.

FREE Parkpop
www.parkpop.nl. **Date** late June.
Loads of European cities claim to hold the largest free festival. The Hague's Parkpop is the Dutch contender: organisers usually expect 300,000 to 500,000 visitors for this family-type affair. Expect some surprisingly big names, Dutch acts and upcoming urban outfits across the event's three side-by-side stages.

Pinkpop
www.pinkpop.nl. **Date** May/June.
Attracting a slightly younger and poppier crowd than Lowlands (*see p254*), Pinkpop is somewhat less adventurous than its indie sister. Still, there are plenty of big names in the worlds of pop, rock, dance and metal at the three-day event.

CLASSICAL & OPERA

One of the most heart-warming aspects of Amsterdam's classical scene is that the city promotes a classless adoration of beautiful music. Attending a concert is not a grand statement of one's arrival in society, but simply about a love of the music.

Concert halls & churches

Bethaniënklooster
Barndesteeg 6b, Old Centre: Old Side (625 0078, www.bethanienklooster.nl). Tram 4, 9, 14, 16, 24, 25 or Metro Nieuwmarkt. **Open** times vary.
Tickets varies. **No credit cards. Map** p326 D2.
Hidden in a small alley between Damstraat and the Nieuwmarkt, this former monastery is a wonderful stage for promising new talent to cut their musical teeth. Amsterdam's top music students deliver regular free concerts, but you'll also find reputable professional ensembles and quartets.

Beurs van Berlage
Damrak 213, Old Centre: Old Side (521 7575, www.berlage.com). Tram 4, 9, 14, 16, 24, 25. **Open** *Box office* 2-5pm Tue-Fri; also from 2hrs before performance. Closed end June-mid Aug. **Tickets** from €12.50. **No credit cards. Map** p326 D2.
The Beurs is a cathedral of culture, comprising a large exhibition room, two concert halls and the offices of the building's three resident orchestras: the Netherlands Philharmonic, the Netherlands Chamber Orchestra and the Amsterdam Symphony Orchestra. Its performance chambers are wonderful, though the music schedule can be surprisingly sparse.

Concertgebouw
Concertgebouwplein 2-6, Museum Quarter (671 8345, www.concertgebouw.nl). Tram 2, 3, 5, 12, 16, 20. **Open** *Box office* 10am-7pm daily; until 8.15pm on performance nights. *Telephone bookings* 10am-5pm daily. **Tickets** from €15. **Credit** MC, V. **Map** p330 D6.
With its beautiful architecture and clear acoustics, the Concertgebouw is a favourite venue of many of the world's top musicians, and is home to the world-famous Royal Concertgebouw Orchestra. For a taster, pop into a free Wednesday lunchtime concert: they often offer a trimmed-down recital from one of the week's key performances.
▶ *The Concertgebouw also holds regular concerts for kids, see p220.*

★ Muziekgebouw aan 't IJ
Piet Heinkade 1, Waterfront (788 2010, www.muziekgebouw.nl). Tram 25, 26. **Open** *Telephone bookings* noon-5pm Mon-Sat.
Admission €8.50-€27.50. **Credit** MC, V. **Map** p327 E1.
Designed by Danish architects 3xNielsen, this is one of the most innovative musical complexes in Europe. The programmers are pleasingly versatile: the weekly schedule typically bustles with all manner of musical delights, from cutting-edge multimedia works to music by composers from throughout the last 150 years.
▶ *The venue plays host to regular jazz concerts; see p253 Bimhuis.*

Muziektheater
Amstel 3, Old Centre: Old Side (625 5455, www.muziektheater.nl). Tram 9, 14 or Metro Waterlooplein. **Open** *Box office* 10am-6pm Mon-Sat; 11.30am-2.30pm Sun; or until start of performance. **Tickets** from €15. **Credit** AmEx, DC, MC, V. **Map** p327 E3.
Home of the Dutch National Ballet, Netherlands Opera and the most recently established Holland Symfonia, the Muziektheater has a reputation for high-quality performances at good prices. Tickets go on sale three months in advance and often sell out fast, so it's advisable to book early.

Muziekgebouw aan 't IJ.

Noorderkerk.

ARTS & ENTERTAINMENT

Noorderkerk

Noordermarkt 48, the Jordaan (620 3119,
www.noorderkerkconcerten.nl). Tram 3, 10
or bus 18, 21, 22. **Open** 11am-1pm Sat; concerts
2-3pm Sat. **Tickets** €10-€30. **No credit cards.**
Map p325 B2.

Sure, the wooden benches in this early 17th-century
church are a bit on the hard side, but the programme of music is great, attracting accomplished
musicians and a host of young talent. Tickets are
available from the venue 45 minutes prior to concert or from the usual ticket outlets.

► *Slip a little classical music into your grocery*
shop with the weekly Saturday classical concerts
held here and Noordmarkt's delicious food market
outside, see p182 and p198.

Stadsschouwburg

Leidseplein 26, Southern Canal Belt (624 2311,
www.ssba.nl). Tram 1, 2, 5, 7, 10. **Open** *Box*
office 10am-6pm or until start of performance
Mon-Sat; from 2hrs before start of performance
Sun. **Tickets** from €11.50. **Credit** AmEx, MC, V.
Map p330 C5.

This resplendent venue on Leidseplein is an
impressive 19th-century building, originally constructed in traditional horseshoe shape. Known primarily for its theatre and opera productions,
contemporary music performances occasionally
manage to break into the schedule.

► *For dance and theatre, see p221 and p276.*

Westerkerk

Prinsengracht 281, Western Canal Belt (624
7766, www.westerkerk.nl). Tram 13, 14, 17.
Open *Office* 10am-3pm Mon-Fri. *Box office*

45mins before concert. **Tickets** varies. **No credit
cards. Map** p326 C3.

This landmark church features a wide range of
lunch and evening concerts, many free of charge.
Cantatas are performed during services, if you want
to hear the music in its proper setting. It's worth visiting to admire the stunning architecture alone.

► *Also worth a visit is the top of Westerkerk's*
tower, where you'll be treated to an incredible view
of the surrounding Jordaan, see pp102-105.

FESTIVALS & EVENTS

Grachtenfestival

Various venues (421 4542, www.grachtenfestival.
nl). **Date** mid Aug.

What started out as a single free concert from an
orchestra floating on a pontoon in front of the Hotel
Pulitzer has grown into the 'Canal Festival'. Handel
would be delighted to hear that this modern water
music has expanded to more than 90 concerts, each
set somewhere near or on the water.

Holland Festival

Various venues (788 2100, www.holndfstvl.nl).
Date June.

This month-long performing arts festival is the
biggest in the country. It takes a refreshing approach
to dance, literature, visual arts, theatre and film, but
there's no doubting that music is its central theme,
particularly in the realms of contemporary classical,
experimental and electronic music. Attracting international stars and composers each year, you're guaranteed a series of groundbreaking premieres and
reworkings that'll move on to make waves in other
cultural capitals around the world.

Nightlife

Amsterdam gets its mojo back.

After years of so-so clubbing, Amsterdam has once more become a great place for creatures of the night. There are more than enough excellent parties to go round in summer, and even in the off-season, Thursdays to Saturdays offer plenty of choice, whatever your musical inclinations.

Don't expect the party to kick off before midnight: before the clock strikes 12, most people are either at home or in a bar (*see pp165-173*) limbering up for the night ahead. And although locals party hard and the scene is enjoyably eclectic, Amsterdam is not a 24-hour city; you'll struggle to keep going after four or five at weekends, or even two or three on weeknights.

Bitterzoet. *See p261.*

CLUBBING IN THE CITY

Amsterdam's nightlife is enjoyably eclectic, and you can find anything from minimalist grooves to maximum noise. The gay scene has plenty of hotspots of its own, too, from the lively, anything goes **Queen's Head** or bohemian **House of Rising** to the unashamedly cruisey **Club Church**; *see pp237-249*.

When it comes to gigs, meanwhile, there has definitely been something of a renaissance in recent years (*see pp250-258*). It's always worth keeping your eyes peeled; you might discover a performance by your favourite band or DJ is but a tram ride away, and the concerts at rock, pop and jazz venues often run into club nights.

In this guide, particular attention has been paid to the most popular club nights held at each venue. While details were accurate at the time of going to press, they are, of course, liable to change, so it's always best to check ahead for specific events. The English-language *Time Out Amsterdam* is an excellent source for the latest city-wide listings, and it's also worth picking up flyers at record stores and bars.

As in any big city, all venues have a bouncer or two standing guard outside. Few – if any – are susceptible to bribery (although you should carry cash since many places don't accept credit cards on the door); you're better off showing up on time and in a mixed boy/girl group.

SEE A NEW SIDE OF THE RED LIGHT DISTRICT

Casa Rosso
Oudezijds Achterburgwal 106
(020 627 8954/casarosso.nl)

Visit the longest-running erotic show in town; it is essential to the ultimate Red Light Experience. Your stay will be unique, fun and unforgettable.
Sunday - Thursday 19.00-2.00
Friday - Saturday 19.00-3.00.

The Bananenbar and Bananenclub
Oudezijds Achterburgwal 37
(020 627 8954/bananenbar.nl)

The most eccentric bar in Amsterdam is the perfect place for friends, lovers, and parties. Not your scene? Head upstairs to Amsterdam's newest and hottest club and hot spot in the Red Light District, the Bananenclub, where the most beautiful women in the Red Light District will dance their way to your heart.
Sunday - Thursday 19.00-2.00
Friday - Saturday 19.00-3.00.

Erotic Museum
Oudezijds Achterburgwal 54
(020 624 7303/janot.nl)

As one of the oldest and historically rich cities in the world, Amsterdam also has some erotic history to offer you. Improve your history and art knowledge on a fun theme.
Sunday - Thursday 11.00-2.00
Friday - Saturday 11.00-3.00.

The Old Centre

Bitterzoet
*Spuistraat 2 (521 3001, www.bitterzoet.com).
Tram 1, 2, 5.* **Open** 8pm-3am Mon-Thur, Sun;
8pm-4am Fri, Sat. **Admission** €5-€12. **No credit
cards. Map** p326 C2.
This busy, comfortable bar triples as a venue for theatre and music. Both bands and DJs tend to embrace
eclectic, laid-back sounds, especially at the regular
Bon Bon Amer gatherings. *Photo p260.*

Dansen bij Jansen
*Handboogstraat 11-13 (620 1779, www.
dansenbijjansen.nl). Tram 1, 2, 4, 5, 9, 14,
16, 24, 25.* **Open** 10pm-4am Mon-Thur; 10pm-
5am Fri, Sat. **Admission** €2 Mon-Wed; €5
Thur-Sat. **No credit cards. Map** p330 D4.
It's a club, Jim, but not as we know it: it says on the
door you'll need valid student ID to get in. DJs spin
cheerful chart tunes and drinks prices are pleasantly
affordable. But if you're over 25, you'll feel like
Barbara Cartland at a booze-infused kindergarten.

Winston International
*Warmoesstraat 125-129 (623 1380,
www.winston.nl). Tram 1, 2, 5, 9, 13, 14, 16, 17,
24, 25.* **Open** 9pm-4am Mon-Thur, Sun; 9pm-5am
Fri, Sat. **Admission** €3-€9. **No credit cards.
Map** p326 D2.
An intimate venue that attracts a mixed crowd with
its alternative rock and indie tronica. Winston's

Escape.

INSIDE TRACK MULTITASKING

Many clubs in Amsterdam are not just
about clubbing. You can play ping-pong
every Tuesday night at **OT301** (*see
p265*); watch music documentaries in
the basement at **Trouw** (*see p265*) early
on Thursday evenings (Seeing Sounds),
or check out **Melkweg** (*see p262*) for
down-to-earth, democratic clubbing.
---

yearly Popprijs gives hope to many student rock
bands and entertainment to unsuspecting civilians.
Cheeky Mondays bring relief to yet another working
week with jungle and drum 'n' bass, while other
nights see bands performing daily, from garage and
folk to funky hip hop and ska, followed by alternative DJs. When relieving yourself, look out for the
enigmatic toilet art gallery.
▶ *The legendary Winston hotel is renowned for its
arty rooms, decorated by local artists; see p134.*

Southern Canal Belt

Air
*Amstelstraat 16 (820 0670, www.air.nl). Tram 4,
9, 14.* **Open** 11pm-4am Thur; 11pm-5am Fri, Sat;
varies Sun. **Admission** €9-€15. **No credit
cards. Map** p327 E3.
Like a phoenix from the ashes, a new club has risen
in the same location as now-defunct Club It.
Musically, the offerings are varied. The 3Hoog event
on Thursdays delivers creative, arty, interactive
nights where house prevails, whereas Fridays have
a more techno feel. On Saturday things tend to be a
bit more commercial, and on Sunday the evening
kicks off early.

Club Up/De Kring
*Korte Leidsedwarsstraat 26-1 (623 6985,
www.clubup.nl). Tram 1, 2, 5, 7, 10.* **Open** 11pm-
4am Thur-Sat. **Admission** €6-€10. **No credit
cards. Map** p330 C5.
Club Up is an intimate venue with a great sound system, connected via a corridor to artists' society De
Kring, which is one floor down. Be sure to visit this
venue when both areas are accessible, as De Kring
provides the laid-back atmosphere that the often-
packed, discotheque-like ballroom of Club Up lacks.
DJs spin disco and house.

Escape
*Rembrandtplein 11 (622 1111, www.escape.nl).
Tram 4, 9, 14.* **Open** 11pm-4am Thur, Sun; 11pm-
5am Fri, Sat. **Admission** €10-€17. **No credit
cards. Map** p331 E4.
With a capacity of 2,000, this is about as big as clubbing gets in central Amsterdam. Ever since club
night Chemistry left, the place has disappeared from

ARTS & ENTERTAINMENT

the national spotlight, resurfacing instead as a venue for a younger, more mainstream crowd. Queues still form on Saturday and Sunday evenings, and the bouncers are wary of groups of tourists, so squeeze into a slinky T-shirt, slap on some hair product and get in line early. *Photo p261.*

Jimmy Woo
Korte Leidsedwarsstraat 18 (626 3150, www.jimmywoo.com). Tram 1, 2, 5, 7, 10. **Open** 11pm-3am Thur, Sun; 11pm-4am Fri, Sat. **Admission** €10-€12. **Credit** AmEx, DC, MC, V. **Map** p330 C5.
Marvel at the lounge area filled with a mixture of modern and antique furniture, and then confirm for yourself the merits of its bootylicious light design and sound system. At times, the place looks just like a music video – and that includes the musicians and actors. If you have problems getting in, cool off across the street at sister cocktail bar, Suzy Wong (Korte Leidsedwarsstraat 45, 626 6769).

Melkweg
Lijnbaansgracht 234A (531 8181, www.melkweg.nl). Tram 1, 2, 5, 7, 10. **Open** 11pm-5am Fri; midnight-5am Sat. **Admission** €5-€32. *Membership* (compulsory) €3/mth or €25/yr. **No credit cards. Map** p330 C5.
Former milk factory 'Milky Way' offers a galaxy of stellar programming and a rebuilt main hall, in addition to the impressive Rabo hall. It's often ridiculously crowded, but great value and down to earth – with a little bit of everything thrown into the mix. Watch out for Saturday's indie-flavoured Gemengd Zwemmen, plus the Klinch nights, where

underground organisations take turns throwing dubstep, acid and techno parties. *Photo below.*
▶ *Melkweg also acts as a gig venue for all sorts of music styles as well as film and dance performances; see also pp221, 228 & 251.*

FREE Minibar
Prinsengracht 478 (422 1935, www.minibar online.com). Tram 1, 2, 5, 7, 10. **Open** 6pm-1am Tue-Thur, Sun; 6pm-3am Fri, Sat. **Credit** AmEx, DC, MC, V. **Map** p330 D5.
Call Minibar a classy sibling of Febo, the local fast-food chain where you grab your food from a hole in the wall. At Minibar, customers are provided with a key to their personal fridge, and pay as they leave. For a venue of its limited size, Minibar has an excellent musical programme, ranging from hip hop and boogie to UK funk and disco. Regular DJs include Cinnaman and FS Green.

Melkweg.

ARTS & ENTERTAINMENT

Profile Isis van der Wel

Night Mayor on fun street.

Year after unexciting year, locals have been complaining that Amsterdam's nightlife was dead in the water. City laws forced clubs and pubs to close early; underground parties were vigorously monitored and often shut down. Even finding food in the wee hours proved difficult. But not everyone was ready to give up and leave.

In 2003, an illustrious group of DJs and party organisers was chosen to collectively don the moniker *Nachtburgemeester* – or 'Night Mayor' – for three years. Though not an official government post, they were tasked with rebuilding bridges of communication between Amsterdam's nocturnal souls and her politicians.

After examining the city's nightlife scene, the group drafted the *Nachtnota* – a 15-page summary of what Amsterdam's nightlife was, is, and possibly could be. Admittedly, they had few achievements beyond words, but they did create a positive atmosphere in which the next Night Mayor might be able to get things done.

In February 2010, Isis van der Wel – a well-known local DJ with nearly 20 years' experience – became Amsterdam's Night Mayor after a controversial election in which the people's favourite, the flamboyant transvestite Jennifer Hopelezz, was passed over by the selection panel.

But Van der Wel isn't letting the controversy get in the way of doing a good job. In addition to her Night Mayor predecessors, she has gathered a team of expert advisers, known as the *Nachtraad* ('Night Council'), to help her campaign for more liberal policies on drugs, a prolonged and extended respect for 'cultural breathing places' where rules are more relaxed

ARTS & ENTERTAINMENT

and – of course – less stringent closing hours for clubs and pubs.

Van der Wel herself is particularly passionate about the cultural breathing places that have been a vital characteristic of the city over the past few decades: 'It's crucial for society not to let these dry up and to provide space for people to create in a state of freedom that's neither controlled nor cultivated by the government.'

Lofty ambitions indeed, but most of the city's night owls would be happy if they could just get a beer after 4am on a Saturday night.

Nachttheater Sugar Factory

Lijnbaansgracht 238 (627 0008, www.sugar factory.nl). Tram 1, 2, 5, 7, 10. **Open** midnight-5am Thur-Sat; 11pm-5am Sun. **Admission** €5-€17. **No credit cards**. **Map** p330 C5.

This 'night theatre' has found its niche as a place where performance meets clubbing. Every night brings a show of some kind, be it classical dancers, MCs in various shapes and sizes, or actors mixing with the crowds. Watch out for Latin-flavoured ¿Que Pasa?, which has built up quite a following. Wicked Jazz Sounds hosts a relaxed Sunday evening, and the cutting-edge Electronation attracts top acts performing synthesizer electro or minimal techno. Sweet it most certainly is.

Paradiso

Weteringschans 6-8 (626 4521, www.paradiso. nl). Tram 1, 2, 5, 7, 10. **Open** 11.30pm-4am Wed, Thur; midnight-5am Fri; 11.30pm-5am Sat. **Admission** from €6. *Membership* (compulsory) €3.50/mth; €25/yr. **No credit cards**. **Map** p330 D5.

An Amsterdam institution, this large ex-church is a safe clubbing bet, with a trusty formula of live show followed by a DJ from around 11pm. Saturdays pull in a youngish, up-for-it crowd, while Noodlanding ('Emergency Landing') on Wednesdays or Thursdays is particularly good for an alternative, indie feel. Bigger concerts by the likes of international superstars such as Lady Gaga or Mark Ronson sell out weeks in advance. *Photo p265.*
▶ *This is a popular venue for 'intimate' concerts by international superstars and lesser-known names alike; see p252.*

Studio 80

Rembrandtplein 17 (www.studio-80.nl). Tram 4, 9, 14. **Open** 10pm-4am Wed, Thur, Sun; 11pm-5am Fri, Sat. **Admission** free-€10. **No credit cards**. **Map** p331 E4.

In the middle of Rembrandtplein's neon glitz and ice-cream-eating crowds lurks this ex-radio studio, a black pearl waiting to be discovered. Dirty disco, deep electronic acid and gritty hip hop are shown off at very reasonable fees. The city's most progressive techno and minimal crowds find their home here and have no trouble bringing disc-spinning or synthesizer-wielding friends from as far afield as Berlin and Barcelona.

The Waterfront, Eastern Islands & Oost

Café Pakhuis Wilhelmina

Veemkade 576 (419 3368, www.cafepakhuis wilhelmina.nl). Tram 26. **Open** varies Wed-Sun. **Admission** €5-€8. **No credit cards**.

Wilhelmina is often overlooked by casual clubbers. Is it the club's IJ-oriented location? The absence of bouncers? Or bottles of beer for only €2.10? In any

Nachttheater Sugar Factory.

case, don't miss it if your heart lies with today's left-field music. For people with a short attention span there's the monthly Page Turner night, which has everything from poetry to electronic performances, all at high speed. Keep an eye on the Beats and Beyond events if you like your funk and boogaloo heavy on the breaks.

Canvas

Wibautstraat 150 (716 3817, www.canvas7.nl). Metro Wibautstraat or tram 3. **Open** 10pm-3am Fri, Sat. **Admission** €5-€9. **Credit** AmEx, MC, V. **Map** p332 H5.

The programming is pretty diverse here, ranging from cutting-edge electronica through hip hop to club house and live jazz musicians. Particularly good are the A La Canvas Fridays, when big local DJs such as Aardvarck and Tom Trago create a 'living room' atmosphere playing anything danceable but house.

Hotel Arena

's Gravesandestraat 51 (850 2400, www.hotelarena.nl). Metro Weesperplein or tram 3, 7, 10. **Open** 10pm-4am Fri, Sat. **Admission** €10-€25. **No credit cards**. **Map** p332 G3.

A truly multipurpose venue, these beautiful buildings were once an orphanage, before becoming a youth hostel. From there, it was only a short step to trendy hotel, bar and restaurant. Big-city folk, used to long treks, will laugh at its accessibility, but Amsterdammers tend to forego the small

detour eastwards, making it hard for the Arena to truly kick clubbing butt – monthly events such as Salsa Lounge, with its sweltering Latin bias, and R&B-drenched Swingbeatz are the exceptions.
▶ *Looking for a place to lay your weary head afterwards? Why not simply check in at the hotel; see p142.*

Panama

Oostelijke Handelskade 4 (311 8686, www. panama.nl). Tram 26. **Open** 11pm-4am Thur-Sat. **Admission** €10-€20. **Credit** AmEx, DC, MC, V. **Map** p327 F1.
A steady force in Amsterdam nightlife, restaurant/theatre/nightclub Panama overlooks the IJ in one of the city's most booming areas. A deserted strip back in 2000 when it opened, the neighbourhood has now been transformed with high-rise offices, steep rents and the shiny Muziekgebouw (*see p256*). Dance to hits at We All Love '80s & '90s (every last Saturday of the month) and look out for the club's irregular UKfunky nights if you like to get your groove on.

★ Trouw Amsterdam

Wibautstraat 127 (463 778, www.trouw amsterdam.nl). Metro Wibautstraat or Tram 3. **Open** 11pm-5am Fri, Sat. **Admission** €10-€18. **No credit cards. Map** p332 G5.
Brought to you by the creative forces behind the dearly departed Club 11, Trouw also features a restaurant for late-night dining and the De Verdieping art gallery. Expect experimental electronica, underground dance music and innovative vibes from hyper-rhythm vanguards Viral Radio. Also have a lookout for the monthly Colors event that brings you the best in house and UK funk.

The Jordaan & Oud-West

★ OT301

Overtoom 301 (412 2954, www.ot301.nl). Tram 1. **Open** varies Fri, Sat. **Admission** €5-€10. **No credit cards. Map** p329 B6.
This former squatted film school serves cheap bottled beer and a wildly varying programme including Matjesdisco (Mullet Disco; be sure to dress accordingly) and not-too-serious electronic new-wave night, Popwave 301.

Outside Amsterdam

'What other place in the world could you find where all of life's comforts, and all novelties that man could want, are so easy to obtain as here – and where you can enjoy such a feeling of freedom?' So wrote René Descartes of Amsterdam in 1628. The same is still true now, but that doesn't stop a good number of clubbers heading out of town, particularly for outdoor events. If you're going further afield, check the website or flyer first and make sure you dress the part.

Bloemendaal Beach Cafés

Beach pavilions, Bloemendaal aan Zee. NS rail to Haarlem or Zandvoort, then taxi (€12.50) or bus 81 to Bloemendaal aan Zee. **Open** varies May-Oct. **Admission** free-€5. **No credit cards.**
Once a wonderful secret, these beach bars now lure clubbers by the thousands each summer weekend. Seven different cafés offer music, fashion and fabulous fixtures and fittings. There's a venue here to suit everyone, from kooky Woodstock through chic Bloomingdale to Ibiza-like Republiek.

ARTS & ENTERTAINMENT

Paradiso.

Sport & Fitness

This small country packs an almighty sporting punch.

Amsterdam is an active city, continually in motion. Every major sport is represented here, with numerous opportunities to get stuck in and keep in shape. For those taking their first steps on the fitness chain, walking and exploring is an ideal start. As well as pounding the city's streets, Noord-Holland's tourist information offices (www.noord-holland.com) can help you explore outlying areas, providing routes of various lengths and types.

Theirs may be a relatively small landmass, but the Dutch people certainly take their sport seriously. Whatever the occasion, when the sons and daughters of the nation step out at competitions, home and abroad, the weight of the world rests expectantly on their fellow countrypeople's shoulders, reflected in the unmistakeable sea of orange cheering from the stands. Football remains the game most special to many, with fans still pining for the 1970s and '80s glory days of Cruyff and Van Basten.

SPECTATOR SPORTS

American football

Full details are available from the sport's governing body, **AFBN** (www.afbn.nl). The **Amsterdam Crusaders** (Sloterweg 1045, West, 617 7450, www.crusaders.nl) are the oldest surviving American-style football club in the Netherlands.

Baseball

The Netherlands is now one of the strongest baseball nations in Europe. Known locally as *honkbal*, international summer competitions such as the **Haarlemse Honkbalweek** (023 525 4545, www.honkbalweek.nl) and **World Port Tournament** in Rotterdam (010 880 8788, www.worldporttournament.nl) attract nations like Cuba, Japan and the USA. The season runs from April to October. For information contact the **KNBSB** (030 751 3650, www.knbsb.nl).

Cricket

At amateur level, cricket is played with fervour and dedication nationwide, with over 100 teams affiliated to the **KNCB** (030 751 3780, www.kncb.nl). Several are in Amsterdam; the biggest is the **VRA** (Nieuwe Kalfjeslaan 21b, Amstelveen, 641 8525, www.vra.nl). Most have junior, veteran and women's teams; newcomers are welcome.

Cycling

Not just a means of transport (or torture device for scaring tourists who stumble into bike lanes), cycling is also a serious sport. Fans turn out in huge numbers for stage, criterium (road circuit) and one-day road races, plus track, field, cyclo-cross and mountain biking varieties. If you have a racing bike, head for **Sportpark Sloten**. Two cycle clubs are based here: **ASC Olympia** (617 7511, www.ascolympia.nl) and **WV Amsterdam** (690 1466, www.wvamsterdam.nl).

Darts

Moves to have darts recognised as an Olympic sport would be supported en masse by the Dutch. Their king of kings, Raymond 'Barney' van Barneveld, has won the BDO world title four times, plus the PDC world championship. Darts fans turn up at national and international competitions, causing the decibel levels to soar. Contact the **Nederlands Darts Bond** (070 36 67 206, www.ndbdarts.nl) for the Dutch tournament calendar.

Football

The Dutch turn out in huge numbers when it comes to football. From international matches played at ArenA, to amateur ones on wet winter afternoons, there's a real devotion that never diminishes through the ups and the downs. In terms of Dutch internationals, it's always a rollercoaster ride in the emotional stakes: just look at the agonising exits faced at every recent major tournament.

Ajax

Amsterdam ArenA, Arena Boulevard 29, Bijlmermeer (311 1444, www.amsterdam arena.nl). Metro Strandvliet, Arena/Bijlmer or NS rail Bijlmer. **Tickets** €49.50-€69.50. **Credit** MC.

The country's most famous club is renowned world-wide for flair on the field and its excellent youth training programme. Although success isn't guaranteed, they're typically there (or thereabouts) and battles with main rivals Feyenoord and PSV are fought fiercely each season in the gladiatorial ArenA. In July, some of the world's biggest teams are invited to take part in the Amsterdam Tournament.
▶ *Who's a lucky boy then? Read up on Ajax's mascot Lucky Lynx, p269.*

Hockey

The Dutch are especially passionate about field hockey and turn up in numbers that prove it. Although the men's team came fourth in the 2008 Olympics, the women are the most successful, having won gold in Beijing and the World Cup eight times.

With around 185,000 players nationwide, the country also boasts the largest number of affiliated teams of any equivalent association in the world. For details on local teams contact **KNHB** (030 751 3400, www.knhb.nl).

Rugby

There are over 100 rugby clubs currently competing throughout the country. Unusually, women's rugby is as popular as men's, and there's also a wealth of youth teams. **AAC** (www.aacrugby.com) in Amsterdam caters for all of the above and welcomes visitors and new players alike. Contact the **National Rugby Board** (480 8100, www.rugby.nl) for schedules. Gay rugby is also quite an international phenomenon: to play or just watch, contact **Amsterdam Lowlanders** www.amsterdamlowlanders.com).

Volleyball

Thanks to the growing success of both men's and women's national teams, volleyball's popularity continues to rise. For details of events and local clubs, contact the Amsterdam office of **NeVoBo** (693 6458, www.holland.nevobo.nl).

FITNESS & LEISURE
Athletics

The *Trimloopboekje* (Dutch Runners' Guide), published every August, lists all running events in the Netherlands. Amsterdam's major road events are the **Vondelparkloop** in January –

Ajax.

ARTS & ENTERTAINMENT

part of the Rondje Mokum series (www.rondje mokum.nl), which includes seven separate ten-kilometre (15-mile) city races and one 15-kilometre (9.3-mile) run, September's **Dam tot Damloop** from Amsterdam to Zaandam and the **Amsterdam Marathon** in October. For club and training facilities, contact **Phanos** (671 6086, www.phanos.org). Details on athletics in Holland are available from the **KNAU** (026 483 4800, www.knau.nl).

Badminton

Following international success from orange-shirted players like Mia Audina and Yao Jie, badminton players and sporting facilities are becoming all the more professional. Contact the **Badminton Union Amsterdam** (697 3758, www.bva-badminton.nl) and **NBB** (030 608 4150, www.badminton.nl) for further information on clubs and courts.

Basketball

Although public basketball courts are a rarity, several clubs in Amsterdam welcome players: contact the **NBB** Amsterdam office (0251 272 417, www.dunk.nl) for more details. Korfball, a mixed-sex sport sharing elements of basketball and netball, is popular: contact the Amsterdam **KNKV** (034 349 9600, www.districten.knkv.nl).

Climbing

The single highest point in the Netherlands, Vaalserberg, is no more than 321 metres (1,053 feet) high. Fortunately, climbing walls are never too far away.

Klimhal Amsterdam

Naritaweg 48, West (681 0121, www.klimhal amsterdam.nl). NS Station Sloterdijk. **Open** 5-10.30pm Mon, Tue, Thur; 2-10.30pm Wed; 4-10.30pm Fri; 11am-10.30pm Sat; 9.30am-10.30pm Sun. **Admission** €12; €9 reductions; €5.50 equipment hire. **No credit cards**.
One of the biggest climbing walls in the whole of the Netherlands, Klimhal Amsterdam is easily recognisable, in a sea of office blocks, by its unusual exterior. It offers courses and great facilities for beginners and advanced climbers.

Golf

While golf isn't a sport that the Dutch have made much of a mark in professionally, it continues to develop as a relaxing game for men, women and children of all backgrounds and levels. Public courses are open to all; many offer driving ranges and practice holes to tune up your game.

Klimhal Amsterdam

De Hoge Dijk

Abcouderstraatweg 46, Zuid-Oost (0294 281 241, www.dehogedijk.nl). Metro Holendrecht then bus 120, 126 to Abcoude. **Open** dawn-dusk daily. **Admission** 18-hole €47, €52 weekend; 9-hole €27, €32 weekend. Short course €24, €27 weekend. **Credit** AmEx, MC, V.
A public, 18-hole polder course, with a par score of 71, plus four par five holes and five par threes to complete the usual glut of par fours. It's on the edge of Amsterdam and reservations are required.

Health & fitness

Amsterdam has a very interesting collection of health clubs thanks to proprietors' willingness to set up shop in the capital's quirky old houses and countless empty office blocks. Look under 'Fitnesscentra' on www.goudengids.nl for full listings. There are also international chains, so ask your home club about options in Amsterdam. The city centre is crawling with health clubs that have day passes from €15 to €25.

Sport City Waterlooplein

Jodenbreestraat 6, Old Centre: Old Side (www. sportcity.nl). Tram 9, 14. **Open** 7am-11pm Mon, Wed; 8.30am-11pm Tue, Thur, Fri; 8.30am-5pm Sat, Sun. **Admission** €17.50. **Map** p327 E3.
Located just a few doors down from Rembrandt's old house, it has the latest fitness machines and

offers a wide variety of classes. After a workout, treat yourself to a sauna, steam bath and solarium.

Horse riding

While it's not particularly sensible to go trotting within the Canal ring, riding is nevertheless fairly accessible. The Netherlands' oldest riding school just off the Vondelpark, the Hollandsche Manege (*see p272* **Horsing Around**), offers classes to young and old.

Saunas

Leave your modesty in the changing room: covering up is frowned upon in most places. Unless stated otherwise, saunas are mixed, but most offer women-only sessions. **Sauna Da Costa** (Da Costakade 200, West, 612 5946, www.saunadacosta.nl) bastes visitors in honey and scented herbs during its Finnish-style *löyly* sauna experience every Monday evening and Saturday afternoon.

Deco Sauna
Herengracht 115, Western Canal Belt (623 8215, www.saunadeco.nl). Tram 1, 2, 5, 13, 17. **Open** noon-11pm Mon, Wed-Sat; 3-11pm Tue; 1-7pm Sun. **Admission** from €20. **No credit cards**. **Map** p326 C2.

This beautiful art deco sauna provides facilities for a Turkish bath, Finnish sauna and cold plunge bath. There's also a solarium. Massages, shiatsu, and beauty and skincare are all available by appointment. Mixed bathing only.

Skateboarding, inline skating & roller skating

Amsterdam is an exciting place if you like spending your days dashing about on various types of tiny wheels. Inline skating is also hugely popular as both a sport and a transport method. **Vondelpark** (*see p112*) is an inline skater's paradise.

Skatepark Amsterdam
NDSM, tt-Neveritaweg 15a (337 5955, 06 4170 0767 mobile, http://skateparkamsterdam.nl).

Lucky Lynx

Mascot with a mission.

Even when the chips are down, Lucky Lynx knows how to rouse a stadium of 50,000 disheartened fans. Lucky, you see, is the official mascot of Amsterdam's AFC Ajax, one of the most successful football teams in the world.

Apparently born on Mount Olympus in Greece, that makes Lucky one of just 100 Balkan lynxes in existence. Small wonder, then, that fans of all ages queue to have their picture taken with him on match day. So popular is Lucky that he even has his own page on social-networking site Hyves.

When he's not pepping up spirits or offering a bosomy hug at a game, Lucky is the face of the Ajax Kids Club, which aims to get children interested in playing football. Given the Dutch obsession with the golden game and the fact that the Ajax youth programme has been turning out world-renowned players – including Johan Cruyff, Dennis Bergkamp and Wesley Sneijder – for years, it's probably not a particularly taxing job...

Het Marnix.

Open 3-10pm Tue-Fri; noon-8pm Sat, Sun.
Admission €5.25.
See p271 **Skatepark**.

Vondeltuin/Rent A Skate
Vondelpark 7, Museum Quarter (06 2157 5885 mobile, www.vondeltuin.nl). Tram 1, 2, 3, 5, 12.
Open 11am-8pm (dry weather only). **Rates** from €5 (€50 security deposit or ID). **No credit cards.**
Map p330 C6.
A skate rental outlet in the bustling Vondelpark that also offers parent-child skating classes. Vondeltuin is also integral to the regular Friday Night Skate sessions (*see below*).

Ice skating

As if the nation were afraid to move at walking pace, the Dutch are as fearless on ice as on bikes, strapping on a pair of blades as soon as temperature permits. Hugely competitive on the international speed-skating circuit, it's not uncommon to see skaters whooshing along narrow city canals the moment they freeze over; even park ponds become rinks when conditions are right.

Head east to the outdoor **Jaap Edenhal** 400-metre (1,312-foot) ice track at **Radioweg 64** (694 9652, www.jaapeden.nl), open October to March. Contact the **KNSB** in Amersfoort (033 489 2000, www.knsb.nl) for details on conditions and events.

Skiing & snowboarding

Although Amsterdam is in the Low Countries, you can still head for the pistes in the heart of this city by going to **Ski Inn** (WG Plein 281, West, 607 0148). With its two pistes and real snow, **Snowplanet** (Recreational Area Spaarnwoude, Heuvelweg 6-8, Velsen-Zuid, 0255 545848, www.snowplanet.nl; *see p220*) is almost like the real thing.

Snooker & carambole

There are a few halls in Amsterdam where you can play snooker or pool cheaply. Carambole, with a pocket-free table, is a popular variation. Traditionally, *biljart* (billiards) is associated

---

INSIDE TRACK SKATE DATES

Check out the popular city-wide tour that is the awesome **Friday Night Skate** (www.fridaynightskate.com; *photo p272*). For an all-weather solution, head to **Skatepark Amsterdam** (www.skatepark amsterdam.nl); *see p271* **Skatepark**.

ARTS & ENTERTAINMENT

Ramp It Up

For those with nerves of iron and wheels of steel.

If you can't live without wheels under your feet, head to **Skatepark Amsterdam** (*see p269*), a 1,750-square-metre (18,800-square-foot) boarders', bikers' and rollerbladers' haven at the top of a seven-metre-high former warehouse on the NDSM.

Besides being the city's largest, it's also the only indoor ramp, so no need to worry about the weather. And don't panic if you forget your board: you can rent one for the ridiculously low price of €2.50, plus you can get all the necessary protective gear.

The adrenalin starts to pump as you glide down the side of this long swathe of smooth concrete, jump over moveable obstacles and slide up and down the miniramp pool, and you can test your skills against better skaters or help out the newbies, since the park is open to beginners and experts alike. Get to know them all at the Friday night Skatepark Disco.

Getting there will also be an important part of this adventure. From Centraal Station get the (free) ferry to NDSM, enjoying a beautiful view of the harbour in the ten to 15 minutes it takes to cross the IJ, after which it's a three-minute walk.

For the right gear, *see p190* **Streetwear**.

with cafés, but there are plenty of bars outside the city centre with tables, too; check www.goudengids.nl under 'Biljartzalen' or contact the **KNBB** (030 600 8400, www.knbb.nl) for details.

Squash

For information on local clubs and competitions, contact the **Dutch Squash Organisation** (079 361 5400, www.squash.nl) or look under 'Squashbanen' on www.goudengids.nl.

Squash City
Ketelmakerstraat 6, Jordaan (626 7883, www.squashcity.nl). Bus 18, 21, 22. **Open** 7am-11pm Mon-Fri; 8.45am-7.30pm Sat, Sun. **Admission** €10.50 before 5pm; €12.50 after 5pm. **Credit** AmEx, MC, V.

An all-round fitness centre where national and international squash champions train.

Swimming

Most Amsterdam hotels barely have space for bedrooms, let alone a pool. Fortunately, the city is well equipped with public baths in each district.

Het Marnix (indoor)
Marnixplein 1, the Jordaan (524 6000, www.het marnix.nl). Tram 3, 10 or bus 18, 21. **Open** 7am-10pm Mon-Thur; 7am-6pm Fri; 7am-8pm Sat, Sun. **Admission** from €3.70. **No credit cards.** This multi-purpose health centre features two pools that, thanks to an advanced filtration system, require very little chlorine. The Tuesday night naturist slot is popular.

Tennis

For details on competitions – including July's **Dutch Open** and the **ABN AMRO World Tennis Tournament** in February – and clubs, contact the **KNLTB** (033 454 2600, www.knltb.nl).

Amstelpark
Koenenkade 8, Amsterdamse Bos (301 0700, www.amstelpark.nl). Bus 170, 171, 172. **Open** *Apr-Sept* 8am-11pm Mon-Fri; 8am-9pm Sat, Sun. *Oct-Mar* 8am-midnight Mon-Fri; 8am-11pm Sat, Sun. **Rates** €25/hr. **Credit** AmEx, DC, MC, V.
A total of 42 tennis courts (16 indoor and 26 outdoor), plus 12 squash courts, a Turkish bath, sauna, swimming pool, shop and racket hire.

Water sports

Away from the canals and pedalos, there are plenty of recreational lakes within easy reach of Amsterdam where seadogs can take to the water. There are rowing clubs on the Amstel and at the Bosbaan in Amsterdamse Bos. Casual canoeists can take a Wetlands Safari tour (06 53 552669,www.wetlandssafari.nl; for more information, call between the hours of 3pm and 10pm or email for info@wetlandssafari.nl).

Friday Night Skate. *See p270.*

Horsing Around

Two legs bad, four legs good.

No need to ask directions to the **Hollandsche Manege** (*see p52*), the stables in the middle of smart Amsterdam-Zuid. The sweet scent of equestrian life serves as its olfactory signpost. For the nasally challenged, two large lanterns on the Vondelstraat beckon visitors to the oldest riding school in the Netherlands, where they can learn the ancient sport of horseback riding.

It's not a pursuit that's much gushed about in the tech-minded fitness mags, but horseriding is a great exercise for the muscles in the dorsal and abdominal areas, and causes less stress to the knees and lower body parts than comparable forms of exercise like walking and swimming. An hour's riding can burn about 300 calories, but most riders are in it for the sheer thrill of gaining control of a powerful beast between their legs.

Not everybody is immediately ready for the saddle. Rider Sanne Locher confided that she had a fear of horses – as a child she'd been thrown many times. Nowadays, the 25-year-old starts her weekends on Friday night partying at the Manege with an hour of horsing around before she and her friends from the Amsterdam Student Equestrian Club head for less smelly pastures.

In the ornate 19th-century foyer overlooking the riding area below, Valeska Groenestein, behind the bar, confesses that for her, 'mastering control over a 600-kilo animal is an enormous adrenaline kick'.

She shares a passion for riding with the other employees and volunteers who take care of the 45 exquisite Arabian, Lipizzaner and Gelderland horses in the stable.

Unlike 40 years ago, riding horses is by no means an elitist sport. Every evening after 7pm, the Manege offers private and group lessons for all ages and levels. And the rates are reasonable too (five lessons for €108). Each week, some 850 participants pass through the stables.

Beginners are first guided through a half hour of basic walking and trotting until they feel comfortable and confident with their horse. Afterwards… giddy up.

Theatre & Comedy

From back-alley box offices to the biggest hits of Broadway.

Amsterdam, like most major cities, has its official monuments to the arts, chief among them the imposing Muziektheater, or 'Stopera' – an opera house, ballet, theatre and civic offices in one. But, as you might expect from this famously open-minded city, this is also a place where performing artists are allowed, indeed encouraged, to experiment. Experimentation happens across all forms and genres, from staged readings to musicals, ballets and improv. The results are worth investigation, so be sure to hunt out smaller, alternative venues and off-centre cultural hubs. The language gap is often surprisingly well bridged by surtitles, audience interaction and strong visuals.

Theatre

Even the flying visitor to Amsterdam will recognise it as a city of artists. Less evident, however, is its active and passionate theatre community that thrives in secret in back-alley venues. Its centrepiece for dance and opera – the **Muziektheater** (*see p222*) – comes bundled with the city hall and therefore resembles an office block rather than a seat for the lavish revivals of Petipa and Tchaikovsky.

Experimentation is common across all genres. If you like cutting-edge performance then the theatres along the Nes are good places to start. For something more mainstream, try **Koninklijk Theater Carré** (*see p275*) or the **RAI Theater** (*see below*). You'll also be well served if commercial musicals are more your thing. And don't worry about the language – the Dutch have a distinctive, visual approach to theatre making, and these days many groups employ English surtitles for their shows.

TICKETS & INFORMATION

Call or visit the **Uitburo** on Leidseplein for information about what's on, or contact the **Amsterdam Tourist Board** (*see p208*). If you prefer to play it by ear, visit the **Last Minute Ticket Shop** on Leidseplein where tickets for that night are sold at half price.

Of the theatres on Nes, **De Brakke Grond** (*see p274*) sells tickets through its own website and box office, while tickets for the **Frascati** (*see p274*) can also be bought at the central box office at De Brakke Grond.

THEATRES

Amsterdam Marionetten Theater

Nieuwe Jonkerstraat 8, Old Centre: Old Side (620 8027, www.marionettentheater.nl). Tram 4, 9. **Box office** *Phone* 10am-5pm Mon-Fri. *In person* from 2hrs before performance. **Tickets** €12-€15. **No credit cards. Map** p327 E2.

Along with Prague and Vienna, famous for their period puppetry and traditions of crafting fine marionettes, Amsterdam remains one of the last outposts of an old European tradition. The Amsterdam Marionetten Theater presents the operas of Mozart and Offenbach, as presented by the more compact performer. Private lunches, dinners and high teas can be booked in advance.

Amsterdam RAI Theater

Europaplein 8-22, Zuid (549 1212, www.rai theater.nl). NS train Amsterdam RAI. **Box office** from 2hrs before performance. **Tickets** €20-€90. **Credit** MC V.

A huge convention and exhibition centre by day, the RAI is an enormous theatre by night and at weekends. Musicals, operas, comedy nights, ballets and spectacular shows can all be enjoyed in this sizeable hall.

De Balie

Kleine-Gartmanplantsoen 10, Southern Canal Belt (553 5155, www.debalie.nl). Tram 1, 2, 5, 7, 10. **Box office** 5-9pm or until start of performance Mon-Fri; from 90mins before performance Sat, Sun. **Tickets** €7-€15. **No credit cards. Map** p330 D5.

DeLaMar Theater.

Theatre, new media, photography, cinema (*see p228*) and literary events sit alongside lectures, debates and discussions about cultural, social and political issues at this influential centre for the local intelligentsia. Add a visit to the café and you've got food for both mind and body. What's culture without a little cake?

De Brakke Grond

Nes 45, Old Centre: Old Side (622 9014, www. brakkegrond.nl). Tram 4, 9, 14, 16, 24, 25. **Box office** *call for details.* **Tickets** *vary.* **No credit cards. Map** p326 D3.

Belgian culture does stretch beyond beer, and the Flemish Arts Centre – De Brakke Grond – is here to prove it. As well as contemporary art productions from Flanders, you'll find visual art, literature, dance and theatre, music, performance, film and new media. Mind you, some good Belgian beer will go down a treat after a fix of progressive Flemish theatre; if you're really lucky you might find an actor or two joining you at the bar of the adjoining café/restaurant.

INSIDE TRACK ACROSS THE GREAT DIVIDE

Don't let the language issue put you off seeing a show. The Dutch have a distinctive, visual approach to theatre-making, and these days many groups, including the award-winning **Toneelgroep Amsterdam** (*see p275*), employ English surtitles for their shows.

DeLaMar Theater

Marnixstraat 402, Southern Canal Belt (0900 33 52 627 premium rate, www.delamar.nl). Tram 1, 2, 5, 7, 10. **Box office** *noon-6pm daily (until 8.15pm on performance days).* **Phone** *10am-10pm daily.* **Tickets** €11.50-€55. **Credit** AmEx MC, V. **Map** p330 C5.

The city's newest theatre and, at a construction cost of around €60 million, one of its most luxurious, the DeLaMar hosts major musicals, opera and drama. Its twin auditoria can accommodate 600 and 900 people respectively, and its managers have plans to make it the key destination of Amsterdam's Leidseplein theatre district.

★ Frascati

Nes 63, Old Centre: Old Side (626 6866, www.theaterfrascati.nl). Tram 4, 9, 14, 16, 24, 25. **Box office** *see p274.* **Tickets** €8.50-€14. **No credit cards. Map** p326 D3.

A cornerstone of progressive Dutch theatre since the 1960s, Frascati gives promising artists the opportunity to stage productions on one of three stages. The mission: to unite trained artists with rugged street artists. The result: a wild selection of theatre and dance events that feature MCs, DJs, VJs and more.

De Kleine Komedie

Amstel 56-58, Southern Canal Belt (624 0534, www.dekleinekomedie.nl). Tram 4, 9, 14, 16, 24, 25. **Box office** *noon-6pm Mon-Sat, or until start of performance.* **Tickets** €9-€20. **No credit cards. Map** p327 E3.

Built in 1786, De Kleine Komedie is Amsterdam's oldest theatre and remains one of its most important. Extremely popular with locals, it is the nation's premier cabaret and music stage, and one of the city's most colourful venues.

★ Koninklijk Theater Carré

Amstel 115-125, Southern Canal Belt (0900 252 5255 premium rate, www.theatercarre.nl). Tram 4, 7, 10 or Metro Weesperplein. **Box office** *Phone* 10am-8pm daily. *In person* 4-8pm daily. **Tickets** €15-€55. **Credit** AmEx, MC, V. **Map** p331 F4.

With a history dating back to the 18th century and an Amstel-side aspect to make property developers drool, this plush former circus is the city's most iconic theatre. The Carré hosts many of the best Dutch cabaret artists and touring plays, as well as

noteworthy musical acts. Its blinking façade makes it the perfect place to see Dutch versions of popular blockbusters, from *Mamma Mia!* to *My Fair Lady*.

Het Rozentheater

Rozengracht 117, the Jordaan (620 7953, www.rozentheater.nl). Tram 13, 17. **Box office** *Phone* 1-5pm Mon-Sat, or until 8pm on performance days. *In person* from 5.30pm until start of performance. **Tickets** €7.50-€14. **No credit cards.** **Map** p325 B3.

The focus of Het Rozentheater is on work for and by young people. Regular performers are a mixture of professionals, theatre students and enthusiastic amateurs from the ages of 15 up to around 30.

Toneelgroep Amsterdam

Creativity and colour abound in Holland's foremost theatre company.

Under the guidance of Flemish director Ivo van Hove, Toneelgroep Amsterdam (795 9900, www.toneelgroepamsterdam.nl) has established itself as the biggest and boldest repertory company in the Netherlands. The 21-strong permanent ensemble has tackled the translated works of Shakespeare and Ibsen, David Mamet and Tony Kushner, among others, and includes many actors who are nationally recognisable for their appearances on Dutch television.

The company is based at the rear of the Amsterdam Stadsschouwburg (where it performs), in a state-of-the-art extension housing rehearsal studios and offices. As might be expected, productions are of a high, national theatre standard and stand apart from drama elsewhere in the world because of their sharp aesthetic choices and frequently anarchic values. Past hits have included Kushner's *Angels in America*, Mamet's *Glengarry*

Glen Ross and a trilingual staging of Alfred Jarry's anarchic *Ubu Roi*, played in Dutch, German and English. The latter production resulted in the decision to employ English surtitles for further main-stage productions, which has made the company more appealing to tourists and expats.

Toneelgroep frequently hosts lectures, symposiums and open rehearsals. The company tours Europe regularly and has longstanding relationships with theatres in Germany, including the Schauspiel Essen, with whom it collaborated on *Ubu*. 'Dutch theatre has learned to be open to new ideas, creative collaborations and different theatre languages,' says resident dramaturg Corien Baart. 'In a world where people are afraid of living together, where people feel powerless and overruled by unjust politics, it's important that theatre reaches out to its neighbours.'

ARTS & ENTERTAINMENT

Stadsschouwburg.

ARTS & ENTERTAINMENT

Performances focus on the trials and tribulations faced by modern youth.

★ Stadsschouwburg
Leidseplein 26, Southern Canal Belt (624 2311, www.ssba.nl). Tram 1, 2, 5, 7, 10. **Box office** 12am-6pm Mon-Sat, or until start of performance; from 2hrs before start of performance Sun. **Tickets** €10-€45. **Credit** AmEx, MC, V. **Map** p330 C5.
The Stadsschouwburg (Municipal Theatre) is a striking 19th-century building in the heart of the theatre, club and restaurant district. It is the chief subsidised venue for new dance, music and drama, and is the home of Toneelgroep Amsterdam (*see p275*). Containing two stages – a traditional proscenium with horseshoe auditorium (which means compromised sightlines if you sit too far to the left or right), and a gaping but flexible black box with raked seats – the venue accommodates local professional companies and pioneering touring ensembles.

▶ *Stadsschouwburg is also one of the main host venues for the Holland Festival (see p278).*

★ Theater Bellevue
Leidsekade 90, Southern Canal Belt (530 5301, www.theaterbellevue.nl). Tram 1, 2, 5, 7, 10. **Box office** 11am-start of performance daily. **Tickets** prices vary. **Credit** AmEx, DC, MC, V. **Map** p330 C5.
The Theater Bellevue dates back to 1840 and is one of the city's most active venues, premiering lunchtime dramas by emerging Dutch playwrights as well as modern dance and cabaret in the evenings – the programme is extensive and its doors are rarely closed. In February, keep an eye out for the recently established Pop Arts Festival for international puppetry, a Bellevue brainchild.

Theater Fabriek Amsterdam
Czaar Peterstraat 213 (522 5260, www.theaterfabriekamsterdam.nl). Tram 10, 26 or bus 42, 43. **Box office** from 2hrs before performance. **Tickets** €25-€55. **No credit cards.**
Housed in an old factory that once built ship engines, Theater Fabriek organises big musical shows, popular operas and Cirque de Soleil-style performances for people who like a mixture of avant-garde and spectacle.

Theater het Amsterdamse Bos
De Duizendmeterweg 7, Amstelveen (643 3286, www.bostheater.nl). Bus 66, 170, 172, 176, 199. **Tickets** €12.50. **No credit cards.**

Profile Boom Chicago

Fantastic, boombastic comedy club.

With its combination of sketch comedy, improv and downright silly behaviour, the Boom Chicago (*see p279*) comedy club has become a staple of the Amsterdam nightlife scene.

Its hybrid sense of humour works well in Anglo-friendly Amsterdam, with American-style comedy (think *Second City* or *The Daily Show*) that comments on Dutch culture and news. Expect gentle ribbing of Dutch social customs and politicians, along with a few jokes about the US. In recent years, shows have become multi-media-tastic, with videos created on the spot as part of the improv and broadcast moments later, to the surprise of participating audience members.

Founded in 1993 by Midwesterners Andrew Moskos, Jon Rosenthal and Ken Schaefle, Boom was initially almost exclusively for tourists but these days audiences can be up to two thirds Dutch. In addition to the regular Boom shows, improvs and cabaret-style reviews (like the 'Best of Boom' shows, featuring popular acts), crowds show up for burlesque shows, weekly Boom! dance parties, queer-friendly clubbing nights, and event-oriented parties on New Year's Eve, Halloween and big American elections.

Boomers were the creative forces behind Comedy Central News (CCN), a breakthrough English-language news show focused on Dutch news ('because we think Dutch news is news too' was the tag), which ran for two seasons on the Dutch Comedy Central network. The star was Boom stage regular Greg Shapiro, who continues to write and perform with Boom and in his own popular solo shows.

Boom has also served as a launching pad for a number of familiar faces in the US including Seth Meyers, a head writer on *Saturday Night Live*, Jason Sudeikis from SNL and the TV show *30 Rock*, and Mad TV performers Jordan Peele, Nicole Parker and Ike Barinholtz.

In late 2010, Boom partnered with nightlife impresario Casper Rynders of Jimmy Woo's (*see p262*), and former owners of club Bitterzoet, to expand the nightlife component. After a renovation in early 2011, Boom will reopen as the 'Chicago Social Club', with new theatre facilities, a bar upgrade and a clubbing programme three nights a week.

Theater het Amsterdamse Bos is the city's answer to the Regent's Park Open-Air Theatre in London and New York's Delacorte Theater in Central Park. In the *Bos* (forest), dreamy midsummer nights can be spent with a picnic hamper and blanket watching a performance of *Twelfth Night*. And if you're like most people who frequent outdoor theatre, you're probably there for the champagne rather than the Shakespeare, so you won't mind listening to iambic pentameter in Dutch translation.

Cultural complexes

Westergasfabriek
Haarlemmerweg 8-10, West (586 0710, www.westergasfabriek.com). Tram 10 or bus 18, 22.
With a wild variety of industrial buildings being reinvented as performance, event and exhibition spaces, the Westergasfabriek is quickly evolving into one of the city's premier cultural hubs; as it was through the 1990s, in fact, when it was a happening underground squat village. It's the new home for Cosmic (606 5050, www.cosmictheater.nl), a theatre troupe that has long been addressing the multicultural realities of the modern world, and Made in da Shade (606 5050, www.shade.nl), a group who make 'theatre for new times in old cities'.
▶ *Complete with acres of water and planted with cypress trees, Westerpark is lovely for a stroll, with plenty of little cafés providing refreshment; see p104.*

Theatre festivals

De Hollandse Nieuwe
Polonceaukade, Central Amsterdam (606 5050, www.cosmictheaters.nl).
The annual Hollandse Nieuwe festival focuses on texts written by established and up-and-coming playwrights from different backgrounds.

★ Het Theaterfestival
Around Amsterdam (624 2311, www.theater festival.be). **Date** end Aug-early Sept.
The Theaterfestival is a jury-selected showcase of the best Dutch and Belgian theatre that has been staged during the previous 12-month season. Like Edinburgh, the Amsterdam Fringe (which runs in tandem) is an uncurated mélange of experimental productions performed in venues large and small, indoors and out.

★ Holland Festival
Around Amsterdam (020 523 77 87, www.hollandfestival.nl). **Date** June.
The Holland Festival is the country's main international arts festival, during which you can see a plethora of international plays, operas, dance troupes, musical acts and exhibitions. Mikhail Baryshnikov performed in 2009, and Sam Mendes

brought his Bridge Project production of *The Tempest* in 2010. Expect 2011 and beyond to fill the city's major venues with theatre gems sourced from around the world.

Over het IJ
NDSM-werf Amsterdam Noord (010 415 9666, www.overhetij.nl). Ferry Amsterdam Centraal to NDSM-werf. **Date** early-mid July.
A summer feast of large theatrical projects and avant-garde mayhem, Over het IJ is usually interesting and frequently compelling. This festival of performance, set in the appropriately apocalyptic setting of NDSM (*see p124*), brings together international troupes united by a love of absurdity and the latest in multimedia.

Parade
Martin Luther Kingpark, Zuid (033 465 4555, www.deparade.nl). Tram 25 or Metro Amstel. **Date** Aug. **Tickets** vary.
This unique event has captured the essence of the old circus/sideshow atmosphere that's usually so conspicuously absent at today's commercial fairgrounds. Parade offers a plentiful selection of bizarre shows, many in beautiful circus tents; spread between them are cafés, bars and restaurants, as well as the odd roving performer. Theatre, music, art, magic, oddities, spectacular shows and all kinds of attractions ring the audience, who are centre-stage instead of the other way around. The event has become very popular and many shows sell out quickly; it's best to go early, have dinner or a picnic, and book your tickets at the Parade Kiosk for the night, though note that some smaller shows sell their tickets separately.

Vondelpark Openluchttheater
Westerstraat 187 (428 3360, www.openlucht theater.nl). Tram 1, 2, 3. **Date** late June-Aug.
Theatrical events have been held in Vondelpark since 1865, and the tradition continues each summer with a variety of (free) shows. Wednesdays offer lunchtime concerts and mid-afternoon children's shows; Thursdays find the bandstand jumping; there's a dance and/or theatre show every Friday evening; various events (including workshops and theatre) take place on Saturdays; and yet more theatrical events and pop concerts are held every Sunday afternoon.

Comedy

While the Dutch have their own cultural history of hilarity, thanks in large part to their own very singular take on the art and practice of cabaret, stand-up is a fairly recent import to the Netherlands in general and Amsterdam in particular. However, it's become more popular in recent years, and shows usually feature a

Comedy Café Amsterdam.

ARTS & ENTERTAINMENT

mix of international and local acts, often performing in English (although it's best to call ahead to check). Theatresports is also popular: audiences throw roses on the stage to register their approval of acts, and wet sponges at the jury when they disagree with the verdict.

If that much interaction isn't for you, then there are always plain old improv shows, at which acts perform without the extra props to help them along.

COMEDY VENUES
★ Boom Chicago
Leidseplein Theater, Leidseplein 12, Southern Canal Belt (423 0101, www.boomchicago.nl). Tram 1, 2, 5, 7, 10. **Box office** 1-9.15pm Mon-Thur, Sun; 1-8.30pm Fri, Sat. **Shows** 8.15pm Mon-Fri, Sun; 7.30pm Sat. **Tickets** €19.50-€39. **Credit** AmEx, MC, V. **Map** p330 C5.
The American improv troupe is one of Amsterdam's biggest success stories. With several different shows running seven nights a week (except Sundays in winter), all in English, the group offers a mix of audience-prompted improvisation and rehearsed sketches. The bar offers cocktails and DJs, and is something of an unofficial meeting point for countless wayward Americans; a restaurant serves lunch from noon until 4pm daily. A genuine cultural movement in an unexpected form. For more details, *see also p277* **Profile**.

Comedy Café Amsterdam
Max Euweplein 43-45, Southern Canal Belt (638 3971, www.comedycafe.nl). Tram 1, 2, 5, 7, 10. **Shows** 9pm daily. **Tickets** €3-€15. **Credit** AmEx, MC, V. **Map** p330 C5.

The Comedy Café has been doing a decent job of bringing the art of stand-up to a wider Amsterdam audience. From Thursday to Saturday, you'll be treated to a stand-up show in a mind-boggling blend of Dutch and English. Monday's shows vary between open-mic and nights under a particular theme (an evening of local comedy, for example). On Tuesdays and Wednesdays comics try out new material at the venue's regular open-mic nights, while Sundays are reserved for English-language improv show In Your Face.

Comedy Theatre
Nes 110 (422 2777, www.comedytheater.nl). Tram 4, 9, 14, 16, 24, 25. **Tickets** €10-€12.50. **Credit** AmEx, MC, V. **Map** p326 D3.
Hyping itself as the 'club house' for comedians, the Comedy Theatre combines ascerbic, politically hard-hitting performers with those who do more straightforward stand-up. Expect local legends like Javier Guzman and international acts such as Tom Rhodes or Lewis Black. To make sure that at least some of the acts are English-speaking, it's best to call in advance before turning up.

Toomler
Breitnerstraat 2, Zuid (670 7400, www.toomler. nl). Tram 2, 5, 16, 24. **Box office** 6-9pm (*phone reservations* 5.15-10pm) Wed-Sat. **Shows** 8.30pm. **Tickets** €5-€15. **No credit cards.**
Located next to the Hilton hotel, this café hosts acts four nights a week. Most programming is stand-up in Dutch, but it's the English-language Comedy Train International, held in January, July and August, that has come to be most closely associated with the venue.

1000s of
things to do…

Escapes & Excursions

Kinderdijk. *See p298.*

Escapes & Excursions

Experience a different kind of green… and yellow, and red.

Before you can say you've truly visited the Netherlands, you must escape Amsterdam's suction and explore 'the real country' a little. Not that hard: it's a small place, where most of the towns and cities worth visiting are under an hour away. Even the country's most remote corners are accessible within a half-day drive or train ride. Just be careful not to fall asleep: you might wake up in Belgium or Germany.

Small historic Dutch towns – the ones that depend on tourism – are experts at capitalising on their traditions, from wooden shoes to windmills. Most are concentrated close to Amsterdam in Noord- and Zuid-Holland, and are also readily accessible by public transport. Then there are the cities, from history-rich Utrecht to the resolutely modern Rotterdam.

Introduction

HELP & INFORMATION

Besides the tourist boards listed under individual destinations, the Netherlands Board of Tourism or **VVV** (Vlietweg 15, 2266 KA Leidschendam, 070 370 5705, www.visitholland.com) can help with information and accommodation. There's also an excellent website, www.goudencirkel.nl, that covers the 'golden circle' of towns that surround the lake (and former sea) IJsselmeer to the north.

For transport listings (trains, buses and the Metro), contact the **OV Reisinformatie** information line (0900 9292 premium rate, www.ov9292.nl), or you can get up-to-date train information at www.ns.nl.

Finally, note that very few of the sights listed in this chapter take credit cards.

GETTING AROUND

Driving

The Netherlands' road system is extensive, well maintained and clearly signposted. For driving advice and detailed information from motoring organisation ANWB, *see p305* **Driving**.

Buses & coaches

The national bus service is reasonably priced, but not as easy to negotiate as the railway. For information and timetables, phone **OV Reisinformatie** (*see left* **Help & Information**).

Cycling

The Netherlands is flat (though windy), so there's little wonder the bike is the country's favourite mode of transport. Cycle paths are abundant and the ANWB and VVV offices sell cycle maps. For bike rental, *see p306* **Cycling**. For bike tours in Amsterdam, *see also p75*.

Rail

Nederlandse Spoorwegen (aka NS, translatable as Netherlands Railway) offers an excellent service in terms of its cost, punctuality and cleanliness. Aside from singles and returns, you can also buy family and group passes, tickets that entitle you to unlimited travel on any given day (Dagkaarten), the OV Dagkaart that entitles you to use buses, trams and the Metro and, for selected places, NS Rail Idee tickets, all-in-one tickets that'll get you to a destination and also include the admission fee to one or more of the local sights. Services are frequent, and reservations are unnecessary.

As a rule, tickets are valid for one day only: if you make a return journey spanning more than one day you need two singles. A weekend return ticket is the exception to the rule: it's valid from Friday night until Sunday night.

NS produces a booklet in English called *Rail Travel for the Disabled*, available from all main stations or from the company direct. There is also disabled access to refreshment rooms and toilets at all stations. For special assistance, call 030 235 7822 at least a day in advance.

Centraal Station Information Desk

Stationsplein 15, Old Centre (0900 9292 premium rate, www.ns.nl). Tram 1, 2, 4, 5, 9, 13, 16, 17, 24, 25, 26. **Open** *Information desk and bookings* 24hrs daily. **No credit cards**. Map p326 D1/2.

Escapes & excursions

AROUND AMSTERDAM

Among many other attractions within easy striking distance of Amsterdam are some of the best of the country's **castles**. Almost 100 of these are open for tourists or business conferences: the 15th-century Stayokay Heemskerk, between Haarlem and Alkmaar, is now a hostel (025 123 2288, www.stayokay.com), while the ultimate in power lunches can be had at Château Neercanne in Maastricht (043 325 1359, www.neercanne.nl) or Kasteel Erenstein in Kerkrade (034 775 0454, www.kasteelerenstein.nl).

Many important events in Dutch history took place in the legendary stronghold **Muiderslot**. This moated castle, situated strategically at the mouth of the River Vecht, was originally built in 1280 for Count Floris V, who was murdered nearby in Muiderberg in 1296. Rebuilt in the 14th century, the fortress has been through many sieges and frequent renovations. The 17th-century furnishings originate from the period of another illustrious occupant, PC Hooft, who entertained in the castle's splendid halls.

The star-shaped stronghold of **Naarden** is not only moated, but has arrowhead-shaped bastions and a very well-preserved fortified town; it was in active service as recently as 1926. All is explained in the **Vestingmuseum**. The fortifications date from 1675, after the inhabitants were massacred by the Duke of Alva's son in 1572; the slaughter is depicted

above the door of the Spaanse Huis (Spanish House). Today, however, Naarden is the perfect setting for a leisurely Sunday stroll.

Meandering down the River Vecht from Amsterdam towards Utrecht, boat passengers can glimpse some of the homes built in the 17th and 18th centuries by rich Amsterdam merchants. Two of the trips afford close-up views of castles, the first stopping on the way for a one-hour tour of **Slot Zuylen**, a 16th-century castle that was renovated in 1752. The collections of furniture, tapestries and objets d'art displayed here give an insight into the lives of the residents. Local tour boat company **Rondvaartbedrijf Rederij Schuttevaer** can arrange English guides with advance notice. Another boat drops passengers in the charming town of **Loenen**, which is home to the spectacular restored castle of Loenersloot; sadly, it's not open to the public.

Muiderslot

Herengracht 1, Muiden (029 425 6262, www.muiderslot.nl). **Open** *Apr-Nov* 10am-5pm Mon-Fri; noon-6pm Sat, Sun. *Nov-Apr* noon-5pm Sat, Sun. **Admission** €12; €6.25 reductions; free under-4s, MK.

Rondvaartbedrijf Rederij Schuttevaer

Oudegracht, opposite no.85, Utrecht (030 272 0111, www.schuttevaer.com). Half-day trips to Rhijnauwen, city tours over the Oudergracht and Singels of Utrecht. Check website for hours and prices. Reservations essential.

Vestingmuseum Turfpoortbastion

Westvalstraat 6, Naarden (035 694 5459, www.vestingmuseum.nl). **Open** *Mid Mar-Nov* 10.30am-5pm Tue-Fri; noon-5pm Sat, Sun. *Nov-mid Mar* noon-5pm Sun. **Admission** €5.50; €3-€4 reductions; free under-4s, MK.

Getting there

Muiderslot

By car 12km (7.5 miles) south-east. By bus 101 or 157 from Amstel Station.

INSIDE TRACK
A GREEN DAY OUT

Just outside Landsmeer, **Het Twiske** is a stunning 650-hectare (1,606-acre) recreation area, with swimming, fishing, water sports, beaches, an adventure playground and plenty of wildlife. To get here, take bus 92 from Amsterdam Centraal Station to Oostzaan Kolkweg (see www.9292ov.nl for details).

Naarden

By car 20km (12 miles) south-east. By train direct from Amsterdam Centraal Station. By bus 136 from Amstel Station.

Tourist information

Naarden VVV

Adriaan Dortsmanplein 1b, Naarden (035 694 2836, www.vvvnaarden.nl). **Open** *Jan-May* 10am-2pm Sat. *May-July* 11am-3pm Mon-Fri; 10am-2pm Sat. *July-Sept* 10am-3pm Mon-Fri; 10am-2pm Sat.

HAARLEM

Lying between Amsterdam and the beaches of Zandvoort and Bloemendaal, **Haarlem** – a gentler and older Amsterdam – is a mere stone's throw from the dunes and the sea, and attracts flocks of beachgoing Amsterdammers and Germans every summer.

To catch up with Haarlem's history, head to **St Bavo's Church**, which dominates the main square. It was built around 1313 but suffered fire damage in 1328; rebuilding and expansion lasted yet another 150 years. It's surprisingly bright inside: cavernous white transepts stand as high as the nave and are a stunning sight. The floor is made up of 1,350 graves, including a dedication to a local midget who died of injuries from a game he himself invented: dwarf-tossing. Then there's the famous Müller organ (1738): boasting an amazing 5,068 pipes, it's been played by Handel and the young Mozart.

Haarlem's cosy but spacious **Grote Markt** is one of the loveliest squares in the Netherlands. Just a few blocks away is the former old men's almshouse and orphanage that currently houses the **Frans Halsmuseum**. Though it holds a magnificent collection of 16th- and 17th-century portraits, still lifes, various genre paintings and landscapes, the highlights are eight group portraits of militia companies and regents by Frans Hals (who's buried in St Bavo's). The museum also has collections of period furniture, Haarlem silver and ceramics and an 18th-century apothecary with Delftware pottery. Nearby is **De Hallen**, whose two buildings, the Verweyhal and the Vleeshal, house an extensive range of modern art between them.

The **Teylers Museum** is also excellent. Founded in 1784, it's the country's oldest museum; fossils and minerals sit beside antique scientific instruments, and there's a superb 16th- to 19th-century collection of 10,000 drawings by masters including Rembrandt, Michelangelo and Raphael. However, Haarlem is more than just a city of nostalgia: it's one of vision, with a truly creative vibe felt all over town. Local illustrator-cartoonist Joost Swarte designed the Toneelschuur theatre in the centre.

Frans Halsmuseum

Groot Heiligland 62 (023 511 5775, www.franshalsmuseum.nl). **Open** 11am-5pm Tue-Sat; noon-5pm Sun. **Admission** €7.50; €3.75 reductions; free under-18s, MK. **Credit** MC, V.

De Hallen

Grote Markt 16 (023 511 5775, www.dehallenhaarlem.nl). **Open** 11am-5pm Tue-Sat; noon-5pm Sun. **Admission** €5; €2.50 reductions; free under-18s, MK. **Credit** MC, V.

Teylers Museum

Spaarne 16 (023 516 0960, www.teylersmuseum.nl). **Open** 10am-5pm Tue-Sat; noon-5pm Sun. **Admission** €9; €2 reductions; free under-5s, MK. **No credit cards.**

Where to eat & drink

At **Hotspot Lambermons** (Korte Veerstraat 1, 023 542 7804, www.lambermons.nl) you can enjoy a French-inspired two-, three- or four-course menu that also features fruits de mer and cheese and charcuterie assortments. For steak that you might well remember for the rest of your life, go to **Wilma & Alberts** (Oude Groenmarkt 6, 023 532 1256, www.wilma-alberts.nl).

If you're more into wooden panelling, leather wallpaper, chaotic conviviality and infinite beer choices, then **In Den Uiver** (Riviervismarkt 13, 023 532 5399, www.indenuiver.nl) is definitely worth investigating.

Where to stay

Carlton Square Hotel (Baan 7, 023 531 9091, www.carlton.nl) is quite posh, with rooms starting at €69-€109. The **Carillon** (Grote Markt 27, 023 531 0591, www.hotelcarillon.com) has doubles starting at €65, while outside the centre, **Stayokay Haarlem** (Jan Gijzenpad 3, 023 537 3793, www.stayokay.com) has B&B starting at €21.

Getting there

By car

10km (6 miles) west on A5.

By train

15mins, direct from Amsterdam Centraal Station.

Tourist information

VVV

Verwulft 11 (0900 616 1600 premium rate, www.haarlem.nl). **Open** 9.30am-5.30pm Mon-Fri; 10am-5pm Sat; noon-4pm 1st Sun of mth.

Flower Power

Tulips from Amsterdam, but also carnations, daffodils, gladioli…

Want a statistic that boggles the mind? Try this: the Netherlands produces a staggering 70 per cent of the world's commercial flower output, and still has enough left to fill up its own markets, botanical gardens, auctions and parades all year round.

The co-operative flower auction – FloraHolland – handles more than 12 billion cut flowers and over half a million plants a year, mostly for export, through a network of six national and international marketplaces (Aalsmeer, Naaldwijk, Rijnsburg, Venlo, Bleiswijk and Eelde). The most impressive is in the world's biggest trading building (120 football fields' worth) in **Aalsmeer** (Legmeerdijk 313, 029 739 7000, www.floraholland.com, closed Sat & Sun), which is a 15-kilometre drive south-west of Amsterdam. (Bus 172 also runs here from Amsterdam Centraal Station.) Its unusual sales method gave rise to the phrase 'Dutch auction'. Dealers bid by pushing a button to stop a 'clock' that counts from 100 down to one; thus, the price is lowered – rather than raised – until a buyer is found. Bidders risk either overpaying for the goods or not getting them if time runs out. The auction is open to the public between 7am and 11am,

Monday to Friday. The earlier you get there, the better it is.

The 'countdown' bidding style was invented at **Broeker Veiling** (Museumweg 2, Broek-op-Langerdijk, 022 631 3807, www.broekerveiling.nl, closed Mon, Tue, Thur Nov-Mar), the oldest flower and vegetable auction in the world. It's a bit of a tourist trap, but nonetheless includes a museum of old farming artefacts, plus a boat trip. The town, Broek-op-Langerdijk, is 36 kilometres (22 miles) north of Amsterdam; if you're not driving, take a train from Amsterdam Centraal Station to Alkmaar, then catch bus 155.

There have been flowers everywhere at the **Keukenhof** since 1949. This former royal 'kitchen garden' dates from the 14th century, and contains tulips and blooms galore (*see p297* **Springtime in Keukenhof**).

For more on the district's history, including a look at the development of the flower bulb business, visit the **Museum de Zwarte Tulp** (Grachtweg 2a, 025 241 7900, www.museumdezwartetulp.nl, closed Mon) in Lisse. Keukenhof and Lisse are a 27-kilometre (17-mile) drive south-west of Amsterdam. Or take the train from Amsterdam Centraal Station to Leiden, then bus 54.

WATERLAND

Until the IJ Tunnel opened in 1956, the canal-laced peat meadows of Waterland, north of Amsterdam, were accessible mainly by ferry and steam railway. This isolation preserved much of the area's heritage; to see a prime example, look around the old wooden buildings at **Broek in Waterland**. This area is best explored by bike before switching over to a canoe or electric motor boat, both of which can be rented from **Waterland Recreatie** (020 403 3209, www.fluisterbootvaren.nl).

Marken, reached via a causeway, was once full of fishermen (some of whom give excellent boat tours), but is now awash with tourists. Visit off-season, however, and you'll likely find it quieter. To protect against flooding, many houses are built on mounds or poles. **Marker Museum** offers a tour of the island's history.

The number of preserved ancient buildings, from Golden Age merchants' houses to the famous herring smokehouses, is what makes **Monnickendam** special. There's also a fine antique carillon on the belltower of the old town hall that's worth hunting down.

Such was **Volendam**'s success as a fishing village that it's said the town flag was flown at half-mast when the Zuider Zee was enclosed in 1932, cutting off access to the sea. The village's enterprise was soon applied to devising a theme park from its fascinating historic features but, sadly, the cheerily garbed locals can barely be seen for the coachloads of tourists dumped there every day – and invariably pointed to the world's biggest collection of cigar bands (11 million in total), all of them on view to a seriously smoke-happy public at the popular **Volendams Museum** (Zeestraat 37, 029 936 9258, www.volendams-museum.com).

De Zaanse Schans is not your typical museum village: people still live here. One of the world's first industrial zones, Zaan was once crowded with 800 windmills that powered the production of paint, flour and lumber. Today, amid the gabled green and white houses, attractions include an old-fashioned Albert Heijn store. Nearby in Zaandam, you can visit **Czaar Peterhuisje**, the tiny wooden house where Peter the Great stayed in 1697 while he was honing his new shipbuilding skills and preparing for the foundation of St Petersburg.

Czaar Peterhuisje

Het Krimp 23, Zaandam (075 681 0000, www .zaansmuseum.nl). **Open** 10am-5pm Tue-Sun. **Admission** €3; €2-€2.50 reductions; free under-4s.

Marker Museum

Kerkbuurt 44-47, Marken (029 960 1904, www.markermuseum.nl). **Open** *Apr-Sept* 10am-5pm daily *Oct* 11am-4pm Sun. **Admission** €2.50; €1.25 reductions.

De Zaanse Schans

Schansend 7, Information Center Pakhuis Vrede (075 681 0000, www.zaanseschans.nl). **Open** 9am-5pm daily. *Museums, Shops & Windmills* hours vary, check website. **Admission** varies, check website.

Getting there

Broek in Waterland

By car 10km (6 miles) north-east. By bus 110, 111, 114, 115 or 118 from Amsterdam Centraal Station. *Photo right.*

Marken

By car 20km (12 miles) north-east. By bus 111 from Amsterdam Centraal Station to Marken, or 110, 114, 115 or 118 to Monnickendam, then boat to Marken.

Monnickendam

By car 15km (9 miles) north-east. By bus 110, 111, 114, 115 or 118 from Amsterdam Centraal Station.

Volendam

By car 20km (12 miles) north-east. By bus 110 from Amsterdam Centraal Station.

De Zaanse Schans

By car 15km (9 miles) north-west. By train Amsterdam Centraal Station to Koog-Zaandijk. By bus 91 from Amsterdam Centraal. *Photo right.*

Tourist information

Volendam & Waterland VVV

Zeestraat 37, Volendam (029 936 3747, www.vvv-volendam.nl). **Open** *Mid Mar-Oct* 10am-5pm Mon-Sat; 11am-4pm Sun. *Oct* 10am-5pm Mon-Sat. *Nov-mid Mar* 10am-3pm Mon-Sat.

WEST FRIESLAND

West Friesland faces Friesland across the northern IJsselmeer. Despite being a part of Noord-Holland for centuries, it has its own customs and far fewer visitors than its near neighbour. One way to get there is to take a train to Enkhuizen, then a boat to Medemblik. From here, take the Museumstoomtram (Museum Steam Train) to Hoorn.

The once-powerful fishing and whaling port of **Enkhuizen** has many relics of its past, but most people come here for the **Zuider Zee Museum**. Wander in either the indoor Binnenmuseum, which has exhibits on seven

Broek in Waterland.

De Zaanse Schans.

The Chain Gang

Cycle north beyond the city bounds for a trip back in time.

Start Centraal Station
Finish Marken (or further to Edam)
Distance Approximately 40km/25 miles
(round trip)
Duration A leisurely 8-10hrs

It's worth following in the tyre tracks of
scores of Lycra-sheathed enthusiasts and
heading north; thanks to the Netherlands'
mercifully flat terrain, it's possible to cover
surprising distances, even without the Lycra.
The eastern Waterland region might be just
20 minutes away by bike from the city
centre, but it's another world – at points,
it feels as if you've cycled into a 17th-
century Dutch landscape painting.

Starting at Centraal Station, catch the
free Buiksloterweg ferry (departures every
five to ten minutes throughout the day), then
follow the packs of competitive road cyclists
(and the signposts when they become tiny
luminous dots on the horizon) to Durgadam.
Riding into the tiny former fishing village,
you'll find a tranquil scene: old painted
wooden houses lining the narrow cobbled
street, pet rabbits grazing in their runs at
the side of the road and hundreds of
bobbing masts on the IJmeer skyline.

Durgadam consists of little more than
this one perfect street, and halfway along
it the village's only brown café, the Oude
Taveerne (Durgerdammerdijk 73, 020 490
4259, www.deoudetaveerne.nl), straddling
the road: café to the left, deck to the right.
With its old-world charm and breathtaking
stepped terrace projecting out into the
tranquil water, it's the perfect place to
stop for a generous portion of *ontbijts*

(breakfast). Make your way down the
gangway-like wooden jetty for the furthest
terrace seats, where you can enjoy a gentle
sea breeze and the sound of lapping water.

From here, set off to the north past the
numerous former sea inlets, which are home
to scores of bird colonies. Just beyond the
village of Uitdam, turn west on to the two-
kilometre causeway – the *Verbindingsdijk*
('Connection') – that has joined the former
island of Marken to the mainland since
1957. It's generally peaceful, bar the
occasional whirring of a neon-clad cyclist
zooming past. The village itself, with its
clusters of traditional green houses built
on piles, is chocolate-box quaint. You can
cycle lazily around the perimeter, taking in
the sturdy lighthouse (nicknamed *de paard* –
'the horse' – for its shape) dating to 1700,
and head out on to the Strekdam, an
unfinished causeway stretching towards,
though not quite meeting, Volendam, to
admire the uninterrupted views.

Riding back up the Strekdam and then
keeping the IJmeer to your right, complete
the circuit of the 'island' to arrive back at
the harbour with its myriad cafés, bars and
restaurants, just in time for a late lunch –
perhaps a *broodje* (sandwich) at the Oude
Marken Lunchroom (Buurterstraat 19)
behind the harbour.

Legs aching, bike moaning, now's the
time to consider your options. You could
catch the ferry to the perfectly preserved
'theme park' village that is Volendam, or
if your legs are up to it, venture as far as
the cheese mecca of Edam; less hardcore
cyclists head back for a well-deserved rest.

centuries of seafaring life around the
IJsselmeer, or the open-air Buitenmuseum,
a reconstructed village (complete with its own
'villagers') of 130 authentic late 19th- and early
20th-century buildings transplanted from
nearby towns.

The Gothic Bonifaciuskerk and Kasteel
Radboud dominate **Medemblik**, a port that
dates from the early Middle Ages. The 13th-
century castle is smaller than it was when it
defended Floris V's realm but retains its
knights' hall and towers. Glassblowers and
leatherworkers show off their skills at the
Saturday market in July and August. Close
nearby is the 'long village' of **Twisk**, with
its pyramid-roofed farm buildings, as well as
the village of **Opperdoes**, built on a mound.

The pretty port of **Hoorn**, which dates from
around 1310, grew rich on the Dutch East
Indies trade; its success is reflected in its grand
and ancient architecture. Local costumes and
crafts can be seen at the weekly historic market,
Hartje Hoorn (9am-5pm Wednesdays in July
and August only). The local **Museum van
de Twintigste Eeuw** (Museum of the 20th
Century), while hardly living up to its name,
does have plenty of interesting exhibits. The
Westfries Museum focuses on art, decor and
the history of the region.

Museumstoomtram Hoorn-Medemblik

*Hoorn-Medemblik; tickets behind the station at
Van Dedemstraat 8, Hoorn (022 921 4862,
www.museumstoomtram.nl), or Hoorn VVV.*
Admission (with boat trip) *Day trip* €19.70;
€14.70 reductions.

Museum van de Twintigste Eeuw

*Bierkade 4, Hoorn (022 921 4001, www.museum
hoorn.nl).* **Open** 10am-5pm Tue-Fri; noon-5pm
Sat, Sun. **Admission** €5; €3.50 reductions.

Westfries Museum

*Rode Steen 1, Hoorn (022 928 0022, www.
wfm.nl).* **Open** 11am-5pm Tue-Fri; 1-5pm Sat,
Sun. **Admission** €5; €3.50 reductions; free
under-5s, MK.

Zuider Zee Museum

*Wierdijk 12-22, Enkhuizen (022 835 1111,
www.zuiderzeemuseum.nl).* **Open** 10am-5pm
daily (outdoor museum closed Nov-Apr).
Admission €14; €8.40-€13.50 reductions; free
under-4s. Half-price during winter season.

Getting there

Enkhuizen

By car 55km (34 miles) north-east. By train direct
from Amsterdam Centraal Station.

> **INSIDE TRACK**
> **HERE LIES VERMEER**
>
> Art-lovers should note that Delft's listing
> **Oude Kerk** (*see p290*) was the final resting
> place of Old Master Vermeer.

Hoorn

By car 35km (22 miles) north-east. By train direct
from Amsterdam Centraal Station.

Medemblik

By car 50km (31 miles) north. By train direct
from Amsterdam Centraal Station.

Tourist information

Enkhuizen VVV

*Tussen Twee Havens 1, Enkhuizen (022 831
3164, www.vvvenkhuizen.nl).* **Open** *Apr-Oct*
8.15am-5pm daily. *Oct-Apr* 9am-5pm Mon-Fri;
10am-4pm Sat.

Hoorn VVV

*Veemarkt 44, Hoorn (022 921 8343,
www.vvvweb.nl).* **Open** *May-Sept* 1-6pm Mon;
9.30am-5pm Tue, Wed, Fri; 9.30am-9pm Thur;
9.30am-5pm Sat; 1-5pm Sun. *Sept-May* 1-5pm Mon;
9.30am-5pm Tue-Sat.

Medemblik VVV

*Kaasmarkt 1, Medemblik (022 754 2852,
www.vvvmedemblik.nl).* **Open** varies, check
website.

DELFT

Imagine a miniaturised Amsterdam – canals
reduced to dinky proportions, bridges narrowed
down, merchants' houses shrunken – and you
have the essence of **Delft**, a student town with
plenty going on.

Delft, though, is of course most famous for
its blue and white tiles and pottery. There are
still a few factories open to visitors – among
them **De Delftse Pauw** and **De Porceleyne
Fles** – but for a more historical overview of the
industry, make for the **Museum Lambert
van Meerten**. The enormous range of tiles,
depicting everything from battling warships
to randy rabbits, contrasts dramatically with
today's mass-produced trinkets.

Delft was traditionally a centre for trade,
producing and exporting butter, cloth, Delft
beer – at one point in the past, almost 200 breweries could be found beside its canals – and,
later, pottery. Its subsequent loss in trade has
been Rotterdam's gain, but the aesthetic
benefits can be seen in the city's centuries-old

gables, hump-backed bridges and shady canals. To appreciate how little has changed, walk to the end of Oude Delft, the oldest canal in Delft (it narrowly escaped being drained in the 1920s to become a sunken tramline), cross the busy road to the harbour, and compare the view to Vermeer's *View of Delft*, now on display in the **Mauritshuis** in the Hague (*see p292*).

Delft also has two spectacular churches. The first, the **Nieuwe Kerk** (New Church; *photo right*) contains the tombs of philosopher Hugo de Groot and William of Orange (alongside his dog, who faithfully followed him to death by refusing food and water). It took almost 15 years to construct and was finally finished in 1396. Across the Markt is Hendrick de Keyser's 1620 **Stadhuis** (City Hall; *Photo right*); De Keyser also designed Prince William's black and white marble mausoleum. Not to be outdone, the town's other splendid house of worship, the Gothic **Oude Kerk** (Old Church; c1200), is locally known as 'Leaning Jan' because its tower stands two metres off-kilter.

Delft's museums have the calming air of quiet private residences. **Het Prinsenhof Municipal Museum**, located in the former convent of St Agatha, holds ancient and modern art exhibitions along with displays about Prince William of Orange, who was assassinated here in 1584 by one of many keen to earn the price put on his head by Philip II of Spain during the Netherland's 80-year fight for independence. The bullet holes are still clearly visible on the stairs.

Though the museums are grand, it's also fun simply to stroll around town. The historic centre has more than 600 national monuments in and around the preserved merchants' houses. Pick up a guide from the VVV and see what the town has to offer: the country's largest military collection over at the **Legermuseum** (Army Museum), for example or the Oostpoort (East Gate), dating from 1394. And while at the VVV, ask if you can pay a visit to the **Windmill de Roos** and the grim torture chamber in **Het Steen**, the 13th-century tower of the historic city hall in the market square – they're both genuinely fascinating.

FREE De Delftse Pauw
*Delftweg 133 (015 212 4920,
www.delftpottery.com).* **Open** *Apr-Oct* 9am-4.30pm daily. *Nov-Mar* 9am-4.30pm Mon-Fri; 11am-1pm Sat, Sun. **Credit** AmEx, DC, MC, V.

Legermuseum
*Korte Geer 1 (015 215 0500,
www.legermuseum.nl).* **Open** 10am-5pm Tue-Fri; noon-5pm Sat, Sun. **Admission** €7.50; €3 reductions; free under-4s, MK & 1st Fri of mth. **Credit** MC, V.

Museum Lambert van Meerten
Oude Delft 199 (015 260 2358, www.lambert vanmeerten-delft.nl). **Open** 11am-5pm Tue-Sun. **Admission** €3.50; €1.50 reductions; free under-12s. **Credit** AmEx, MC, V.

De Porceleyne Fles
Rotterdamseweg 196 (015 251 2030, www.royal delft.com). **Open** *Apr-Oct* 9am-5pm daily. *Nov-Mar* 9am-5pm Mon-Sat. **Admission** €8, free under-12s; €2 guided tour. **Credit** AmEx, DC, MC, V.

Het Prinsenhof Municipal Museum
Sint Agathaplein 1 (015 260 2358, www. prinsenhof-delft.nl). **Open** 11am-5pm Tue- Sun. **Admission** €7.50; €4 reductions; free under-12s. **Credit** AmEx, MC, V.

Where to eat & drink

Don't miss **Kleyweg**'s **Stads Koffyhuis** (Oude Delft 133, 015 212 4625, www.stads-koffyhuis.nl), which has a terrace barge in the summer and serves Knollaert beer, a local brew that is still made to an old medieval recipe. **De Wijnhaven** (Wijnhaven 22, 015 214 1460, www.wijnhaven.nl) and **Vlaanderen** (Beestenmarkt 16, 015 213 3311, www. vlaanderen.nl) provide delicious meals and excellent views at good prices.

Where to stay

De Ark (Koornmarkt 65, 015 215 7999, www.deark.nl) is upmarket, with rooms priced from €143 for a double room. **De Plataan** (Doelenplein 10, 015 212 6046, www.hotelde plataan.nl) is more reasonable, costing €114 for a double.

Getting there

By car
60km (37 miles) south-west on A4, then A13.

By train
1hr from Amsterdam Centraal Station, changing at the Hague if necessary.

Tourist information

Toeristische Informatie Punt (Tourist Information Point)
Hippolytusbuurt 4 (0900 515 1555 premium rate, www.delft.nl). **Open** *Apr-Sept* 10am-5pm Mon; 9am-6pm Tue-Fri; 10am-5pm Sat; 10am-4pm Sun. *Oct-Mar* 11am-4pm Mon; 10am-4pm Tue-Sat; 10am-3pm Sun.

Delft

THE HAGUE

The Hague (Den Haag) is the nation's power hub and centre for international justice. It began life as the hunting ground of the Counts of Holland before being officially founded in 1248, when William II built a castle on the site of the present parliament buildings, the Binnenhof. It was here that the De Witt brothers were lynched after being accused of conspiring to kill William of Orange; they were brutalised nearby in Gevangenpoort, now a grimly evocative torture museum (no children under nine).

Queen Beatrix arrives at the Binnenhof in a golden coach every Prinsjesdag (third Tuesday in September) for the annual state opening of parliament. Guided tours are organised daily to the Knights' Hall, where the ceremony takes place. The **Mauritshuis**, a former regal home, is open to the public with one of the most famous collections in the world: masterworks by Rubens, Rembrandt (namely, *The Anatomy Lesson of Dr Tulp*) and Vermeer (namely, *The Girl with a Pearl Earring*).

The Hague's city centre is lively, with a good selection of shops lining the streets and squares around the palaces and along Denneweg. The city is also one of the greenest in Europe and has a number of lovely parks. Clingendael has a Japanese garden; Meijendael, further out, is part of an ancient forest; and the Scheveningse Bosje

is big enough to occupy an entire day. Between the Bosje and the city is Vredes Paleis (the Peace Palace), a gift from Andrew Carnegie that is now the UN's Court of International Justice. On Churchillplein, the grand International Criminal Tribunal was the setting for former dictator Slobodan Milosevic's sulky theatrics – and, later, his death.

Beyond Scheveningse Bosje is Scheveningen, a former fishing village and now a resort. The highlight is the **Steigenberger Kurhaus Hotel**: built in 1887, it's a legacy of Scheveningen's halcyon days as a bathing place for European high society. Also here is the 'Sculptures by the Sea' exhibition, a multi-dimensional collection of statues at the **Museum Beelden aan Zee**. The renovated **Panorama Mesdag** houses not only the single largest painting in the country (120 metres, 400 feet, in circumference), from which it takes its name, but also works from the Hague (most of them seascapes) and Barbizon (landscapes and pastoral scenes from peasant life) schools.

None, though, is worth as much as *Victory Boogie Woogie*, Piet Mondrian's last work, which sold for a cool ƒ80 million (€36 million) in 1998. It's now on display at the **Haags Gemeentemuseum**, which holds the world's largest collection of works by Mondrian as well as many works of paradoxical art by MC Escher. The Haags Gemeentemuseum is next

The Hague.

Say Cheese

In search of the yellow stuff.

Few things are held higher in national affections than cheese. When they're not munching on it or exporting more than 400,000 tonnes of it every year, the Dutch are making a tourist industry of it.

One ritual for both tourists and members of the cheese porters' guild is the **Alkmaar Cheese Market** – the oldest and biggest cheese market in the world – which runs from 10am to noon every Friday between April and mid September. Pristine porters, wearing odd straw hats with coloured ribbons denoting their competing guilds, weigh the cheeses and then carry them on wooden trays hung from their shoulders. Then buyers test a core of cheese from each lot before the ceremony, which takes place at the Waag (Weigh House); here you can also find a variety of craft stalls and the cheese museum, **Het Hollands Kaas Museum** (De Waag, Waagplein 2, 072 515 5516, www.kaasmuseum.nl, closed Sun & all Dec-Mar).

But Alkmaar has more than cheese on offer and the VVV provides a walking tour of the medieval centre. Among the attractions at the **Biermuseum** (Houttil 1, 072 511 3801, www.biermuseum.nl, closed Mon & Sun) is a cellar in which to taste various beers, and the **Stedelijk Museum** (Canadaplein 1, 072 548 9789, www.stedelijkmuseumalkmaar.nl, closed Mon) has impressive art and toy collections. For more on the town's attractions visit the tourist information office, the **VVV** (Waagplein 2, 072 511 4284, www.vvv web.nl, closed Sun).

The Netherlands' famous red-skinned cheese is sold at **Edam**'s cheese market,

held every Wednesday in July and August from 10am until noon. Though the town, a prosperous port during the Golden Age, tells many stories through its exquisite façades and bridges, they can't compete with the cheese. In 1840, edams were used as cannon balls in Uruguay to repel seaborne attackers (imagine the humiliation of dying from a cheese injury). Then in 1956 a canned edam, a relic from a 1912 expedition, was found at the South Pole – and, when opened, proved to be merely a trifle 'sharp'. The town itself added to this lore in 2003 by building a colossal cheese cathedral from 10,000 of the unholy orbs to raise repair funds for its ancient Grote Kerk (Big Church). There's more information at **Edam VVV** (Stadhuis, Damplein 1, 029 931 5125, www.vvv-edam.nl, closed Dec-Mar & Sun, bar July & Aug).

Meanwhile, over in **Gouda**, golden wheels of cheese go on sale at the market every Thursday from 10am in July and August. Near the town, there are also many thatched-roof *kaasboerderijen* (cheese farms), several of which are on the picturesque River Vlist. Look out for *kaas te koop* signs (cheese for sale) and you may be able to peer behind the scenes as well as buy fresh gouda.

Still, Gouda does have other things going for it besides the yellow stuff. It's darn scenic and its candles are another classic: 20,000 of them light the square during the Christmas tree ceremony. **Gouda VVV**, the tourist information office, is at Lange Tiendeweg 29-31 (0900 4683 3288 premium rate, www.vvvgouda.nl, closed Mon morning & all day Sun).

door to the excellent **Museum of Photography** (Stadhouderslaan 43, 070 338 1144, www.fotomuseumdenhaag.nl) and linked to the **Museon**, an excellent science museum that induces wonder in both kids and adults, and the **Omniversum IMAX Theatre**, a state-of-the-art planetarium. The Gemeente's brand new sister museum, **Escher in het Paleis** on Lange Voorhout, is filled with yet further examples of the mind-melting art of MC Escher and supplemented with much interactive multimedia.

On the off-chance that your stopover in the country consists of one afternoon only, one way of seeing everything is by visiting **Madurodam**, an insanely detailed miniature city that dishes up every Dutch cliché in the book. Windmills turn, ships sail and trains speed around on the world's largest model railway. But if you happen to visit on a balmy summer's evening, when the models are lit within by 50,000 miniature lamps, then Madurodam leaves behind any hint of ironic appreciation and becomes a place of wonder.

Binnenhof

Binnenhof 8a (070 364 6144, www.binnenhof bezoek.nl). **Open** 10am-4pm Mon-Sat. **Tours** start at €4. **No credit cards.**

Escher in Het Paleis

Lange Voorhout 74 (070 42 77730, www.escher inhetpaleis.nl). **Open** 11am-5pm Tue-Sun. **Admission** €7.50; €5 reductions; free under-7s, MK. **No credit cards.**

Gemeentemuseum

Stadhouderslaan 41 (070 338 1111, www. gemeentemuseum.nl). **Open** 11am-5pm Tue-Sun. **Admission** €10; free under-18s, MK. **Credit** AmEx, MC, V.

Gevangenpoort Museum

Buitenhof 33 (070 346 0861, www.gevangen poort.nl). **Open** 10am-5pm Tue-Fri, *hourly tours start at 10.45am*; noon-5pm Sat, Sun, *hourly tours start at 12.45pm.* **Admission** €7.50; €5.50 reductions, MK. **No credit cards.**

Madurodam

George Maduroplein 1 (070 416 2400, www.madurodam.nl). **Open** *Apr-June* 9am-8pm daily. *July, Aug* 9am-11pm daily. *Sept-Apr* 9am-6pm daily. **Admission** €14.50; €10.50-€13.50 reductions; free under-3s. **No credit cards.**

Mauritshuis

Korte Vijverberg 8 (070 302 3456, www.mauritshuis.nl). **Open** 10am-5pm Tue-Sat; 11am-5pm Sun. **Admission** €10.50 incl audio tour; free under-18s, MK. **Credit** AmEx, MC, V.

Museum Beelden aan Zee

Harteveltstraat 1 (070 358 5857, www. beeldenaanzee.nl). **Open** 11am-5pm Tue-Sun. **Admission** €9.50; €4.75 reductions; free under-13s. **Credit** AmEx, MC, V.

Panorama Mesdag

Zeestraat 65 (070 364 4544, www.mesdag.nl). **Open** 10am-5pm Mon-Sat; noon-5pm Sun. **Admission** €6.50; €3-€5.50 reductions; free under-3s. **No credit cards.**

Where to eat & drink

Beer fans should try **De Paas** (Dunne Bierkade 16a, 070 360 0019, www.depaas.nl). The living-room feel at **Murphy's Law** (Dr Kuyperstraat 7, 070 427 2507, www.murphysjazz.nl) attracts a friendly if unlikely mix of alternative folk and drunk diplomats.

Where to stay

Le Meridien Hotel Des Indes (Lange Voorhout 54-56, 070 361 2345, www.hague. lemeridien.com) is the most luxurious hotel in town, with prices to match (doubles start at €275). The hostel **Stayokay Den Haag** (Scheepmakersstraat 27, 070 315 7888, www.stayokay.com) charges around €25-€30 for a bed and €52-€70 for doubles.

Getting there

By car

50km (31 miles) south-west on A4, then A44.

By train

50mins from Amsterdam Centraal Station to Den Haag Centraal Station; change at Leiden if necessary.

Tourist information

VVV

Hofweg 1, outside Centraal Station (0900 340 3505 premium rate, www.denhaag.com). **Open** 9.30am-6pm Mon-Fri; 9.30am-5pm Sat; 11am-5pm Sun.

LEIDEN

Canal-laced **Leiden** derives a good deal of its charm from the Netherlands' oldest university, which was founded here in 1575 and which includes such notable alumni as René Descartes, US president John Quincy Adams and many a Dutch royal. The old town teems with bikes and bars and contains the most historic monuments per square metre in the country and so a very rewarding place to visit.

Windmill & drawbridge in **Leiden**.

In the Dutch Golden Age of the late 16th and 17th centuries, Leiden thrived on textiles. It also spawned three great painters of that era: Rembrandt van Rijn (born in a mill on the Rhine River), Jan van Goyen and Jan Steen. Although few works by these three Masters remain in the Leiden of today, the **Stedelijk Museum de Lakenhal** (Lakenhal Municipal Museum), where the Golden Age cloth makers met, does have a painting by Rembrandt, as well as works by other Old Masters and collections of pewter, tiles, silver and glass. Perhaps Leiden's most notable museum, though, is the **Rijksmuseum van Oudheden** (National Museum of Antiquities), which houses the largest archaeological collection in the Netherlands: in particular, the display of Egyptian mummies should not be missed. The excellent **Rijksmuseum voor Volkenkunde** (National Museum of Ethnology) showcases the cultures of Africa, Oceania, Asia, the Americas and the Arctic.

The ten million fossils, minerals and stuffed animals exhibited at **Naturalis** (Natural History Museum) make it the country's largest museum collection, and the 6,000 species of flora at the **Hortus Botanicus**, one of the world's oldest botanical gardens, include descendants of the country's first tulips. If Dutch clichés are the things that you came here to see, head straight to the **Molenmuseum de Valk** (the Falcon Windmill Museum), a windmill-turned-museum where you can see living quarters, machinery and a picturesque view out over Leiden. But an even better panorama can be had from the top of the Burcht, a 12th-century fort on an artificial mound in the city centre.

Hortus Botanicus Leiden
Rapenburg 73 (071 527 7249, www.hortus leiden.nl). **Open** *Apr-Oct* 10am-6pm daily. *Nov-Mar* 10am-4pm Tue-Sun. **Admission** €6; €2-€3 reductions; free under-4s, MK. **Credit** AmEx, MC, V.

Molenmuseum de Valk
2e Binnenvestgracht 1 (071 516 5353, www.molendevalk.leiden.nl). **Open** 10am-5pm Tue-Sat; 1-5pm Sun. **Admission** €3; €1.70 reductions; free under-6s, MK. **No credit cards.**

Naturalis
Darwinweg (071 568 7600, www.naturalis.nl). **Open** 10am-5pm daily. **Admission** €11; €7-€10 reductions; free under-4s, MK. **Credit** MC, V.

Rijksmuseum van Oudheden
Rapenburg 28 (071 516 6163, www.rmo.nl). **Open** 10am-5pm Tue-Sun. **Admission** €9; €5.50-€7.50 reductions; free under-12s, MK. **Credit** AmEx, DC, MC, V.

Rijksmuseum voor Volkenkunde
Steenstraat 1 (071 516 8800, www.rmv.nl). **Open** 10am-5pm Tue-Sun. **Admission** €7.50; €3-€5 reductions; free MK. **Credit** AmEx, MC, V.

Stedelijk Museum de Lakenhal

Oude Singel 28-32 (071 516 5360, www.lakenhal.nl). **Open** 10am-5pm Tue-Fri; noon-5pm Sat, Sun. **Admission** €7.50; €4.50 reductions; free under-18s, MK. **No credit cards.**

Where to eat & drink

A traditional cosy atmosphere is to be had at **De Hooykist** (Hooigracht 49, 071 512 5809, www.dehooykist.nl) and **In Den Bierbengel** (Langebrug 71, 071 514 8056, www.indenbier bengel.nl), which specialise in meat, fish and wines. Bar-restaurant **Annie's Verjaardag** (Hoogstraat 1a, 071 512 5737, www.annies verjaardag.nl) occupies eight candle-lit cellars underneath a bridge in the centre of town: its main selling point is the canal barge terrace.

Where to stay

The **Golden Tulip** (Schipholweg 3, 071 522 1121, www.goldentulipleidencentre.nl) is the town's poshest hotel, with rooms costing between €133 and €210. Rather cheaper is the **Mayflower** (Beestenmarkt 2, 071 514 2641, www.hotelmayflower.nl), where rooms start at €75.

Getting there

By car
40km (24 miles) south-west on A4.

By train
35mins from Amsterdam Centraal Station, direct.

Tourist information

VVV
Stationsweg 2d (0900 222 2333 premium rate, www.leidenpromotie.nl). **Open** 11am-5.30pm Mon; 9.30am-5.30pm Tue-Fri; 10am-4.30pm Sat.

ROTTERDAM

The antithesis of Amsterdam, both visually and in vibe, this port city brings an urban grit to the Dutch landscape. Almost completely flattened in World War II, it has blossomed as a concrete-and-glass jungle.

Rotterdam is a haven for artists, musicians, designers and cutting-edge architecture. Its citizens also love a good party – among its many festivals, multicultural celebration **Summer Carnival** (www.zomercarnaval.nl) draws no fewer than 900,000 spectators each July.

The city also remains in a continual state of regeneration, including a futuristic skyline along the banks of the River Maas. The **Oude Haven** (Old Harbour) is a work of imaginative modernism, the pinnacle of which is Piet Blom's witty bright yellow cubic houses such as **Kijk-Kubus**. Across the splendid white asymmetrical **Erasmus Bridge**, nicknamed 'the swan', don't miss activities in **Las Palmas** (Willeminakade 66), a remnant of the 1950s cruise ship era that's been restored as a cultural beacon, housing the **Dutch Photography Museum**, among other institutions.

Across town, architectural wizard Rem Koolhaas designed his city's cultural heart, the Museumpark, where you'll find outdoor sculptures and five museums. The top three are the **Netherlands Architecture Institute**, which gives an overview of the history and development of architecture, especially in Rotterdam; the **Museum Boijmans Van Beuningen**, with a beautiful collection of traditional and contemporary art (including works by Bruegel, Van Eyck and Rembrandt); and the **Kunsthal**, which deals with art, design and photography, with regular travelling exhibitions. The adjoining street, Witte de Withstraat, offers contemporary art hub **TENT** (Witte de Withstraat 50, 010 413 5498, www.tentplaza.nl), many smaller galleries and a variety of excellent restaurants and bars too. A bird's eye view of it all can be had from the nearby **Euromast**, if you can handle the height (185 metres, or 607 feet).

The vastly sprawling **Historical Museum Rotterdam** includes the Dubbelde Palmboom (Double Palm Tree), housed in an old granary in Delfshaven and exploring life and work in the Meuse delta from 8000 BC to the present, and Het Schielandshuis, a palatial 17th-century mansion, another of the few buildings spared in the bombing.

The neighbouring town of **Schiedam** (VVV, Buitenhavenweg 9, 010 473 3000) houses the world's five tallest windmills and the planet's largest collection of Dutch gins and liqueurs in the tasting house of its distillery museum.

If you're a backpacker, take advantage of **Use-it** (Schaatsbaan 41-45, 010 240 9158, www.use-it.nl), just moments from the exit of the station. It offers great tips for what to do in the city, as well as free lockers in which to ditch your bag.

A short drive from Rotterdam is the town of **Alblasserdam**, where a posse of 19

Springtime in Keukenhof

Tiptoe through the tulips.

Twenty-eight hectares (70 acres) of lush parkland; 4.5 million tulips in 100 varieties; 80,000 visitors in just eight weeks. No doubt about it, the **Keukenhof** is the jewel in the region's crown.

Nowhere is the Dutch cult of the tulip celebrated in more glorious fashion than at this 'garden of Europe', located in South Holland's dune and bulb region. Open for just eight weeks each year (in accordance with the tulip's natural flowering season), the garden boasts a staggering 4.5 million of them. There are other flowers, of course – crocuses, hyacinths and narcissi from late March; lilies and roses in early summer – but the tulip is the star, standing to attention in regimental rows of glorious colour that extend as far as the eye can see.

The Keukenhof (literally, 'kitchen garden') is one of the most spectacular flower gardens in the world, welcoming more visitors per day in its short open season than any other attraction in the Netherlands. Located on the site of the former 15th-century Slot Teylingen estate, owners Baron and Baroness Van Pallandt commissioned landscape architects JD and LP Zocher, who designed Amsterdam's Vondelpark, to lay the grounds out in the English landscape tradition and that design has remained the standard ever since.

In 1949, the Keukenhof as we know it was born as a showcase for local bulb growers, who still donate the 7 million bulbs planted by hand each year. In the 60 years since its opening, the Keukenhof has become not only a great showcase for the bulb industry but one of the most photographed locations in the world – and for good reason. Riotous colours and inventive landscaping make the displays fresh and new every year.

The park's five restaurants cater to every taste, whether you're looking for a coffee on the go or a long, leisurely lunch to rest your weary limbs. At the Oranje Nassau Pavillon, you can witness the three most characteristic features of the Dutch landscape from the terrace: dune, polder and dyke. And of course, your trip wouldn't be complete without a visit to the gift shop for bulbs to create your own mini Keukenhof back home.

You've got eight weeks to make the trip. Ready, set... go!

Located in the bulb region between Amsterdam and the Hague (025 246 5555, www.keukenhof.nl).

ESCAPES & EXCURSIONS

ESCAPES & EXCURSIONS

Erasmus Bridge, Rotterdam. *See p296.*

Kinderdijk Windmills, called a gang, can still be seen. Clustered to drain water from reclaimed land, they are now under sail for the benefit of tourists (1.30-5.30pm on Saturdays in July and August, and the first Saturday in May and June). During the second week in September they're illuminated from 9.30pm to 11pm.

Euromast
Parkhaven 20 (010 436 4811, www.euro mast.nl). **Open** *Apr-Sept* 9.30am-11pm daily. *Oct-Mar* 10am-11pm daily. **Admission** €8.90; €5.70 reductions; free under-4s. **Credit** AmEx, DC, MC, V.

Historical Museum Rotterdam
Korte Hoogstraat 31 (010 217 6767, www.hmr.rotterdam.nl). **Open** 11am-5pm Tue-Sun. **Admission** €5; free under-17s, MK. **No credit cards.**

Kijk-Kubus
Overblaak 70 (010 414 2285, www.kubus woning.nl). **Open** 11am-5pm daily. **Admission** €2.50; €1.50-€2 reductions; free under-4s. **No credit cards.**

Kinderdijk Windmills
Molenkade, Alblasserdam (06 52 08 34 86 mobile, www.kinderdijk.com). **Open** *Apr-Sept* 9.30am-5.30pm daily. *Off-Season* weekends only, 11am-4pm. **Admission** €3.50; €2 reductions.

Kunsthal
Westzeedijk 341 (010 440 0301, www.kunsthal.nl). **Open** 10am-5pm Tue-Sat; 11am-5pm Sun. **Admission** €12.50; €2-€5.50 reductions; free under-6s. **No credit cards.**

Museum Boijmans Van Beuningen
Museumpark 18-20 (010 441 9400, www.boijmans.nl). **Open** 11am-5pm Tue-Sun. **Admission** €15; €10 reductions; free under-18s, MK, Wed. **Credit** AmEx, MC, V.

Netherlands Architecture Institute
Museumpark 25 (010 440 1358, www.nai.nl). **Open** 10am-5pm Tue-Sat; 11am-5pm Sun. **Admission** €8; €5 reductions; free under-18s, MK. **Credit** AmEx, MC, V.

Where to eat & drink

Less than a minute from Centraal Station, **De Engel** (Eendrachtsweg 19, 010 413 8256, www.hermandenblijker.nl) offers a wide range of international cuisine. For veggies there's **Bla Bla** (Piet Heynsplein 35, 010 477 4448, www.bla-bla.nl), while **El Faro Andaluz** (Leuvehaven 73-74, 010 414 6213, www.elfaroandaluz.nl) serves Spanish tapas.

Bars-wise, **De Schouw** (Witte de Withstraat 80, 010 412 4253) is a stylish brown café that now attracts artists and students. A lofty range of beers draws locals and tourists to **Locus Publicus** (Oostzeedijk 364, 010 433 1761, www.locus-publicus.com).

Where to stay

Hotel New York (Koninginnenhoofd 1, 010 439 0500, www.hotelnewyork.nl) is one of the most luxurious and historical places in town, with 72 rooms including two tower rooms and a loft with a terrace. Happily it's not unreasonably priced: doubles start at €145. **Hotel Bazar** (Witte de Withstraat 16, 010 206 5151, www.hotelbazar.nl) is also a little out of the ordinary: the rooms come decorated in a variety of Middle Eastern, African and South American styles, and it also hosts an excellent Middle Eastern restaurant. Doubles range from €75 to €120.

Getting there

By car
73km (45 miles) south on A4, then A13.

By train
1hr from Amsterdam Centraal Station, direct.

Alblasserdam
By car 20km (12 miles) south-east (enter Nederwaard 1, 2961AS Kinderdijk in GPS).

Euromast, Rotterdam. *See p296*

Tourist information

Alblasserdam VVV
Cultureel Centrum Landvast, Haven 4, Alblasserdam (078 691 2923, www.vvv alblassedam.nl). **Open** 10am-10pm Mon-Fri; 11am-10pm Sat; 1-10pm Sun.

Rotterdam VVV
Coolsingel 195 (0900 403 4065 premium rate, www.rotterdam.info). **Open** 9am-5.30pm Mon-Thur, Sat; 9am-9pm Fri; 10am-5pm Sun.

UTRECHT

One of the oldest cities in the Netherlands, **Utrecht** was also, in the Middle Ages, the biggest, and was a religious and political centre for hundreds of years – at one point there were around 40 houses of worship in the city, all with towers and spires. From a great distance, it must have looked like a pincushion.

But there's more to Utrecht than mere history alone: the university is one of the largest in the Netherlands – still expanding and employing architects such as Rem Koolhaas (who designed the Educatorium) – and the centre bustles with trendy shops and cafés.

Bikes can be hired from **U-Stal** (Stationsplein 7, 030 231 7656, www.u-stal.nl), but the city is so compact that practically everything is within short walking distance. A starting place is the **Domtoren**, the cathedral tower. At over 112 metres (367 feet), it's the highest tower in the country and, with over 50 bells, the largest musical instrument in the Netherlands too. The tower can be climbed and the panorama is worth the 465 steps: vistas stretch 40 kilometres (25 miles) to Amsterdam on a clear day. Buy tickets across the square at **VVV** (Domplein 9; *see p300*), where you can also get details on the rest of the city and the castles on its outskirts.

The space between the tower and the Domkerk was originally occupied by the nave of the huge church, which was destroyed by a freak tornado in 1674; the exhibition inside the Domkerk shows interesting 'before' and 'after' sketches.

Another fascinating place to explore is the **Oudegracht**, the canal that runs through the centre of the city, and its cafés and shops make excellent places for snacks and boat-watching.

Of the city museums, Utrecht's **Catharijneconvent** (St Catharine Convent Museum) is situated in a beautiful late-medieval building. Mainly dedicated to Dutch religious history, it also has a great collection of paintings by Old Masters, including Rembrandt. The **Centraal Museum** has a varied collection, from paintings by Van Gogh to contemporary art and cutting-edge fashion. One wing is

ESCAPES & EXCURSIONS

...dicated to illustrator Dick Bruna, who created ...at charming bunny, Nintje (known to some as Miffy). Another Utrecht-born celebrity in the collection is de Stijl architect and designer Gerrit Rietveld, known for his rectangular chairs and houses: the **Rietveld-Schröderhuis**, just outside the city centre, can be reached on the Centraal Museum's tour bus. The world's single biggest collection of automated musical instruments can be found at the fun **Nationaal Museum van Speelklok tot Pierement**. The **Universiteitsmuseum** (University Museum) focuses on science education and also has a centuries-old botanical garden.

Utrecht is in an area rich with castles, forests and arboretums. **Slot Zuylen** (Zuylen Castle, Tournooiveld 1, Oud Zuilen, 030 244 0255, www.slotzuylen.com) presides over some exquisite waterfalls and gardens. Check the concerts and shows in **Kasteel Groeneveld**'s gorgeous gardens (Groeneveld Castle, Groeneveld 2, Baarn, 035 542 0446, www. kasteelgroeneveld.nl), north-east of Utrecht. Stroll in the **Arboretum von Gimborn** (Vossensteinsesteeg 8, 030 253 1826, www.gimbornarboretum.nl) in Doorne, then to **Kasteel Huis Doorn** (Langbroekerweg 10, 034 342 1020, www.huisdoorn.nl), where Kaiser Wilhelm II lived until his death in 1941.

Centraal Museum

Nicolaaskerkhof 10 (030 236 2353, www. centraalmuseum.nl). **Open** 11am-5pm Tue-Sun. **Admission** €9; €4-€7.50 reductions; free under-12s, MK. **Credit** MC, V.

Museum Catharijneconvent

Lange Nieuwstraat 38 (030 231 3835, www.catharijneconvent.nl). **Open** 10am-5pm Tue-Fri; 11am-5pm Sat, Sun. **Admission** €11.50; €7 reductions; free under-5s, MK. **No credit cards.**

Nationaal Museum van Speelklok tot Pierement

Steenweg 6 (030 231 2789, www.museumspeelklok.nl). **Open** 10am-5pm Tue-Sun. **Admission** €9; €5-€8 reductions; free under-4s, MK. **No credit cards.**

Rietveld-Schröderhuis

Prins Hendriklaan 50 (030 236 2310, www.rietveldschroderhuis.nl). **Open** By appt 11am, 1pm, 2pm, 3pm, 4pm Wed-Sun. **Admission** €12; €3-€10.50 reductions. **Credit** MC, V.

Universiteitsmuseum

Lange Nieuwstraat 106 (030 253 8728, www.museum.uu.nl). **Open** 11am-5pm Tue-Sun. **Admission** €7; €3.50 reductions; free MK. **No credit cards.**

Where to eat & drink

De Winkel van Sinkel (Oudegracht 158, 030 230 3030, www.dewinkelvansinkel.nl) is a grand setting for coffee or food, especially at night, when its catacombs open for club nights and as a late-night restaurant. Those looking for dinner on the verge of a Michelin star ought to stop in on **Wilhelminapark** (Wilhelminapark 65, 030 251 0693, www.wilhelminapark.nl), at the centre of a beautiful green that makes an ideal summer hangout.

With a gaggle of local students, there's a feeling one should be hitting the books rather than the local beers. **ACU** (Voorstraat 71, 030 231 4590, www.acu.nl) has cheap eats and some of the city's edgier music events; **België** (Oudegracht 196, 030 231 2666) serves over 300 types of beer; the **Ekko** (Bemuurde Weerd Westzijde 3, 030 231 7457, www.ekko.nl) focuses on indie and dance.

Where to stay

The four-star **Malie Hotel** (Maliestraat 2, 030 231 6424, www.maliehotel.nl) is a beautiful old merchant's house: a double costs from €79, including breakfast. Those on a tighter budget should try small hostel **Strowis** (Boothstraat 8, 030 238 0280, www.strowis.nl), with shared rooms for €16 to €18.

Getting there

By car

40km (25 miles) south-east.

By rail

30mins from Amsterdam Centraal Station, direct.

Tourist information

VVV

Domplein 9 (0900 128 8732 premium rate, www.utrechtyourway.nl). **Open** noon-6pm Mon; 10am-6pm Tue-Wed, Fri; 10am-8pm Thur; 9.30am-5pm Sat; noon-5pm Sun.

AROUND UTRECHT

Though **De Haar** looks the quintessential medieval castle, it's actually relatively recent. In 1892, the baron who inherited the ruins of De Haar (dating from 1391) re-created the original on a majestic scale, moving the entire village of Haarzuilens 850 metres (259 feet) to make room for Versailles-styled gardens. The lavish interior is only visible on one of the informative guided tours.

Reitveld Schröderhuise, Utrecht.

Schoonhoven has been famous for its silversmiths since the 17th century, giving it its nickname of Zilverstad (Silver City). You can see antique pieces in the **Nederlands Goud-, Zilver- en Klokkenmuseum** and also at the former synagogue **Edelambachtshuis** (Museum of Antique Silverware). Olivia van Noort, the first Dutchman to sail around the world, and Claes Lourenz Blom, who, locals believe, introduced the windmill to Spain in 1508, are in fact buried in the 14th-century **Bartholomeuskerk**, whose tower leans 1.6 metres. Not buried here is Marrigje Ariens, the last woman to be burned as a witch in the country – but a circle of coloured stones by the city hall marks where she died in 1591.

Dating from the 11th century, **Oudewater** (north of Schoonhoven), once famed for its rope-making, also has a rich witch-hunting past. Reaching its peak in the 1480s, the fashion didn't die out until the beginning of the 17th century and Oudewater achieved fame for its weighing of suspected witches and warlocks in the **Heksenwaag** (Witches' Weigh House); today, swarms of tourists step on the scales.

De Haar
Kasteellaan 1, Haarzuilens, Utrecht (030 677 8515, www.kasteeldehaar.nl). **Open** *Check website for opening hours and tour times. Grounds* 9am-5pm daily. Sometimes closed for special events so best to call ahead. **Admission** *Castle & grounds*

€9.50; €6 reductions; free under-3s. *Grounds only* €3; €2 reductions; free under-3s.

Edelambachtshuis
Haven 13, Schoonhoven (0182 382614, http://rekkoert.nl). **Open** 10am-5.30pm Tue-Fri; 10am-5pm Sat. **Admission** call for details.

Heksenwaag
Leeuweringerstraat 2, Oudewater (034 856 3400, www.heksenwaag.nl). **Open** *1 Apr-1 Nov* 11am-5pm Tue-Sun. **Admission** €4.25; €2 reductions; free under-4s.

Nederlands Goud-, Zilver- en Klokkenmuseum
Kazerneplein 4, Schoonhoven (0182 385612, www.ngzbm.nl). **Open** noon-5pm Tue-Sun. **Admission** €6; €5 reductions; free under-12s.

Getting there

De Haar
By car 15km (9 miles) west. Bus 127 from Utrecht.

Oudewater
By car 30km (19 miles) west. Bus 180 from Utrecht.

Schoonhoven
By car 30km (19 miles) south-west. Bus 195 from Utrecht.

urist information

udewater VVV
Leeuweringerstraat 10, Oudewater (034 856 4636, www.vvvoudewater.nl). **Open** *Apr-Sept* 10am-4pm Tue-Sat; 11am-3pm Sun (July, Aug). *Oct* 10am-1pm Tue, Thur; 10am-4pm Wed, Fri, Sat. *Nov-Mar* 10am-1pm Tue, Thur-Sat; 10am-4pm Wed.

Schoonhoven VVV
Stadhuisstraat 1, Schoonhoven (0182 385009, www.vvvschoonhoven.nl). **Open** *May-Oct* 1.30-4.30pm Mon; 9.30am-4.30pm Tue-Fri; 10am-3pm Sat. *Oct-May* 1.30-4.30pm Mon; 9.30am-4.30pm Tue-Fri; 10.30am-3.30pm Sat.

GRONINGEN

The northern capital city of **Groningen** is the furthest one can get from Amsterdam without leaving the country itself. Called the 'Amsterdam of the North', it packs a similarly contemporary punch while still retaining plenty of old-world charm.

Groningen is a city that rocks – especially at night. But it's not just another student town. It's been around since BC became AD, when it was quick to evolve into a bustling walled city with a major grain market and high stakes in sugar and shipbuilding. Its history as a natural gas reserve is reflected in the **Aardgas Headquarters** (Concourslaan 17), a classic example of organic architecture. In fact, you're greeted by several architectural classics as soon as you arrive. **Centraal Station** is across the street from the **Groninger Museum**, the funkiest art gallery on the planet – even Bilbao's Guggenheim looks prefabricated by comparison. Also nearby is an early work by superstar architect Rem Koolhaas: the **Urinoir**, featuring both stainless steel toilets and the homoerotic photography of Erwin Olaf. It's located on Kleine Der A in the scenic Westhaven district, also home to the **Nederlands Stripmuseum** (Comics Museum), which covers everything from Asterix to Zorro and beyond.

If you proceed up Folkingestraat you'll soon find yourself at **Vismarkt** and **Grote Markt**. The latter's image-defining church and tower are the **Martinikerk** and **Martinitoren**. Historians claim they are named after St Martin rather than the cocktail, but suspicions rise, given that the surrounding square kilometre has the highest density of alcohol licences in the country. If all that isn't enough, the tower of nearby church **Jozefkerk** is nicknamed 'Drunken Man's Tower': each of its six faces has a clock and therefore at least two are always visible, creating a sense of double vision. Yep, it's a student town all right.

Groningen also provides the perfect base to explore nature. There's much within cycling distance – for instance, the moated manors of **Menkemaborg** or **Fraeylemaborg** – but you can also take a bus to the nearby port towns, whence ferries go to the Wadden islands of **Schiermonnikoog** and **Ameland**.

Groninger Museum
Museumeiland 1 (050 366 6555, www.groningermuseum.nl). **Open** 10am-6pm Tue-Sun. **Admission** €10; €6-€9 reductions; free under-12s, MK. **Credit** AmEx, DC, MC, V.

Nederlands Stripmuseum
Westerhaven 71 (050 317 8470, www.stripmuseumgroningen.nl). **Open** 10am-5pm Tue-Sun. **Admission** €7.95; €6.95 reductions; free under-4s. **Credit** MC, V.

Where to eat & drink

For drinking all year round, there are two main strips. **Peperstraat** is middle of the road, while **Poelestraat** is the trendier alternative. **Jazzcafe de Spieghel** (Peperstraat 11, 050 528 0588, www.jazzcafedespieghel.nl) features jazz of both the trad and acid varieties.

For eats, **'t Feithhuis** (Martinikerkhof 10, 050 313 5335, www.feithhuis.nl) is open all day, while **De Drie Gezusters** (Grote Markt 36, 050 312 7041) also offers reasonable food. Many consider the Italian-inspired **Groninger Museum Restaurant** (*see above*, book via 050 360 3665) to be the best place to eat in town.

Where to stay

For a bit of class, try the **Hotel de Ville** (Oude Boteringestraat 43-45, 050 318 1222, www.nh-hotels.com), where doubles range from €105 to €190. Meanwhile, the central **Martini Budget Hotel** (Gedempte Zuiderdiep 8, 050 312 9199, www.martinihotel.nl) offers doubles from €67.50. On a budget, check **Simplon Youthhotel** (Boterdiep 72-73, 050 313 5221, www.simplonjongerenhotel.nl).

Getting there

By car
190km (120 miles) on A7.

By train
2hrs from Amsterdam Centraal Station, direct.

Tourist information

VVV
Grote Markt 25 (0900 202 3050, www.vvvgroningen.nl). **Open** *Sept-June* 9am-6pm Mon-Fri; 10am-5pm Sat. *July, Aug* 9am-6pm Mon-Fri; 10am-5pm Sat; 11am-3pm Sun.

Directory

NDSM. *See p124.*

Getting Around

ARRIVING & LEAVING

By air

There are always plenty of **taxis** at the main exit, but be sure to take a recognised taxi and check the price before you set off. Don't accept rides from drivers soliciting within the airport – they're not official taxi drivers and you could end up paying way above the odds. Alternatively, use the following bus or rail links.

Connexxion Airport Hotel Shuttle
Connexxion counter, Arrivals Hall 4, Schiphol Airport (038 339 4741, www.airporthotelshuttle.nl). **Times** every 30mins 6am-9pm. **Tickets** *Single* €15. *Return* €24; 50% reduction 4-14s; free under-4s. **Credit** AmEx, MC V.
This door-to-door bus service from Schiphol to Amsterdam is available to anyone prepared to pay, but you'll have to get yourself to one of the 100-odd allied hotels. Return trips must be booked at least 2 hours prior to departure.

Schiphol Airport Rail Service
Schiphol Airport/Centraal Station (www.9292ov.nl, www.ns.nl). **Times** every 10mins 6am-12.30am; every hr 1-5am; approx every 30mins 12.30-1am & 5-6am. **Tickets** *Single* €3.70; €2.20 reductions; free under-4s. *Same-day return* €7.10; €4.30 reductions. **Credit** MC, V.
Takes about 20 minutes to Centraal Station. Make sure you buy your ticket before boarding, otherwise you'll incur a €35 fine in addition to the fare. Tickets can be bought at the yellow machines (cash or Dutch cash card only) and at the ticket office in the airport's main hall. Return tickets are valid for that day only.

Airports

Schiphol Airport 0900 0141 (€0.40/min), www.schiphol.nl.
AerLingus 0900 265 8207 (cost unspecified), www.aerlingus.com.
British Airways 346 9559, www.britishairways.com.
EasyJet 0900 265 8022 (€0.80/min), www.easyjet.com.
KLM 474 7747, www.klm.com.

By car

Options for crossing the channel with a car ferry include: Harwich to Hook of Holland with Stena Line (www.stenaline.nl); Newcastle to Amsterdam (IJmuiden) with DFDS Seaways (www.dfdsseaways.co.uk); Hull to Rotterdam or Zeebrugge with P&O Ferries (www.poferries.com); or Dover to Calais with P&O Ferries or SeaFrance (www.seafrance.com). Ferries from Ireland go from Rosslare to either Roscoff or Cherbourg in France (www.irish ferries.com). Another option is the Eurotunnel to France (www.euro tunnel.com).

By coach

International coach services arrive at Amstel station. To reserve, see the Eurolines website (www.euro lines.nl), which is in English. Fares start from around €45 for a single journey from London Victoria Coach Station to Amsterdam.

By rail

The fastest and simplest route from London is Eurostar (www.eurostar.com) from St Pancras International, taking you to Brussels. There you change for an InterCity or Thalys high-speed train to Amsterdam.

The 'Dutch Flyer' train and ferry service incorporates a train from Liverpool Street Station to Harwich, Stena Line's superferry crossing to Hook of Holland, and then train to Rotterdam where you change for a train to Amsterdam Centraal.

If you live in the North of England or Scotland, take the ferry from Hull or Newcastle (*see above* **By car**). Transfer buses take you from the port to either Rotterdam Centraal or Amsterdam Centraal train stations.

PUBLIC TRANSPORT

For information, tickets, maps and an English-language guide to all types of public transport tickets, visit the GVB, Amsterdam's municipal transport authority in person or use its useful website (*see below*). The 9292ov service (www.9292ov.nl) groups national bus, train, taxi, tram and ferry information, and its 'door-to-door' journey planner is invaluable.

For a basic map of the tram network, *see p336*; for details of NS, the Netherlands' rail network, *see pp282-283*.

GVB *Stationsplein, opposite Centraal Station (0900 8011 premium rate, www.gvb.nl).* Tram *1, 2, 4, 5, 9, 13, 16, 17, 24, 25, 26.* **Open** *Telephone enquiries* 8am-7pm daily. *In person* 7am-9pm Mon-Fri; 10am-6pm Sat, Sun. **Map** p326 D1.
The GVB runs Amsterdam's Metro, bus, tram, Stop/Go and ferry services. OV-Chipcards (*see below*) can be bought here.
Other locations *Head Office*: Arlandaweg 100 (lost articles); Bijlmer ArenA station; Metro stations; Rembrandtplein; Leidseplein (night buses only, midnight-6am Fri, Sat).

Fares & tickets

Don't travel on a bus or tram with no ticket. Uniformed inspectors make regular checks and passengers lacking a valid ticket will be fined €37.50 on the spot. Playing the ignorant foreigner won't work.

OV-Chipcard

The comprehensive OV-Chipcard ticketing system covers the tram, Metro and bus services. You simply scan your card against the readers located at the doors/gates of your chosen mode of transport at the start and end of each journey. It's worth noting, however, that if you don't scan your card when you leave, it won't be valid any more.

For visitors, there are one- to seven-day disposable OV-Chipcards available (€7-€29), which allow for unlimited day and night travel for the duration of the card (from the moment you first scan it). These must be purchased in advance and are available from GVB Ticket and Info outlets (*see above*) and various other locations (check GVB website for full list). A one-hour OV card (€2.60) can also be purchased on trams, buses and Metros. See www.ov-chipkaart.nl.

Trams & buses

Buses and trams run from 5.30am Monday to Friday, 6.30am Saturdays and 7.30am Sundays, with a special night bus service taking over once they've stopped. Yellow signs at stops indicate the tram and bus number as well as the name of the stop. There are usually maps of the entire network in the shelters and route maps on the vehicles themselves.

Night bus stops are indicated by a black square at the stop with the bus number printed on it, and they run from 12.30am to 5.30am Monday to Friday, or until 6.30am on weekends.

Other road users should be warned that trams only stop if absolutely necessary. Listen out for tram warning bells and cyclists should cross tramlines at an angle to avoid the front wheel getting stuck.

Remember to always scan your OV-Chipcard at the reader by the doors when getting in and out. If you're buying the one-hour card onboard, you can get it from the driver (or the conductor near the back on trams).

The Stop/Go service is a convenient mode of transport that circles the city, and connects with many bus or tram routes. Cruising along Prinsengracht, it only has four designated stops – Oosterdok, De Ruijterkade Oost, Centraal Station and Waterlooplein – but you can get on and off on request by waving one down or asking the driver to stop when you want to get off. The Stop/Go runs daily (around every 12mins, 9am-5.30pm), and costs €1 for a one-hour ticket (available from the driver and only valid on the Stop/Go) or you can use your OV-Chipcard. Take note: obstructions such as roadworks and removals vans mean the bus may temporarily deviate from its normal route so pay some attention to your journey when on board, and take a stroll to the nearest junction if you've been waiting too long.

Metro

The Metro uses the same OV-Chipcard system as the trams and buses (see left), and provides a fast link between all the areas around Amsterdam. There are three lines – 51, 53 and 54 – which terminate at Centraal Station (CS), while the line 50 runs from the north-west through to the south-east. Trains leave CS from around 6.30am Monday to Friday (6.45am Sat, 7.45am Sun) to about 12.45am daily. See www.gvb.nl for full timetables.

TAXIS

Since it was decentralised, there are more independent taxi companies in the market to help break the monopoly of Taxi Centraal Amsterdam, which unfortunately means there are some opportunist drivers out there, while others have

no idea where they're going. Your best bet is to opt for a cab that has the red and black 'TCA/7x7' rooflight on it whenever you can, or phone for one (777 7777).

Sometimes it's hard to hail a taxi in the street, but ranks are dotted around the city. The best central ones are outside Centraal Station, alongside the bus station (at Kinkerstraat and Marnixstraat), Rembrandtplein and Leidseplein.

Always ask your driver how much your journey will cost before you set off – they should be able to give you an approximate figure; that way you'll know if you've been ripped off. Make sure the metre starts at the minimum charge (€7.50 for 1-4 passengers); your initial €7.50 includes 2km, after that you pay €2.20/km for the first 25, and €1.75/km thereafter. If you feel you've been ripped off, ask for a receipt before handing over cash. If the fee seems too high, phone the central taxi office (650 6506, 9am-4pm Mon-Fri) or contact the police.

Wheelchairs will only fit in taxis if they're folded. If you're a wheelchair user, you can call the special car transport service (633 3943, 7am-5pm daily). You'll need to book one or two days in advance and it costs around €2.20/km.

Alternatively, hail a 'bicycle cab' – basically a high-tech rickshaw – or order one (06 1859 5153 same day, 06 4158 5012 booking; www.wieler taxi.nl, €1/3min per person, €0.50 reductions, free under-2s). There's a €2.50 surcharge for phone orders.

DRIVING

If you're coming by car to the Netherlands, it's wise to join a national motoring organisation beforehand. To drive in the Netherlands you'll need a valid national driving licence; ANWB (see below) and many car-hire firms favour photocard licences (Brits need the paper version as well for this to be legal). You'll need proof that your vehicle has passed a road safety test in its country of origin, an international identification disk, vehicle registration papers and insurance documents.

The Dutch drive on the right. Motorways are labelled 'A'; major roads 'N'; and European routes 'E'. Seatbelts are compulsory for drivers and all passengers. Speed limits are usually 50kmph (31mph) within cities, 80kmph (50mph) outside, and 100kmph (62mph) on motorways. Speeding and other traffic offences are subject to heavy on-the-spot fines.

If you're driving in Amsterdam, look out for cyclists; they're unforgiving and act like they have right of way. Always check carefully before you make a turn and when you open your door. Many streets in Amsterdam are one-way – for cars that is, not bikes, so don't be surprised to see them cycling against the traffic flow.

Strict drink driving laws only allow 0.5 milligrams of alcohol per millilitre of blood.

Royal Dutch Automobile Club (ANWB) *Buikslotermeerplein 307-311, Noord (088 269 3080, 088 269 2222 customer services, 088 269 2888 24hr emergency line, www.anwb.nl). Bus 31, 38, 46, 230, 245.* **Open** *Customer services* 8am-8pm Mon-Fri; 8.30am-5pm Sat. **Credit** MC, V. **Map** p330 D6.
An annual membership fee (€49.50-€69.50) covers the cost of assistance if you break down. Members of a foreign motoring organisation may be entitled to free help. Crews may not accept credit cards at the scene.

Car hire

Dutch car hire (*autoverhuur*) firms generally expect at least one year's driving experience and will want to see a valid national driving licence (with photo) and passport before they lend vehicles. All will require a deposit by credit card, and you generally need to be over 21. Prices given below are for one day's hire of the cheapest car available excluding insurance and VAT.

Adam's Rent-a-Car *Nassaukade 344-346, Oud West (685 0111, www.adamsrentacar.nl). Tram 7, 10, 17.* **Open** 8am-6pm Mon-Fri; 8am-8pm Sat. **Credit** AmEx, MC, V. **Map** p330 C5.
One-day hire costs from €32; the first 100km (62 miles) are free, and after that the charge is €0.14/km. Branch at Middenweg 51.

Dik's Autoverhuur *Van Ostadestraat 278-280, De Pijp (662 3366, www.diks.net). Tram 3, 4, 25.* **Open** 8am-7.30pm Mon-Sat; 9am-12.30pm, 8-10.30pm Sun. **Credit** AmEx, MC, V. **Map** p331 F4.
Prices from €36 per day. The first 100km are free, then it's €0.16/km.

Hertz *Overtoom 333, Oud West (612 2441, www.hertz.nl). Tram 1.* **Open** 8am-6pm Mon-Fri; 8am-2pm Sat; 9am-2pm Sun. **Credit** AmEx, MC, V. **Map** p329 B6.
Prices from €50 per day. The first 300km are free, then it's €0.15/km.

DIRECTORY

DIRECTORY

Clamping & fines

Wheel-clamp (*wielklem*) teams are swift and merciless, and the minimum fine is €103.60. You can pay by credit card by calling 251 3322 (24-hour pay-and-go service) and someone will come and remove the clamp upon payment. To pay in cash, visit any of the Stadstoezicht offices listed (after business hours, go to the head office, *see below*). Once you've paid, return to the car and wait for the clamp to be removed. Thankfully, de-clampers normally turn up fairly promptly.

If you fail to pay the fine within 24 hours, your car will be towed away; call the City Surveillance Service (251 3322, 24hrs daily) to find out if it has. You can collect your car from the pound at Daniël Goedkoopstraat 9; take proof of identity, your licence number and payment. It will cost a minimum €150, plus parking fine, plus a tariff per km to reclaim it from the pound if you do so within 24 hours, and around €58 for every 12 hours thereafter.

Head office *Daniël Goedkoopstraat 9, Oost (251 2121, www.stadstoezicht.amsterdam.nl). Metro 51, 53, 54.* **Open** 8am-5pm daily; 24hrs daily if your car has been towed. **Credit** AmEx, MC, V. **Map** p327 F3.
Other locations *Beukenplein 50, Oost (251 2121). Tram 3, 9, 10, 14.* **Open** 9am-5.30pm Mon-Fri. **Map** p332 H4.
De Clercqstraat 42-44, Oud West (251 2121). Tram 3, 12, 13, 14. **Open** 8am-4.30pm Mon-Sat. **Map** p329 B4.

Parking

All of central Amsterdam is metered from 9am until at least 7pm – and in many places to midnight – and spaces are difficult to find. Buying day or evening tickets from the machines is cheaper than paying hourly rates. Rates for the centre are €30 9am-7pm, €36 9am-9pm Mon-Sat and €21 noon-7pm, €27 noon-9pm Sun. Tickets valid for 24 hours (€45 Mon-Sat, €36 Sun), one week (€180 9am-7pm, €216 9am-9pm, €270 24hrs) or one month (€648 9am-7pm, €777.60 9am-9pm, €972 24hrs) can be bought from the Cition service points (*see below*).

Car parks (*parkeren*) are indicated by a white 'P' on a blue square. After controlled hours, parking at meters is free. Below is a list of central car parks where you're more likely to find a space at peak times, although prices can be rather prohibitive.

When leaving your car anywhere across the city, be sure to empty it of valuables and leave your glove box open: cars with foreign plates are vulnerable to break-ins.

Cition service points
Cition (251 3737, http://cition.nl). **Open** 8am-6pm Mon-Fri.
Daniël Goedkoopstraat 9, Oost (251 3322, www.stadstoezicht.amsterdam.nl). Metro 51, 53, 54. **Open** 7am-11pm Mon-Fri. **Credit** AmEx, MC, V. **Map** p327 F3.
De Clercqstraat 42-44, West (251 2121). Tram 3, 12, 13, 14. **Open** 8am-4.30pm Mon-Sat. **Map** p329 B4.
Burgerweeshuispad 301, Zuid (251 2121). Metro 50, tram 16, 24, or bus 62. **Open** 9am-7pm Mon; 9am-2pm Tue; 9am-4pm Wed-Fri.
ANWB Parking Amsterdam Centraal *Prins Hendrikkade 20a, Old Centre: New Side (638 5330).* **Open** 24hrs. **Rates** €5/hr; €55/24hrs. **Credit** AmEx, MC, V. **Map** p326 D2.
Many nearby hotels offer a 10% discount on parking here.
Europarking *Marnixstraat 250, Oud West (0900 446 6880 rate €0.45/min).* **Open** 6.30am-1am Mon-Wed; 24hrs 7am Thur-1am Mon. **Rates** €3.50/55mins; €38/24hrs. **Credit** AmEx, DC, MC, V. **Map** p329 B4.
De Kolk Parking *Nieuwezijds Kolk, Old Centre: New Side (427 1449).* **Open** 24hrs. **Rates** €4/52mins; €50/24hrs. **Credit** AmEx, MC, V. **Map** p326 C2.

Petrol

There are 24-hour petrol stations (*tankstations*) at Gooiseweg 10, Sarphatistraat 225, Marnixstraat 250 and Spaarndammerdijk 218.

WATER TRANSPORT

Amsterdam is best seen from the water. Sure, there are canal cruises, but they don't offer the freedom to do your own exploring. For ways to get around on the water, *see pp75-79* **Tour Amsterdam**. Upon rental, don't ignore the introductory rules of the water (put simply: stick to the right and beware canal cruisers).

CYCLING

Cycling is the most convenient means of getting from A to B: there are bike lanes on most roads, marked by white lines and bike symbols. When cycling, unless indicated otherwise by signs, the right-before-left rule applies and

watch out for pedestrians stepping into your path. Bike lights are compulsory in the dark; police set up periodic checkpoints and will fine you on the spot if you don't have any. Avoid getting your tyre in the tram rails, always cross them at an angle and never leave a bike unlocked; Amsterdam has one of the highest bicycle theft rates in the world. If someone on the street offers you a bike for sale (*fiets te koop*), don't be tempted: it's almost certainly stolen, and there are plenty of good and cheap bike hire companies around, of which we list a selection below and in **Tour Amsterdam** (*see p75*). Apart from these, check the www.goudengids.nl under the section 'Fietsen en Bromfietsen Verhuur'.

Note that almost every bicycle in Amsterdam now uses the reverse-pedal braking system rather than a pair of manual brakes attached to handlebars. Those who are used to the latter will find that it takes some time to adjust, so be sure to allow some time to practise before setting out on the streets.

Bike City *Bloemgracht 68-70, the Jordaan (626 3721, www.bikecity.nl). Tram 10, 13, 14, 17.* **Open** 9am-6pm daily. **Rates** from €13.50/day 9am-5.30pm. *Deposit* €25. **Credit** AmEx, MC, V. **Map** p325 B3.
Mac Bike *For listing, see p75* **Tour Amsterdam.**
Mike's Bike Tours *Kerkstraat 134, Southern Canal Belt (622 7970, www.mikesbiketours.amsterdam.com). Tram 1, 2, 5.* **Open** 9am-6pm daily. *Oct-Mar* 10am-6pm daily. **Rates** from €7/day. **No credit cards**. **Map** p330 D4.
Guided tours available.
Rent-A-Bike *Damstraat 20-22, Old Centre: Old Side (625 5029, www.bikes.nl). Tram 4, 9, 14, 16, 24, 25.* **Open** 9am-6pm daily. **Rates** €7 till 6pm; from €9.50 24hrs; €25 deposit and passport/ID card or credit card photocopy. **Credit** AmEx, MC, V. **Map** p326 D3.

WALKING

Amsterdam is a compact city, and everything is easy to reach by foot. The canals, cobbled streets, stunning architecture and amount of cafés make a stroll through the city a truly pleasant experience. Know that cyclists are ruthless; they stop for nothing and no one, so don't get in their way. For details on walking tours, *see p78* **Tour Amsterdam**.

Resources A-Z

ADDRESSES

Addresses take the form of street then house number, such as Damrak 1.

AGE RESTRICTIONS

In the Netherlands, only those over the age of 16 can purchase alcohol (over 18 for spirits); you have to be 16 to buy cigarettes (18 to smoke dope). Driving is limited to over-18s.

ATTITUDE & ETIQUETTE

Amsterdam's reputation as a relaxed city is well founded, as anyone will find out after a wander around the Red Light District. However, not everything goes. Smoking dope is not OK everywhere: spliffing up in restaurants is usually frowned upon, and while most restaurants don't have dress codes, many nightclubs ban sportswear and trainers.

BUSINESS

The construction of a new Metro line linking north and south Amsterdam is indicative of the city's status as a big business centre. The south of Amsterdam is where most of the action is, with corporate hotels rubbing shoulders with the World Trade Center and the RAI convention centre. www.amsterdampartners.nl is a mine of useful information.

Banking

ABN-Amro *0900 0024 (€0.10/min. 8am-9pm Mon-Fri; 9am-5pm Sat), www.abnamro.nl.*
Locations all over Amsterdam.
Fortis Bank *0900 8172 (€0.10/min. 24hrs daily), www.fortisbank.nl.*
Full facilities in 50 banks.
ING Group *0900 0933 (€0.10/min. 8am-9pm Mon-Fri; 9am-5pm Sat), www.ing.com.*

Rabobank *777 8899 (8am-9pm Mon-Fri; 9am-5pm Sat), www. rabobank.nl.* Some 30 locations.
For information on currency exchange, *see p311.*

Couriers & shippers

FedEx *0800 0222 333, www.fedex. com/nl_english.* **Open** *Customer services* 8am-6.30pm Mon-Fri. **Credit** AmEx, MC, V.
TNT *0800 1234, www.tnt.com.* **Open** 24hrs daily. **Credit** AmEx, DC, MC, V.

Office hire & business services

Many tobacconists and copy shops have fax facilities.

Euro Business Center
Keizersgracht 62, Western Canal Belt (520 7500, www.eurobc.nl/eu). *Tram 1, 2, 5, 13, 14, 17.* **Open** 8.30am-5pm Mon-Fri. **Credit** AmEx, DC, MC, V. **Map** p326 C2.
Office leases from one day to two years, virtual offices, meeting rooms and secretarial services.
World Trade Center
Strawinskylaan 1, Zuid (575 9111, www.wtcamsterdam.com). *Tram 5 or NS rail Amsterdam Zuid-WTC Station.* **Open** *Office & enquiries* 9am-5pm Mon-Fri.
Long or short term lets and business services available.

Translators & interpreters

Amstelveens Vertaalburo
Ouderkerkerlaan 50, Amstelveen (645 6610, www.avb.nl). *Bus 65, 170, 172.* **Open** 9am-5pm Mon-Fri.
No credit cards.
Translation and interpreter services.
Mac Bay Consultants
PC Hooftstraat 15, Museum Quarter (24hr phoneline 662 0501, *www.macbay.nl).* *Tram 2, 3, 5, 12.* **Open** 9am-7pm Mon-Fri. **No credit cards. Map** p330 C6.
Specialists in financial and legal document services.

Useful organisations

For details of embassies and consulates, *see p308.*

Commissariaat voor Buitenlandse Investeringen Nederland *Juliana van Stolberglaan 148, 2595 CL, The Hague (070 602 8818, www.nfia.nl).* **Open** 8am-6pm Mon-Fri. The Foreign Trade Agency is the first port of call for businesses relocating to the Netherlands.
EVD: Economische Voorlichtingsdienst *Juliana van Stolberglaan 148, 2595 CL, The Hague (070 602 8093, www. hollandirade.com).* **Open** 8am-5pm Mon-Fri (appt necessary).
The Dutch Agency for International Business and Co-operation includes the Netherlands Council for Trade Promotion (NCH), both handy sources of information. Call in advance to make an appointment.
Home Abroad *Weteringschans 28, Southern Canal Belt (625 5195, www.homeabroad.nl).* **Open** 10am-5.30pm Mon-Fri. **Map** p331 E5.
Assistance with all aspects of life and business in the Netherlands.
Kamer van Koophandel (Chamber of Commerce)
De Ruyterkade 5, the Waterfront (531 4000, www.kvk.nl). *Tram 1, 2, 4, 5, 9, 13, 16, 17, 24, 25.* **Open** 8.30am-5pm Mon-Fri, Wed until 8pm. **Map** p326 C1.
Offers lists of import/export agencies, trade representatives and companies by sector. Essential.
Ministerie van Buitenlandse Zaken *Bezuidenhoutseweg 67, Postbus 20061, 2500 EB, The*

DIRECTORY

Hague (070 348 6486, www.min buza.nl). **Open** 7am-8pm Mon-Fri for the legalisation of documents. The Ministry of Foreign Affairs. Detailed enquiries may be referred to the EVD (*see p307*).
Ministerie van Economische Zaken *Bezuidenhoutseweg 30, 2594 AV, The Hague (0800 8051, www.rijksoverheid.nl).* **Open** 9am-5.30pm Mon-Fri.
The Ministry of Economic Affairs: helps with general queries about the Dutch economy. Detailed queries may be referred to the EVD (*see p307*).
Netherlands-British Chamber of Commerce *Oxford House, Nieuwezijds Voorburgwal 328l, Old Centre: New Side (421 7040, www.nbcc.co.uk).* Tram 1, 2, 5, 13, 14, 17. **Open** 9am-5pm Mon-Fri. **Map** p326 D3.

CONSUMER

If you have any complaints about the service you received from Dutch businesses that you were unable to resolve, contact the National Consumentenbond (070 445 4545, www.consumentenbond.nl; 8am-8pm Mon-Thur; 8am-5.30pm Fri, Dutch only) for one-off advice at cost.

CUSTOMS

EU nationals over the age of 17 may import limitless goods into the Netherlands for personal use, but non-EU countries may still have limits. Check the rules for the particular country you're visiting/returning to to find out what you can bring. The import of meat or meat products, fruit, plants, flowers and protected animals to the Netherlands is illegal. Call the toll-free Customs Information Line (0800 0143, 8am-8pm Mon-Thur; 8am-5pm Fri) for more information.

DISABLED

The most obvious difficulty people with mobility problems face here is negotiating the winding cobbled streets of the older areas. Pavements are often poorly maintained, and canal-house steps usually steep. But the pragmatic Dutch can generally solve any problems quickly.
Most large museums have facilities for disabled users but little for the partially sighted and hard of hearing. Most cinemas and theatres are accessible, but do check in advance. The AUB (www.aub.nl) and the Amsterdam Tourist Board (*see p312*) have brochures on places and attractions with disabled facilities.

Wheelchair users travelling on public transport should bear in mind that some tram and bus stops are not suitable (check the GVB leaflets or timetables found at the stops), and that the Metro is only accessible to those who 'have normal arm function'. For the special taxi service, *see p305*.

DRUGS

Locals have a relaxed attitude to soft drugs, but smoking isn't acceptable everywhere. Use discretion. Outside Amsterdam, public consumption of cannabis is largely unacceptable. For more on drugs, *see pp65-71*.
Foreigners found with hard drugs should expect to face prosecution. Organisations offering advice can do little to help foreigners with drug-related problems, although the Jellinek Drugs Prevention Centre is happy to provide help in several languages, including English. Its helpline (590 1515, 3-5pm Mon-Thur) offers advice and information. There's a 24-hour crisis/detox emergency number too: 590 5000.

ELECTRICITY

The voltage is 220, 50-cycle AC and compatible with British equipment, but because the Netherlands uses two-pin continental plugs you'll need an adaptor. American visitors may need a transformer.

EMBASSIES

American Consulate General *Museumplein 19, 1071 DJ (575 5309, 0900 872 8472 premium rate, http://amsterdam.usconsulate.gov/).* Tram 3, 5, 12, 16. **Open** US citizens services 8.30-11.30am Mon-Fri. *Immigrant visas* 1.30-3pm. **Map** p330 D6.
Australian Embassy *Carnegielaan 4, 2517 KH, The Hague (070 310 8200, 0800 0224 794 Australian citizen emergency phone, www.australian-embassy.nl).* **Open** 8.30am-5pm Mon-Fri. *Visa & immigration information* 9am-noon Mon-Fri.
This embassy cannot issue you with visas or accept visa applications. The nearest Department of Immigration and Multicultural Affairs outpost is at the embassy in Berlin, Germany. Note that only general visa information is available from the Visa Information Officer.
British Consulate General *Koningslaan 44, 1075 AE (676 4343, www.britain.nl).* Tram 2. **Open** British citizens 8.30am-1.30pm Mon-Fri. *Phone enquiries* 2-5pm Mon-

Thur; 2-4.30pm Fri. *Visa enquiries* by appt only 3-4.30pm Mon-Fri.
British Embassy *Lange Voorhout 10, 2514 ED, The Hague (070 427 0427, www.britain.nl).* **Open** 9am-5.30pm Mon-Fri.
For visa and tourist information, contact the Consulate.
Canadian Embassy *Sophialaan 7, 2514 JP, The Hague (070 311 1600, www.canada.nl).* **Open** 9am-1pm, 2-5.30pm Mon-Fri. *Consular and passport section* 10am-1pm, 2-4.30pm Mon-Fri.
Irish Embassy *Dr Kuyperstraat 9, 2514 BA, The Hague (070 363 0993, www.irishembassy.nl).* **Open** 10am-12.30pm, 2.30-5pm Mon-Fri. *Visa enquiries* 10am-12.30pm Mon-Fri.
New Zealand Embassy *Eisenhowerlaan 77N, 2517 KK, The Hague (070 346 9324, visas 070 365 8037, www.nzembassy.com/netherlands).* **Open** 9am-12.30pm, 1.30-5.30pm Mon-Fri.

EMERGENCIES

In an emergency, call 112 (free from any phone) and specify police, fire service or ambulance. For helplines and hospitals, *see right*; for police stations, *see p311*.

GAY & LESBIAN
Help & information

COC Amsterdam *Rozenstraat 14 (626 3087, www.cocamsterdam.nl).* Tram 13, 14, 17. **Open** *Phone enquiries* 10am-4pm Mon-Fri. **Map** p325 B3.
For the social side of gay life here.
COC National *Rozenstraat 8 (623 4596, www.coc.nl).* Tram 13, 14, 17. **Open** 9.30am-5pm Mon-Fri. **Map** p326 C3.
COC's head office deals with all matters gay and lesbian.
Gay & Lesbian Switchboard *623 6565, www.switchboard.nl.* **Open** noon-6pm Mon-Fri.
For general information or safe-sex advice, the friendly English-speakers here are well informed.
Homodok-Lesbisch Archief Amsterdam (Gay & Lesbian Archives) *Centrale Bibliotheek, 6th floor, Oosterdokskade 143 (523 0837, www.ihlia.nl).* Tram 10, 12, 14. **Open** noon-5pm Mon-Fri; 1-5pm Sat, Sun. **Map** p327 E1.
Non-lending library of books and articles, and a large video collection.
IIAV *Obiplein 4, Oost (665 0820, www.iiav.nl).* Tram 3, 7, 10, 14 or bus 22, 37, 59, 65. **Open** noon-5pm Mon; 10am-5pm Tue-Fri.

DIRECTORY

This women's archive, started after the war, has a lot of other resources, including several online databases.
Het Vrouwenhuis (The Women's House) *Nieuwe Herengracht 95, Southern Canal Belt (625 2066, www.akantes.nl). Tram 7, 9, 14 or Metro Waterlooplein.* **Open** *Office* 10am-5pm Mon-Fri. *Library, internet café* noon-5pm Wed, Thur. **Map** p327 F3.

Other groups & organisations

Dikke Maatjes *Postbus 15456, 1001 ML (www.dikkemaatjes.nl).* Means 'close friends' – a gay club for chubbies and their admirers.
Mama Cash *Postbus 15686, 1001 ND (515 8700, www.mamacash.nl).* **Open** 9am-5pm Mon-Fri.
Helps to fund women's groups and women-run businesses, and sponsors lesbian organisations and events.
Sportclub Tijgertje *Postbus 10521, 1001 EM (06 1024 9026, www.tijgertje.nl).*
Organises a wide variety of sports activities for gays and lesbians, plus an HIV swimming group.

HEALTH

As for any trip abroad, take out medical insurance before you leave.

Afdeling Inlichtingen Apotheken *694 8709.*
A 24-hour service that can direct you to your nearest chemist.
Centraal Doktorsdienst/Atacom *592 3333, www.atacom.nl.*
A 24-hour English-speaking line for advice about symptoms.

Accident & emergency

Go to the *eerste spoedhulp* (A&E) of any hospital (*ziekenhuis*). The Dutch emergency number is 112; *see left*.

Academisch Medisch Centrum (AMC) *Meibergdreef 9, Zuid (566 9111, 566 3333 first aid). Metro Holendrechp or bus 59, 60, 120, 126.*
Boven IJ Ziekenhuis *Statenjachtstraat 1, Noord (634 6346, 634 6200 first aid). Bus 34, 36, 37, 39, 171, 172.*
Onze Lieve Vrouwe Gasthuis (OLVG) *'s Gravesandeplein 16, Oost (599 9111, 599 3016 first aid). Tram 3, 10 or Metro Weesperplein or Wibautstraat.*
St Lucas Andreas Ziekenhuis *Jan Tooropstraat 164, West (510 8911, 510 8161 first aid). Tram 13 or bus 19, 47, 80, 82, 97.*

VU Ziekenhuis *De Boelelaan 1117, Zuid (444 4444, 444 3636 first aid). Metro Amstelveenseweg or bus 142, 147, 148, 149, 170, 171, 172.*

Contraception & abortion

The morning-after pill is available from pharmacies (*see below*) over the counter.

Amsterdams Centrum Voor Seksuele Gezondheid *Louwesweg 6, 1066 EC (512 4903, www.acsg.nl). Tram 9, 10, 14 or bus 22.* **Open** 8.30am-5pm Mon-Wed, Fri. **Map** p332 G3.
An abortion clinic. Besides giving information on health, the staff at this family-planning centre can help with prescriptions for contraceptives. Prescription charges vary. You must make an appointment.
Polikliniek Oosterpark *Oosterpark 59, Oost (693 2151, 592 3809 emergencies after hours, www.oosterparkkliniek.nl). Tram 3, 9.* **Open** *Advice* 8.30am-5pm daily. **Map** p332 H4.
Advice on contraception and abortion. Non-residents will be charged for an abortion. Check the website for details.

Dentists

For a dentist (*tandarts*), call the 24-hour helpline TBB or the AOC.

AOC *Wilhelmina Gasthuisplein 167, Oud West (616 1234). Tram 1, 2, 3, 5, 12.* **Open** 9am-noon, 1-4pm Mon-Fri. **Map** p329 B5.
Emergency dental treatment. Call 686 1109 (Dutch language only) to find out where a walk-in clinic will be open at 11.30am and 3.00pm that day.
TBB *570 9595, 0900 821 2230 (premium rate).*
A 24-hour service that can refer you to a dentist. Operators can also give details of chemists open outside normal hours.

Opticians

For our favourite opticians, *see p201*; otherwise, check under 'Opticiens' at www.goudengids.nl.

Pharmacies

For pharmacy hours, *see below*. For select pharmacies, *see p203*.

Prescriptions

Chemists (*drogists*) are usually open from 9.30am to 5.30pm Monday to Saturday. For prescription drugs,

go to a pharmacy (*apotheek*), usually open from 9.30am to 5.30pm, Monday to Friday. Outside these hours, phone Afdeling Inlichtingen Apotheken (*see left*). Details are also posted at local *apotheken*.

STDs, HIV & AIDS

The AIDS Helpline (689 2577, open 2-10pm Mon-Fri) offers advice and can put you in contact with every department you need. Also, the city's health department, the GGD, runs its own free STD clinics that are anonymous and open to all.

GGD *Weesperplein 1 (555 5822, www.ggd.amsterdam.nl). Tram 9, 14 or Metro Waterlooplein.* **Open** 8.30-10.30am, 1.30-3.30pm Mon-Fri. **Map** p327 E3.
Examinations and treatment of STDs, including an HIV test, are free and anonymous.
HIV Vereniging *1e Helmersstraat 17 B3, Oud West (689 3915, www.hivnet.org, www.hivsite.nl). Tram 1, 2, 3, 5, 12.* **Open** 9am-5pm Mon-Fri. **Map** p330 C5.
The Netherlands HIV Association supports those who are HIV positive, including offering legal help. You can get HIV test results in one hour. Call 689 2577 (2-6pm Mon-Fri) to make an appointment for the Friday evening clinic or walk in Fridays between 7pm and 9pm.
Schorer Gay & Lesbian Health *Sarphatistraat 35, Southern Canal Belt (573 9444, www.schorer.nl). Tram 7, 10.* **Open** 9am-5pm Mon-Fri. **Map** p331 F4.
This state-funded agency offers support for gays and lesbians in Amsterdam. The staff are all very well informed, and they all speak excellent English.
Stichting AIDS Fonds *Keizersgracht 390-392, Western Canal Belt (626 2669, www.aids fonds.nl). Tram 1, 2, 5.* **Open** 9am-5pm Mon-Fri. **Map** p330 C4.
This organisation runs an AIDS/STD information line for gay- and lesbian-specific health questions (0900 204 2040, 2-10pm Mon-Fri) and runs workshops on anal sex. Parts of its website are in English.

HELPLINES

Alcoholics Anonymous *625 6057, www.aa-netherlands. org.* **Open** 24hr helpline.
A lengthy but highly informative message in English/Dutch details times and dates of meetings, and contact numbers for counsellors. The website is in English.

Narcotics Anonymous *662 6307.*
Open 24hr answerphone with
contact numbers of counsellors.
SOS Telephone Helpline *675
7575.* **Open** 24hrs daily.
Volunteer-run counselling service for
anyone with emotional problems. If
English isn't understood at first, keep
trying and someone will help you.

ID

Everyone has to carry some sort of
identification all the time. If you're
moving to Amsterdam, you have to
register with the local council, in the
same building as the Aliens' Police
(*see p312* **Visas & immigration**).

INTERNET

All global ISPs have a presence
here (check websites for a local
number). For a selection of useful
local websites, *see p313.*

Internet cafés

Easy Internet Café *Damrak 33,
Old Centre: Old Side (no phone,
www.easyeverything.com). Tram
4, 9, 16, 24, 25.* **Open** 9am-10pm
daily. **Rates** from €2.50/unit.
(Passes for 1-30 days also available).
No credit cards. Map p331 D4.
Freeworld *Nieuwendijk 30, Old
Centre: New Side (620 0902).
Tram 1, 2, 5, 13, 17, 20.* **Open**
9am-1am Mon-Thur, Sun; 9am-
3am Fri, Sat. **Rates** €1/30min.
No credit cards. Map p326 D2.
Buying refreshments is compulsory
for customers wanting to go online.
Internet Café *Martelaarsgracht
11, Old Centre: New Side (no phone,
www.internetcafe.nl). Tram 4, 9, 16,
20, 24, 25.* **Open** 9am-1am Mon-
Thur, Sun; 9am-3am Fri, Sat. **Rates**
around €1/30min. **No credit cards.
Map** p326 D2.
Compulsory drinks are offered
frequently by the staff.

LEFT LUGGAGE

There is a staffed left-luggage
counter at Schiphol Airport (601
2443, www.schiphol.nl, 7am-
10.45pm daily, €6/item/24hrs).
There are also lockers in the arrival
and departure halls, while in
Amsterdam there are lockers at
Centraal Station (from €4/24hrs).

LEGAL HELP

ACCESS *Herengracht 472, 2nd
floor (423 3217, www.access-nl.org).*
Open *Helpline* 10am-4pm Mon-Fri.
Visits by appointment only.

The Administrative Committee
to Co-ordinate English Speaking
Services gives assistance in English.
Juridisch Loket *Vijzelgracht 21-25,
Old Centre: New Side (0900 8020
premium rate, www.hetjl.nl). Tram
1, 2, 5.* **Open** 9am-5pm Mon-Fri.
Map p326 C3.
Qualified lawyers offering free
or low-cost legal advice.

LIBRARIES

You'll need to show proof of
residence in Amsterdam and ID
to join a library (*bibliotheek*). It
costs €23 (23-64s) or €13.50 (19-22s,
over-65s) per year and is free for
under-18s. However, in public
libraries (*openbare bibliotheek*)
you can read books, papers and
magazines without membership.

Centrale Bibliotheek (OBA)
*Oosterdokseiland 587, Old Centre:
Old Side (523 0900, www.oba.nl).
Tram 1, 2, 4, 5, 9, 13, 16, 17, 24,
25, 26.* **Open** 10am-9pm Mon-Fri.
Map p327 E1.
Anyone can use the main public
library for reference purposes.
There's also a variety of English-
language books and activities for
children (*see p218*).

LOST PROPERTY

Report lost property to the police
(*see right*). Inform your embassy
or consulate too, if you lose your
passport. For things lost at the
Hoek van Holland ferry terminal
or Schiphol Airport, contact the
company you're travelling with.
For lost credit cards, *see right.*

Centraal Station *Stationsplein
15, Old Centre: Old Side (0900 321
2100 premium rate, www.ns.nl).
Tram 1, 2, 4, 5, 9, 13, 16, 17, 24,
25, 26.* **Open** 8am-6pm Mon-Fri;
7am-5pm Sat. **Map** p326 D1.
Items found on trains are kept here
for three days (it's easiest to just go
to any window where tickets are
sold and ask), before being sent
on to Centraal Bureau Gevonden
Voorwerpen (Central Lost Property
Office), 2e Daalsedijk 4, 3551 EJ
Utrecht (030 235 3923, 8am-5pm
Mon-Fri). Items are held for three
months. To pick up items costs
€10, posting costs €15 or more.
GVB Lost Property *Arlandaweg
100 (0900 8011 premium rate).
Tram 12.* **Open** 9am-4pm Mon-Fri.
Map p326 C1.
Wait a day or two before you call,
describe what you lost on bus, Metro
or tram, and leave a number. Staff

will call you back if it is found.
Alternatively, there is an online
form at www.gvb.nl (in Dutch).
Police Lost Property
*Stephensonstraat 18, Zuid (559
3005). Tram 12 or Metro Amstel
Station or bus 14.* **Open** *In person*
9.30am-3.30pm Mon-Fri. *By phone*
noon-3.30pm Mon-Fri.
Before contacting the office, check
at the local police station.

MEDIA

Newspapers & magazines

There are many Dutch-language
newspapers and magazines. Foreign
magazines and papers are widely
available, but pricey.
For Anglophones, the local
Tourist Board publishes the
monthly *Day by Day*, a basic
listings guide available at VVV
Tourist offices (€1.95). *Time Out
Amsterdam* is published monthly
and is available from newsagents
and bookshops.

Broadcast media

Besides the national basics (Ned 1,
Ned 2 and Ned 3), Amsterdam also
has its own 'city CNN' – the really
quite cool AT5 (its site www.at5.nl
has some English) – as well as Salto
(www.salto.nl), which broadcasts
typically local and low-budget
culture/cult stuff. There are also
about a dozen national commercial
stations and extra channels on cable.
The wall-to-wall porn is largely an
urban myth, so don't expect any
late-night thrills unless your
hotel has the 'extended service',
which usually also features films,
Discovery, Eurosport and other
cable stalwarts. Dutch radio
is generally bland but Radio
Netherlands (www.rnw.nl) often has
interesting programming in English.

MONEY

Since January 2002 the Dutch
currency has been the Euro.

ATMs

If your cash card carries the Maestro
or Cirrus symbols, you should be
able to withdraw cash from ATMs.
You may get charged by your bank.

Banks

Amsterdam is a capital that has
more than its fair share of enormous
banks. Most banks are open 9am to
5pm, Monday to Friday, with the

Postbank opening on Saturday mornings as well. For a full list of banks, *see p307* **Banking**, or check www.goudengids.nl under 'Banken'.

Bureaux de change

GWK Travelex *Centraal Station, Old Centre: Old Side (0900 0566 €0.25/min, www.gwktravelex.nl). Tram 1, 2, 4, 5, 9, 13, 16, 17, 24, 25, 26.* **Open** 8am-10pm daily (Sun from 9am). *Telephone enquiries* 8am-11pm daily. **Map** p326 D1. **Other locations** Leidseplein 107-109 (8.30am-10pm daily); Schiphol Airport (7am-10pm daily); Damrak 86 (10am-10pm daily); Dam 23-25 (9.15am-7pm Mon-Sat, 10.15am-5.45pm Sun); Damrak 1-5 (9am-8pm daily); Leidseplein 31A (9.15am- 5.45pm daily).

Credit cards

Credit cards are widely used. Most restaurants will take at least one type of card; they're less popular in bars and shops, and most supermarkets don't accept them at all, so always check first and carry some cash. The most popular cards are Visa, MasterCard (aka Eurocard), American Express and Diners Club. If you lose your card, call the relevant 24-hour number immediately.

American Express *504 8666, 0800 023 3405 (freephone).* **Diners Club** *654 5511.* **Mastercard/Eurocard** *030 283 5555 if card was issued in the Netherlands; otherwise, 0800 022 5821 (freephone).* **Visa** *660 0611 if card was issued in the Netherlands; otherwise, 0800 022 3110 (freephone).*

Tax

Sales tax (BTW) – 19 per cent on most items, six per cent on goods such as books and food, more on alcohol, tobacco and petrol – will be included in prices quoted in shops.

OPENING HOURS

As a general rule, shops are open from 1pm to 6pm on Monday (if they're open at all); 10am to 6pm Tuesday to Friday, with some open until 9pm on Thursdays; and 9am to 5pm on Saturdays. Smaller shops are more erratic; if in doubt, phone.

The city's bars tend to open at various times during the day and close at around 1am throughout the week, except for Fridays and Saturdays, when they stay open

until 2am or 3am. Restaurants generally open in the evening from 5pm until 11pm (though some close as early as 9pm); many are closed on Sunday and Monday.

POLICE STATIONS

For emergencies, call 112. There is a 24-hour police service line 0900 8844 for the Amsterdam area. You can also call 0800 7000 to report a crime anonymously. If you are a victim of a crime, require practical or medical support, or have lost your documents – anything really that might go wrong as a tourist – the Police Station on Nieuwezijds Voorburgwal has a special Amsterdam Tourist Assistance Service (ATAS; *see below*).

Dutch police (www.politie-amsterdam-amstelland.nl) are under no obligation to grant a phone call to those they detain – they can hold people for up to six hours for questioning for minor crimes, 24 hours for major matters – but they'll phone the relevant consulate on behalf of a foreign detainee.

Hoofdbureau van Politie (Police Headquarters) *Elandsgracht 117, the Jordaan (0900 8844 premium rate). Tram 7, 10.* **Open** 24hrs daily. **Map** p330 C4. **Amsterdam Tourist Assistance Service (ATAS)** *Nieuwezijds Voorburgwal 104-108 (625 3246). Tram 1, 2, 5, 13, 17.* **Open** 10am-10pm daily. **Map** p326 C2.

POSTAL SERVICES

The national postal service is TNT Post (www.tntpost.nl), and the national postal information phone line is 058 233 3333. Most post offices are open 9am to 5pm, Monday to Friday. Stamps (*postzegels*) can also be bought from tobacconists, Albert Heijn and souvenir shops across Amsterdam. For post that is destined outside Amsterdam, use the *overige postcodes* slot in regular letterboxes.

Post offices

To find a post office, look under 'Postkantoren' on www.gouden gids.nl. One of the handier central branches is Waterlooplein 10 (Jodenbuurt, 0900 767 8526, 9am-6pm Mon-Fri, 10am-2pm Sat).

Main Post Office *Singel 250, Old Centre: New Side (0900 767 8526 premium rate). Tram 1, 2, 5, 13, 14, 17.* **Open** 9am-6pm Mon-Fri; 10am-2pm Sat. **Map** p326 C3.

RELIGION

Catholic

St John & St Ursula *Begijnhof 30, Old Centre: New Side (622 1918, www.begijnhofamsterdam.nl). Tram 1, 2, 4, 5, 16, 24, 25.* **Open** *Chapel* 1-6.30pm Mon; 9am-6.30pm Tue-Fri; 9am-6pm Sat, Sun. *Adoration of the Eucharist* 4-5pm, 5.30-6.30pm Mon-Fri; 5-6pm Sat, Sun. *Services* phone for details. **Map** p326 D3.
Check out the Begijnhof Shop tourist information and also religious books and souvenirs.

Dutch Reformed Church

Oude Kerk *Oudekerksplein, Old Centre: Old Side (625 8284, www. oudekerk.nl). Tram 4, 9, 16, 24, 25.* **Open** 11am-5pm Mon-Sat; 1-5pm Sun. **Map** p326 D2. *See also p89.*

Jewish

Liberal Jewish Community Amsterdam *Jacob Soetendorpstraat 8, Zuid (540 0120, office rabbinate 540 0136, www.ljgamsterdam.nl). Tram 4.* **Open** *Rabbi's office* call for appt. *Services* 8pm Fri; 10am Sat. **Orthodox Jewish Community Amsterdam** *Van der Boechorststraat 26, Zuid (646 0046, www.nihs.nl). Bus 69, 169.* **Open** 9am-5pm Mon-Fri by appt only.
Information on the city's Orthodox synagogues and Jewish facilities.

Muslim

THAIBA Islamic Cultural Centre *Kraaiennest 125, Zuid (698 2526). Metro Gaasperplas.*
Phone for details of mosques, prayer times and cultural activities.

Reformed Church

English Reformed Church *Begijnhof 48, Old Centre: New Side (624 9665, www.ercadam.nl). Tram 1, 2, 4, 5, 9, 16, 24, 25.* **Services** in *English* 10.30am Sun. **Map** p326 C3.
The main place of worship for the local English-speaking community.

SAFETY & SECURITY

Amsterdam is a relatively safe city, but that's not to say you shouldn't be vigilant. The Red Light District is rife with expert pickpockets and always lock your bike. Take care on the train to Schiphol, especially at stops, as suitcases get pulled off just as the doors are closing.

SMOKING

Smoking is not allowed in clubs, bars, restaurants etc. While on the street and in the open, you'll have almost no problems sparking up. For more on Amsterdam's dope laws, *see pp65-71*.

TELEPHONES

The code for Amsterdam is 020. To call within the city, just dial the seven-digit number. There are other types of numbers that appear in this book. 06 numbers are for mobile phones; 0800 numbers are freephone numbers; and 0900 numbers are charged at premium rates. The latter two cannot be reached from abroad.

Dialling codes

From the Netherlands
Australia: 00 61
Irish Republic: 00 353
UK: 00 44 (then drop the first '0' from the area code)
USA & Canada: 00 1

To the Netherlands
Dial the appropriate international access code, followed by the area code (without the first '0'), then the number as it appears after. The first 0 on mobiles is also dropped.
From Australia: 00 11 31
From UK & Irish Republic: 00 31
From USA: 011 31

Within the Netherlands
National directory enquiries: 0900 8008 (€1.15/call)
International directory enquiries: 0900 8418 (€1.15/call)
Local operator: 0800 0101
International operator: 0800 0410

Making a call

Listen for the dialling tone (a hum), insert the phonecard, dial the code (none for calls within Amsterdam), then the number. On public phones, a digital display indicates credit left.

International calls can be made from all phone boxes. For information on rates, phone international directory enquiries (*see above*).

Public phones

Amsterdam payphones are green and grey 'poles', with a KPN logo. Cards are available from stations, the Amsterdam Tourist Board, post offices and tobacconists. You can also use credit cards in many phones across the city.

Mobile phones

Check with your service provider before leaving about service while you're in the Netherlands.

TIME

The Netherlands is an hour ahead of Greenwich Mean Time (GMT). All clocks on Central European Time (CET) now go back and forward on the same dates as GMT. The Dutch use the 24hr system.

TIPPING

It's usual to tip ten per cent, leaving the extra in change, not on your card.

TOILETS

For men, there are the historic green metal urinals; peeing into canals is an offence. For the ladies, public loos are rare, but some cafés and department stores allow you to use theirs for a few cents.

TOURIST INFORMATION

Amsterdam Tourist Board (VVV)
Stationsplein 10, Old Centre: New Side (0900 400 4040 €0.40/min, www.visitamsterdam.nl). Tram 1, 2, 4, 5, 9, 13, 16, 17, 24, 25. **Open** 9am-5pm daily. **Map** p326 D1/2.
The main office of the VVV is right outside Centraal Station. English-speaking staff can change money and provide details on transport, entertainment, exhibitions and day-trips in the Netherlands. They also arrange hotel bookings for a fee, and excursions or car hire for free. There is a good range of brochures for sale, and VVV's monthly listings magazine *Day by Day* is sold for €1.95. The information line features an English-language service.

Other locations Leidseplein 1 (9.15am-5pm Mon-Thur, Sun; 9.15am-7pm Fri, Sat); Centraal Station, platform 2B 15 (8am-8pm Mon-Sat; 9am-5pm Sun); Schiphol Airport, Arrivals 2 (7am-10pm daily).

VISAS & IMMIGRATION

Citizens from the EU, USA, Canada, Australia and New Zealand need only a valid passport for stays of less than three months. Citizens of other countries must have a tourist visa.

For stays longer than three months, apply for a residents' permit at the Dienst Vreemdeling-enpolitie (Aliens' Police Station, Johan Huizingalaan 757, Slotervaart, 559 6161, www.ind.nl).

WHEN TO GO

See below **The Local Climate**.

Public holidays

Called *Nationale Feestdagen* in Dutch, the public holidays are: New Year's Day; Good Friday; Easter Sunday and Monday; Koninginnedag (Queen's Day, 30 April; *see p209*); Remembrance Day (4 May); Liberation Day (5 May); Ascension Day; Whit (Pentecost) Sunday and Monday; Christmas Day; Boxing Day.

WOMEN

Central Amsterdam is fairly safe for women: use your common sense when travelling alone.

De Eerstelijn and Meldpunt Vrouwenopvang *611 6022.* **Open** 24hrs.
Call this number for support if you have been a victim of rape, assault, sexual harassment or threats.

THE LOCAL CLIMATE

Average temperatures and monthly rainfall in Amsterdam.

	°C/°F	Rainfall (mm/in)	Sun (hrs/day)
Jan	4/39	68/2.7	1.8
Feb	6/43	48/1.9	2.8
Mar	9/48	66/2.6	3.7
Apr	13/55	53/2.1	5.5
May	17/63	61/2.4	7.2
June	20/68	71/2.8	6.6
July	22/72	76/3.0	6.9
Aug	22/72	71/2.8	6.7
Sept	19/66	66/2.6	4.4
Oct	14/57	73/2.9	3.3
Nov	9/48	81/3.2	1.9
Dec	6/43	84/3.3	1.5

Further Reference

BOOKS

Fiction

Baantjer *De Cock series* Crime novels by a local ex-cop. Also a TV series.
Albert Camus *The Fall* Man recalls his Parisian past in Amsterdam's 'circles of hell'.
Tracy Chevalier *Girl with a Pearl Earring* Inspired by Vermeer's painting and set in 17th-century Delft.
Arnon Grunberg *Blue Mondays* Philip Roth's *Goodbye Columbus* goes Dutch in this 1994 bestseller.
David Liss *The Coffee Trader* Thriller focused on a 17th-century Portuguese Jewish financier, tempted into the emerging coffee trade.
Alistair MacLean *Puppet on a Chain* Interpol narcotics agent flies into town on the trail of a dope king.
Deborah Moggach *Tulip Fever* A love triangle in 1630s Amsterdam, at the beginning of the tulip boom.
Harry Mulisch *The Assault* A boy's perspective on World War II. Also a classic film.
Multatuli *Max Havelaar, or the Coffee Auctions of the Dutch Trading Company* A colonial officer and his clash with the corrupt government.
Janwillem van der Wetering *The Japanese Corpse* An off-the-wall police procedural set in Amsterdam.
Manfred Wolf (ed) *Amsterdam: A Traveller's Literary Companion* The country's best writers on the city.

Non-fiction

Ian Buruma *Murder in Amsterdam: The Death of Theo van Gogh and the Limits of Tolerance* An analysis of tensions over immigration and tolerance in the Netherlands
Timothy Brook *Vermeer's Hat: The 17th Century and the Dawn of the Global World* An exploration of the Golden Age via various works of art.
Sean Condon *My 'Dam Life* Offbeat insights by Australian wit.
Anne Frank *The Diary of Anne Frank* Still-shocking wartime diary.
RH Fuchs *Dutch Painting* A comprehensive guide.
Zbigniew Herbert *Still Life with a Bridle* The Polish poet and essayist meditates on the Golden Age.
Etty Hillesum *An Interrupted Life: The Diaries and Letters 1941-1943* The moving wartime experiences of a young Amsterdam Jewish woman who died in Auschwitz.

Lisa Jardine *Going Dutch: How England Plundered Holland's Glory* Cultural interaction between British and the Dutch in the Golden Age.
Geert Mak *Amsterdam: A Brief Life of the City* The city's history told through the stories of its people.
Simon Schama *The Embarrassment of Riches* A lively social and cultural history of the Netherlands.
David Winners *Brilliant Orange: the Neurotic Genius of Dutch Football* Much more than just a football book: a delve into the Dutch psyche.
Russell Shorto *The Island at the Center of the World: The Epic Story of Dutch Manhattan* The Dutch as seen through their influence in the New World.
Wim de Wit *Amsterdam School: Dutch Expressionist Architecture*

MUSIC

Arling & Cameron *Music for Imaginary Films* (2000) Eclectic duo reinvent the history of the soundtrack.
Chet Baker *Live at Nick's* (1978) In front of his favourite rhythm section, Chet simply soars.
The Beach Boys *Holland* (1973) Californians hole up in Holland and start recording.
The Ex Starters *Alternators* (1998) Anarcho squat punks/improv-jazzsters team up with Steve Albini.
Human Alert *Ego Ego* (2005) Hysterical punk legends go orchestral.
Osdorp Posse *Origineel Amsterdams* (2000) Nederhop maestros' primer in local street talk.

FILMS

Amsterdam Global Village *dir Johan van der Keuken* (1996) A long, meditative and arty cruise through the city's streets and people.
Amsterdamned *dir Dick Maas* (1987) Psychotic frogman, lots of canal chase scenes and continuity problems that lead to characters turning an Amsterdam corner and ending up in Utrecht.
Black Book *dir Paul Verhoeven* (2006) A Jewish singer goes undercover for the Dutch Resistance.
The Fourth Man *dir Paul Verhoeven* (1983) Mr Basic Instinct's melodrama seethes with homoerotic desire.
Hufters en Hofdames (Bastards and Bridesmaids) *dir Eddy Terstall* (1997) Amsterdam as a backdrop to twentysomething relationship pains.

Karacter (Character) *dir Mike van Diem* (1997) An impeccable father–son drama.
De Noorderlingen (The Northerners) *dir Alex van Warmerdam* (1992) Absurdity and angst in a lonely Dutch subdivision.
Ocean's Twelve *dir Steven Soderbergh* (2004) Star-cast heist series comes to Europe.
Turks Fruit (Turkish Delight) *dir Paul Verhoeven* (1973) Sculptor Sculptor Rutger Hauer's rich young wife is killed by a brain tumour.
Yes Nurse! No Nurse! *dir Pieter Kramer* (2002) Musical cult classic for connoisseurs of camp.
Zusje (Little Sister) *dir Robert Jan Westdijk* (1995) A family affair with voyeuristic overtones.

WEBSITES

www.9292ov.nl GVB's excellent door-to-door route-planner.
www.amsterdam.nl Advice on living in and visiting Amsterdam, with searchable maps.
www.archined.nl News and reviews of Dutch architecture.
www.channels.nl Virtual tour of Amsterdam's streets, with reviews of hotels, restaurants and clubs.
http://collectie.ahm.nl/search. aspx The city through images, from the Amsterdam Historical Museum.
www.dutchnews.nl Dutch news summarised in English.
www.englishbreakfastradio.nl Early morning radio show on Amsterdam, with podcast archive.
www.expatica.com English news and reviews aimed at expats.
www.gayamsterdamlinks.com
www.holland.com National tourism board website.
www.iamsterdam.nl Official Amsterdam Tourist Board website.
www.nisnews.nl English-language Dutch news, running since 1965.
www.panoramsterdam.nl Over 300 360-degree shots of Amsterdam.
www.radionetherlands.nl Dutch and international news in English.
www.simplyamsterdam.nl Aimed at the 'independent traveller'.
www.subba-cultcha.com All things counterculturally musical.
www.theessenceonline.com/ amsterdam-the-essence Influential 'dammers interviewed.
www.timeoutamsterdam.nl That's us. Look for updates from our monthly English magazine.

Content Index

INDEX

Venue Index

INDEX

INDEX

Advertisers' Index

Please refer to the relevant pages for contact details.

INDEX

Maps

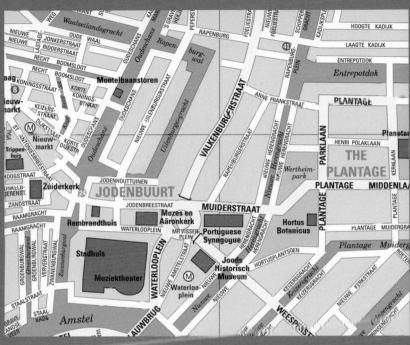

Legend

Major sight or landmark	
Hospital or college	
Railway station	
Parks	
Canal	
Motorway	
Main road	
Main road tunnel	
Pedestrian road	
Airport	✈
Church	✚
Area name	DE PIJP

SPAARNDAMMERSTRAAT TASMANSTRAAT

Het IJ

WESTERDOKSDIJK

DE RUIJTERKADE

PIET

HAARLEMMER HOUTTUINEN

PRINS HENDRIKKADE

See p325
See p326

Centraal Station

RED LIGHT DISTRICT

HAARLEMMERWEG

Noorderkerk

WESTERN CANAL BELT

DAMRAK

SPUISTRAAT

Waag

Nieuw-markt

Oude Kerk

THE OLD CENTRE

BOS EN LOMMER

THE JORDAAN

NASSAUKADE

Singelgracht

Prinsengracht

Keizersgracht

Herengracht

Nieuwe Kerk

Dam

Nationaal Monument

OLD SIDE

Muziektheater

Anne Frankhuis

Koninklijk Paleis

ROKIN

NEW SIDE

Damrak

Amstel

Begijnhof

AMSTEL

ROZENGRACHT

Herengracht

REMBRANDTPLEIN

Herengracht

Keizersgracht

JAN VAN GALENSTRAAT

Singelgracht

DE CLERCQSTRAAT

NASSAUKADE

Ketzersgracht

SOUTHERN CANAL BELT

ADMIRAAL DE RUIJTERWEG

Prinsengracht

VIJZELGRACHT

JAN EVERTSENSTRAAT

HOOFDWEG

LEIDSEPLEIN

DE BAARSJES

OUD WEST

OVERTOOM

Singelgracht

STADHOUDERSKADE

Rijksmuseum

Heineken Experience

HOBBEMAKADE

See p329
See p330

Van Gogh Museum

Stedelijk Museum

MUSEUM QUARTER

Concertgebouw

OVERTOOM

Vondelpark

HOOFDWEG

A10 To A8 & Zaandam

ZUID

HAARLEMMERMEERSTR.

STADIONWEG

To A4 & Schiphol ✈

Amsterdam Overview

To KNSM Eiland

Java Eiland

Sporenburg   Borneo

OOSTELIJKE HANDELSKADE

HEINKADE

IJ-TUNNEL

See p327

THE WATERFRONT

ZEEBURGERDIJK

MOLUKKENSTRAAT

INSULINDEWEG

KATTENBURGERSTRAAT

OOSTENBURGERGRACHT

MAURITSKADE

VALKENBURGERSTRAAT

THE PLANTAGE   Artis

PLANTAGE MIDDENLAAN

LINNAEUSSTRAAT

Muiderpoort

Tropenmuseum

WATERLOOPLEIN

MAURITSKADE

WEESPERSTRAAT

Oosterpark

MIDDENWEG

THE OOST

HUGO DE VRIESLAAN

MIDDENWEG

Prinsengracht

Amstel

WIBAUTSTRAAT

GOOISEWEG

Singelgracht

STADHOUDERSKADE

AMSTELDIJK

See p332

GOOISEWEG

VAN WOUSTRAAT

Amstel

Amstel

DE PIJP

FERDINAND BOLSTRAAT

See p331

AMSTELDIJK

SPAKLERWEG

ROOSEVELTLAAN

RIJNSTRAAT

RIVIEREN-
BUURT

WIELINGENSTR

PRESIDENT KENNEDYLAAN

To A8 & Volendam A10

0   1 km

0   0.5 mile

A2 *To Utrecht*

© Copyright Time Out Group 2011

A12 *To A4 & Schiphol* ✈

The Netherlands

0   50 km
0   30 miles
© Copyright Time Out Group 2011

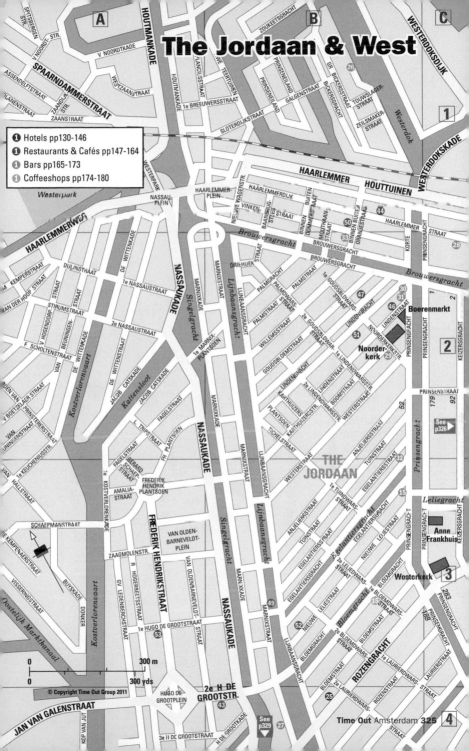

The Jordaan & West

A **B** **C**

- 1 Hotels pp130-146
- 1 Restaurants & Cafés pp147-164
- 1 Bars pp165-173
- 1 Coffeeshops pp174-180

SPAARNDAMMERSTRAAT

HAARLEMMERWEG

Westerpark

NASSAUKADE

THE JORDAAN

Boerenmarkt

Noorderkerk

Anne Frankhuis

Westerkerk

HAARLEMMER HOUTTUINEN

Brouwersgracht

Prinsengracht

See p326

See p329

© Copyright Time Out Group 2011

300 m

300 yds

JAN VAN GALENSTRAAT

2e H DE GROOTSTR.

4

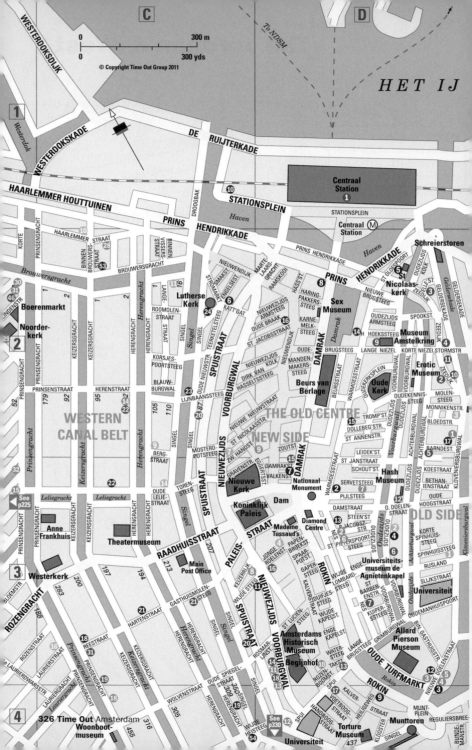

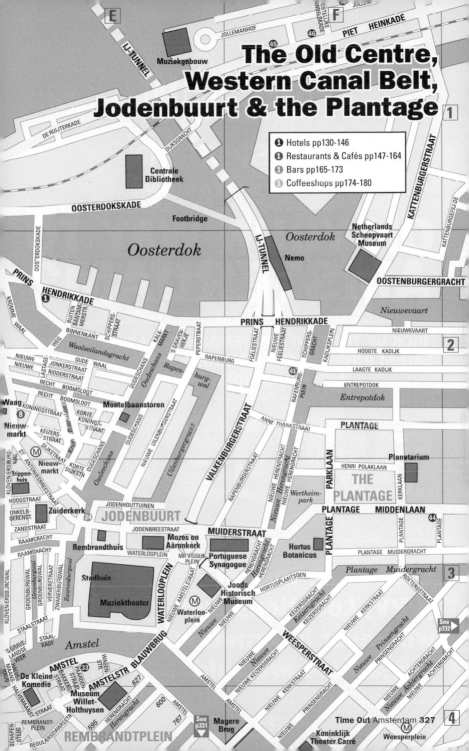

Oud West

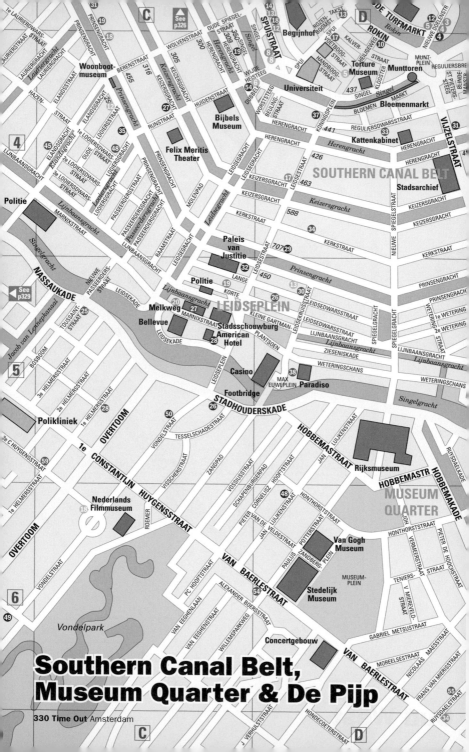

Southern Canal Belt, Museum Quarter & De Pijp

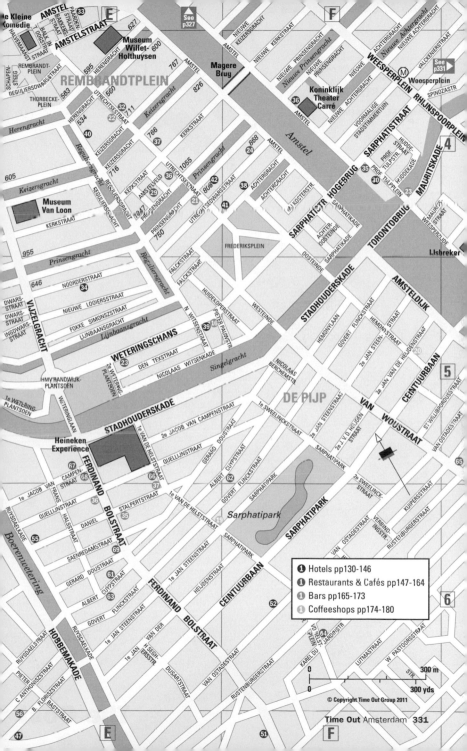

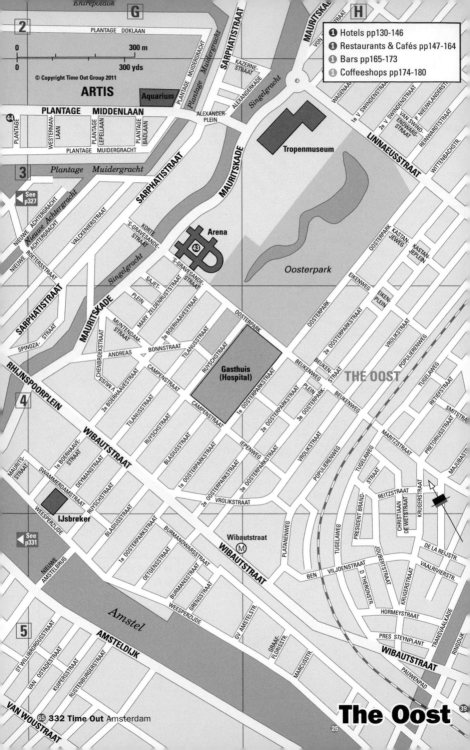

G

2

PLANTAGE DOKLAAN

Entrepotdok

0   300 m

0   300 yds

© Copyright Time Out Group 2011

ARTIS

Aquarium

PLANTAGE MIDDENLAAN

44

PLANTAGE

WESTERMAN-LAAN

PLANTAGE LEPELAAN

PLANTAGE BADLAAN

PLANTAGE MUIDERGRACHT

3

Plantage Muidergracht

◀ See p327

ALEXANDER-PLEIN

SARPHATISTRAAT

KAZERNE-STRAAT

ALEXANDERKADE

Singelgracht

H

Von

MAURITSKADE

1 Hotels pp130-146
1 Restaurants & Cafés pp147-164
1 Bars pp165-173
1 Coffeeshops pp174-180

WAGENAAR

1e V. SWINDENSTRAAT

2e V. SWINDENSTRAAT

V. SWINDENSTR.

V. NIEUWLANDERSTR.

REINWARDTSTRAAT

VAN SWIND. EINDHUES STRAAT

LINNAEUSSTRAAT

WITTENBACHSTR.

Tropenmuseum

Arena
43

Singelgracht

NIEUWE ACHTERGRACHT

Nieuwe Achtergracht

VALCKENIERSTRAAT

'S-GRAVESANDE-STRAAT

KORTE 'S-GRAVESANDE-STRAAT

'S-GRAVESANDE STRAAT

NIEUWE HUIDERSTRAAT

SAJET. PLEIN

MARY ZELDENRUSTSTRAAT

Oosterpark

OOSTERPARK KASTAN-JEWEG

KASTAN-JEPLEIN

EIKENWEG

EIKEN-PLEIN

THE OOST

SARPHATISTRAAT

SPINOZA-STRAAT

MAURITSKADE

MUNTENDAM-STRAAT

CHENBROEKSTRAAT

V. MUSSC

ANDREAS BONNSTRAAT

2e BOERHAAVESTRAAT

CAMPENSTRAAT

1e BOERHAAVESTRAAT

TILANUSSTRAAT

2e BOERHAAVE STRAAT

4

RHIJNSPOORPLEIN

1e BOERHAAVE-STRAAT

DEYMANSTRAAT

RUYSCHSTRAAT

WIBAUTSTRAAT

MAURITS-STRAAT

SWAMMERDAMSTRAAT

WEESPERZIJDE

IJsbreker

◀ See p331

NIEUWE AMSTELBRUG

BLASIUSSTRAAT

BURMANDWARSSTRAAT

OETGENSSTRAAT

BURMANSTRAAT

GRENSSTRAAT

WEESPERZIJDE

Amstel

AMSTELDIJK

ST WILLIBRORDUSSTRAAT

VAN OSTADESTRAAT

KUIPERSSTRAAT

RUSTENBURGERSTRAAT

GV AMSTELSTR.

GV AMSTELSTRAAT

GRAAF FLORISSTR.

MARCUSSTR.

5

TILANUSSTRAAT

RUYSCHSTRAAT

BLASIUSSTRAAT

OOSTERPARK

RUYSCHSTRAAT

Gasthuis (Hospital)

OOSTERPARKSTRAAT

1e OOSTERPARKSTRAAT

CAMPENSTRAAT

IEPENWEG

1e OOSTERPARKSTRAAT

VROLIKSTRAAT

2e OOSTERPARKSTRAAT

3e OOSTERPARKSTRAAT

VROLIKSTRAAT

BEUKENWEG

BELKEN-WEG

BEUKENWEG

PLEIN

OOSTERPARKSTRAAT

VROLIKSTRAAT

POPULIERENWEG

TUGELAWEG

Wibautstraat
Ⓜ

PLATANENWEG

BEN

VILJOENSTRAAT

TUGELAWEG

PRESIDENT BRAND-STRAAT

REITZSTRAAT

D. THERONSTR.

JOUBERTSTRAAT

CHRISTIAAN DE WETSTRAAT

KRUGERSTRAAT

MARITZSTRAAT

PRETORIUSSTRAAT

RETIEFSTRAAT

SMITSTRAAT

MAJUBASTR.

DE LA REIJSTR.

VAALRIVIERSTR.

HORMEYSTRAAT

PRES STEYNPLANT

TRANSVAALKADE

RINGDIJK

WIBAUTSTRAAT

PAUWENPAD

VAN WOUSTRAAT

65 **332 Time Out** Amsterdam

25

39

The Oost

Street Index

STREET INDEX

STREET INDEX

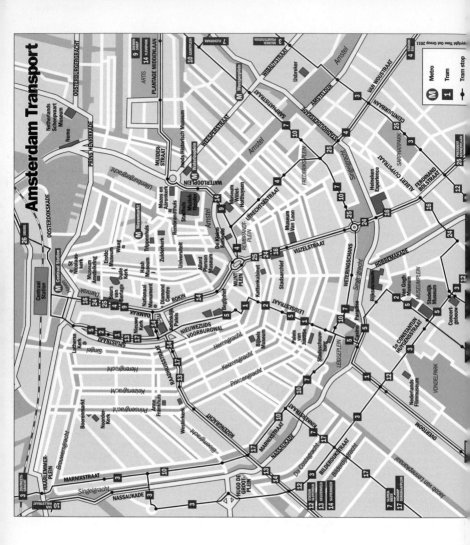

Amsterdam Transport